101 890 221 X
D1486485

COMMUNIST TERROR IN ROMANIA

DENNIS DELETANT

Communist Terror in Romania

Gheorghiu-Dej and the Police State, 1948-1965

HURST & COMPANY, LONDON

First published in the United Kingdom by
C. Hurst & Co. (Publishers) Ltd.,
38 King Street, London WC2E 8JZ

Printed in India
ISBN 1-85065-386-0

CONTENTS

Preface and Acknowledgements *page* vii

Abbreviations xii

Map xiii

Chapters

1. The Early Years of the Romanian Communist Party 1
2. The Communist Party in Romania, 1930–1944 11
3. The Communist Party and the Coup of 23 August 1944 34
4. The Path to Power of the Romanian Communist Party 53
5. Imposition of the Totalitarian Model and Persecution of the Church 74
6. The *Securitate* and the Use of Terror 114
7. Dej's Struggle for Dominance 146
8. The Downfall of Lucreţiu Pătrăşcanu 170
9. The Romanian Gulag 195
10. Armed Resistance 225
11. Dej Emerges Supreme, 1952–1956 235
12. From Subservience to the Soviet Union to Autonomy, 1957–1965 269
13. Conclusion 289

Appendixes

1. Account by Emil Bodnăraş of his Actions between November 1942 and April 1944 297
2. The Report of V. Leskov 309
3. Statement by Gheorghe Pintilie presented to the Party Commission investigating the death of Ştefan Foriş 314

4. The Formation of the Groza Government 319
5. The Romanian Foreign Ministry 322
6. Conditions in the Aiud Central Penitentiary 324
7. The Organisation of the Romanian Security Service, 1948-1965 328
8. The Arrest and Interrogation of Herbert (Belu) Zilber 331

Bibliography 335
Index 345

PREFACE AND ACKNOWLEDGEMENTS

There is no major study of the entire period of Communist rule in Romania. Inside the country, domestic historiography had to conform to the party's ideological constraints. Outside, historical inquiry has concentrated on the Romanian Communist Party (RCP) as an institution and on Nicolae Ceauşescu. Gheorghe Gheorghiu-Dej, Ceauşescu's predecessor, who built up and maintained the Communist system between 1944 and 1965, has received less attention.

Accordingly this book focuses on Dej's rise to prominence in the RCP and the purges which were an instrument of that ascent. It therefore complements my study *Ceauşescu and the Securitate: Coercion and Dissent in Romania, 1965-1989* (Hurst, 1995). As with that volume, the files of the *Securitate* provide much of the evidence. Little of this material has been used in work published outside Romania; articles published in the Romanian press and in Romanian academic journals have drawn upon some of the *Securitate* archives, but no single-volume study on the repressive aspect of Dej's rule has appeared or, as far as I am aware, is being prepared. Since 1990, as well as secret police documents, much memoir literature on the prisons and prison camps has been published and has enabled me to compare and confront the accounts of the jailers and the jailed.

Before 1990, studies of Communism in Romania were forced to rely upon fragmentary secondhand sources for their treatment of the repressive core of the Communist regime – Ghiţa Ionescu's excellent study says virtually nothing about the extent of the *gulag* and has only a couple of references to the secret police. Historians now have access to a wealth of untapped archival documentation, which sheds greater light upon the intrinsic coercion of the Dej era, and thereby provides confirmation of what has long been suspected about the nature of Communism in Romania.

The new written material is supplemented by interviews which I have conducted with witnessess to these events. Extracts from the minutes of some of the RCP Politburo meetings during the period under discussion have appeared in Romanian secondary sources and are quoted where appropriate. Until full access to these documents is available, it will not be possible to verify some of the evidence offered here. Of course, the official party record has its own limitations. My research into the archives of the Romanian Ministry of the Interior revealed interrogation minutes submitted in the early 1950s to Gheorghiu-Dej for approval, which contained substantive deletions in red pencil in the latter's own hand. Whether minutes of the Politburo meetings were doctored in a similar way remains for the time being a matter of speculation. Caution is also advisable in handling oral testimony. The respondents are often subjective and seek to justify their past behaviour, often by hiding the unsavoury aspects of their past. Some interviewees do indeed provide information which corroborates written sources, while others give illuminating details for which the researcher can find no corroboration. By contrast, there are yet others who, in an effort to inflate their own importance, are unwilling to admit that they do not have the answers to certain questions and instead have recourse to invention. The task of the researcher is to establish the reliability of the respondent and I have indicated the status of the oral information obtained in the footnotes. In my own experience of interviewing notable party figures from this period one thing struck me in particular: an aversion to talking about the Party's links with the Soviet Union and particular Soviet officials.

This study, I hope, will offer students of Communism in Eastern Europe an additional comparative angle for their research, and Romanians themselves an authoritative study of a past that is still largely denied them. Evidence of this denial is afforded by the recent 586-page single-volume *A History of Romania*, published in Romania (Iaşi: Centre for Romanian Studies, Romanian Cultural Foundation, 1995), which achieves the remarkable feat of covering the forty years of Communist rule in thirty-six pages and devotes precisely fourteen pages to the Dej era (pp. 528-42). Even more astonishing is that the Romanian *gulag* is dealt with in less than 100 words. Similarly scant in its treatment of the repression is Silviu Brucan's autobiography *The Wasted Generation* (Boulder, CO: Westview Press, 1993). Brucan, a qualified dissident of the late 1980s and self-styled *éminence grise* of the 1989 Romanian revolution, is silent about the arch-Stalinist Brucan of the late 1940s. He does not hide the fact that there were two faces to

Communist society, the 'nice and kind face' of a prosperous, egalitarian future, trumpeted by the media, and 'the other face' of the *gulag*, but to his account of Communist terror in the twenty years of Dej's rule, when he himself was a senior figure in the party, he devotes less than three pages (pp. 86-8). Brucan presents a one-sided appreciation of Dej as an enlightened despot, endowed with natural intelligence, tact and extraordinary self-control, who showed 'respect for professional competence and generally for educated people, whose knowledge and expertise he highly appreciated' (p. 39).

Vladimir Tismăneanu, in his sparkling collection of essays on Dej entitled *Fantoma lui Gheorghiu-Dej* (Bucharest: Univers, 1995), recognises this distortion:

> In the avalanche of articles which point the finger at Romanian Communism, in the host of incriminating material relating to Ceauşescu family dictatorship, it seems to me that we lose sight of the nature of totalitarianism in Romania. But even more than this, there is a tendency to forget who presided over the Stalinisation and Sovietisation of the country, and how and in what circumstances it took place.[...] The name of Gheorghe Gheorghiu-Dej has only been mentioned occasionally, without any attempt being made to penetrate those obscure and even dark areas of the political biography of the man who led the Romanian Communist Party between 1944 and March 1965 (p. 105).

Tismăneanu does in fact go a long way in penetrating these 'dark areas' in his essays. What emerges from them is a picture of an unscrupulous, gregarious criminal, whose cruelty and cunning remain unsurpassed in twentieth-century Romanian history: 'Dej's Stalinism was instinctive, not ideological. He loved power, it had a voluptuous whiff, and he chose his victims with the agility of a feline. He was adept as simulating kindness and even tenderness, only in order to strike more surely and without hesitation when his target least expected it' (p. 107). These personal traits are crucial to an assessment and interpretation of his motives and explain Dej's use of terror as an instrument of political power. Anyone who may think that the phrase 'use of terror' is an exaggeration will discover in the following pages that, alongside the punitive measures that Dej took to reduce Romanian society to servitude and which led to the deaths of thousands of political prisoners, he personally gave the order for the murder of at least three persons, of whom two were political rivals and the third was his daughter's lover. He inaugurated and controlled that use of terror whose impact upon Romanian society is analysed in this study.

The entry of Soviet troops into Romania in 1944 transformed the Communist Party of Romania into a major political force, and it was on the back of Soviet power that Gheorghiu-Dej and his colleagues were installed in government. Initially, Romania shared with all the Communist regimes of Eastern Europe a total reliance upon terror as an instrument of political power. This terror was wielded in two stages: the first to eliminate opponents in the drive to consolidate power; the second to ensure compliance once revolutionary change had been effected. In Romania's case the first stage, broadly speaking, encompassed the period 1945 to 1964 (the year in which an amnesty for political prisoners was completed), and the second from 1964 to 1989. There was a perceptible change in the degree of repression exercised by the regime in 1964. Until this final year of Dej's rule as general secretary of the Romanian Workers' Party, terror embraced the whole of Romanian society in a search for actual or potential opponents of totalitarian conformity, and imparted to many throughout the population the sense that they were being hunted. It is vital to our understanding of the period to realise that, irrespective of the evolution in relations between Bucharest and Moscow, the repressive nature of Dej's regime remained essentially the same, as did the level of violence used against those who were arrested and subjected to interrogation. After 1964 Romanians were marked by fear, rather than terror, of the *Securitate*, and the Ceauşescu regime, for all its appalling abuses of human dignity and contempt for human rights, never used the tactics of mass arrests and wholesale internal deportations that were a feature of most of the Dej era. It did not have to. Dej had done his work well.

Acknowledgements

Maurice Pearton's copious comments and criticisms have helped to make this study what it is. Romanian friends have given generously of their time in providing personal accounts of their experience of the Dej era, both inside and outside jail and the labour camp.

Among them are my late father-in-law Andrei Caracostea, the late Corneliu Coposu, Ana Blandiana and Romulus Rusan, Seta, Alexandru and Aristide Ionescu, Şerban Papacostea, Paul Cernovodeanu, Alexandru Zub, Constantin Ticu Dumitrescu, Ion Gavrilă-Ogoranu, the late Traian Borcescu, and Alexandru Salca.

Mircea and Rodica Dumitrescu, relations by marriage and the dearest of friends, have given me over the last twenty-five years invaluable insights into the Romanian experience of Communist rule as well as unstinting hospitality. Marius Oprea, Claudiu Secaşiu and Robert Levy, members of the new generation of scholars, offered me solid support in my research by sharing with me the fruits of their own labours in the Romanian archives, while Florin Constantiniu and Ion Chiper did the same in respect of certain foreign archives.

A Nuffield Small Grant gave me the wherewithal to spend time in the archives of the SRI, the Romanian Security Service, to consult material on the organisation and membership of the *Securitate*. I here extend my gratitude to Virgil Măgureanu, the former Director of the SRI, for facilitating access to those archives.

November 1998 DENNIS DELETANT

ABBREVIATIONS

The term *Securitate* is used in this book to denote the Romanian State Security organisation during the period of Communist rule. This organisation went through various permutations between 1948 and 1989. Those permutations, and the Soviet State Security model which usually inspired them, are reflected in the following abbreviations:

DGIE	*Direcţia Generală de Informaţii Externe* (Romanian Foreign Intelligence Service, 1963-72, March 1978-October 1978, subordinated to the *Securitate*)
DGSP	*Direcţia Generală a Securităţii Poporului* (Romanian Security Service, 1948-51)
DGSS	*Direcţia Generală a Securităţii Statului* (Romanian Security Service, 1951-56)
DS	*Departamentul Securităţii* (Romanian Security Service, 1956-78)
KGB	Soviet Security Service, 1954-
MGB	Soviet Security Service, 1946-54
NKGB	Soviet Security Service, 1943-46
NKVD	Soviet Security Service, 1934-43

1

THE EARLY YEARS OF THE ROMANIAN COMMUNIST PARTY

Until the end of the Second World War, the Romanian Communist Party (RCP) was on the fringes of Romanian politics. Its identification with the doctrines of Communism, and the threat posed by the Soviet Union as a hostile neighbour, deprived it of any popular support.[1] The interventions of the Moscow-based Communist International (Comintern) in the party's affairs were invariably disastrous, and further marginalised the party since it was considered subservient to Soviet interests. Two Comintern policies gave particular offence – the demands for the return of Bessarabia to the Soviet Union and for self-determination for the minorities in Romania. This view of the party as 'alien' and as a tool of the Soviet Union led the Romanian government to ban it, on 11 April 1924. This ban remained for twenty years and crippled the party's activity. The faithful were obliged to work clandestinely and they were liable to be caught by the *Siguranţa*, the secret police. Jail was therefore a common experience of party activists in the interwar period. Prison crystallised their beliefs and convinced many of them of the righteousness of their cause. In these circumstances, the party became more like a sect, its members deprived of any check on their convictions which overt participation in politics might have promoted.

Some of the problems which the party faced were not unique.

[1] Until it was legalised on 23 August 1944, the RCP was known by its Comintern designation 'the Communist Party of Romania'. For the early history of the party see: Ghita Ionescu, *Communism in Rumania, 1944-1962*, London: RIIA/Oxford University Press, 1964, pp.1-28; Stephen Fischer-Galaţi, *The New Rumania: From People's Democracy to Socialist Republic*, Cambridge, MA: MIT Press, 1967, pp. 1-16; Robert R. King, *History of the Romanian Communist Party*, Stanford, CA: Hoover Institution Press, 1980, pp.9-38; and Michael Shafir, *Romania: Politics, Economics and Society*, London: Pinter, 1985, pp.9-28.

The parties of the left in general exerted little influence on political life in the interwar years. Romania, being a predominantly agricultural country, lacked a powerful indigenous working class upon which these parties might have formed a base, while the electoral strength of the National Peasant Party (formed in 1926 from the union of the Peasant Party and the National Party of Transylvania) demonstrated its attractiveness to the peasantry with its programme of peasant control of the means of production in agriculture, and of devolution of government administration in the village. In the 1926 general elections, the NPP won 727,000 votes (28% of the votes cast), in 1928 2,209,000 (78%), in 1932 1,204,000 (40%), and in 1937 627,000 (20%).

The Social Democratic Party (SDP), the principal democratic party of the left, had been rent by dissension during the First World War and emerged from it split into two factions dubbed 'maximalists' and 'minimalists'.[2] The former parallelled the Bolsheviks by advocating the immediate dictatorship of the proletariat through revolution, and were led by Alexandru Dobrogeanu-Gherea, Boris Ştefanov and Alecu Constantinescu.[3] Among the

[2] Ionescu, *Communism in Rumania*, pp.10-11.

[3] Ştefanov (conspiratorial name I. Draganov) was born on 8 October 1883 and was the nephew of Christian Rakovsky, one of the founders of the Romanian SDP. He joined the Romanian SDP in 1913 and in the following year was coopted into the party's council as a representative for the Dobrogea. Elected to parliament in May 1920 as a SDP candidate, he was arrested after the general strike of October. Immediately after his release from jail following a general amnesty in June 1922, Ştefanov was elected to membership of the Central Committee at the Second Congress of the RCP. After the proscription of the party in April 1924, he was sent to Paris as the party's representative on the Balkan Communist Federation, and in spring 1925 returned clandestinely to Romania. In winter 1925, he went to Moscow with all the members of the Romanian Politburo on the orders of the Comintern. Three months after returning to Romania he was arrested on 5 August 1926, tried and sentenced in February 1928 to eight years' imprisonment for being active in an illegal organisation. On his release in August 1933, the Politburo sent him to Moscow as the party's representative on the Executive Committee of the Comintern, and in December 1934 (according to an official obituary, 1935 according to Ştefanov) he was appointed general secretary of the RCP, a position he held till early 1940 while resident in the Soviet Union. His place as Romanian representative to the Comintern was taken by Ana Pauker in 1941 and at the end of the year Ştefanov was sent to a Russian prisoner of war camp to act as political instructor to Romanian prisoners. Twelve months later, he was recalled to Moscow to work as a Romanian editor in the Foreign Languages Publishing House. On 15 May 1945, he was

younger members of this group were Marcel Pauker and his future wife, Ana Rabinsohn.[4] Their differences with the minimalists were more of emphasis than of substance, with the minimalists taking a more cautious line on the need for violent change. Further fragmentation occurred with the emergence of a third faction, the 'centrists', who supported affiliation to the Comintern, provided that it did not vitiate Romania's independence.

The creation of the Comintern in March 1919 profoundly changed the course of the socialist movement in Romania for it exerted an irresistible attraction to those in the SDP who sought change by revolution. The maximalists argued for immediate affiliation with the Comintern but were thwarted by the minimalists who, at a SDP congress held in May 1919, persuaded the participants to adopt a programme of democratic socialism; the transfer of all means of production from the private sector to state control but within the existing political system. The conflict between the two factions came out into the open again in November 1920, when a six-member delegation of maximalists and minimalists was sent to Moscow to negotiate Comintern affiliation. When Bukharin and Zinoviev criticised the SDP for its unwillingness to adopt a revolutionary programme, the minimalists responded by complaining about Comintern interference with the composition of the SDP's leadership.

When the delegation returned from Moscow in January 1921, its members put a motion to the party's General Council recom-

---

sent by Gheorghe Dimitrov, Comintern secretary, to Sofia where he remained till his death on 11 October 1969; see V. Smârcea, 'Boris Ştefanov', *Anale de Istorie*, vol.19 (1973), no.5, pp.143-6). A letter from Ştefanov dated 29 September 1956, addressed to the Central Committee of the RCP, gives a brief autobiography (I am grateful to Marius Oprea for passing me a photocopy). This letter also contains a request from the author that he be allowed to contribute to a history of the RCP which he understands is being compiled by the newly-founded Institute of Party History in Bucharest. The letter is marked 'for the attention of comrade Pîrvulescu'. Whether a reply was sent is not known. Others sources give June 1936 as the date of Ştefanov's appointment as party secretary.

4 Marcel Pàuker's son-in-law, Gheorghe Brătescu, has assembled a fascinating collection of documents from the Russian Centre for the Preservation and Study of Documents of Contemporary History in Moscow relating to Pauker and published them in *Lichidarea lui Marcel Pauker*, ed. G. Brătescu, Bucharest: Univers Enciclopedic, 1995. They include 400 pages of autobiographical material written in October and November 1937 in Pauker's own hand while he was under arrest in Moscow.

mending affiliation. The vote highlighted the divisions within the party: the proposal received the endorsement of the maximalists and the centrists, who together formed a majority, while the minimalists, who opposed affiliation, decided to leave the party. The council decided to convene a party congress in May where the principal item on the agenda was to be affiliation to the Comintern. This became what is regarded as the First Congress of the RCP, which opened in Bucharest on 8 May 1921. It was scheduled to run for five days, but police raids and arrests forced the abandonment of the congress on 12 May, the day after it voted to declare affiliation to the Comintern. According to C. Titel Petrescu, a leading socialist in the interwar period, three of the most fervent advocates of affiliation were police agents who aimed thereby to provide justification for the arrests.[5] The unfinished business, which included the adoption of a programme and the election of senior officials, was continued at a second congress, held in Ploieşti on 3-4 October 1922, when those participating took the name of the 'Communist Party of Romania, section of the Communist International'. This is indeed how the party is styled in the records of the Comintern. Gheorghe Cristescu was elected general secretary.

Membership of the Comintern gave the kiss of death to the fortunes of the Romanian Communists during the interwar period. By the time of the party's second congress, the impact of affiliation to the Comintern had become clear. At the insistence of Moscow, the 'centrists' were expelled in early 1922; Comintern sources indicated that whereas the SDP had over 45,000 members before the split, the RCP retained only 2,000 members in 1922.[6] On 11 April 1924, shortly after negotiations for resuming diplomatic relations between Romania and the Soviet Union collapsed over the Russian refusal to accept any formula which might be interpreted as an acknowledgement of Romanian sovereignty over Bessarabia, the Romanian government issued an order banning the RCP.

Henceforth the party was forced to conduct its activities underground or through surrogate organisations. Both means were impediments to recruitment and to the exercise of the democratic

5 Ionescu, *Communism in Rumania*, p.19.

6 Mary Ellen Fischer, *Nicolae Ceauşescu: A Study in Political Leadership*, Boulder, CO: Lynne Rienner, 1989, p.20. For the sake of consistency I refer to the party throughout this period as the RCP.

conduct of party affairs. Even though it was reduced to a marginalised heap, the party was required to behave by the Comintern as a 'proper' Communist Party by holding congresses and implementing a party line. Congresses were duly held, but in secret and outside Romania – the third in Vienna (1924), the fourth in Kharkov (1928), and the fifth and final pre-war congress in Moscow (1931).

Most damaging to the RCP's hopes of winning new recruits were Comintern directives which constituted an attack on Romania's national integrity. These were diametrically opposed to the sentiments of the vast majority of Romanians, including those in the industrial working class. The directives also provoked divisions within the RCP. Cristescu, a Romanian by birth, recognised that the adoption of such a policy by the party could lead to proscription, while the Transylvanian Hungarians Elek Koblos (Romanian pseudonym Bădulescu) and Sandor Korosi-Krizsan (Georgescu), were in favour. To resolve the conflict, Alexandru Dobrogeanu-Gherea proposed the despatch of an RCP delegation to Moscow to discuss the issue with the Comintern executive. The visit in September 1923 resulted in defeat for Cristescu, who was replaced in the following year as general secretary by the non-Romanian Koblos.

Typical of the directives was the call from the fifth Comintern Congress, held in June and July 1924, for 'the political separation of oppressed peoples from Poland, Romania, Czechoslovakia, Yugoslavia, and Greece'; the demand that Bessarabia, northern Bukovina, and the Western Ukraine be united with the Soviet Union; and that Transylvania and the Dobrogea be made independent states.[7] With the RCP now outlawed, there was nothing to be lost by adopting this position and, as if to emphasise its non-national character, the party installed Koblos as general secretary at the third RCP congress held in Vienna. The delegates accepted a resolution proclaiming the right of the minorities to secede from the newly-enlarged Romania, a stance it was to reiterate at its fourth and fifth congresses. The resolution effectively endorsed Soviet claims to Bessarabia by declaring the hope of 'workers and peasants of Bessarabia that their national revolution would unite

[7] *Ibid.*, p.21. Details of the some of the money given to the RCP by the Comintern for the publication of propaganda of this nature can be found in G. Buzatu, 'Cominterniştii români se pregătesc', *Magazin Istoric*, vol.28, no.2 (February 1994), pp.37-8.

them with the USSR'.[8] The Romanian parliament responded in December by passing a law making Communist activity an offence. As a result, over 'eight hundred members of the party were arrested and an entirely new party apparatus had to be erected', according to Comintern reports.[9]

The party's policy of self-determination for the minorities inevitably drew members of these groups to the party's ranks in disproportionate numbers and this, in turn, reinforced its 'alien' image.[10] That image was underlined by the facts that between the late summer of 1924 and the spring of 1944 its general secretaries were not ethnic Romanians, and that its fourth and fifth congresses were staged in the Soviet Union. At the former Vitali Holostenko, a one-time member of the Ukrainian Communist Party, was elected general secretary to replace Koblos but the party continued to be rent by factional disputes, generated by personality clashes rather than ideological conflict. Holostenko's authority was challenged by Marcel Pauker who, under his conspiratorial name of Luximin, claimed to represent the party. He was supported by Alexandru Dobrogeanu-Gherea, Boris Ştefanov and Laszlo Luka (Vasile Luca), a Transylvanian Hungarian worker who at the Kharkov Congress had been elected to the party's Central Committee. With the party paralysed by this confusion, the Comintern intervened to convene the fifth congress in Moscow in 1931, imposing yet another non-Romanian, Alexandru Stefanski (Gorun), as general secretary. Stefanski was a member of the Polish Communist Party and served as leader of the RCP from his base in Berlin for three years before Eugen Iacobovici took his place. In June 1936, the Bulgarian Ştefanov took over and held office until December 1940 when the Transylvanian Hungarian Ştefan Foriş was appointed by the Comintern.[11]

Foriş was born on 9 May 1892 in the village of Tărlungeni

[8] Shafir, *Romania*, p.24.

[9] Fischer, *Nicolae Ceauşescu* p.16, quoting from G.D. Jackson, *Comintern and Peasant in Eastern Europe, 1919-1930*, New York: Columbia University Press, 1966, p.254.

[10] Even key party documents were written not in Romanian, but in German or Russian e.g. Marcel Pauker's 'self-criticism' addressed to the party's Central Commitee in May 1932; see Brătescu, *Marcel Pauker*, pp.304-6.

[11] According to an autobiographical letter of Sţefanov, he was appointed general secretary of the RCP in 1935: see n.3.

near Braşov in Transylvania, which at that time was under Hungarian rule. After completing a degree in physics and mathematics at Budapest University, he returned to Braşov in September 1919 and joined the Hungarian-language socialist newspaper *Munkas* (Worker) as an editor. He became a member of the Communist Party in 1921 and in the following year moved to Bucharest where, after the proscription of the party, he worked underground as an agitator. In 1926 he became secretary of *Ajutorul Roşu* (Red Aid), the Romanian section of the Comintern-controlled International Organisation for Aiding the Fighters of the Revolution, known by its Russian initials MOPR *(Mezhdunarodnaia organizatsiia pomoshchi bortsam revoliutsii)*. The MOPR provided food and legal aid to Communist activists in prison. In 1927 Foriş was coopted as a member of the Central Committee and took part in the fourth party congress the next year. He was arrested and imprisoned in July 1928 but a rapid deterioration in his health led to his release and he went to Moscow. At the end of 1930 he returned to Romania and was arrested once more on 26 August 1931. Freed in 1935, he was appointed in 1938 to the secretariat of the Central Committee, and in February 1940 was summoned by the Comintern to Moscow and returned in December as general secretary of the party.[12]

The ethnic composition of the party's leadership made it particularly vulnerable in the ultranationalist arena of Romanian politics in the 1930s, when the myth of 'Judeo-Bolshevism' was propagated by Corneliu Codreanu's Iron Guard and other movements of the extreme right such as the National Christian Party led by Octavian Goga and Alexandru C. Cuza. In an effort to present a more indigenous image, some Jewish party members took Romanian cover names, among them Ion Roitman (Chişinevski), Lev Oigenstein (Leonte Răutu), and Ernst Neulander (Valter Roman). Those like Ana and Marcel Pauker, Bela Brainer and Remus Kofler who did not confirmed suspicions in the public mind about their real loyalties.[13] Their presence, coupled with that of Tran-

[12] A.G. Savu, 'Ştefan Foriş. Schiţă pentru o viitoare biografie', *Magazin Istoric*, no.7, 1968, pp.53-8. This issue of *Magazin Istoric* was withdrawn from circulation by the authorities because of this article on Foriş. I am grateful to Marian Ştefan for providing me with a copy; see also N.I. Florea, 'Ştefan Foriş', *Analele de Istorie*, vol.18 (1972), no.3, pp.150-3.

[13] As M. Shafir points out (*Romania*, p.26), some of the leading Communists

sylvanian Hungarians such as Elek Koblos and Ştefan Foriş, and the Bulgarians Gheorghe Crosneff and Dimitur Kolev (Dumitriu Coliu), invited the conclusion that the use of 'Romanian' in the title of the party was a fiction. Most Romanians ignored the fact that the majority of Jews in Romania did not belong to the RCP, and that a number of these leaders, such as Dobrogeanu-Gherea and Marcel Pauker, were victims of Stalin's purges in the Soviet Union.[14]

An analysis of membership figures for the 1930s shows that the Hungarians, who made up less than 8% of the country's population, were some 26% of the RCP; the analogous figures for Jews were 4% of the population and 18%, for Russians and Ukrainians 3% and 10%, and for Bulgarians 2% and 10%. Romanians, by contrast, made up 72% of the population yet only 23% of party members.[15]

It has been argued that for those Jews who embraced Communism, its special attraction was its universal ideology which promised a new identity transcending the ethnic or the national. Nurturing the belief that assimilation was the answer to their crisis of identity, the Jewish Communists saw the need for a fundamental change in society as a necessary condition of that assimilation[16] These views led one analyst to offer the graphic description of the interwar Romanian Communists as 'political sleepwalkers, possessed by the quasi-religious belief that the Soviet Union personified their most sacred dreams of social justice and human freedom.'[17]

---

were doubly tainted in being, in the case of Chişinevski and Răutu, not only Jews but from Bessarabia to boot.

14 Alexandru Dobrogeanu-Gherea was executed at Lublianka prison in Moscow on 4 December 1937; see Marius Mircu, *Dosar Ana Pauker*, Bucharest: Editura Gutenberg, 1991, p.93. Tatiana Pauker was informed by the Praesidium of the USSR in 1959 that her father died on 16 August 1938 (author's interview with Tatiana Brătescu, 30 July 1994). This news received partial confirmation in 1993 when Tatiana was informed by the Ministry for Security of the Russian Federation that 'in all probability' Marcel Pauker was executed on 16 August 1938 on a shooting range in the Moscow suburb of Butovo (Brătescu, *Marcel Pauker*, p. 297).

15 Shafir, *Romania*, p.26.

16 King, *History of the RCP*, p.34.

17 Vladimir Tismăneanu, 'The Tragicomedy of Romanian Communism', *East European Politics and Societies*, vol.3, no.2 (spring 1989), p.341.

Those close to Ana Pauker admit that she worshipped Stalin and believed that, in spite of his mistakes, the future lay with the Soviet Union.[18]

The membership of the party, nevertheless, remained small. In 1922 the party had 2,000 members but according to Comintern data that figure had fallen by 1925 to 1,661 members. In 1927 the number collapsed dramatically to barely 300, probably because the party's stance on Bessarabia had become well known, but membership was to rise slowly throughout the 1930s, reaching its highest point in 1937 with 1,635 activists.[19] Despite this exiguous membership the party did manage to exercise influence through front organisations. The most significant of these was the Worker-Peasant Bloc *(Blocul Muncitoresc-Ţărănesc)*, which was founded in 1925 as a legal body. The bloc won between 32,000 and 39,000 votes in the parliamentary elections of 1926, 1927 and 1928, and achieved its greatest success in that of June 1931, when it secured 73,716 votes and five seats in parliament, although its victories were later invalidated. Among the five deputies was Lucreţiu Pătrăşcanu, a young lawyer, who became a leading figure in the party in the 1940s. The bloc's strongest support came from Transylvania and the Banat, territories with large Hungarian, German

[18] Author's interview with Gheorghe Brătescu, Pauker's son-in-law, 30 July 1994. That Pauker was not blind to Stalin's crimes is evident from the following anecdote. When Mr Brătescu discussed Khrushchev's denunciation of Stalin in 1956 with Pauker, he asked her whether she did not share his belief that Khrushchev was lying. To his self-confessed surprise, she said that it was all probably true.

[19] Membership of the RCP from 1925 to 1937 was as follows:

1925	1,661
1926	1,500
1927	300
1928	500
1929	461
1930	700
1936	1,083
1937	1,635

The breakdown of membership on ethnic affiliation for the year 1933 was: Hungarians 440, Romanians 375, Jews 300, Bulgarians 140, Russians 100, Moldavians 70, Ukrainians 70, others 170. (Comintern files in RTsKhIDNI [Russian Centre for the Preservation and Study of Documents on Contemporary History], fond 495, opis 25, dos.744; I am grateful to Prof. Ioan Chiper for this information.)

and Jewish minority populations. Both provinces had only been united with Romania in 1918, and insensitive integrationist policies since union disaffected large segments of the minorities. But factors other than ethnic protest must also be taken into account when considering the party's appeal. Both Transylvania and the Banat were more industrialised than other areas of the country and the party's stance on social and economic grounds boosted its vote. Support for the bloc waned after 1931, and two years later the government ordered its dissolution and that of other front organisations.

2

THE COMMUNIST PARTY IN ROMANIA, 1930-1944

The Romania in which the Communist Party operated was radically different from the country in which socialism first appeared.[1] As a result of its participation in the First World War, it more than doubled in area and increased in population from 7.5 million to more than 17 million. The enlarged Romania included areas formerly ruled by Russia, Hungary and Bulgaria – which left Romania with two neighbours unreconciled to their losses and bent on revision of the treaties which legalised them, and a third, the Soviet Union, refusing to recognise the loss of Bessarabia. By these additions of territory, the new Romania had minorities, amounting to 29% of the population, which the centralising policies of governments in the 1920s did little or nothing to reconcile to their new status. Both before and after the War, there were the Jews, largely concentrated in Moldavia, whose arrival, often under duress, from Russia and the Ukraine nevertheless made them widely regarded, especially among peasants, as 'Russians'. Sephardic immigrants from the south, largely settled in Wallachia, were less

[1] Before the First World War, the two leading figures in the Romanian socialist movement were Constantin Dobrogeanu-Gherea, born Konstantin Katz, who was forced to flee his native Ukraine in 1875 because of his involvement in revolutionary activity, and Christian Rakovsky, a Bulgarian from the Dobrogea who later became a prominent member of the Soviet Communist Party. Gherea was quick to recognise that Romanian did not offer propitious ground for the dissemination of socialist ideas, lamenting that socialism was regarded by Romanian intellectuals as an 'imported exotic plant', and confessing, in a letter to Karl Kautsky in 1894, that when he had 'first arrived in Romania as a Russian refugee, not even the word "socialism" was known there'. (Shafir, *Romania*, p. 12; for biographical details of Dobrogeanu-Gherea and a discussion of his indebtedness to Marx in his writings see Michael Kitch, 'Constantin Dobrogeanu-Gherea and Romanian Marxism', *Slavonic and East European Review*, vol.133, no.1, p.87).

resented, and indeed were much more integrated, especially in finance and industry.

Industrial development was confined to an east-west axis from Timişoara to Braşov in Transylvania, and a north-south axis from Sighişoara in Transylvania to Ploieşti and Bucharest in Wallachia. This left the country a prominently agricultural one, with great discrepancies between town and country. According to the 1930 census, 80% of the population of 18 million lived on the land in villages that were poorly served by transport and communications. Few villages had piped water or electricity, health services were primitive, especially in the more backward regions of Moldavia and Bessarabia, and in such conditions it is hardly surprising that infant mortality was among the highest levels in Eastern Europe.

These problems were of a complexity which would have taxed the most far-sighted government and the most thoroughgoing cadres of administration: in the interwar period, Romania had neither. The greatest discrepancy, from a Western point of view, lay in the gulf between word and deed. Behind the façade of political institutions copied from the West the practice of government was subject to patronage and to narrow sectional interests. Under the constitution of 1923 the king had the power to dissolve parliament and to appoint a new government. That government was charged with seeking a popular mandate by organising elections whose conduct was entrusted to the county prefects. Invariably the new government appointed new prefects to secure the desired result. By general consensus the only elections deemed to have been relatively free of such manipulation were those of 1928.

Institutionalised corruption was matched by a personal variety. The exploitative rule of foreign princes in Wallachia and Moldavia in the eighteenth and early nineteenth centuries had helped to create a culture among the dominant élite in which rapacity was regarded as proof of dexterity and cunning, and therefore corruption of principles had become widespread. This culture had been assimilated by the small, bureaucratic middle class who as political appointees expected to rely on unofficial remuneration in the form of bribes to supplement their meagre salaries. There was no native economic middle class to act as a check on the élite since commerce had fallen largely into the hands of the largely disenfranchised Jews who were barred from public service.

Idealism was scorned, and those who searched for it – the young

–were driven to the only parties which seemed to have any on offer, those of the Right. Although a radical land reform was introduced soon after the War, many peasants were unable to afford the loans necessary to buy agricultural machinery. The economic recession of the 1930s ushered in a decade of instability in which the xenophobia of the impoverished peasantry was exploited by right-wing movements, principally the Iron Guard, and directed against the Jews. Disillusion with the failure of parliamentary government to solve economic problems fuelled support for the Guard, with its promise of spiritual regeneration and its programme of combatting 'Jewish Bolshevism'.

The Communist Party, despite its proscription, responded to these conditions by being active on the labour front. It organised a number of strikes, one of which was to bring to the fore a railway worker who, after the imposition of Communist rule in Romania, became Romania's leader. Gheorghe Gheorghiu was something of a rarity among RCP members, being at once an ethnic Romanian and from a working-class background (his father was a manual worker). His lack of a formal education marked him out from the intellectuals in the party, such as the Paukers and Pătrăşcanu, and even from his later close friend, Emil Bodnăraş, who had passed out from a Romanian officers' school.

Gheorghiu was born in Bîrlad in Moldavia on 8 November 1901. His parents, Tănase and Ana, sent him to work at the age of eleven as a porter in the Danube port of Galaţi. He managed to complete three years of secondary education in a trade school, qualifying as an electrician. According to one source, he took a series of jobs in a timber mill, a textile mill and then in coopers' yards in Piatra Neamţ and Moineşti. From 1919 to 1921 he worked as an electrician in the town of Câmpina, after which he returned to Galaţi where he signed on as an electrician in a railway yard. Between 1923 and 1925, he did his military service, being promoted to sergeant. In 1927 he married Maria Alexe, a local girl whose father was a local trader, and the couple had two daughters.[2]

2 Vasilica (Lica) (born in Galaţi on 28 August 1928 and died in Bucharest on 15 March 1987) and Constantina (Tanţi) (born in Galaţi on 23 April 1921). In 1933, Maria Gheorghiu divorced Dej and later remarried. In November 1938, Dej, according to a police report, asked the party for permission to marry Elena Sârbu, a Communist activist, but he later withdrew this request, (J. Enache, 'Căsătorii, divorţuri, iubiri, copii şi nepoţi', *Dosarele Istoriei*, no.3(8), 1997, p.

Accusations of 'Communist agitation' led Gheorghiu to be transferred from the railway yards in Galaţi to Dej on 15 August 1931 and it was his association with the town which led him to attach the suffix Dej to his name. (For reasons of conciseness we use the surname Dej throughout the book).

Various dates have been given for Dej's initiation into the Communist Party – 1928, 1930 and 1932. As state employees railway workers were denied the right to strike, and this merely added to their disaffection. Gheorghiu took up his colleagues' grievances and on 20 March 1932 attended a national meeting of railwaymen in Bucharest where he was elected to the Central Action Committee. On 2 February 1933, the railway workers at the Griviţa yards in Bucharest went on strike after the government withdrew from earlier agreements on working conditions with the men. The strike spread to railwaymen in Cluj and Iaşi. Dej

11). Maria was allegedly a heavy drinker and after his release from internment Dej took custody of his daughters. He did not remarry. Lica Gheorghiu made a name for herself as an actress, starring in a number of Romanian films in the early 1960s. She was married twice, first to Marcel Popescu whom Gheorghiu-Dej made minister for foreign trade (19 March 1957-17 August 1959). After Dej's death, he was vice-president of the Chamber of Commerce. He died in 1979. Lica and Marcel had two children: Sanda, born in 1950, who is a notary; Camilia Mândra, born in 1955, also a notary. In the late 1950s, Lica met and fell in love with a doctor, Gheorghe Plăcinţeanu. Their affair infuriated Dej and he ordered Alexandru Drăghici, the minister of the interior, to 'remove' the doctor. Drăghici duly obliged by having Plăcinţeanu murdered. After divorcing Marcel, Lica married Gheorghe Rădoi who at the time was a director of the 'Red Flag' tractor plant in Braşov. He was made a member of the Central Committee. For a brief period, Rădoi was vice-president of the Council of Ministers (18 March-21 August 1965). In 1975, Radoi failed to secure nomination for election to the Central Committee. Tanţi, the younger daughter, trained as an engineer and became a lecturer at Bucharest Polytechnic. In 1953, she fell in love with a popular singer called Cezar Grigoriu. Dej frowned upon this liaison as well and in 1956 ordered Grigoriu's arrest. The singer was interrogated and beaten by Isidor Hollinger, head of the counter-espionage directorate of the *Securitate* and accused of working for the Americans and British. He was released after twenty-four hours and told by Hollinger to explain his disappearance by saying that he had got drunk. Tanţi is said to have frantically tried to trace her lover by telephone from Marcel Popescu's office in the Central Committee. Grigoriu followed Hollinger's instructions, whereupon Popescu turned to Tanţi and said: 'See, you didn't upset the chief too much. Look, they didn't arrest him after all!' Tanţi later married Stamate Popescu, a sculptor by whom she had a daughter (M. Oprea, 'Lica şi Tanţi Dej se iubeau cu doi burgheji', *Cuvîntul* (25-31 May 1992).

and other members of the committee were arrested on 14 February and on the following day there were violent clashes at the yards between workers and police which left several railwaymen dead. Although he was in jail during these disturbances, Dej was put on trial as one of the instigators alongside Constantin Doncea, Chivu Stoica, Dumitru Petrescu, Ilie Pintilie and Gheorghe Vasilichi, all later to be involved in the upper echelons of the party, and over 100 other 'agitators'. He was sentenced on 19 August 1933 to twelve years' hard labour.[3] His wife divorced him the previous year and married a policeman.

He was sent to the Doftana prison near Câmpina where in 1936 he was joined by all the other jailed Communists following a decision by the authorities to incarcerate all of them together. If the aim was to supervise them more effectively, it was a patent failure, as a police report from September 1936 indicated: 'At Doftana the Communists, though isolated in their cells, carry on political work...hold daily conferences and...discuss subjects of communist agitation. [...] The prisoners are organised in a collective which includes all Communist prisoners. [...] In addition, there is a Communist group...which leads the collective.'[4] Imprisonment at Doftana, like the Griviţa strike and the coup of 23 August 1944, was accorded a sacred place in Gheorghiu-Dej's career by postwar Communist historiography and continued to enjoy mythical status in the annals of the Communist movement compiled under Nicolae Ceauşescu, who also served a two-year sentence there for Communist agitation between 1936 and 1938. The prison experience of the Communists in Doftana was presented as an integral part of the class struggle between the proletariat and an alliance of the bourgeoisie and landowners in which the latter, faced with the prospect of defeat, resorted to the use of legislation 'of a repressive nature' in order to stifle the growth of 'the revolutionary movement of the proletariat'. The conditions in which the Communists were held in Doftana, one party historian claimed,

3 Mircea Chiriţoiu, 'Radiografia unui stalinist', *Dosarele Istoriei*, no.3(8), 1997, pp.4-5 and Fischer, *Nicolae Ceauşescu*, p.23. Among those arrested with Dej were Constantin Agiu who was released shortly afterwards, Vasile Bîgu, Constantin Doncea (alias Victor Pandelescu), Dumitru Petrescu, Chivu Stoica, and Gheorghe Vasilichi. In 1938 Agiu was re-arrested and spent six months in Doftana.

4 *Ibid.*

revealed, in direct contrast to the police report of 1936, 'the premeditated aim of destroying them physically and morally through the use of pressure, solitary confinement, beatings and starvation'.[5]

So sweeping a condemnation is not supported by reliable evidence. While isolation cells were occasionally used in which the prisoners were kept in total darkness and solitary confinement, prisoners in ordinary adjacent cells could communicate with each other. The Doftana prisoners were allowed visitors, food parcels, money and reading matter.[6] Even correspondence was smuggled in, and this allowed Gheorghiu-Dej to keep in touch with the party leadership, for he was coopted to its Central Committee (CC) *in absentia* in 1935.[7] In terms of his ethnic and social background he was, as a CC member, unique, apart from Ilie Pintilie who was also a railwayman. Unlike Constantin Pîrvulescu, Iosif Chişinevski, Petre Borilă and Gheorghe Stoica, from among the Romanian Communists, or Klement Gottwald, Erno Gero, Boleslaw Bierut or Iosip Broz Tito from among the other East European Communist Parties – later his coevals – Dej did not study at the Comintern school in Moscow.

In Doftana the young Communists looked to Gheorghiu-Dej for leadership and he provided it. He cultivated an avuncular image, being addressed as 'the old man', even though he was only in his mid-thirties. Among their number were Gheorghe Apostol, Nicolae Ceauşescu, Alexandru Drăghici and Alexandru Moghioroş, all of whom were to be promoted after 1944 to senior party and state positions as Gheorghiu-Dej's trusted lieutenants. Alongside this group of young activists he attracted a parallel set of friends who were all Soviet agents: Pintilie Bondarenko, Vasile Bucikov, Petea Goncearuk, Serghei Nikonov and Misha Posteuca. It was from the latter group that Dej learned his halting Russian.[8]

[5] Olimpia Matichescu, *Doftana: Simbol al Eroismului Revoluţionar*, Bucharest: Editura Politică, 1979, pp.12-13.

[6] Author's interview with Gheorghe Apostol, 7 May 1990.

[7] Mircea Bălănescu, an assistant to Ştefan Foriş, related how Foriş kept in touch with Gheorghiu-Dej by using couriers, known as 'technicele'. These were attractive young women to whom letters from Foriş were passed on by Mircea Bălănescu for delivery to Iosif Şraier, Gheorghiu-Dej's legal representative, who took them to his client in Doftana (interview with M. Bălănescu, televised on Romanian TV on 28 July 1994).

[8] Letter from Mircea Oprişan to the author, 3 January 1996. Oprişan, who

Nevertheless, prison was hardly a place from which Gheorghiu-Dej could translate his authority into effective action. It also cut him off from the Comintern and meant that he did not pass through the hands of its instructors, either in Moscow or elsewhere. This marked him out from those in the Communist Party in Romania who did and made him an unknown quantity to Stalin.

The opposite was true of the figure who was to become Gheorghiu-Dej's main rival after 1944. Ana Pauker was born on 13 December 1893 in the village of Codaieşti in Moldavia into a middle-class family called Rabinsohn. Her father was a *haham*, a Jewish cantor and teacher of Hebrew at the local school. At the turn of the century, the Rabinsohns moved to Bucharest. Details of Ana's youth and education are sketchy and largely anecdotal, and the first mention of any professional activity concerns her employment as a teacher of Hebrew at the Brotherhood of Zion primary school in Bucharest.[9] Shortly afterwards, in September 1915, she joined the socialist movement. According to an autobiographical pamphlet, published in 1951, Ana helped to distribute literature produced by the Romanian SDP. She was more forthcoming about her activity in this period to Corneliu Coposu, the private secretary of NPP leader Iuliu Maniu, whom she encountered at Cluj prison in the mid-1930s. There, she revealed that after leaving her post as a schoolteacher, she found a position as a secretarial assistant at the independent newspaper *Dimineaţa* where she had responsibility for the library. It was while working there that in 1921 she met the son of one of the major shareholders of the newspaper, Marcel Pauker, who was three years her junior and had just returned from Paris where he had taken a doctorate in law.[10]

The two took part in the founding congress of the RCP in May 1921, but the arrest of its leading members prompted them to flee to Zurich where they were married on 1 June. Marcel

---

knew Dej from his time in Caransebeş jail, said that Dej also learned some Yiddish from Simion Zeiger, a lawyer who became a close friend of Dej and served as his personal secretary when he acquired ministerial office.

9 For this largely anecdotal account of Ana's background see Mircu, *Dosar Ana Pauker*, pp.12-23. Another source places her in the northern Moldavian town of Buhuşi as a schoolteacher (Corneliu Coposu, *Dialoguri cu Vartan Arachelian*, Bucharest: Editura Anastasia., 1992, p.63).

10 *Ibid.*, p.63.

enrolled as a student of engineering at the École Polytechnique Federale while Ana began a course in medicine. A few months after the wedding, Ana returned to Bucharest to give birth to her first child, a daughter Tania, who died of dysentery before she was one year old. At the second RCP congress, held at Ploieşti in October 1922, both Marcel and Ana were elected to the Central Committee of the party. After the proscription of the party and the suppression of its newspaper *Socialismul* in April 1924, Ana was given the task of publishing underground propaganda and she became a target of the *Siguranţa*, the security police. She was arrested with four female colleagues and held in Văcăreşti prison. At Ana's instigation the four went on hunger strike and were beaten, after which they, and Ana, were released till the date of their trial, fixed for July 1925.[11]

The defendants absconded and Ana Pauker was sentenced *in absentia* to ten years' imprisonment. The Paukers managed to flee abroad in 1926, staying in Berlin, Paris and Prague, and in the same year Ana's son Vlad was born in Vienna. From there they went to Moscow where Ana attended the Comintern training school in order to become an instructor. In Moscow Ana produced a second daughter, Tatiana, in 1928. Her husband returned to Romania clandestinely in the spring of 1929, only to be arrested on 4 May, but he was to benefit from an amnesty of which he took advantage to work underground for two years before returning to Moscow. In December 1932 he was again sent by the Comintern to Romania, this time to organise Communist activity in Transylvania, and in the following year he was recalled to Moscow.

Ana, too, was given a mission by the Comintern. She was attached in turn to the Czechoslovak, German and French Communist Parties (from 1931 to 1932) as an instructor, with the cover name of Marina.[12] In March 1934 she was sent back by the Comintern to Romania in the company of other comrades

[11] Mircu, *Dosar Ana Pauker*, p.43.

[12] It was in Paris that she had an affair with Albert Fried (Clément), a fellow instructor for the French Communist Party, as result of which she gave birth to a daughter, Maria, in Moscow in December 1932. Marcel was similarly wayward in his affections at this time. He had an affair in Bessarabia with an RCP activist, Rosa Elbert, who bore a son named Iacov in 1931 (author's interview with Tatiana Brătescu, 30 July 1994).

in an attempt to revive clandestine activity which had been severely curtailed following the Griviţa strike. She was eventually arrested in Bucharest in the early hours of 13 July 1935. Her trial and that of eighteen other Communists who included Alexandru Moghioroş, his future wife Stela (Esther Radoshovetsky), Alexandru Drăghici and Liuba Chişinevski was scheduled to be held in the capital but street demonstrations in support of the defendants led the authorities to move it to Craiova. Proceedings opened on 5 June 1936, and were attended by several foreign press correspondents and observers. Among the twenty-four lawyers for the defence were Lucreţiu Pătrăşcanu and Ion Gheorghe Maurer, as well as leading advocates from Bucharest.[13]

Ana was found guilty of being a leading member of an outlawed organisation and sentenced on 7 July to ten years' imprisonment. She spent five in the prisons of Dumbrăveni, Rîmnicu-Sărat and Caransebeş before being exchanged on 3 May 1941 for Ion Codreanu, a sixty-two-year-old Romanian from Bessarabia who had been arrested for 'anti-Soviet agitation' in the previous July following the Soviet annexation of the province.[14] While Ana was in prison, her husband was arrested in Moscow in 1937 together with other senior members of the RCP: Alexandru Dobrogeanu-Gherea, Ecaterina Arbore, Pavel Tcacenko, Elek Koblos and David Fabian.[15] All became victims of Stalin's purges.

These blows to the RCP did not prevent it from mounting a successful operation to recruit volunteers for the International Brigades during the Spanish Civil War. Volunteers were also raised by the NPP and the SDP. 'Committees in Support of Republican Spain' were set up by all three parties to help provide food and clothing

[13] Ion Gheorghe Maurer was born in Bucharest on 23 September 1902. His mother was Romanian but his father was from Alsace and was employed as French tutor to Prince Carol (later King Carol II). After studying law at Bucharest University, he practised at the bar. He developed Marxist sympathies and often appeared for the defence of Communists. According to his own testimony, he joined the Party 'somewhat before 1936'. (L. Betea, *Maurer şi lumea de ieri*, Arad: Fundaţia Culturală Ion Slavici, 1995, p.13).

[14] Details related by Codreanu to Archibald Gibson, Kemsley Newspapers correspondent, in 1945 and recorded in Gibson's private papers (in possession of this author).

[15] Dobrogeanu-Gherea was executed on 4 December 1937 at the Lubîianka prison in Moscow. For a biography of Fabian see *Anale de istorie*, vol.16, 1970, no.6, p.174.

for the republican forces. The Liberal government espoused a policy of non-intervention and instructed the passport authorities not to issue passports to volunteers, but many left without them. More than 500 Romanian Communists fought on the Republican side, and their passage to Spain was organised by a network covering Romania, Czechoslovakia, Austria, Switzerland and France.[16] Among those who fought were Petre Borilă, Mihai Burcă, Constantin Doncea, Mihail Florescu, Valter Roman and Gheorghe Stoica. After the Republican defeat in the Civil War, a number of the Romanian volunteers were interned in the south of France but some, such as Mihail Florescu and Mihai Patriciu, escaped and fought in the French resistance till 1944, after which they found their way back to Romania.[17]

[16] It included Eduard Mezincescu, Gheorghe Rădulescu, and Leonte Răutu in Romania, and Alexandru Buican in France (Tismăneanu, 'Tragicomedy', p.356, n.62). Răutu was born in 1910 in Bessarabia. Like his fellow townsman Iosif Roitman Chişinevski (they were both from Bălţi), he joined the Agitprop (Agitation and Propaganda) section of the RCP in the early 1930s.

[17] Not all the Romanian Communist volunteers travelled to Spain from Romania. In October 1936, a group of émigré Romanian Communists from France left directly for Spain. Among them was Valter Roman, who had been forced to leave Romania in 1934 after the collapse of the Communist student movement there. Roman was a mechanical engineer who commanded a volunteer regiment of artillery during the Civil War. In October 1938, the volunteers were withdrawn from Spain. Some were interned in the south of France, but Roman went to the Soviet Embassy in Paris from where he was taken to Le Havre and sent by steamer to Leningrad. He spent the war years in Moscow and returned to Romania with the Horia, Cloşca and Crişan division of NKVD-trained troops in 1945 (interview with Mihail Florescu, 12 August 1996).

The part played by Romanian Communists in the French resistance is recalled in a series of personal recollections in *Les Roumains dans la Résistance française*, Bucharest: Meridiane, 1971.

It was Stalin's intention, according to Eduard Mezincescu, a veteran Communist and senior official in the Romanian Foreign Ministry in 1948, to use the Spanish Civil War in order to establish a bridgehead of Communism in that country and with this in mind he despatched 'volunteers'. Many of them were, in fact, NKVD agents who were given orders to eliminate all those considered unreliable in the Spanish Party. Mezincescu was sent to Cluj in 1936 and helped to coordinate a network which helped 'volunteers', among whom were Soviet agents (Pavel Cristescu, Grigore Naum, Minea Stan) pass into Czechoslovakia from where the Czech party sent them on to France. At the end of the Civil War, the volunteers were interned in the south of France. From these camps the NKVD extracted only their agents and those of the Comintern and sent them to Moscow. The rest were left to languish in the camps (interview with

Internment in France, imprisonment in Romania and liquidation by Stalin all dealt crushing blows to the RCP. The party's financial position was also disastrous. From a report compiled by a certain Scevortzov, described as one of the Romanian party leaders, which reached the Executive Committee of the Comintern in January 1940, it emerged that members' contributions were totally insufficient to cover the costs of the party's activities in Romania. According to the report, in 1939 there were only twenty-six paid activists, seven in Bucharest and the rest in regional branches. The financial support required to maintain the remnants of the party came from the Comintern which used different channels through which to filter the funds. From Moscow the money was sent to the Romanian Communists in France who then despatched it to Romania. At the beginning of 1939 Boris Ştefanov, the general secretary of the RCP living in Moscow, wrote to the Comintern secretary Georgi Dimitrov alerting him that two party members, Bela Brainer and Gheorghe Vasilichi, based in France, had complained to him about a shortage of money. Dimitrov approved the despatch of US $1,000 to be shared by the two men. On 4 August 1939 Vasilichi informed Ştefanov that he was sending a man to Romania to pass on the latter's instructions.[18]

Up till the summer of 1939 the Comintern, whose principal executives were the Bulgarian Georgi Dimitrov and Dmitri Manuilsky, a member of the Central Committee of the Soviet Communist Party, had conducted a crusade against Hitler and Fascism as the main enemy of peace and of socialism in Europe, and in this context the RCP had launched a slogan calling for 'defence of the frontiers'. But no sooner had Molotov and Ribbentrop signed the Nazi-Soviet Pact in August 1939 than the Comintern changed its line. Hitler and Fascism were no longer the enemy; instead, Britain and France were to be blamed for the Second World War. A Comintern manifesto published in October 1939 avoided any attack on the Nazi dictatorship and echoed Molotov's and Ribbentrop's call for a negotiated peace. An article published in December 1939 in the *Communist International* by Ştefanov accused

Eduard Mezincescu, 7 April 1993).

18 Details of this correspondence and of relations between the Comintern and the Communist Party in Romania in this period are to be found in T.A. Pokivailova, '1939-1940: Cominternul şi Partidul Comunist din România', *Magazin Istoric*, vol.31, no.3 (March 1997), pp.45-8.

Britain and France of attempting to drag Romania into the imperialist war. He maintained that Romania's interests required a treaty of mutual assistance with the Soviet Union and directed the RCP to work for the right of self-determination in the annexed provinces of Bessarabia, Bukovina, Transylvania and Dobrogea, even if this meant their separation from Romania. Few Romanians believed the Soviet Foreign Ministry's denial that Ştefanov represented the views of the Soviet government, and most were convinced that the article revealed a Soviet interest in Romania that went beyond the recovery of Bessarabia.[19]

Ştefanov's difficulties were compounded by a report submitted to the Comintern in January 1940 by party activists in Romania criticising him for giving the Comintern inaccurate information about the political situation in Romania. Ştefanov in response accused the local party leaders of opportunism, 'rightist deviation' and 'Trotskyism'. Imposing the Comintern line at a distance (and a changing one in the circumstances of the Molotov-Ribbentrop Pact), especially in the absence of regular communication between Moscow and Bucharest, was difficult for Ştefanov. Dimitrov was dissatisfied with him, it appears, and this led to his replacement in early 1940 as general secretary of the RCP by an ailing Bela Brainer.[20]

The territorial losses suffered by Romania in the summer of 1940 almost eradicated the party. Stalin, annexing Bessarabia and Northern Bukovina in June 1940, and Hitler, with his award of Northern Transylvania to Hungary in August, reduced Romania's total area and population by almost a third. The cession of these provinces was catastrophic for the RCP's membership since it removed areas where loyalty to it was strong. According to Comintern figures, the RCP's membership of 4,210 dropped to about 1,000 as a result of the Soviet annexation of Bessarabia and Northern Bukovina and the partition of Transylvania and the Dobrogea.[21]

[19] Henry L. *Roberts, Rumania: Political Problems of an Agrarian State*, New Haven: Yale University Press, 1951, p.258.

[20] L. Betea, 'Testamentul lui Foriş', *Magazin Istoric*, vol.31, no.4 (April 1997), p.42.

[21] A document of 8 July 1940 signed by Ilin gave the breakdown of RCP membership by districts as follows: Transylvania 780, Prahova 160, Oltenia 170, Dobrogea 260 (mostly Bulgarians), Lower Danube 90, Moldavia 250, Bukovina (end of March 1940) 380, Bessarabia (end of May 1940) 280, and Bucharest

The desire of Dimitrov to ensure that the RCP remained a slave to the Comintern's bidding led him to summon Ştefan Foriş and Teohari Georgescu for consultation with Comintern officials in October 1940.[22] Both Foriş and Georgescu crossed secretly

---

(including students) 440. An additional 1,200 members were listed as being in the army, and 200 in the Union of Communist Youth. The total number of RCP members was thus 4,210. With the loss of Bessarabia and Northern Bukovina the numbers dropped to 3,260, and the subsequent amputation of Northern Transylvania and the Dobrogea reduced them still further to about 1,000 (Moscow, RTsKhIDNI, fond 495, opis 180, dos. 482). I am grateful to Professor Ioan Chiper for this information.

[22] Teohari Georgescu was born on 31 January 1908 in Bucharest. After four years of elementary school he became a printer's apprentice and in 1923 entered the printing plant of *Cartea Românească*. In 1928 he joined the printers' union and helped to organise a strike. His role in the strike brought him to the attention of the *Siguranţa* who placed him under surveillance. In the following year, he joined the Communist Party. In November 1933, he was arrested for distributing Communist manifestos and detained for several months before being released on grounds of 'insufficient proof'. He was rearrested in June 1934 for Communist activity but released on bail. He was arrested once again in Ploieşti in January 1935 for failing to appear at his trial, and held for several months before being released until the trial date was fixed. His trial was postponed on more than ten occasions between 1937 and 1940 when he was finally sentenced to two months' imprisonment. From 1937 to 1938 he worked as a printer for the daily *Adevărul* and the National Printing Office. In August 1940, he was sent to Moscow to receive instruction from the NKVD, on orders from George Dimitrov, secretary of the Comintern, on how to code messages and how to use a special technique of writing them on glass. He was arrested in April 1941 as part of the Bucharest party cell led by Iosif Chişinevski (Riotman) and sentenced in May to ten years in jail. The first part of his sentence was carried out at Caransebeş jail. In April 1942, he was moved to Văcăreşti prison to work in the printing-shop and returned to Caransebeş at the end of August where he stayed until his release at the end of August 1944 (*Archive of the Romanian Security Service* (henceforth abbreviated to ASRI), fond Y, dosar 40009, vol.21, pp. 111-37). An appraisal of Georgescu, made by the British political mission in 1946, shed some interesting light on his family background: 'Several responsible reports claim, although baptised Orthodox, [Georgescu] is of Jewish origin and [his] actual name is Burah Tescovici. Married for a second time to Jewess, Eugenia Samoila, a former dressmaker. He has one daughter. His family furnishes [an] interesting example of nepotism. He is [the] brother-in-law of General [Nicolae] Pârvulescu, under-secretary of supplies, who through Georgescu entered into contact with the Communists. He has [a] brother who is [the] police chief of 31st Bucharest district. His wife has two brothers, one of whom was [a] press chief of [the] People's Court during war criminal trials, while the second on returning from Russia started in January 1946 a police information bureau under the name of 'Documentary Bureau.' (Public Record Office, FO 371/59190/

into newly-occupied Bessarabia to receive instructions. Foriş was appointed general secretary of the party after the death of Bela Brainer, and Georgescu was allegedly designated Foriş's successor should anything befall him.[23]

The annexation of Bessarabia had other consequences for individual RCP members. Leonte Răutu and Alexandru Bîrlădeanu, both from the province, were accorded Soviet nationality and instructed to go to Moscow.[24] There they joined Vasile Luca –arrested as a Communist activist in Cernăuţi (Czernowitz) in 1940 but released after the Soviet occupation of Northern Bukovina –and Valter Roman.[25] With the arrival of Ana Pauker in May

R7847/6181/37). General Nicolae Pârvulescu was appointed secretary-general of police in the Ministry of the Interior by Georgescu on 6 March 1945. Dissatisfied with this post, he was made under-secretary at the Ministry of Supplies in summer 1945. The claim that Georgescu was Jewish is not borne out by his party file.

23 Author's interview with Eduard Mezincescu, 7 April 1993. Ştefanov, in Moscow since 1939, had had no direct contact with the rump of the RCP.

24 Bîrlădeanu was born at Comrat in Bessarabia in 1911. He completed his secondary schooling at Iaşi and in 1932 was taken on as a lecturer in political economics at the University of Iaşi. He appears to have been active in the NPP at this time since Corneliu Coposu, its youth leader, recalls Bîrlădeanu being presented to him during a visit he made to the town (Coposu, *Vartan Arachelian*, p.67). Bîrlădeanu admitted to being a Communist from his student days and having flirted with the NPP but he left the latter after its handling of the Griviţa strikes. The Soviet annexation of Bessarabia caught him there on holiday at his mother's house and he remained in the province. He worked at an economics institute in Chişinău until the outbreak of war in 1941, when he was evacuated to Kazakhstan. Poor eye-sight saved him from conscription and he was sent down a coal mine in Caraganda for several months before persuading a local party boss to assign him to a secondary school in the town teaching mathematics. In 1943, he was sent to Moscow for doctoral studies and returned to Romania in 1946. Bîrlădeanu's unusually long stay in the Soviet Union led to rumours that he was in fact a Russian and a member of the Soviet Communist Party, but he denied this, claiming that he joined the Romanian Communist Party in 1946 (Betea, *Maurer*, pp.289-90).

25 Vasile Luca was the Romanianised name of Laszlo Luca, a Hungarian born in the commune of Cătălina in Covasna county in Transylvania on 8 June 1898. He lost his parents at the age of seven and was placed in an orphanage in Sibiu. When he was thirteen he became apprentice to a local padlock maker. In 1915, he secured a job in the railway yards in Braşov but at the end of the year was called up into the Austro-Hungarian army and sent to the front. He resumed his railway job in 1919 when he also joined the trade union movement. In 1924, he became regional secretary of the Communist Party in Braşov. Arrested

1941, this group constituted the so-called 'Moscow bureau' of the RCP. All were contributors to the Comintern-backed Romanian radio station *România liberă*. In 1943 Pauker was given the task of assisting in the recruitment of the 'Tudor Vladimirescu' division of the Red Army, formed from Romanian prisoners of war, and together with Vasile Luca and two captured officers, Colonel Captaru and Colonel Nicolae Cambrea, she visited prison camps to attract volunteers.[26]

---

in the same year for membership of an illegal organisation, he spent three years in jail. In 1928 he was elected to the party Central Committee. As a result of the internal struggles within the party he was sent to do basic party work in Moldavia. In 1933, he was arrested for organising trade union activity, tried and imprisoned for five years. After his release from jail he was coopted on to the party Central Committee and delegated to present a report to the Comintern about the party's activity. On 4 April 1940, he was caught while trying to cross the frontier into the Soviet Union and detained in Cernăuţi in Northern Bukovina. He was released from custody following the Soviet occupation of the province at the end of June ('Documentarul referitor la procesul privind pe Vasile Luca', *Arhiva Comitetului Executiv al CC al PCR (Archive of the Executive Committee of the Central Committee of the Romanian Communist Party)*, no.264/19, 18 Feb. 1972. I am grateful to Marius Oprea for locating this document.) By virtue of his presence on Soviet territory, Luca was offered the right to claim Soviet citizenship which he exercised. He spent the next four years in Moscow, working for the Romanian section of Radio Moscow and for the Comintern-backed Romanian radio station *România liberă* (Ionescu, *Communism in Rumania*, p.353); see also Buzatu, 'Cominterniştii', pp.41-2, who in Moscow consulted a register belonging to Aná Pauker with 185 names of Romanian Communists who sought refuge in the Soviet Union during the war.

26 The first camp Pauker visited was at Oranki in July 1943; see N. Fuiorea, *Divizia Stalinistă 'Tudor Vladimirescu' în Umbra Steagului Roşu*, Bucharest: Pan-Arcadia, 1992, p.17. Two army divisions, named 'Tudor Vladimirescu' and 'Horia, Cloşca and Crişan', were formed respectively in October 1943 and April 1945 from Romanian prisoners of war in the Soviet Union. They were organised on the Soviet model in which political allegiance to the Communist Party was paramount. This was ensured by a political command which, in the 'Tudor Vladimirescu' division was composed as follows: Major Ştefan Iordanov, political officer for the division; Major Dumitru Petrescu, head of the section for education and culture; Captain Mihai Burcă, political officer for the 1st Infantry Regiment; Captain Dumitru Coliu, political officer for the 2nd Infantry Regiment; Captain Gheorghe Stoica, political officer for the 3rd Infantry Regiment; Captain Petre Borilă, political officer for 1st Artillery Regiment; Captain Sergiu Sevcenko, political officer for the anti-tank batallion; Alexandru Paraschiv, political officer of the reconnaisance section; Ştefan Rab, political officer for the signals company. They were Communists who had been given military rank. Petrescu and Stoica had taken part, alongside Ana Pauker, in the conference held on 3 and 4

September 1943 at Krasnogorsk, where a series of measures designed 'to improve anti-Fascist activity' in the prisoner-of-war camps was taken. The most important took the form of the creation, in the following month, of the 'Tudor Vladmirescu' division from prisoners from various camps. They wère encouraged to join on the instigation of Ana Pauker, Vasile Luca and other Romanian Communists living in the Soviet Union. Colonel Nicolae Cambrea, one of the prisoners, was appointed the division's commander. The Soviet High Command decided to prepare the division for action on 29 March 1944, and on that day General Kovalenko and General Melnikov visited the division. They resolved that the division should swear its oath on 30 March. This included the promise to 'faithfully respect the brotherhood of arms with the Soviet Union' and 'to fight for a lasting peace with the Soviet Union which has given me the power to fight with a weapon in my hand for the destruction of the common enemy, Nazi Germany' (A.D. Duţu, 'Politizarea armatei române', *Dosarele Istoriei*, vol. 1, no.4, (1996), p.30). However, sensitivity over the delicate problem of avoiding contact with Romanian units led the Soviets to keep the division away from the front line. It was moved to Vapniarka in Transnistria and on 9 May was visited once more by Ana Pauker and Vasile Luca. The 23 August coup removed the danger of a direct confrontation between the division and Romanian forces and it was ordered to move straight to Bucharest. To this end, it was provided with 150 lorries and on 30 August the advance units of the division entered Bucharest. Major Dumitru Petrescu immediately contacted Gheorghiu-Dej and other Communist leaders. The division went on to fight, as part of the Red Army, in Transylvania, Hungary and Slovakia. After being placed in the reserve on 20 March 1945, it was withdrawn from operations and sent back by train to Bucharest where it was received by Gheorghiu-Dej. Almost 1,000 officers and men were selected from the division and given training by party activists. On 26 April, they were incorporated into the Romanian army, promoted and decorated. At the beginning of May, 986 of them were sent to units at the front where they were given the newly-created posts of political officers. On 8 May 1945, the new command to which they were responsible, namely the Higher Directorate for Education, Culture and Propaganda of the Army, was established. This was the instrument by which the Communist Party imposed its policy on the army.

The second division of Romanian volunteers, the 'Horia, Cloşca and Crişan' division, was formed at Kotovsk in the Soviet Union on 12 April 1945 by order of Stalin. Its commander was General Mihail Lascăr, who had been taken prisoner at Stalingrad. A Soviet counsellor was appointed to the division, in the person of Colonel Novikov Stepanovici, who was given the task of 'helping the volunteers to familiarise themselves with Soviet weaponry'. The political officer was Lt.-Col. Dumitru Petrescu (who had fulfilled the same function with the 'Tudor Vladimirescu' division), while the head of the education and cultural section was Major Valter Roman. The division's mission was, in the words of Lascăr, 'to be a model for the organisation of the entire Romanian army for the purpose of building a new army, with a new spirit, the Romanian Democratic Army...' (Duţu, 'Politizarea', p.3). It was formally integrated into the Romanian army, together with the 'Tudor Vladimirescu' division on 15 August 1945.

Romania's participation in the German attack on the Soviet Union in June 1941 perpetuated the divisions within the RCP. From this date jailed Communists, as their prison sentences expired, were transferred from Caransebeş to the internment camp in Tîrgu-Jiu, established in the autumn of 1939 for Polish refugees.[27] Among them was Teohari Georgescu, who was caught by the police and jailed in Caransebeş in early 1941. These Communists were thus no longer held, legally speaking, as prisoners but as 'internees'. Dej emerged as the leader of this second group, the 'prison group' as it is sometimes known.[28] Despite internment they were able, by bribing the camp authorities, to maintain contact with the remnants of the party who had avoided arrest. The principal figures in this third group, the rump of the party, were Ştefan Foriş, confirmed as secretary-general of the RCP by the Comintern in 1940, his deputy Remus Kofler (who took over, it seems, from the arrested Georgescu), Constantin Agiu, Lucreţiu Pătrăşcanu, Constantin Pîrvulescu and Iosif Rangheţ.

At Tîrgu-Jiu discipline was even less strict than in the prisons. While in Caransebeş, Dej had managed to get on the right side of the governor, Dobrian, who allowed him to listen to the radio, thereby following the progress of the war.[29] Gustav Corbu, a British subject of Romanian origin interned at Tîrgu-Jiu between October 1941 and November 1943, distinguished three groups of internees: those who could afford to pay for their keep (the equivalent of £8 per month at 1945 prices); needy intellectuals who could only meet part of the costs; and the destitute and

27 Jailed Communists had been moved to Caransebeş in November 1940 after the destruction of Doftana jail in an earthquake.

28 It included Gheorghe Apostol, Nicolae Ceauşescu, Iosif Chişinevski, Miron Constantinescu, Alexandru Drăghici, Teohari Georgescu and Alexandru Moghioroş. Dej's leadership of the imprisoned Communists was initially contested. Pavel Câmpeanu, a young Communist jailed at Caransebeş, recalled how three fellow prisoners, Ion Meţiu, Tănase Bratosin, and Virgil Fulgescu, who were also railwaymen, tried unsuccessfully to take over from Dej as leader of the Communist faction in the jail (P. Câmpeanu, 'Note asupra PCR în anii 40-50', *Sfera Politicii*, vol.1, no.2 (January 1993), p.18). Other notable internees in Tîrgu-Jiu were the industrialist Max Auschnitt, the poet Tudor Arghezi and General Nicolae Rădescu.

29 After 23 August 1944, Constantin Dobrian was promoted to the rank of general and served as prosecution counsel in the trial of Marshal Antonescu in May 1946.

Communists who were made to work. Up till 1942 the camp commandant was Colonel Zlătescu, who was alleged to have made a fortune while in charge. Those who could pay fully lived in clean and comfortable huts and were given good food. However, they had to pay Zlătescu for the smallest service.[30] Newspapers and books approved by the censor were allowed into the camp, but no radios.

After a quarrel with Zlătescu, Corbu was sent to do hard labour on the Tîrgu-Jiu-Petroşani railway. He was quartered, with fifty others, in a hut 3 metres by 10, and helped to hew eight tunnels through solid rock. A Lieutenant Trepăduş, who was in charge of the gangs, was said by Corbu to have been brutal to Jewish Communists. Corbu saw a Jew tied to a cross and left on it for twenty-four hours in the bitter cold, and also witnessed beatings administered to Jews, some of whom died.[31] Zlătescu's malpractices came to the notice of the Ministry of the Interior and he was dismissed, being replaced by Colonel Şerban Leoveanu, who nevertheless is said by other internees to have continued them.[32]

On 8 September 1942 almost all the Jews among the Communists interned in Tîrgu-Jiu were deported to Transnistria, the Romanian-administered territory between the Dniester and the Bug which had been overrun by German and Romanian armies in the autumn of 1941. The Jews were gathered in the camp at Vapniarka in the county of Jugastru.[33] A total of 1,312 Communists and Socialists

[30] His tariffs were fixed on a sliding scale, the equivalent of £15 (at 1945 prices) being charged for five or six days' 'leave' in Bucharest or a telephone call to the capital, £5 for permission to receive a visitor or for permission to go into Tîrgu-Jiu, and £3 for sending a letter by private messenger. Corbu had been educated at Glasgow High School and University, had worked in a Scottish shipyard as an engineer, had lived in Britain for twenty-nine years, and had married an Englishwoman. He failed to leave Romania before the outbreak of war between Britain and Romania in December 1941 and was interned.

[31] Recorded in the private papers of Archibald Gibson, the Kemsley Newspapers correspondent in Romania.

[32] A People's Tribunal sentenced Zlătescu and Trepaduş on 22 May 1945 to death and life imprisonment respectively. Zlătescu's sentence was commuted a few days later to life imprisonment.

[33] An exception was Iosif Chişinevski who remained in Caransebeş. Born in 1905 in Bessarabia, Iosif Chişinevski is believed to have studied at the Communist Party academy in Moscow during the late 1920s. He was arrested in 1941 as the head of a Bucharest Communist cell and sent to Caransebeş jail. He was

from all over Romania were assembled in this camp.[34] The poor diet, which included a type of pea used for feeding cattle, caused permanent paralysis of the lower limbs in 117 detainees. A further fifty-two, after being transferred to a prison in Rîbniţa, were shot by a retreating German SS unit on 18 March 1944.[35] The remainder survived the war and several of them, including Simion Bughici and Aurel Rottenberg (Ştefan Voicu), went on to occupy ministerial positions in the Communist government.

After the battle of Stalingrad and the advance of the Soviet armies the rules were relaxed for the Communist detainees in Tîrgu-Jiu. At the same time, labour shortages meant that construction teams made up of Communists were sent to do repair work in the vicinity of the camp, and it was during such tasks that the Communists outside the camp were able to pass messages to those on labour detachment. Among those who did electrical repairs in homes near the camp was Nicolae Ceauşescu.

It was in the Tîrgu-Jiu camp that the 'prison faction' under Gheorghiu-Dej took a decision to remove Ştefan Foriş as general secretary of the party in April 1944. The circumstances in which this decision was taken are not entirely clear, for the mists of politically-engineered distortion still linger over the matter. According to the official version propagated subsequently, a meeting was held on 4 April in the camp hospital involving Dej, Emil Bodnăraş, Constantin Pîrvulescu, Iosif Rangheţ and Chivu Stoica at which Dej demanded the removal of Foriş on the grounds that he was a police informer. In his place a provisional secretariat of Bodnăraş, Pîrvulescu and Rangheţ was appointed by those present.[36]

---

spared deportation to Transnistria because only Jews with sentences under ten years were sent to the province. Those with heavier sentences, like Chişinevski, Simion Zeiger, and Radu Mănescu, stayed in Caransebeş until their release on 23 August 1944 (see Pavel Câpeanu, 'Pe marginea unei recenzii. Mistere şi pseudo-mistere din istoria PCR', *22*, no.34 (23-30 August), 1995, p.12).

34 The number of persons held in Vapniarka on 5 May 1943 was 1,312 of whom 1,092 were Jewish internees and 198 Christian internees. The remaining 22 were classified as criminals and were Christians. Of the Jews, 835 were males, 136 females, and 5 children (Archive of the Romanian Ministry of the Interior, pachet 91, dosar 569, p.445).

35 Dora Litani, *Transnistria*, Tel Aviv, 1981, p.77 (in Romanian).

36 Eduard Mezincescu, 'Polemici', *România literară*, no.27 (9-15 September 1992), p.2. Mezincescu asserts that Pîrvulescu remained in Romania, was expelled from

What were the grounds for thus accusing Foriş? Did Dej and his associates act on their own initiative or on instructions from Moscow, channelled to them by the Soviet agent Bodnăraş? After all, Foriş had been confirmed in his position as party secretary-general by the Comintern, but links with the Comintern were broken during the war.

Contact between Foriş and the Comintern had been assured via Soviet agents in Sofia who travelled to Bucharest, but this link was broken after Romania's entry into the war against the Soviet Union in June 1941. Instead, messages were relayed from Moscow to Foriş through Petre Gheorghe, the secretary of the party in Bucharest.[37] Relations between Foriş and Gheorghe became strained when the latter, apparently on orders from the Comintern, instructed Foriş to organise sabotage actions behind the Romanian lines. Foriş refused, arguing that such a request was unrealistic since most of the party members were either interned or under house arrest.[38]

This difference of opinion led Foriş to remove Gheorghe as head of the party organisation in Bucharest. Gheorghe, however, refused to hand over the lists of passwords. In 1942, Gheorghe was arrested by Romanian counter-espionage agents and accused of spying for the Soviet Union. His arrest laid Foriş open to the charge of treachery, especially as Foriş, like all of the senior party figures who were not in internment, was regularly hauled in by the secret police, the *Siguranţa*, for questioning and, as in the case of Pătrăşcanu and perhaps even Foriş, consulted by General Piki Vasiliu, under-secretary at the Ministry of the Interior, about the attitude of the party regarding the conduct of the war. Indeed, it was precisely this charge which was levelled at Foriş posthumously by Dej in 1951 when he accused him of being a collaborator of

---

the secretariat of the RCP in 1942 by Foriş for indiscretion, and stayed hidden in a safe house of the party with his consort at that time, Ana Toma, until 4 April 1944 when he and Bodnăraş met Dej and other members of his group in the prison hospital in Tîrgu-Jiu and decided upon Foriş's dismissal as a traitor. Furthermore, Bodnăraş, Mezincescu claims, was not involved in preparations for the 23 August coup until 13 June 1944.

37 Gheorghe was of Bulgarian background and had been active in the Communist Party in the southern Dobrogea. Sent to Moscow for training as an NKVD agent in the mid-1930s, he was posted to Bucharest on the eve of the war.

38 Mezincescu, 'Polemici', p.2.

the *Siguranţa*[39] Foriş refused to give any legal help to Gheorghe, an act which would have offered proof of the latter's party membership, and without this Gheorghe was tried, not as a Communist, but as a spy.[40] After Stalingrad, Marshal Antonescu commuted the death sentences of Communists (the last Communist was executed in October 1942) but not those convicted of espionage and in 1943 Gheorghe was executed.[41] Clearly, Foriş's behaviour, if true, would have made him a target not only of the party but also of the NKVD.[42]

Foriş was held responsible by Dej for a string of arrests which had debilitated RCP activity since 1940.[43] On the face of it, there

39 Ionescu, *Communism in Rumania*, p.80. By the same token, the charge of collaboration with the *Siguranţa* was made against Pătrăşcanu at his trial in April 1954 and continued to be repeated parrot-fashion by Dej and his colleagues. For example, at the Central Committee plenum of November 1961 Maurer claimed that he was interned in Tîrgu-Jiu 'because of Patraşcanu's treacherous activities' (*ibid.*). The party commission, set up to investigate the Pătrăşcanu case in 1965, reported that he had received an invitation in spring 1944 from General Vasiliu to discuss the situation in Romania with Marshal Antonescu, and that he had received permission from the party leadership to accept. In the event, Antonescu changed his mind about seeing him ('Raportul Comisiei de partid, constituită în vederea clarificării situaţiei lui Lucreţiu Pătrăşcanu', *Cuvîntul*, no.36 (8-14 September), 1992, p.6).

40 Lawyers to represent arrested Communists, and money and food for those imprisoned or interned were provided by the International Red Aid Organisation, known from its Russian initials as MOPR. The secretary-general of the Romanian branch during the war was Eduard Mezincescu. In the autumn of 1944 the organisation's name was changed to 'Patriotic Defence' *(Apărarea patriotică)*.

41 Mezincescu, 'Polemici', p.2.

42 According to another scenario, Foriş may have been acting under instructions from Moscow. Foriş, it is argued, had Moscow's backing in autumn 1943 to conclude a deal with Antonescu which involved the sacrifice of the Communists in Romania. (Fischer-Galaţi, *New Rumania*, p.21). With plenty of examples of Soviet cynicism from the interwar period to point to, Dej and his interned colleagues decided to preempt this move by removing Foriş and taking over the party before the arrival of the Red Army and the Moscow bureau. The subsequent murder of Foriş may well have suited Stalin, for any public revelations about attempts to forge a deal with Antonescu, not to mention one made at the expense of the interned Communists, would have exposed them to charges of duplicity before the Romanian public, have severely embarrassed the Dej faction in the party, and damaged Stalin's relations with the western Allies.

43 Dej always spoke with great animosity about Foriş as he regarded him as a *Siguranţa* agent. He formed this view after an experience he had in Doftana jail

was little to link Foriş and his deputy, Remus Kofler, with any of them, the arrests being the result either of the diligence of the *Siguranţa*, or of the inepitude of the activists themselves, or of information received from informers within the party itself. Nevertheless, at the trial of Kofler and Lucreţiu Pătrăşcanu in April 1954, Kofler, Pătrăşcanu and Foriş were all blamed for keeping known police informers in positions of responsibility in the party who betrayed much of its activity to the *Siguranţa*.[44]

Much use was made of Foriş's actions – whether justifiably or not is impossible to determine – by Gheorghiu-Dej and his associates in Tîrgu-Jiu when plotting his removal, as is indicated by a memoir of Bodnăraş. Bodnăraş gave his own account of his actions between the time of his release in November 1942 and the removal of Foriş from the party leadership on 4 April 1944, in discussions with Valter Roman, Gheorghe Zaharia and Ada Grigorian on 18 and 20 January 1960. This group had been charged by Dej with examining the background to the 23 August coup in the light of the publication in the West of a book by General Hans Friessner, former commander of the German forces in Romania during the war, which had been partially serialised in a Soviet journal. Dej had also been stung by criticism in Soviet publications of Romania's part in the war against the Soviet Union and the RCP's alleged 'inactivity' during the war. Bodnăraş's account has never been made public and since it reveals that he was the key figure in the removal of Foriş from the party leadership, it is reproduced in appendix 1 to this book.

The arrest of Petre Gheorghe in somewhat suspicious circumstances and his execution, together with the ambiguous nature of the relations of Foriş and Kofler with the *Siguranţa*, provided the

in 1940 when, according to Alexandru Bîrlădeanu, Dej told his lawyer, Ion Gheorghe Maurer, that he wanted to escape from the prison. Maurer relayed Dej's wishes to no one but Foriş. Dej was summoned a few days later to the prison commandant who told him that he had heard that he [Dej] wanted to escape. Author's interview with Alexandru Bîrlădeanu, 8 August 1996.

44 Under cross-examination at his trial, Kofler stated that the man behind the arrest of more than sixty Communist activists in 1942 was a certain Melinte who was secretary of the Ilfov party organisation. After serving a six-month sentence in 1941, he was re-appointed to his position as Ilfov party secretary, even though, Kofler claimed, he was known to be a police informer. *Principiul Bumerangului. Documente ale Procesului Lucreţiu Pătrăşcanu*, Bucharest: Editura Vremea, 1996, p.576.

grounds for Dej's move against Foriş. The ambiguity was an inevitable consequence of Foriş's attempt to preserve the party and some form of clandestinity. For its part, the *Siguranţa* hoped, through Foriş, to keep a track on Moscow's intentions, especially after Stalingrad when it became clear that Stalin was going to play a major role in determining Romania's future.

The removal of Foriş in April 1944 and his subsequent brutal murder on the orders of Dej, symbolise, as Vladimir Tismăneanu has noted, 'the essentially repressive, anti-democratic character of Romanian Communism'.[45] Dej's actions were characteristic of the inability of the Romanian Communists to follow any democratic procedures in implementing a change in leadership. Rumour and whispered denunciation were preferred to reasoned dialogue with Foriş, and Dej's *post factum* attempt to engineer a justification for his actions through the Pătrăşcanu-Kofler trial represented the height of cynicism. Foriş's removal was to herald a decade-long mafia-like struggle for power in the party.

45 V. Tismăneanu, *Arheologia Terorii*, Bucharest: Editura Eminescu, 1992, p.106.

3

THE COMMUNIST PARTY AND THE COUP OF 23 AUGUST 1944

The impulse for the coup of 23 August 1944 was provided by the Axis defeat at Stalingrad in January 1943. In the course of the Soviet counter-offensive two German armies, two Romanian armies and one Italian army were decimated. The Romanian losses in the period from 19 November 1942 to 7 January 1943 were put at 155,010 dead, wounded and missing, most of the latter having been taken prisoner.[1] This represented over a quarter of all Romanian troops engaged on the Eastern Front. Hitler had lost the initiative in the war against the Soviet Union and his forces now began to be thrown back across Europe. The consequences of Stalingrad were equally momentous for Antonescu. He now realised that Hitler could no longer win the war. On the advice of his chief-of-staff, General Ilie Şteflea, he had wisely not committed all his forces to the campaigns in the Soviet Union, holding half in reserve to protect his country's territorial integrity. As the military situation steadily deteriorated Antonescu tolerated the emission of peace feelers via his vice-president, Mihai Antonescu, or via Iuliu Maniu, but all these soundings foundered on the Anglo-American insistence upon 'unconditional surrender', announced by Roosevelt and accepted by Churchill at the Casablanca Conference in January 1943.

The acceptance of unconditional surrender by the Romanians, be it Maniu or Antonescu, was the stumbling-block in all subsequent negotiations held between Maniu's representatives and the Allies in Cairo in the spring of 1944. Yet approaches made in December 1943 by Soviet officials to Romanian diplomats in Stockholm suggested that their government wished to set up independent

[1] *România în anii celui de-al doilea război mondial*, vol.1, Bucharest: Editura Militară, 1989, p.489.

contacts with Antonescu and Maniu and was prepared to accept less than unconditional surrender. A curious situation thus emerged in which both the Romanian government and opposition were seeking to obtain the best possible terms for an armistice in parallel negotiations, one in Cairo with the Allies collectively and the other, in Stockholm with the Russians separately. Not surprisingly, both Antonescu and Maniu believed that they were in a position to bargain over unconditional surrender, hence the misunderstanding that arose between the Allies and Maniu, and the increasing British irritation with the latter. Maniu wanted some assurance as to what conditions he could get before making any plans to overthrow Antonescu. In particular, he was anxious to prevent Soviet occupation of Romania. The Russians, on the other hand, took the pragmatic view that it was more realistic to treat with Antonescu since he controlled the army and an about-turn by the latter against the Germans would preclude the need for a coup by the opposition.

For his part Antonescu, aware of the fragility of Romania's territorial integrity in the face of the Soviet advance, sought armistice terms which would guarantee Romania's independence of Soviet authority. Yet the more he delayed, the closer the Red Army moved and the greater the threat of occupation. Only King Michael and his advisers seemed to grasp the fact that Stalin would be tempted to withhold his assent to armistice conditions if he manoeuvred himself into a position to impose them through military might. Antonescu's refusal to accept what he considered to be unsatisfactory terms from the Allies, coupled with his reluctance as an officer to abandon his German ally who was now on the defensive, made the king, in concert with the opposition leaders, determined to plot his overthrow. It was the young king who took the initiative in arresting Antonescu on the afternoon of 23 August 1944, thus taking Romania out of the Axis.

It is one of the many tragedies in the history of the Romanians that the principal architects of the coup of 23 August 1944, King Michael and the democratic leaders, overthrew a military dictatorship only to be virtually overthrown themselves within six months by another incipient totalitarian order. In the Soviet zone of Germany and Poland, where the ravages of war had removed all political structures, it was relatively simple for Stalin to bring his client Communist parties to power, but in Romania the imposition of the new order required the removal of surviving structures. King Michael's coup had pre-empted any Soviet move to seize immediate power and when Soviet troops entered Bucharest eight days later they found a Romanian government without significant Communist representation ready to negotiate an armistice and hold elections.

The coup had a crucial impact upon the course charted by Stalin for the RCP. It was also responsible for bringing Dej into the forefront of political events, and thereby launching him on the road to power. Since Dej emerged first as the leader of that wing of the party which was most closely involved with the coup and went on to secure his domination of the entire party, the coup was accorded a sacred place in party history. Even before Dej achieved supremacy within the party and was able to control its historiography, his Communist colleagues sought to deny the credit gained by the king and the major democratic parties for the coup by assuming it exclusively for themselves, thereby claiming legitimacy for their rule.

To this end, the role of the Romanian Communists in the coup was deliberately exaggerated by the party. King Michael was relegated to the position of a mere spectator. In this endeavour Communist apologists were abetted by the suppression by the Communist authorities of any accounts of the coup which did not fit into their scenario of the events. Therefore the accounts of key participants in the events, that is of the king and of members of his entourage who escaped to the West, which described the king's crucial act in ordering the arrest of Marshal Antonescu on 23 August 1944, were largely unknown in Romania before the overthrow of the Communist regime.[2]

An example of this distortion was Lucreţiu Pătrăşcanu's account of the preparations for the coup, published on its first anniversary in *România liberă*. Pătrăşcanu claimed that 'three meetings were held at the palace with King Michael in the chair to prepare for the coup of 23 August' at which he [Pătrăşcanu] was 'the only

[2] These included A. G. Lee, *Crown against Sickle*, London: Hutchinson, 1950; R.H. Markham, *Rumania under the Soviet Yoke*, Boston, MA: Meador Publishing, 1949; R. Bishop and E.S. Crayfield, *Russia astride the Balkans*, London: Evans, 1949. The historiography of the coup is presented in King, *History of the RCP*, pp.40-3, and in Shafir, *Romania*, pp.30-7.

representative of the entire opposition'.[3] This is untrue. Preparations for the coup were discussed simultaneously at the palace, where the king consulted with his personal advisers, and by the so-called National Democratic Bloc (NDB), formed on 20 June 1944 from representatives of the National Peasant, National Liberal, Social Democratic, and Communist parties, who met at various houses.

While it is true that even before the formation of the NDB, Pătrăşcanu and Titel Petrescu, the leader of the Social Democrats, were taking part in secret preparations for the coup under the king's chairmanship, all the subsequent coup plans were discussed at meetings of the NDB, and the last meeting held before the coup, on 21 August, was attended by the king, his palace advisers, the leaders of the major opposition parties, and Pătrăşcanu.[4] Today with the recent publication of eye-witness accounts of the coup and the disclosure by contemporaries of Pătrăşcanu and Dej of fresh information about the activities of the RCP during the war and its relationship to Moscow, the part played by the Communists in the coup can be determined with greater accuracy, and in the process the mystification of the coup perpetrated at Dej's behest can be dispelled.[5]

Following the disaster which befell Romanian troops at Stalingrad, King Michael called for peace in his 1943 New Year

[3] L. Pătrăşcanu, 'Cum s-a pregătit actul de la 23 august 1944', *România liberă*, p.9.

[4] In a conversation in December 1944 with V. Morev, the TASS correspondent in Romania, Pătrăşcanu claimed that 'the first meeting in connection with the preparations for the coup took place with the king in May 1944. At the meeting, apart from the king, were Generals Sănătescu, Mihail, Răşcanu and Aldea, Niculescu-Buzeşti, Styrcea, Pătrăşcanu and Bodnăraş. The last two were the only representatives of a political party.' (Foreign Policy Archive, Moscow, fond 0125, opis 33, file 6, folio 127, pp.128-34). I am grateful to Dr Florin Constantiniu for showing me this document. Niculescu-Buzeşti, however, is reported to have met Pătrăşcanu and Bodnăraş for the first time on 13 June; I. Hudiţa, 'Pagini. de Jumal', *Magazin Istoric*, vol.28, no.7 (July 1994), p.41.

[5] The most lucid account of the coup and preparations for it is given by Ivor Porter, *Operation Autonomous: With S.O.E. in Wartime Romania*, London: Chatto and Windus, 1989. 'Autonomous' was the code-name for a three-man Special Operations Executive mission, parachuted into Romania on 22 December 1943. The team, consisting of Lt.-Col. A.G.G. de Chastelain, Cpt. Ivor Porter and a Romanian radio operator Silviu Meţianu, was arrested almost immediately by Romanian gendarmes and taken to police headquarters in Bucharest where they remained until their release on 23 August 1944.

broadcast to his people. Irritated by what he considered to be the indecisiveness of the opposition, led by Maniu and Brătianu, the young king declared later that he had been ready to take Romania out of the war against the Allies in February 1944 but that 'whenever plans appeared to be maturing he was prevented from taking action by objections raised by the opposition'.[6] The king's impatience was doubtless a sign of his youth (he was only twenty-two), and the veteran Maniu advised more prudently against a coup at that time on the grounds that there were too many German troops in the country. Nevertheless, the king could turn to the wise counsels of his mother, Queen Helen, of General Sănătescu, the head of the military household, and of Grigore Niculescu-Buzeşti, the head of the cypher and communication section of the Foreign Ministry.

At the time Maniu was in regular radio contact with the British via a radio operator called Nicolae Ţurcanu (code-named 'Reginald') who had been sent into Romania in June 1943 by the Special Operations Executive. At the end of October 1943, Maniu had expressed a desire to leave Romania in order to contact the Russians with British assistance. In response the Foreign Office told Maniu that any approaches from Romania, be they from individuals or from the government, should be addressed to all three Allies and that they should take the form of an offer by a duly-authorised emissary to sign an unconditional surrender to the three principal Allies.[7] The Foreign Office told the Soviet government about Maniu's request. In December 1943 the Romanian Counsellor in Stockholm George Duca contacted the British and American ministers in the name of Maniu about peace terms, unaware that his own minister, Frederick Nanu, had been approached, on 26 December, by what Nanu took to be an NKVD officer, with an offer to deal with the Romanian government.[8]

[6] 'Report of Lt.-Col. A.G.G. de Chastelain on the "Autonomous" Mission, dated September 1944', in *23 August 1944. Documente,* eds I. Ardeleanu, V. Arimia, M. Muşat, vol.II, Bucharest: Editura Ştiinţifică şi Enciclopedică, 1984, p.802.

[7] The National Archives of the United States, Washington, DC, General Records of the Department of State (R.G. 59), European War, 74000119, EW 1939/2057. Reproduced in *23 August 1944. Documente,* vol.I, doc.456.

[8] The Soviet official in question was a man named Spitchkine whom the Special Operations Executive surmised was acting independently of his minister, Madame

Contact was maintained for several months on a clandestine basis. Nanu was told that the Russians would keep the Western Allies informed and that strict secrecy should be maintained. On 13 April armistice terms agreed by the representatives of the American, British and Soviet governments in Cairo were transmitted to the marshal and to Maniu. They called for a Romanian *volte-face* against the Germans, the payment of reparations to the Russians, the confirmation of Bessarabia and Northern Bukovina as Soviet territory, the restoration of Northern Transylvania to Romania and the granting to Soviet troops of unrestricted movement, although not occupation, throughout Romania during the period of the armistice.[9]

The receipt of the terms seems to have caused a breach to open up between the marshal and Maniu. In a letter he wrote in mid-April, Maniu stated that Antonescu 'wished to continue the war at the side of the Germans'; Maniu accepted the terms, however, and stated that once he was certain that Antonescu could not be moved, he would act in conjunction with the king.[10] Even so, the suspicion that the Western Allies, and in particular Britain, had abandoned Romania to the Russians, troubled Maniu who used the Romanian emissary to Cairo, Constantin Vişoianu, to voice these concerns to Christopher Steel, the British representative, at the end of May. This provoked Antony Eden, the foreign secretary, to instruct Steel to tell Vişoianu that there was no use in his trying to obtain assurances about British policy 'as distinct from that of the Soviet government'.[11] But there was no rebuke from Eden when Steel, in answer to a further question from Vişoianu as to whether Maniu should form 'a democratic coalition embracing the Romanian Communist Party', replied that in his own view a broad national union of this kind would be 'warmly welcomed by Allied public opinion'.[12]

This cautious advice probably confirmed Maniu in his view

Alexandra Kollontay (Elisabeth Barker, *British Policy in South-East Europe in the Second World War*, London: Macmillan, 1976, p.229.

9 *Foreign Relations of the United States, 1944*, vol.IV, Washington, DC: US Department of State, p.170.

10 Barker, *British Policy* p.233.

11 *Ibid.*, p.237.

12 *Ibid.*, p.238.

that it would be good politics to bring the Communists into a coalition and when Vişoianu asked Daniel Semionovici Selod, the assistant to Nikolai Novikov, the Soviet representative in Cairo, to suggest a name, Selod replied 'Lucreţiu Pătrăşcanu'.[13] Although held under house arrest throughout 1943 and early 1944 at a mountain village called Poiana Ţapului near Sinaia, the king's summer residence, Pătrăşcanu was kept informed of plans to take Romania out of the war by Colonel Octav Ulea, master of ceremonies at the palace.[14] In April 1944 Pătrăşcanu negotiated

[13] Interview with Corneliu Coposu, 31 October 1991. In a paper presented at a symposium in Paris on 22 May 1994, Coposu disclosed, in his capacity as Maniu's secretary and the person responsible for enciphering and deciphering Maniu's telegrams in the British code sent via Ţurcanu to Cairo, that in response to Novikov's suggestion to Vişoianu that the Romanian opposition should involve the section of the Comintern in Romania, Novikov was told that the number of Communists in Romania identified by the SSI (Romanian Intelligence) was 845, of whom 720 were not ethnic Romanians.

In reply, Maniu was told that it was common knowledge that a section of the Comintern in Romania did not exist but that public opinion abroad had to have the impression of the existence of a homogeneous opposition embracing all social and political categories. Maniu said that, in that case, he had nothing against the enlargement of the opposition. However, none of the Communists contacted in Romania claimed to be the true representatives of the RCP. With some satisfaction Maniu cabled Novikov for his direction as to who was official representative of the Comintern in Romania and Novikov replied: 'Lucreţiu Pătrăşcanu'; 'Exilul Românesc: Identitate şi Conştiinţă istorică', *Lupta,* no.232 (7 Oct. 1994), p.5. According to Communist historiography the meeting of 4 April in Tîrgu-Jiu is alleged to have instructed Pătrăşcanu, Bodnăraş and Ion Gheorge Maurer to join the other political parties in an effort to extract Romania from the war with the Soviet Union. A few days later Pătrăşcanu negotiated an agreement with Titel Petrescu, the leader of the SDP, to set up a United Workers' Front. Bodnăraş made his first appearance at a sub-committee charged with the preparation of plans for the defence of Bucharest on 13 June, although according to one account the main purpose was to discuss future relations with Moscow (Ioan Hudiţă, *op. cit.*, p.41).

[14] Iosif Şraier, the Communist Party's legal representative, conducted negotiations with Iuliu Maniu and Prince Ştirbey in preparation for the 23 August coup. One source claims that he received full authority from Moscow in his conversations with Maniu which initially he conducted alone. Later he acted as Lucreţiu Pătrăşcanu's liaison in the negotiations between the Communist Party and the other members of the NDB. Before the Groza cabinet was reorganised in January 1946 he hoped to become minister of the interior but with his political ambitions frustrated, he left Romania later that year ('List of Roumanian Personalities, 1947', Report no.262, 3 November 1947, Public Record Office, London, FO/371/67272 B).

an agreement with Titel Petrescu, the leader of the Social Democrats, to set up a United Workers' Front, thus giving the Communist Party greater authority. Both men took part in the secret preparations for the coup under the king's chairmanship. Pătrăşcanu was brought into meetings of a sub-committee under Colonel Dumitru Dămăceanu which prepared plans for the defence of Bucharest and at the beginning of June he suggested that the Communist Party's military representative, Emil Bodnăraş (code-named Engineer Ceauşu), should attend since he could organise small bands of armed workers who could assist in a *volte-face*.

Bodnăraş was no ordinary official of the Communist Party: he was also an NKVD agent whose role in the preparations for the coup remains shadowy and has consequently fomented speculation, including the suggestion that he was used by Marshal Antonescu as a clandestine conduit to the Soviet authorities.[15] After the Axis defeat at Stalingrad, it was clear to Antonescu that it would be

15 There are many question-marks over Bodnăraş's real loyalties. According to his party file he was born in Colomea (now in the Ukraine) on 10 February 1904 of Ukrainian-German parentage. (I am grateful to Claudiu Secaşiu for this information). Bodnăraş studied law at Iaşi University where, according to his official obituary, he first came into contact with Marxist groups. He then joined the officers' academy in Timişoara where he completed his training in 1927 (*Anale de istorie*, vol.22 (1976), no.1, p.189). His obituary says nothing about the following seven years until his arrest and his sentencing in 1934 to ten years' hard labour. The gap has been filled from other sources. In 1927, he was posted to Craiova with the rank of lieutenant and later transferred to a barracks at Sadagura in northern Romania only 30 km. from the river Dniester and the border with the Soviet Union. From there he defected to the Soviet Union. Two questions arise at this point. Why should Bodnăraş, with his Ukrainian background, be posted so close to the Soviet frontier? Was he perhaps recruited by Romanian military intelligence and his defection planned? Information from the KGB archives now sheds some light on these questions. It claims that Bodnăraş was sent into the Soviet Union in 1931 as the military intelligence officer of the 12th Artillery Regiment based in Sadagura but was turned by the Soviets and was trained as a Soviet agent at a school in the town of Astrakhan (G. Iavorschi, 'Pentru cine a lucrat "inginerul Ceauşu"?', *Magazin Istoric*, vol.28, no.9 [September 1994], p.18). Bodnăraş admitted as much in a meeting of the Romanian Politburo held on 13 and 14 March 1961: 'Towards the end of 1933 [Vyacheslav] Menzhinsky was still alive [and] he headed the special agency where I worked [...] my contact was one of the deputy heads of this service.' Menzhinsky was head of the OGPU (Soviet Security Service) from 1926 until his death in May 1934, when he was succeeded by his first deputy, Genrikh Yagoda, who may have been the assistant to whom Bodnăraş was referring. In July 1934,

the OGPU was integrated into the NKVD (People's Commissariat for Internal Affairs), headed by Yagoda, which directed the activities of the political police, the regular police, criminal investigation, border troops, and internal troops. Though only a part of the NKVD, the political police was usually referred to as the NKVD (C. Andrew and O. Gordievsky, *KGB: The Inside Story of its Foreign Operations from Lenin to Gorbachev*, London: Sceptre, 1991, p.146). Foreign intelligence gathering was directed by INU, the Foreign Intelligence Department of the NKVD, which was set up in 1921. Bodnăraş's activities would have been supervised by Artur Artuzov, head of INU from 1929 until 1934, and then by Abram Slutsky, Artuzov's successor, who was poisoned during the purges in February 1938. Bodnăraş fondly reminisced about his treatment by the Soviets: 'The Soviet secret services were particularly considerate towards me and took care to brief me, giving me access to books and papers so that I didn't get cut off from events in Romania. I also received the daily *Universul*. When the strike at the Griviţa yards took place (February 1933), the Soviets brought me from my lodgings to their headquarters where I spent several days following the information which they received from their secret services who were noting what was happening.' (Stenogram of the RWP Politburo Meeting of 13-14 March 1961). My thanks to Marius Oprea for passing on a copy of this record. A number of officers who served in Romanian counter-intelligence during and immediately after the Second World War have stated that Bodnăraş's fluent knowledge of German allowed him to be used on various espionage missions by the OGPU/NKVD in Poland and the Baltic republics before he was sent to Bulgaria in 1934. En route through Romania he was recognised in the Gara de Nord station in Bucharest and arrested. He was tried for desertion, for stealing documents and for crimes against the country's security, and sentenced to ten years' imprisonment. Other questions arise. Why was he sent by his Soviet masters to Bulgaria by train through Romania, with all the risks of recognition that the journey entailed, when he could have travelled direct by boat from Odessa to Burgas? Was he sent deliberately by train in the hope that he would be caught by the Romanians as a Soviet spy and imprisoned with the Romanian Communists whom he could infiltrate on behalf of the NKVD? Was he, in fact, a double agent? His mission from the Soviets may well have been to evaluate Gheorghiu-Dej because the latter, unlike other leading figures in the RCP, had not studied in the Soviet Union. Serghei Nikonov, the Soviet-trained head of the SSI (the Romanian Intelligence Service) from 1946 to 1951, expressed the conviction in a conversation in 1988 with Titu Simon, a former officer in Romanian military intelligence, that Bodnăraş had been recruited in the 1920s by an officer in the SSI named Florin Becescu (cover-name Georgescu) to penetrate the Soviet security and intelligence services and that this was the purpose of his mission to the Soviet Union. In 1947, information was passed to Bodnăraş by the Russians that Georgescu had worked as a double agent, for both the Romanians and the Soviets, and Bodnăraş gave orders for his liquidation before Nikonov could investigate the charges. The reason for Bodnăraş's haste, Nikonov believed, was to prevent the emergence of any details of his recruitment by Becescu (T. Simon, *Pacepa: Quo Vadis?*, Bucharest: Odeon, 1992, pp.77-8).

prudent to establish closer links with the Russians and Bodnăraş was an obvious channel. Unlike his colleagues Dej, Apostol, Chişinevski and Georgescu, he had been exempted from internment at the Tîrgu-Jiu prison camp after being released from Caransebeş prison in November 1942 on the grounds of having been an officer in the Romanian army. Bodnăraş made his first appearance at one of the meetings to prepare the coup at a house on Calea

---

Simon's account of Bodnăraş's hand in Becescu's death is corroborated by Traian Borcescu, head of the counter-intelligence section of the SSI between 1941 and 1944. Becescu joined the Communist Party after 23 August 1944 and was appointed head of counter-intelligence in the SSI (he had held this post previously until 1941). However, he released information about Ana Pauker's private life as a young woman and lost the confidence of Bodnăraş. It was for this indiscretion that Bodnăraş, according to Borcescu, ordered Becescu's removal. While travelling to attend a meeting in Sinaia on the orders of Bodnăraş, Becescu's car was ambushed and he was shot dead by Communist agents (author's interview with Traian Borcescu, 8 March 1995). Bodnăraş served his sentence at Doftana, Aiud, Galaţi and Braşov according to the official obituary. He was also held at Caransebeş jail, for he was seen there by a fellow inmate Mircea Oprişan, in 1942 (letter to the author from M. Oprişan, 29 August 1994). In Doftana Bodnăraş formed a close friendship with Gheorghiu-Dej and became a member of the Communist Party. He was released from prison on 7 November 1942 at the suggestion of the SSI and settled in the town of Brăila near the mouth of the Danube. It was here that, in return for payments made to Rânzescu, the local inspector of police who was a friend of SSI head Eugen Cristescu, he was able to wander freely around the town and its outskirts and consequently to pick up instructions dropped by Soviet planes on the outskirts of town. Using the cover of a commercial representative for a small company based in Brăila and the name of 'Engineer Ceauşu', Bodnaraş travelled freely, albeit under the surveillance of the *Siguranţa*, and he was a frequent visitor to Bucharest. Here Bodnăraş collected information from an agent named Kendler, a timber-merchant, who on instructions from Bodnăraş paid a sum of 30,000 lei monthly in 1943 to Col. Enache Borcescu, a member of the Romanian General Staff, for information about Romanian and German troop movements. Kendler's regular meeting-place with Borcescu was a Greco-Catholic church in Bucharest (author's interview with Traian Borcescu, 8 March 1995).

Bodnăraş was also a frequent visitor to Tîrgu-Jiu where, by suborning Colonel Şerban Lioveanu, the commandant of the internment camp, he was able to consult Gheorghiu-Dej on several occasions. Drawing on secret Communist Party funds, Bodnăraş bought weapons from German soldiers based in Romania in order to arm Communist detachments which he formed in Bucharest in the early summer of 1944. This activity did not escape the attention of the Gestapo who requested his arrest but Colonel Traian Borcescu, the head of counter-intelligence in the SSI, resisted on the grounds that Bodnăraş 'could be of use in Romania's exit from the war' (Iavorschi, 'Ceauşu', p.19).

Moşilor on the night of 13 June 1944. Even members of the king's circle were impressed by Bodnăraş's dedication[16] and the latter, in his turn, was sufficiently convinced by the thoroughness of the plans to be able to satisfy his Communist colleagues that the RCP only stood to enhance its position by joining the National Peasant, National Liberal and Social Democratic parties in the formation of the NDB on 20 June 1944.

A week later the Allied representatives in Cairo received the plan drawn up by the king and the NDB for the coup. To be successful, Maniu argued, the coup had to be accompanied by three Allied actions. First, there should be a major Soviet offensive on the Romanian front within twenty-four hours of the *volte-face*; second, three airborne brigades, either Anglo-American or Soviet, with an additional 2,000 parachute troops should be dropped at the time of the coup; third, there should be a heavy bombardment of communications with Hungary and Bulgaria. The plan met a favourable response from both the British and American representatives, yet when the American suggested a tripartite meeting to discuss it, the Soviet representative Nikolai Novikov said that this would be premature.

Novikov waited in vain for instructions from Moscow. The Russians had nothing to lose by pinning their hopes on a bilateral deal with Marshal Antonescu; this had the double advantage for them of dealing directly with Romania's military leader, thereby obviating the need to negotiate with Maniu, and of giving them time, in view of the marshal's hesitancy, to prepare for their military occupation of Romania. Indeed, at the beginning of June, Madame Alexandra Kollontay, a veteran revolutionary and the Soviet minister in Stockholm, had offered improved armistice conditions to Nanu which, in addition to an unconditional promise to return Transylvania, pledged to allow 'free areas' where the Romanian government would be sovereign and where no foreign troops would be allowed to enter, to show leniency over reparations and to allow fifteen days between the signing of an armistice and a Romanian declaration of war on Germany.[17]

Soviet hopes toward Antonescu were dashed when the marshal saw Hitler on 5 August. To Hitler's leading question as to whether

16 Porter, *Operation Autonomous*, p.175.

17 Barker, *British Policy*, p.239.

Romania intended to fight on, Antonescu temporised by saying that this depended upon Germany's commitment to assist Romania stem the Russian advance and upon the attitude of Hungary and Bulgaria. The marshal returned to Bucharest in deep depression and did nothing about the Soviet terms. In the meantime Maniu was desperately seeking a reply from Cairo to the coup plan sent on 27 June. On 7 July the king and his advisors, including the opposition leaders, fixed 15 August as the date for action, hoping to synchronise their action with a Soviet offensive. The longer the coup was delayed, the greater the chance that the Red Army would push forward, occupying more Romanian territory and giving Moscow a reason for preferring a straightforward military conquest of the country without any help from the king and the opposition. Moreover the increasingly frequent Anglo-American air raids on the oilfields around Ploieşti and on Bucharest were a reminder to the Romanians of the cost of the alliance with Germany. Still Maniu heard nothing from Cairo, and the coup was postponed. Finally on 20 August the long-awaited Soviet offensive came, prompting Maniu to inform Cairo that the king and his group had decided to take action.

The Soviet Generals Malinovsky and Tolbukhin successfully launched a massive assault of almost one million troops and 1,500 tanks against the combined German and Romanian forces straddling the Prut. The front south of Iaşi was breached and the king rushed from Sinaia to Bucharest to consult his advisors. The representatives of the political parties could not be located. The king asked Colonel Dămăceanu how long he needed to get his part of the plan, namely to seize the telephone exhange and the radio station, ready, and was told 'five days'. The coup was therefore fixed for 26 August at 1 p.m. The marshal and Mihai Antonescu would be invited to lunch, after which there would be an audience to discuss the course to be adopted. If the marshal refused negotiation with the Allies, the king would dismiss him and appoint a new government to be drawn from the opposition parties. This government would invite the Germans to evacuate Romania and empower its emissaries in Cairo, Barbu Ştirbey and Constantin Vişoianu, to sign an armistice.

On the following evening, 21 August, the plans agreed by the king and his advisors the day before were approved by the members of the NDB at their last full meeting before the coup. It was attended by the king, Maniu, Brătianu, Pătrăşcanu, Titel Petrescu, Grigore Niculescu-Buzeşti, the head of Foreign Ministry communications, Ion Mocsony-Styrcea, the marshal of the king's household, General Constantin Sănătescu and Mircea Ionniţiu, the king's private secretary.[18] Pătrăşcanu came with a draft proclamation for the king's approval and argued, with Petrescu's backing, for a government of national unity led by Maniu. Maniu refused and pressed for a government of technicians, headed by a soldier, to handle the armistice conditions and the presence of the Red Army. The matter was left in the hands of Maniu and Pătrăşcanu who were to draw up a list of ministers by 23 August. It was agreed that the politicians should disperse until the projected day of action, 26 August.

Yet once again unforseen circumstances intervened in the timing of the coup. Antonescu, dismayed by the rapid advance of the Soviet forces, was moving back and forth between the front in southern Moldavia and Bucharest and decided to return to the front on 24 August. This meant that he would probably be absent from the capital on the day fixed for the coup. The news, which had been picked up fortuitously by Styrcea, was quickly transmitted to the king who was able to get word to Maniu that the coup should be brought forward to 23 August. Mihai Antonescu, the prime minister, was unnerved by the deteriorating military situation and decided, on his own initiative, to negotiate an armistice with the Allies. He told the marshal on the evening of 22 August and the latter raised no objections. That same evening the marshal told the German minister Clodius that he would make one last effort to halt the Russians, and that in the event of failure, he reserved the right to act as he saw fit. After the meeting with Clodius, Mihai Antonescu sent a courier to Stockholm instructing Nanu to tell Madame Kollontay of the Romanian government's willingness to conclude an armistice. In the event the courier arrived on 24 August, the day after the coup.[19]

[18] Porter, *Operation Autonomous*, pp.192-3.

[19] See Nicholas Baciu, *Sell-Out to Stalin: The Tragic Errors of Churchill and Roosevelt*, New York: Vantage Press, 1984, p.147. The courier in question, Neagu Djuvara, made it quite clear to his audience at the fiftieth anniversary symposium, '23 August 1944 in the history of Romania' held in Bucharest on 8-9 October 1994 (to which King Michael had accepted an invitation but was refused entry to Romania by the authorities), that Mihai Antonescu, with the marshal's approval,

On the morning of 23 August, in a last-ditch effort to get the marshal to conclude an armistice, Maniu and Constantin Brătianu asked the historian Gheorghe Brătianu, the Liberal leader's nephew, to use the respect he enjoyed with the Romanian leader to persuade him to see the king that afternoon. The marshal listened to Brătianu's arguments and apparently agreed to go to the palace, but on condition that Maniu and Gheorghe Brătianu send him a letter by 3 p.m. confirming that they stood behind him in signing an armistice. The marshal then gave instructions that an audience should be sought with the king at 4 p.m. Mihai Antonescu was granted a separate one at 3.30.

The king now convened his advisors and decided that the show down with the marshal should take place at his audience that afternoon. Niculescu-Buzeşti and Mocsony-Styrcea left the palace to warn Maniu and Pătrăşcanu respectively but Maniu was not at home and Pătrăşcanu's contact said that he and Titel Petrescu would come to the palace, but only after nightfall. Similarly, George Brătianu could find neither his uncle nor Maniu and was therefore unable to meet the marshal's condition that he should bring a letter from both by 3 p.m. When George Brătianu turned up to see the marshal empty-handed the latter was furious and said that Mihai Antonescu could go to the palace alone and pass on the marshal's apologies to the king.[20]

Mihai Antonescu arrived for his audience at the appointed time and was received by the king and General Sănătescu. He offered Marshal Antonescu's apologies, at which point Sănătescu left the

---

had merely told Nanu to approach Madame Kollontay to ask whether the earlier conditions given by the Russians were still valid or would have to be negotiated. At the same time, Djuvara revealed, Mihai Antonescu instructed Nanu not to tell the British and Americans of this approach to the Soviets. Mihai Antonescu did not, as Nanu later claimed, tell him that the marshal was ready to withdraw and had given Mihai a free hand to sign the armistice (F.C. Nano, 'The First Soviet Double-Cross: A Chapter in the Secret History of World War II', *Journal of Central European Affairs*, vol.12, no.3 [Oct. 1952], pp.236-58). As Djuvara remarked, the events in the three-month period since the issue of the Russian conditions had rendered many of them irrelevant and the mere raising of the question as to whether they were still valid showed how out of touch with reality the two Antonescus were.

20 This account of events on 23 August is taken from M. Ionniţiu, '23 August 1944. Amintiri şi reflecţiuni', *Revista istorică*, vol.2, nos 9-10 (1991), pp.557-75, and Porter, *Operation Autonomous*, pp.198-202.

room and telephoned the marshal, saying that there was no point in snubbing the king at this critical time. The marshal relented and agreed to come. He was escorted into the drawing room to meet the king who was with Mihai Antonescu and Sănătescu. The marshal proceeded to give a detailed account of the situation at the front and said that he would only conclude an armistice after obtaining Hitler's consent. The king replied that the military situation would brook no further delay; since Soviet troops were already in occupation of part of the country an armistice should be signed immediately. Asked by the king whether he would stand aside for someone who would contact the Allies, the marshal replied 'Never'. After withdrawing briefly to his study to inform his advisors, Styrcea, Buzeşti, Ionniţiu and General Aurel Aldea, that the moment had now come for the marshal's arrest, the king returned to the drawing room and told the marshal that, in concordance with the wishes of the Romanian people as expressed through the four democratic parties, he was taking the country out of the war to save it from disaster. If the marshal refused to implement the king's wish that an armistice be concluded, then he should consider himself dismissed.

When the marshal retorted that he took orders from no one, the king replied that, in that case he was dismissed and left the room. As he did so he signalled to his aide, Colonel Emilian Ionescu, to arrest the marshal and Mihai Antonescu. Ionescu summoned the four-man guard that had been prepared for such an eventuality and amid the protests of the marshal the two Antonescus were escorted upstairs and locked in the king's strongroom.

Back in his study the king consulted with his advisors as to the immediate steps to be taken. The leaders of the political parties had to be informed of the arrests, the Allies had to be notified, the military plan for the coup had to be executed and most important of all, a prime minister had to be named to replace Mihai Antonescu. In the absence of Maniu, it was decided to appoint General Sănătescu, who enjoyed the respect of the army. Ionniţiu typed out a decree to this effect, the king signed it, and the new prime minister set out for army headquarters to transmit the order for Romanian troops under Colonel Dămăceanu to take up positions at strategic points in Bucharest and to cease hostilities against the Soviet forces at the front. Proof that the army placed their loyalty to their supreme commander, the king, above that to Marshal

Antonescu, was the fact that not a single senior officer disobeyed Sănătescu's orders and not one of them defected to the marshal.

Since Maniu and Pătrăşcanu had failed to agree on a list of ministers, and neither was at the palace, the new government had to be formed on the spot from the king's advisers. Niculescu-Buzeşti, a counsellor in the Foreign Ministry, was elevated to foreign minister, and General Aldea became minister of the interior, while the representatives of the four parties in the NDB – Maniu, Brătianu, Petrescu and Pătrăşcanu – were appointed ministers of state without portfolio. Ionniţiu was doubtless not alone in his feeling at the time that the politicians had, at this crucial moment, shown themselves to be 'a pathetic bunch'.[21]

The first of them to appear at the palace was Pătrăşcanu, who arrived shortly after 8 pm. He brought with him the king's proclamation, which was approved after amendments by Buzeşti and Sănătescu, and the texts of two decrees, previously agreed at meetings of the NDB, granting an amnesty to political prisoners and abolishing the internment camps in which many Communists and other political detainees had been held. At the same time, Pătrăşcanu asked the king for the post of minister of justice. Since none of the other political leaders had cabinet seats, the king did not want to risk an accusation of partiality, but given Pătrăşcanu's legal background, his diligence in producing the draft proclamation and the decrees, and that he was the first member of the NDB to appear at the palace, the king offered him a compromise: minister of justice *ad interim*. The fact that Pătrăşcanu alone among the political representatives secured this temporary position gave rise in accounts about the formation of this new government to the supposition that he was acting on orders from the Communist Party and this, in turn, helped to cement the fiction in Communist historiography of the dominant role of the party in the coup. In the circumstances it was the most immediately plausible appointment for Pătrăşcanu, given the speed of events on the afternoon of 23 August and the lack of time in which to contact the leaders of the Communist Party.[22]

Pătrăşcanu was followed shortly afterwards by Titel Petrescu and then, an hour or so later, by Emil Bodnăraş who was presented

[21] Ionniţiu, '23 August 1944', p.570.

[22] This is the view of Ionniţiu.

to the king under the name of 'Engineer Ceauşu' and as head of a group of Communist-trained armed civilians known as the 'Patriotic Guards'. About an hour after the recording of the king's proclamation to the country announcing the coup and the immediate cessation of hostilities with the Allies had been broadcast over the radio at 10.12 p.m., Marshal Antonescu who was still locked in the palace strong room, asked for paper and made his will. At about 1 a.m. Bodnăraş and a group of armed workers took charge of the two Antonescus and drove them away to a safe house in the Bucharest district of Vatra Luminoasă.[23]

Even today, political opponents of the king have joined admirers of Antonescu in seeking to make capital at the expense of the king over this transfer of the marshal to the Communists, accusing the monarch of 'treachery'. The truth of the matter is that the first consideration for the king and the NDB in planning the coup had been, to prevent the marshal from reaching the German forces and thereby setting up a 'rebel' pro-German government. In this respect they were faced with a problem: they did not want to hand Antonescu over to the police, whom the marshal had used to harass the opposition leaders, for fear that the police might release him. Pătrăşcanu proposed instead that a civilian guard, drawn from trusted persons from all four opposition parties, should take custody of Antonescu until the police was purged. He was ready to offer volunteers from within the Communist Party and invited the other parties to do the same. This idea found favour with Maniu and Brătianu. At a subsequent meeting at the palace on 17 August Maniu announced that he had a team of NPP volunteers ready to undertake this role. However on the evening of the coup this team was not available, having been sent to Transylvania according to Maniu to assist in the fighting against the Germans. Custody of the marshal was therefore left in the hands of Bodnăraş whose group was the only one to appear at the palace.[24]

Also taken to the house in Vatra Luminoasă were Antonescu's fellow ministers, General Constantin Pantazi, minister of defence,

[23] Pătrăşcanu, '23 august 1944'. Among this group of armed civilians was Ştefan Mladin, who for a period after 23 August was one of those in charge of the bodyguard of Gheorghiu-Dej.

[24] Ionniţiu, '23 August 1944', p.574.

General Dumitru Popescu, minister of the interior, General Constantin Vasiliu, under-secretary of state at the Interior Ministry, and Colonel Mircea Elefterescu, head of Bucharest Police. On 31 August, two days after Soviet troops entered Bucharest, the group was handed over by Bodnăraş into the custody of Lieutenant-General Tevcenkov and Major-General Nikolai Burenin, the commander of Soviet forces in Bucharest, on orders issued by General (later Marshal) Rodion Malinovski, commander of Soviet operations in Romania.[25]

King Michael was still at a mountain retreat in the Carpathians, having left the capital for fear that it might fall to the Germans in the early hours of 24 August. With or without the king's presence once the Antonescus had been handed over to them the Soviet authorities were in a position to impose their will without hindrance. Romania was now an occupied country and it is difficult to see how the king could have intervened against his new ally to prevent them taking a leader who had conducted hostilities against them during the previous three years. Those who argue that the king should have done so ignore the realities of the time.

What emerges from this description of the preparations for the coup and its implementation is that the Romanian Communists were but one of a number of players involved. Their part was defined by a number of considerations. As a party with little popular support within Romania, the Communists' importance in shaping the country's future depended on the influence their sponsor, Stalin, was able to wield in Romanian affairs. As the war progressed that importance was magnified by the advance of

[25] On the following day, the group was taken by train to Moscow and held until May 1946 in a castle some 60 km outside the Russian capital. According to an account written by Pantazi's son, they were well treated (Ion Pantazi, 'O mărturie indirectă despre 23 august', *Apoziţia*, 1980-1, Munich, pp.20-30). At the end of April 1946 all six were sent back to Bucharest to stand trial as 'war criminals'. On 17 May Marshal Antonescu, Mihai Antonescu, Pantazi, Vasiliu, Gheorghe Alexianu, the former governor of Transnistria, Radu Lecca, former chief of Jewish affairs, and Eugen Cristescu, head of intelligence service were sentenced to death. All, except the marshal, lodged appeals and Cristescu, Lecca and Pantazi had their sentences commuted by the king, with the consent of government acting on the advice of the Soviet authorities. The marshal's mother appealed to the king for clemency but, on the advice of the government, the king denied her request. The two Antonescus, Alexianu and Vasiliu were executed by firing squad in the grounds of Jilava prison at 6 pm on 1 June 1946.

the Red Army. The inclusion of representatives of the RCP in the NDB was regarded as sound politics by the king and the major opposition leaders in view of the impending entry of the Red Army onto Romanian soil and the lead that the Soviet Union would take in determining the conditions of an armistice. But having said that, the Communists were allowed to play a significant part in the coup because of the lapses of the other parties which were compounded by the Communists' superior organisation on the evening of the coup: Pătrăşcanu was the first party representative to appear at the palace on 23 August; Maniu and Brătianu could not be contacted; and Bodnăraş and his 'Patriotic Guards' were the only civilian militia to arrive to take charge of Antonescu. These facts were used by the Communists to underpin their exaggerated claim to have played the leading role in the coup.

The coup of 23 August transformed the status of the Communist Party in Romania. At the beginning of 1944, after twenty-three years' existence, the party was a small faction-ridden political group with little or no effective resonance in Romania, its leadership scattered over three main centres and constrained to respond to policies decided in Moscow which were relevant to Soviet political strategies rather than Romanian political conditions. By the autumn of that year, the RCP had become an influential factor in the Romanian political scene. By the end of 1944 it had been thrust into the forefront of events by the occupying Soviet power, its factional rivalry blurred by the need to prepare itself for the role assigned to it by Stalin in Romania's future. In adjusting to that role the Communists found it hard to shake off the legacy of clandestinity. Their leading figures were, as elsewhere, habituated to dogmatism and dissimulation. Mindful of the Stalinist purges of 1937 and 1938, Gheorghiu-Dej and Ana Pauker considered deviousness to be an important element in survival and it was to characterise their struggle for leadership of the party.

4

THE PATH TO POWER OF THE ROMANIAN COMMUNIST PARTY

Immediately after the coup Romania's external position was that of an independent state waging war against its former allies on the side of its former enemies. So when Soviet troops entered Bucharest on 30 August they found an interim Romanian government ready to negotiate an armistice and hold free elections. The British had suggested that as part of the Armistice Agreement an Allied Control Commission be set up to oversee the implementation of the terms, but the Soviet determination to have the main say in this matter was carried through in their armistice draft of 31 August which stated that the terms would be implemented 'under the control of the Soviet High Command, hereinafter called Allied (Soviet) High Command, acting on behalf of the Allied powers'. As if to stress the point Soviet Foreign Minister Vyacheslav Molotov in conversation with American Ambassador Averell Harriman implied that the Western allies could only have political contact with the Romanian government through the Russians.[1]

The Russians refused to concede any matters of principle in their draft proposals to the British and the Americans, and were adamant about fixing a definite sum for reparations. Both the British and American ambassadors, however, were told by their governments that in the event of Soviet insistence they were to agree to their proposals in order to present a show of unity to the Romanians. The Romanian delegation, led by Lucreţiu Pătrăşcanu, had arrived in the Soviet capital on 29 August, but the sparring among the Allies meant that the agreed armistice terms could not be presented to it before 10 September. If the Russians hoped that they would find Pătrăşcanu, as a Communist, more acquiescent in the discussions, they were mistaken, and his

[1] Paul D. Quinlan, *Clash over Romania: British and American Policies towards Romania: 1938-1947*, Los Angeles: American-Romanian Academy of Arts and Sciences, 1977, pp.106-7.

sharp exchanges with Molotov may well have marked him out as an unreliable figure to the Kremlin.[2] The agreement was signed at 5 a.m. on 13 September.[3]

In effect Stalin used the armistice to subvert the effects of the coup of 23 August which had threatened to wrest the initiative in Romanian affairs from him. In order to regain that initiative the Soviet leader fashioned from the armistice a legal framework for securing a dominant political and economic interest in Romania.[4]

[2] The record of the second meeting between the Soviet, British and US delegations, and the Romanian delegation on the armistice terms, held on 11 September at 10 p.m., indicates the friction between the two men. Here is a sample:

> Mr Molotov observed that Roumania had been defeated and must recognise the fact. It must be included in the armistice terms.
>
> Mr Pătrăşcanu argued that the present Roumanian government was not the government which had been waging war against the Russians. It had overthrown that government.
>
> Mr Molotov pointed out that Roumania had only asked for an armistice after they had been forced to do so by the breaking of the Roumanian front by the Red Army. The argument was finished; the preamble stood in its present state; he would only add that the armistice would be signed by Marshal Malinovski.
>
> Mr Pătrăşcanu said that the Roumanians had wished to accept the armistice since last July.
>
> Mr Molotov said that to wish was one thing, to act, another.

(PRO, FO 371/44011, ff.22-52; see also V. F. Dobrinescu, *România şi Organizarea Postbelică a Lumii, 1945-1947*, Bucharest: Editura Academiei Republicii Socialiste România, 1988, p.199). The Romanian diplomatic minute of the negotiations was published in G. Buzatu, *România cu şi fără Antonescu*, Iaşi: Editura Moldova, 1991, pp. 259-71.

[3] Nevertheless, dated the 12th.

[4] The significance attached by the Soviets to the armistice was publicly spelled out at a lunch given by the Romanian Foreign Minister Constantin Vişoianu for Andrei Vyshinski, the Soviet deputy foreign minister on 14 October 1944 in Bucharest. In his speech, Vişoianu declared that 'On 23 August, at the command of His Majesty the King and the call of the democratic parties, the Romanian nation and its army rose to a man against the dictator government.' Vyshinski, in reply, yoked 23 August and 12 September together and avoided reference to the king: 'On 12 September were laid the foundations of good relations between the Russian people and the Romanian people. [...] It was not by chance that another day, 23 August, was its forerunner. [...] On that day the revolutionary action of the Romanian people, led by the democratic parties of the country, put an end to the criminal war [...] great importance of the date for Romania's home policy. I believe I'm entitled to say that 12 September has equal significance for Romanian foreign policy.' Quoted from report of speeches in Public Record

By its terms, Romania was to provide twelve infantry divisions for the Allied cause and to allow free passage to Soviet troops. She was to pay in kind a sum in reparations of $300 million over a six-year period and restore property taken from the Allies. Articles 13 and 14 provided for the arrest of war criminals and the dissolution of 'Fascist-type' organisations. Censorship was to be imposed if the Soviet authorities considered it necessary. The territorial clauses recognised the Soviet annexation of Bessarabia and Northern Bukovina, and the Vienna award which had given Northern Transylvania to Hungary was annulled.

Since the Soviet Union had a monopoly over its interpretation, the Armistice Agreement became the mechanism for the takeover of Romania. Article 18 established an Allied Control Commission, under the general direction and order of 'the Allied (Soviet) High Command acting on behalf of the Allied Powers'. In practice, it functioned under statutes drawn up by the Russians, under which, until Potsdam, American and British officers were treated as delegations to the commission, and not as structurally part of it. Hence rights formally granted to the Allies under the Armistice Agreement were defined and enforced by the Russians. Stalin, therefore, had two satisfactory instruments for pursuing his objectives in Romania: a Communist Party which was an acknowledged part of the country's political structure, and an agreement with his Allies which gave the Red Army all the scope it needed.

The takeover of Romania resulted from the interaction between these two instruments: the Red Army, as any army, while fighting was still in progress, required order behind the front, but in Romania the only order acceptable to the Russians was that guaranteed by the RCP. The party's role was to prevent the post-coup régime from establishing order on any other terms. That requirement implied firstly, neutralising the existing means of maintaining the social order, *viz.* army, judiciary and police and redesigning them on the Soviet model; secondly, creating mass support which the RCP totally lacked, and which would provide the new régime with the necessary theoretical legitimation. Both activities involved reliance on terror, and both could be relied upon to destroy any vestiges of support for the monarchy and for 'Western' democracy.

Office. FO 371/43984. Vyshinski's emphasis upon 12 September may well be the first 'official' announcement of the Party line.

In the caretaker government of General Sănătescu (23 August-2 November 1944), set up to direct Romania's new war course, the majority of ministerial posts had gone to military officers, with only the Ministry of Justice being secured by the Communists in the person of Pătrăşcanu. While several senior officers of the intelligence service, the SSI *(Serviciul Special de Informaţii)*, were arrested in September 1944, the committee charged with screening the 600 personnel of the SSI employed nationally concluded, in a report of 20 October, that they could find only two officers against whom charges could be levelled and these were 'abusive behaviour and unseemly conduct'.[5] The personnel of the Ministry of the Interior and of the security police, the *Siguranţa*, remained largely unchanged.[6] It was the failure to replace these figures that provided a pretext for the Communists to set about torpedoing the Sănătescu government. At the same time the Soviet authorities set about weakening Romania's army and police force.

On 2 October the Soviet High Command demanded the reduction of the police force from 18,000 to 12,000. On 6 October it forced the resignation of General Gheorge Mihail, the chief of the Romanian General Staff, because of his opposition to the Soviet order that all Romanian units should be disarmed, except for the twelve divisions fighting alongside the Russians. Mihail's successor, General Nicolae Rădescu, consented under protest to the Soviet demand (26 October) that the Romanian army in the interior be reduced from thirteen full-strength to three skeleton divisions with a total complement of 10,000, and that the numbers of frontier guards and gendarmerie be cut from 74,086 to 58,018. This process was continued over the next three years, leading to a fall in the strength of the Romanian armed forces from 419,000 in May 1945 to 136,000 in December 1947.[7]

[5] *Cartea Albă a Securităţii*, vol. 1, Bucharest: SRI, 1995, p.92. The officers arrested were Eugen Cristescu, the head of the SSI, Gheorghe Cristescu and Nicolae Trohani, both department heads, Florin Begnescu, an officer in the counter-espionage section, and Eugen Haralamb.

[6] The policing and public order duties were carried out by the Directorate General of the Police (to which the security police, the *Siguranţa* was subordinated), the Corps of Detectives, and the General Inspectorate of the Gendarmes. The latter were responsible for public order in rural districts. All three bodies came under the aegis of the Ministry of the Interior.

[7] A. Duţu, 'Comisia Aliată de Control Destructurează Armata Românâ (3)',

These actions by the Soviet authorities ensured that the party could proceed without fundamental interference. Its first task was to broaden its bridgehead in government. That in itself demanded admission to crucial ministries – Interior, Defence Justice – and the creation of mass support, which could be used to demand radical political change. On 2 October the Communist Party and the Social Democratic Party joined forces to form the National Democratic Front (NDF). Members of the front threatened workers at the major factories in Bucharest and elsewhere with arrest by the Soviet army if they refused to vote out the old works' committees and elect NDF representatives in their place. The new committees then took charge of the workers' canteens and the rationing procedures and soon the NDF had much of industry in its grip, forcing workers to accede to its will under pain of withdrawing rations and special ration cards.

In industry and elsewhere, the threats were given weight by the 'Guards of Patriotic Defence', since enlarged from the nucleus of armed workers who took charge of Antonescu after his arrest. Enlargement, in September 1944, was supervised by the Soviet Security Service, the NKGB, and placed under the command of Emil Bodnăraş. It provided the ideal cover for the training of agents and thugs who were to be infiltrated into the police and security forces when the Communists gained access to the Ministry of the Interior. The Guards were used to root out 'Fascists' and encourage recalcitrants to see the error of opposition. When necessary they enjoyed the logistic cooperation of the Russian command. Their recruits included gaolbirds and former Iron Guardists, whose intimidatory skills had, of course, been honed in the late 1930s.[8] On 15 January 1945 Prime Minister General Rădescu ordered the Guards' disbandment, but Georgescu and Bodnăraş simply

Revista de Istorie Militară, no.5, 1992, p.221.

[8] One of the advantages of a class theory of politics is that it legitimates casual murder. The Guards' victims, who were killed or later died of their injuries, have yet to be counted. Apart from their role as 'shock troops', the Guards (known in Romanian as *Formaţiunile de Luptă Patriotice*) also played an intelligence role and infiltrated the SSI and Romanian Military Intelligence (Section II of the Romanian General Staff). These FLP agents went on to occupy senior positions in the Communist *Securitate* and militia: see Claudiu Secaşiu, 'Serviciul de Informaţii al PCR; Secţia a II-a Informaţii şi Contrainformaţii din cadrul Comandamentului Formaţiunilor de Luptă Patriotice (FLP) – Penetrarea Serviciilor Oficiale de Informaţii (23 August 1944-6 Martie 1945)' in *6 martie 1945*, pp.146-57.

ingored the instruction. With the truncated Romanian army absent or disarmed, the government had no countervailing power.

The Armistice Agreement had stipulated the dissolution of 'all pro-Hitler organisations (of a Fascist type)' (Art.15). This, widely drawn, was liberally interpreted. In early September, the foreign minister, Niculescu-Buzeşti, and Stârcea, the marshal of the palace (both leading figures in the coup of 23 August), called for the immediate establishment of a tribunal for the trial of war criminals and of pro-Germans holding responsible positions. Maniu raised legalistic objections and the proposal was dropped.[9]

Hence what the proposers had feared came to pass; the liquidation of Fascism fell to the Russians and to their local minions. We should at this point recall that the war against the Axis still in progress was widely accepted as an anti-Fascist' crusade; that there were many in Romania who, in some sense or other, qualified as 'Fascist' and that the governments immediately after the coup appeared to be dilatory in dealing with them. So an agitation to get rid of Fascists could count on some popular support. Events soon demonstrated that, in practice, 'Fascist' came to mean what the Communists said it was, and that they could say it through 'spontaneous' demonstrations and through a press which was rapidly being brought under control.[10]

On 8 October the NDF organised its first mass meeting in Bucharest, at which some 60,000 demonstrators called for the resignation of the Sănătescu government for having failed to remove 'Fascists' from public life. On the following day General Vinogradov,

[9] See the digest of OSS reports in the Public Record Office, FO to Minister Resident, Cairo, no.3251, 16 Sept. 1944 (WO 201 1602).

[10] The fate of *Viitorul* – the old National Liberal organ – is instructive. Between the armistice and February 1945, publication was frequently suspended by order of the Control Commission in consequence of its exposure of official communiqués claiming the liberation by Russian troops of towns already freed by Romanian units and of its editorials attacking Communist leaders. Within the enterprise, from November a self-appointed Communist committee prevented printing of articles critical of the NDF. The workers capitulated, on the threatened withdrawal of their ration cards, and of possible deportation. The editor received death threats. Finally, the Control Commission ordered the paper's suppression on 15 February when all non-Communist journals were closed down. One of the charges was that the paper was printing suspicious abbreviations. They turned out to be the distinctions of Air Vice-Marshal Stevenson, head of the British Military Mission, his 'CBE, DSO, MC' being interpreted as a coded message.

head of the Russian Military Mission, demanded that the government arrest forty-seven Romanians as war criminals, among them two cabinet ministers, General Gheorghe Potopeanu, the minister of the national economy who had served for a brief period as military governor of Transnistria, and General Ion Boiteanu, the minister of education. The slowness with which Sănătescu acted against Antonescu's officials provided ammunition to the Communist Party and the Soviet authorities, and both accused the Romanians of not respecting articles 14 and 15 of the armistice. In their defence Romanian officials argued that the bureaucracy would not be able to function if large scale purges of the kind demanded by the Russians were implemented.[11] Confirmation of the Communists' charges came from an American OSS (Office of Strategic Services) report of February 1945 which stated that during the first six weeks after the August coup the Sănătescu government dismissed only eight Romanian officials.[12]

Demonstrations also focused on specific political figures whom the Communists wanted removed. One such was the new Minister of the Interior Nicolae Penescu, a National Peasant who was vehemently anti-Soviet. Mass demonstrations were organised to shout 'Down with Penescu'. At the end of November the NDF seized upon a suburban brawl as a pretext for demanding his resignation.[13] A group of drunken Romanian soldiers shot dead

[11] The same argument was invoked forty-five years later by former Communists in Romania in defending the retention of the Ceauşescu bureaucracy after the revolution of 1989.

[12] Quinlan, *Clash over Romania*, p.116, n.58.

[13] James Marjoribanks, assistant to the British political representative on the Allied Control Commission, sent a minute to the Foreign Office on 2 December 1944 describing a conversation with Penescu. 'Penescu said that he had taken office with two aims: (*a*) to ensure order in the country; (*b*) to hold communal elections. The Communists had agreed to his appointment because they considered him an agrarian member of the National Peasant Party's left wing. Mr Penescu had positive evidence: (*a*) that the shooting incident which was being used to discredit his ministry involved a man who was not a simple workman but a wealthy ex-legionary (Iron Guardist – author's note) who had been shot because he was having an affair with someone else's wife; (*b*) that ex-legionaries (Iron Guardists), were encouraged to join the Communist party (he said that he would send me a photostatic copy of the order to this effect); (*c*) that a considerable quantity of arms – machine guns, rifles, grenades etc. of which he had the exact location and particulars – had been supplied to the Communist Guards by the Soviet Army (FO 371/48547. R/95/28/37).

two trade unionists, for whom the NDF organised a huge funeral. The Communist press raged about 'Hitlerist Fascist bullets from automatic rifles of the Fifth Column supported by leaders of the National Peasant Party'. The Peasant Party ministers and their National Liberal colleagues withdrew from the cabinet of Sănătescu whom they felt was too tolerant of the Communists' harassment. On 2 December the king asked General Nicolae Rădescu, formerly chief of the General Staff and a non-party figure, to form a cabinet.[14]

Rădescu received strong backing from King Michael, who on 4 December warned Andrei Vyshinski, the Soviet deputy foreign minister, that the Communists' activities threatened to throw the country into anarchy. Among these was an unremitting press campaign in the party newspaper *Scînteia* condemning the Romanians' alleged failure to fulfil the principal conditions of the armistice. *Scînteia* reprinted (6 December 1944) Soviet charges that the Romanian Government had systematically shirked its direct debt to the Soviet Union and had openly supported the administration which sabotaged the Armistice Convention. The leaders of the so-called 'historic parties' in Romania (the NPP and NLP) who were widely represented in the Sănătescu government, were responsible. The conclusion was ominous:

> 'The Soviet Command in this part of the Soviet-German front is displaying the utmost patience which is being abused by those Romanian politicians who have transformed this region of the front into an area of intrigue which is undermining the mobilisation of the forces of the Romanian people and basic order in the country'. [...][15]

The king told Vyshinski that if the Soviet Union continued

[14] Rădescu (1874-1953) won the Order of Michael the Brave, the highest Romanian military decoration, during the First World War. From April 1926 to July 1928 he served as Romanian military attaché in London. Upon his return to Romania, he became a member of the military household of the royal palace. In 1930 he was discharged from the army on grounds of age. In November 1941 he was interned on Antonescu's orders for writing a defiant letter to Baron Killinger, Hitler's envoy, in reply to disparaging remarks made by the Baron about Romania. On 15 October 1944 he was appointed chief of the General Staff and held this position until the beginning of December. On 6 December he was appointed prime minister and minister of the interior.

[15] 'In Bucureşti acum 50 ani', *Magazin Istoric*, vol.28, no.12 (December 1994), pp.49-50.

to support the Communists in this way, he would find himself forced to abdicate and leave the country. Vyshinski was said to have been surprised by the king's boldness and denied any Soviet responsibility. In the government reshuffle the Communist-dominated NDF had hoped to secure the Ministry of the Interior, but Rădescu reserved the post for himself. Thereupon the party leaders, Ana Pauker and Vasile Luca, refused even to discuss NDF participation in the new government. However, under instructions from Vyshinski, they now backed down.[16] Rădescu did, however, concede the position of deputy minister of the interior to the Communists, appointing Teohari Georgescu, a member of the party's Central Committee; his Communist colleagues in the cabinet were Pătrăşcanu, minister of justice, and Gheorghiu-Dej, minister of communications and public works.

Vyshinski's decision throws some light on Soviet intentions at this time. His long-term mission was to prepare Romania for Sovietisation, but the short-term priority was to conclude the war against Germany as quickly as possible. Instability in Romania would compromise that aim. Furthermore the RCP was still not strong enough to take over the administration of the country where the bulk of the population was hostile to Communism; therefore, should the king abdicate, the Russians were likely to have to assume part of the administration themselves. Such a move would expose their motives to Britain and the United States. Consequently Vyshinski lowered the temperature in Romania. He left the country as he had come, without notice, on 8 December.[17]

So for a brief period NDF meetings and street demonstrations ceased, but Communist penetration of institutions continued unabated. Teohari Georgescu installed his own men in nine of the

16 Dinu C. Giurescu, *Romania's Communist Takeover: The Rădescu Government*, Boulder, CO: East European Monographs, 1994, p.135. Pătrăşcanu, in conversation with the Tass correspondent in late December 1944, considered that the Communist Party had made a mistake in provoking the fall of the Sănătescu government since the more energetic Rădescu had replaced him. 'If before we had a prime minister whom the NDF had in its pocket, now we have a prime minister who is in someone else's pocket.' When asked to explain what he meant by this, Pătrăşcanu declared that hostile internal and external forces were behind Rădescu. 'He meant the British,' the Tass correspondent told Moscow (F. Constantiniu, A, Duţu, M. Retegan, *România în război, 1941-1945*, Bucharest: Editura Militară, 1995, p.285).

17 *Ibid.*, p.137.

sixteen prefectures in the provinces with strict orders to ignore government instructions and do only his bidding. He also ignored an undertaking to Rădescu to disband the 10,000 strong Communist militia and introduced into the *Siguranţa* agents trained in the 'Patriotic Guards'. The relative calm ended with the publication of the NDF's New Year's appeal to the people in which they condemned the Rădescu government for failing to fulfil the terms of the armistice, and called for agarian reform of all property exceeding an area of 50 hectares within six weeks.

It was soon evident that the RCP's moves were Soviet orchestrated. In early January 1945 Ana Pauker and Gheorghiu-Dej returned from Moscow claiming that they had 'received Soviet approval for the bringing into power of a Communist government'.[18] The actions of the NDF bore this claim out. The NDF attacked its NLP and NPP partners in the government by denouncing them as 'Fascists' who opposed the will of the people. On 29 January the NDF published its government programme which denounced the NLP and NPP as 'reactionaries' who opposed the will of the people, and called for a new government, immediate agrarian reform and the democratisation of the army.[19] When the Liberals and Peasants attempted to answer these charges, their newspapers ceased to appear owing to the refusal of the Communist-controlled printing union to produce them and the appearance of 'activist' committees in workshops.

Acting on instructions from Vyshinski, Gheorghiu-Dej approached the dissident liberal leader Gheorghe Tătărescu with an invitation to enter the NDF in order to give it the appearance of a broader base. On 31 January Gheorghiu-Dej told the NDF council of his talks with Tătărescu who had stated his readiness to enter the NDF. 'There are opinions', Gheorghiu-Dej stated 'in very competent places [i.e. Moscow], which indicate to us the need to bring Tătărescu close to us and not to reject him.' Vasile Luca agreed; for him Tătărescu 'represented economic power'. Lothar Rădăceanu, however, was less enthusiastic. He criticised Tătărescu's tolerance of the Iron Guardists and the fact that 'he was their greatest protector'. Gheorghiu-Dej saw the

18. Quinlan, *Clash over Romania*, p.120.

19 Programul de Guvernare al Frontului National Democrat, *Viaţa politică în Documente*, eds Ioan Scurtu *et al.*, Bucharest: Arhivele Statului, 1994, pp.93-6.

attraction of Tătărescu not merely in the advantages he could bring to the NDF but also in terms of the damage he could do to Maniu: 'Maniu wants to get rid of him [Tătărescu] as a dangerous adversary... Let us think seriously of breaking the National Peasant front,' Gheorghiu-Dej concluded.[20]

The Communist press accused Rădescu of sabotaging the armistice by allegedly failing to cleanse Romanian public life of 'Fascism' but omitted to point out that it had failed to put its own house in order in those ministries headed by Communists. Teohari Georgescu sent an open letter to the press accusing Rădescu of having hindered the 'decontamination' of the Ministry of the Interior. In a stormy cabinet meeting on 14 February Rădescu requested Georgescu's resignation for acts of insubordination. Georgescu, supported by his Communist colleagues in the cabinet, refused to go and the prime minister responded on 16 February by publishing three circulars calling on the commission charged with compiling the list of officials liable for dismissal to complete its task. Rădescu was able to point out that the commission for purging the Ministry of the Interior, of which Teohari Georgescu himself was a member, had taken three months to examine seventy-five cases out of 300, and that following the general's intervention 137 cases had been dealt with in twelve days. In fact, under the Rădescu government 780 officers (i.e. employees of the Interior Ministry) out of a total estimated at 14,000 were purged.[21]

Aware of the power which Georgescu and Bodnăraş were amassing, Rădescu ordered the disbandment of the 'Patriotic Guards' on 15 January but the two Communists simply ignored his instruction. Georgescu still refused to leave his post. He continued to go to his office and issued a telegram to prefects, informing them that 'in compliance with the decision of the NDF council, he would remain in office'. 'I advise you most emphatically', he continued, 'not to carry out orders directed against the people, given by General Rădescu, who has proved himself by his dictatorial action to be the enemy of our people.'[22] In the meantime, Deputy

20 Stenograma Şedinţei Consiliului FND, *Viaţa politică în Documente*, pp.97-119.

21 *Cartea Albă* pp.12, 92. The number of police officers remained virtually the same until the reorganisation of the police according to the Soviet model in August 1948.

22 Text in private papers of Mr Ivor Porter, to whom I am grateful for a sight

Prime Minister Petru Groza was encouraging peasants to anticipate land reform by seizing the land of large estate owners, An article in *Scînteia* of 13 February 1945 reported the expropriation of estates by peasants in the counties of Prahova and Dâmboviţa. Two days later Rădescu accused Groza at a cabinet meeting of preparing civil war. Both Rădescu and King Michael feared that the Left was preparing a coup amidst reports that the Russians were sending NKGB troops to Bucharest.[23]

The NDF staged demonstrations in several towns, among them Brăila and Constanţa on the Black Sea, Craiova in the south, Roman in Moldavia, and Târgu-Mureş in Transylvania, calling for the resignation of the Rădescu government. Although many of the participants came of their own accord, the NDF also used blackmail to mobilise demonstrators. Workers who did not join trade unions were refused ration cards. A police report of 4 February stated that in many factories works' committees were paralleled by so-called 'sacrifice committees' composed of members of parties of the Left. These committees were set up to ensure that the workers followed the orders of the Communist Party and did not join any other parties or non-Communist organisations.[24]

Any hopes that the Romanian people might have had from the declaration on Liberated Europe, issued at the Yalta Conference, that 'sovereign rights and self-government' would be restored 'to

---

of this document. A similar disregard for Rădescu had been shown one month earlier by Georgescu and Bodnăraş.

[23] Quinlan, *Clash over Romania*, p.120. Doubts about Dej even meeting Stalin during his visit to Moscow are conveyed in a telegram from the Earl of Halifax, British ambassador in Washington, to the Foreign Office, dated 3 February 1945. Burton Berry, the senior American political representative on the Allied Control Commission in Romania, had reported on 30 January a conversation with the marshal of the court in which the latter stated that King Michael 'had talked with Gheorghiu-Dej who confessed that he had not (repeat not) had interviews with Soviet leaders but had "gained the general impression" that the Romanians' position *vis-à-vis* the Russians would be improved if a Communist government were installed.' Commenting on the telegram, a Foreign Office hand notes, 'Dej's confession suggests that he and Pauker have claimed Russian support for their programme without having really received it' (Public Record Office, FO 371/48547. R2516/28/37).

[24] N. Tampa, 'Starea de spirit din România la începutul anului 1945 [The Atmosphere in Romania at the Beginning of 1945]', *6 martie 1945. Inceputurile Comunizării României,* Bucharest: Editura Enciclopedica, 1995, pp. 312-18.

those peoples who have been forcibly deprived of them' were soon dispelled. Organised thuggery was practised by the 'Patriotic Guards' in support of NDF committees whose hold over several key factories in Bucharest was challenged by non-NDF workers. This particular campaign of Communist-inspired violence began at the ASAM defence works early in February and spread to the Official Gazette and Stella works where the NDF committees were thrown out. At the union elections at the ASAM shops only fourteen of the 600 workers voted for the Communist candidates while 180 voted for the non-party list (the remainder abstained). On 6 February, sixty members of the 'Patriotic Guards' and two NKGB soldiers drove to the ASAM works, beat up those who had voted for the independent list and took eleven of them away to the NKGB headquarters. On 19 February 3,600 of the 5,500 employees at the Malaxa steel and armament works in Bucharest signed a resolution calling for the resignation of the NDF committee headed by Vasile Mauriciu, a former Iron Guardist. Voting on the resolution on the following day was interrupted when the NDF committee called on railwaymen and tramway employees to defend them at the factory. Fighting broke out between the Malaxa workers and the outsiders during which several workers were killed and the Communist labour leader Gheorghe Apostol was wounded. After the affray all those whose identity cards showed that they had voted were arrested and taken to NDF branches.[25]

25 A broadsheet issued by the workers at the Malaxa factory on 23 February read:

> We protest most strongly at the terror tactics which irresponsible persons from outside the factory are employing at the Malaxa works in support of the committee of dishonourable agitators which has been kept in place against the workers' will. We protest at the violence of the armed mercenaries who were brought in by lorries under the direction of Gheorghiu-Dej, who has come to impose the will of a disparate minority which has even shot its own supporters. We denounce the hooligans who wish to halt with gun fire the free expression of the workers' will. We demand the arrest of the armed bands of NDF supporters, who have been brought in from outside and have no place amongst us. We demand the arrest of Gheorghiu-Dej and the other Trotskyist agitators. We want free elections and a secret ballot. We want trade unions based on professions and not politically manipulated hordes. We demand that the government ensure freedom and the secret ballot, and prevent the terror practised against us by irresponsible criminals. We want work and order. We want peace. Down with the terror in the trade unions!

The situation escalated as travesty was added to injury. *Scînteia* accused Rădescu of attempting to foment a civil war; its attacks were echoed by *Graiul Nou*, the Red Army newspaper in Romania, and *Pravda*. Anatoli Pavlov, the Soviet political representative on the Allied Control Commission, followed the script by advising the chief American on the commission that unless the Rădescu government 'rid itself of...Fascist elements... the people themselves can be expected to take necessary corrective action'.[26] Matters came to a head on 24 February. At the end of a large NDF demonstration the crowd moved into the palace square in front of the Ministry of the Interior where Rădescu had his office. Shots were fired and several people were killed. On orders from Rădescu the Romanian troops guarding the building fired into the air to disperse the crowd. The American historian Henry Roberts, then serving as an officer in the OSS,

> [....] watched the procession and was in the crowd no more than fifty feet from the first shots. Yet at that time and since I have been unable to discover precisely what happened. I do know that government had kept Romanian troops off the streets that day to avoid inciting trouble. The crowd did move toward the Ministry of the Interior building, although it showed little signs of direction. The first shots were fired from a small piece and from somewhere in the crowd, but by whom and for what purpose I do not know.[27]

What was clearly established later by a joint Romanian-Russian commission of doctors was that the bullets extracted from the victims were not of a calibre used by the Romanian army, but these findings came too late for Rădescu. Unable to contain his

[26] *Cartea Albă,* vol.1, p.122.

[27] Roberts, *Rumania*, p.263, n.29. Rear-Admiral L. Bogdenko, vice-chairman of the Allied Control Commission, wrote in a report sent to Moscow that 'Romanian troops who were guarding the Ministry of the Interior opened fire. Some of the demonstrators responded with fire. Simultaneously, shooting started from the building of the prefecture in Bucharest.' At 1700 hours Bogdenko demanded that Prime Minister Rădescu order all troops, gendarmes and police to cease firing from their side. The same ultimatum was given to the Romanian military commander as well as to the head of the gendarmerie. It was accepted (see T. A. Pokivailova, 'A.Y. Vyshinski, first deputy Commissar for Foreign Affairs of the USSR, and the Establishment of the Groza Government' in *6 martie 1945*, pp. 53-4).

anger at the provocation, the prime minister broadcast to the nation and denounced the Communist leaders Ana Pauker and Vasile Luca as 'hyenas' and 'foreigners without God or country', a reference to their non-Romanian origins and their atheism.[28] The Russians now intervened. Soviet Deputy Foreign Minister Vyshinski arrived unexpectedly in Bucharest on 27 February and went straight to the palace to demand that Rădescu be replaced. King Michael hesitated and told the Russian that constitutional procedures had to be respected. On the following afternoon Vyshinski returned and demanded to know what action the king had taken. When Michael again announced that he was consulting political leaders, the deputy minister shouted his dissatisfaction and gave the king until six pm that evening to announce Rădescu's dismissal. The king was intimidated into consenting.

Michael turned to the British and American representatives for help and advice, but despite the lodging of Western protests in Bucharest and Moscow at Vyshinski's behaviour, the deputy foreign minister continued to force the pace:

> All the truly democratic forces in Romania must be represented in the government and such a government will be able to ensure order and peace in Romania, which is behind the front of the Red Army, whilst at the same time ensuring the honourable and conscientious fulfilment of the armistice conditions.[29]

Military pressure was soon added to political. On 28 February, Colonel-General Ivan Susaikov, the deputy-commander of the southern group of armies, replaced Lieutenant-General V. Vinogradov as deputy chairman of the Allied Control Commission.[30] Without consulting his British and American colleagues he ordered some Romanian units stationed in and around Bucharest to the front and disbanded others. Their place was taken by Soviet tanks and troops who occupied the Prefecture of Police, the Central Post

28 The text of the speech can be found in Scurtu, *Viaţa politică in Documente*, pp.149-50.

29 Photocopies Russia, packet XIII, document 5, p.21. Quoted in M. Ignat, 'Implicaţiile Convenţiei de armistiţiu asupra evoluţiei vieţii politice româneşti' in *6 martie 1945*, p.33.

30 The nominal Chairman, Marshal Rodion Malinovsky, as commander of the second Ukrainian front, was preoccupied with hostilities in Hungary and Czechoslovakia.

Office, and the Romanian General Staff Headquarters. Two Romanian bomber groups and two fighter squadrons based in the capital were disbanded, and the rest of the Romanian air force was grounded. Hundreds of plain-clothes and uniformed police were dismissed and Soviet troops patrolled the streets of Bucharest, checking the documents of pedestrians and of drivers and their vehicles, and using the opportunity to commandeer even more Romanian vehicles.

On 1 March Vyshinski informed the king that Petru Groza, Rădescu's deputy and a trusted nominee of the Russians, 'was the Soviet choice'. Michael reluctantly gave Groza the go-ahead to form a government but the Liberals and Peasants refused to join a government controlled by the NDF. Groza's first cabinet was rejected by the king. On 5 March Vyshinski informed Michael that unless a Groza government was accepted he 'could not be responsible for the continuance of Romania as an independent state'.[31] Fearing a coup the king acquiesced on the following afternoon. Thereafter the Communist take-over of Romania proceeded rapidly.[32]

Susaikov later explained to the British and American representatives, respectively Air Vice-Marshal Stevenson and Brigadier

[31] Quinlan, *Clash over Romania*, p.128.

[32] Following his dismissal Rădescu was taken under British protection and lived in the legation building for nine weeks until an agreement was reached between the British and Soviet governments assuring the former that Rădescu would not be harmed on returning home. On 11 November he received orders from the Ministry of the Interior to stay at home, from which he did not move till the spring of 1946 when the police provided him with a car, a driver and a detective. An incident on 15 March 1946 persuaded him to leave Romania as soon as possible. That day, while attending a function at the Athenaeum in Bucharest, he was attacked by a group of men armed with clubs, and he and his detective were injured. His escape was arranged by his secretary, Barbu Niculescu. On 15 June Rădescu, together with his secretary and four other persons, including a Romanian airman, took off from Cotroceni airfield and flew to Cyprus. He settled in New York in 1947 where he helped to found the anti-Communist Romanian National Committee under the patronage of King Michael. Its work was financed by several million dollars secreted out of Romania for this purpose between 1945 and 1946. In February 1950, Rădescu requested that this money be publicly accountable but other committee members disagreed and he resigned. He died in New York on 16 May 1953. The committee, whose chairmanship was taken over by Constantin Vişoianu, remained active until 1975 (*Free Romanian Press*, vol.29, no.3 [March 1984].

Schuyler, that the Groza government was indeed imposed by force on the orders of Marshal Malinovski who feared an uprising at the rear of his front. Susaikov had been sent to Bucharest to prevent a Romanian *volte-face* by disarming Romanian troops and bringing in Groza.[33] This argument is not entirely without substance.

[33] Susaikov gave this explanation at the end of October 1945, asking Stevenson and Schuyler whether they would have done otherwise. They agreed that they would not, but thought that it was a pity that this had not been explained before (H. Hanak, 'The Politics of Impotence: The British Observe Romania, 6 March 1945 to 30 December 1947' in *Românii în istoria universală, vol.III/1*, eds I. Agrigoroaie, Gh. Buzatu and V. Cristian, Iaşi, 1988, p.433). Soviet sensitivity to disorder behind their lines had been conveyed to Schuyler at the time by A. Pavlov, the Soviet political representative. At a meeting of the Allied Control Commission on 14 February 1945, Pavlov had told Schuyler that 'no disorder can be permitted to occur in the rear of the Soviet armies...nor can any Fascist activities within the state of Romania be permitted' (Giurescu, *Romania's Communist Takeover*, p.67). Soviet unease about the possibility of a Romanian uprising had been fuelled by the infiltration of German agents and German-held Romanian prisoners of war into Romanian units in order to instigate mutinies. Roland Gunne, an SD officer from Transylvania, joined the staff of the Romanian Fourth Army which was fighting in Hungary. The commander of the Fourth Army was General Gheorghe Avramescu who, before the 23 August coup, had fought against the Russians in the Crimea and whose son-in-law, Ilie Vlad Sturdza, was the son of the foreign minister of the Iron Guard government in exile set up in Vienna on 10 December 1944. Avramescu's anti-Russian sentiments made him a prime candidate for German manipulation and Gunne and Iron Guard sympathisers persuaded the general to defect with his forces to the German side in the event of a successful German counter-offensive (P. Biddiscombe, 'Prodding the Russian Bear: pro-German Resistance in Romania, 1944-5', *European History Quarterly*, vol.23, no.2 [April 1993], pp.205-12, and G. Klein, 'Inceputurile rezistenţei antisovietice în România (23 august 1944-6 martie 1945)' in *6 martie 1945*, pp.295-311. On 3 March 1945, Avramescu and his chief-of-staff, General Nicolae Dragomir, were arrested at the command post of the second Ukrainian front at Divin in Czechoslovakia on the orders of Marshal Malinovski by Soviet Army counter-espionage officers. Avramescu's fate is unclear. According to a report presented to Stalin by Beria and his deputy Abakumov, he was killed in a German air attack on Budapest (Klein, 'Inceputurile rezistentei', p.309). This is confirmed by a reply sent in summer 1963 by the USSR Supreme Court to a request from the Romanian Ministry of Justice for information about Avramescu's fate. The letter stated that the general had died on 3 March 1945 near the town of Iasbereni following a German air attack and was buried in Soshalom, a district of Budapest. (A. Duţu, and F. Dobre, 'S-a mai dezlegat o enigmă în cazul Avramescu?' *Magazin Istoric*, vol.31, no.5 [May 1997], pp.7-8). No mention was ever made by the Soviet authorities of his arrest. His wife and daughter were arrested on the same day. The daughter committed suicide three days later, and Avramescu's wife spent eleven years in Soviet labour camps

Soviet sensitivity to disorder behind the lines had been conveyed to Schuyler at the time by A. Pavlov, the Soviet political representative. At a meeting of the Allied Control Commission on 14 February 1945, Pavlov had told Schuyler that 'no disorder can be permitted to occur in the rear of the Soviet armies...nor can any Fascist activities within the state of Romania be permitted.'[34]

From the archival evidence now available, there appears to have been some disagreement within the Communist Party leadership over the composition of the Groza government. The decisive voice in the matter appears to have been Vyshinski. In a note dated 21 January 1945 to Serghei Dangulov, senior assistant to the head of the political department of the Allied Control Commission, Vyshinski told him 'to maintain contacts and relations with Gheorghe Tătărescu', a former prime minister under King Carol and a dissident Liberal.[35] Vyshinski's influence with Gheorghiu-Dej persuaded the latter to reject calls late in February from the NLP representative Constantin (Bebe) Brătianu for the Communists to continue to work with the NLP and NPP in government. Instead, Gheorghiu-Dej pressed for an alliance both with Tătărescu and with a dissident NPP faction led by Anton Alexandrescu. At an NDF council meeting held on 26 February Gheorghiu-Dej made his position clear. He had told Brătianu that he did not have a mandate to hold discussions with him and told him bluntly that his proposal [for continued cooperation] was unacceptable. 'We see no reason for the present government to carry on.' Reviewing the current political situation Gheorghiu-Dej said that although the NDF had consolidated its position in the government it had not succeeded in resolving the political crisis.

before being allowed to return to Romania (J. Urwich-Ferry, *Fără Paşaport prin URSS* [In the USSR without a Passport], Munich: Iskra, 1977, vol.II, pp.51-7). Dragomir was taken straight to the Soviet Union where he was tried and sentenced to eight years' hard labour. After completing his sentence, he was sent on 4 April 1953 to work as a veterinary assistant on a state farm in the region of Kustanai. He requested repatriation to Romania and was returned on 10 January 1956. On 11 January 1957, he was re-arrested in Bucharest for no apparent reason. He appealed unsuccessfully against his arrest on numerous occasions and was held in various prisons until his release on 27 July 1964. He died in 1981 aged 83. (A. Duţu, F. Dobre, 'Opt ani muncă silnică pentru un post de felcer veterinar', *Magazin Istoric*, vol.30, no.6 [June 1996], pp.47-52).

34 Giurescu, *Romania's Communist Takeover*, p.67.

35 Pokivailova, *1939-40*, p.52.

> What we proposed was to enlarge our political base. The forces which today make up the NDF are not sufficient, new alliances must be found. We have found these in the progressive elements among the National Peasants [...] and secondly in the political grouping of Tătărescu. We can no longer make the same kinds of combinations with the representatives of the so-called 'historic' parties as we have made to date.[36]

Gheorghiu-Dej's views were not shared by other leading Communists. Vasile Luca, speaking at a meeting of the NDF council held on 5 March, insisted that despite the NDF's dislike of holding talks with the NLP and NPP 'we must do everything that is humanly possible to form a government in a constitutional manner in the interests of the country and in the current international situation, [and] we must not, in our haste, destroy everything.'[37] Ana Pauker, according to Anton Alexandrescu the NPP dissident, was in favour of a new government formed in collaboration with Maniu and Brătianu and had allegedly received the backing of General Susaikov.[38]

The new Groza government was dominated by the NDF, which held fourteen of the eighteen cabinet posts. Communists controlled the Ministries of the Interior, Justice, War, and the National Economy. Dissident Liberal and Peasants held the other four portfolios, the most notorious being King Carol's former prime minister, Gheorghe Tătărescu, once an opponent and now a

[36] 'Meeting of the NDF Council, 26 February 1945', Central Archive of the Institute of Party History of the Central Committee of the Romanian Workers' Party, fond 80, inventory 1, file no.16, pp.7-8, 11. Gheorghiu-Dej was to claim later, at a plenary meeting of the Central Committee held on 9-10 June 1958, that 'he alone worked' for a limited coalition with Tătărescu while Pauker, Pătrăşcanu and Soviet officials on the Allied Control Commission argued 'that we should continue with the National Peasants and the National Liberals' (R. Levy, 'Power Struggles in the Romanian Communist Party Leadership During the Period of the Formation of the Groza Regime' in *6 martie 1945*, p. 88). Gheorghiu-Dej's words may have been a retrospective attempt to show that he had acted independently of the Soviet Union and the so-called 'Muscovite faction' of Pauker and Luca and in doing so omitted any mention of Vyshinski's decisive role.

[37] 'Stenograma Şedinţei Consiliului Partidului Naţional Democrat' in Scurtu, *Viaţa politică în Documente*, pp.170-1.

[38] 'Piese Noi la "Dosarul Ana Pauker"', *Magazin Istoric*, no.10 [October], 1992, pp.26; see also Levy, 'Power struggles', p.88.

sycophant of the Soviet Union, who was made deputy prime minister and foreign minister. Teohari Georgescu was elevated to the position of minister of the interior. Immediately after his appointment Georgescu announced that 'in order to carry out its tasks...the Ministry of the Interior must rely on a powerful police apparatus that had been purged of all Fascist, collaborationist or compromised elements who had been perverted by anti-democratic and venal customs and practices.'[39] Of the 6,300 Ministry of the Interior personnel employed on 6 March 1945, 2,851 were placed on reserve and 195 dismissed. In their place were brought in 'honest, democratic and capable elements'.[40]

The police, the *Siguranţa*, the gendarmerie, and the corps of detectives, were reorganised, the latter body being given the special task of tracking down and arresting members of the Iron Guard who were still active.[41] Under the direction of an NKVD agent Alexandru Nicolski, the corps was to provide the nucleus of the *Securitate*.[42] Georgescu's colleague, Emil Bodnăraş, was promoted to secretary-general to the prime minister. Bodnăraş occupied a key position, for various strands in the Communist take-over intersected in his office. He was also an agent of the NKGB and

39 *Cartea Albă*, vol.1, p.92.

40 *Ibid.* In June 1946 Georgescu reported that the numbers of Ministry of Interior personnel had risen to 8,500, of whom only 4,084 had been employed before 23 August 1944.

41 *Ibid.*, vol.1, p.13.

42 The number of officers in the Corps of Detectives was, according to the available documents, halved from 221 in March 1945 to 101 in January 1947. Enrolled in the Corps after March 1945 were a number of Romanian-speaking Soviet agents, most of whom, like Nicolski, had been captured by the Romanian authorities and had been released from jail after 23 August. Among these agents were Andrei Gluvakov, Vladimir Gribici, Mişa Protopopov, Vanea Didenko, Iaşka Alexeev, Mihail Postanski (Posteucă), Mişa Petruc, Alexandru Şişman and Pyotr Gonciaruc (P. Ştefănescu, *Istoria Serviciilor Secrete Româneşti*, Bucharest: Divers Press, 1994, p.163). A serialised biography of Nicolski was published in the Romanian weekly *Cuvîntul* (April and May 1992) by Marius Oprea. In October 1944 he joined the police and after the imposition of the Groza government was named head of the Corps of Detectives. On 17 April 1947 he was appointed inspector general of the security police and when the *Securitate* was established on 30 August 1948, he was named as one of the two deputy directors. For further details see Dennis Deletant, 'The *Securitate* and the Police State in Romania, 1948-64', *Intelligence and National Security*, vol.8, no.4 [October 1993], pp.13-14.

reported faithfully to his masters in Moscow on the attitudes of senior figures in the new government as well as on the manoeuvring within the RCP.

On 7 March Groza announced that there would be a purge of 'Fascists' from public life and on 2 April the Party daily *Scînteia* declared that several hundred police and counter-espionage officers who were 'guilty of the disaster which had befallen the country' (Communist jargon for the alliance with Germany) had been arrested. The arrests were carried out on 20 March by Bessarabian-born Soviet agents, newly conscripted into the police. Most of them had been captured by the Romanian authorities during the interwar years and had been released from jail after 23 August. To complete Soviet control over the forces of repression Groza signed an order on 27 April giving the secretary-general control of the intelligence service, the SSI. The danger of any opposition to the Soviet and Communist presence by trained and armed forces was eliminated, and the new instruments for Communising Romanian society were in place.

5

IMPOSITION OF THE TOTALITARIAN MODEL AND PERSECUTION OF THE CHURCH

The establishment of the Groza government brought with it the total subordination of the forces of order to the Communists. Citizens' committees were formed to assist the police, which had been reduced by Soviet order on 28 February and purged, and these arrogated to themselves the right to check people's documents in the street, to search homes for goods allegedly removed from the Soviet Union during the war or which had formerly belonged to Germans and Hungarians, and to inspect houses with a view to billeting refugees or Soviet officers. There was no legal supervision of these random intrusions into people's lives and the rapidity with which the police degenerated into a force of repression under Groza generated a widespread fear of authority.

In order to obtain the verdicts that he required Vyshinski ordered Pătrăşcanu, the minister of justice, to dismiss more than 1,000 magistrates in April 1945 and replace them with pliant zealots.[1] It was not just the retributive aspect of these purges that was important but also the instrumental use of them. The two were linked: the threat of retribution was deployed to press people to become tools of the Communists. Groza himself told the British journalist Archie Gibson on 23 May 1945 that in the two months since he had taken office 90,000 Romanians had been arrested,[2]

[1] Communist activists were appointed as public prosecutors in the Ministry of Justice in April 1945. They were Stroe Botez, Avram Bunaciu, Alexandru Drăghici, H. Leibovici, M. Mayo, C. Mocanu, M. Popilian, I. Pora, I. Raiciu, Ştefan Ralescu, Dumitru Săracu, Alexandru Sidorovici, V. Stoican, Camil Suciu and C. Vicol. Drăghici, who in 1952 became minister of the interior, acted as a public prosecutor in the trial of Ion Antonescu in May 1946.

[2] Unpublished Gibson MS in possession of the author.

but there is no information to hand to confirm this figure. For some there were good grounds for arrest, as in the case of Nicolae Sturdza and Nelly Ostroveanu, two members of an Iron Guard group who were found to be housing nineteen German soldiers living under assumed names in Bucharest and who were arrested in March. For others the opposite was true; thirteen Poles were held in the internment camp at Caracal without being questioned. Persons convicted of atrocities during the Romanian administration of Transnistria were harshly punished. People's Tribunals were introduced by Pătrăşcanu to try alleged war criminals and on 22 May twenty-nine war criminals, including Generals Nicolae Macici, Constantin Trestioreanu and Cornel Calotescu, were sentenced to death, and a further eight to various terms of imprisonment.[3] The death sentences were commuted to life imprisonment on 5 June.[4] In August 1945 the discovery of two 'terrorist' plots led to the arrest of about twenty 'hirelings of ex-Premier Rădescu', and of a second group of seventeen people who had allegedly

[3] Macici, Trestioreanu and Calotescu were charged with carrying out reprisals against the Jewish population of Odessa in October 1941. On 22 October 1941 a huge explosion destroyed the Romanian military headquarters in Odessa, killing 128 soldiers and civilians, including General Ioan Glogojanu, the town commander. Marshal Antonescu immediately gave the order for reprisals: for every Romanian and German officer killed, 200 Communists were to be hanged; for every soldier, 100 Communists. During the night of 22 October the military authorities carried out the order and by daybreak 450 Jews, considered Communists, were left hanging on the streets of Odessa. In addition about 50,000 Jews were force-marched to Dalnik, about 8 km. outside the city, to be executed. On the intervention of Odessa's mayor, Gherman Pântea, and General Macici, the column was sent back to Odessa, but not before those Jews at the head of the column were herded into four large sheds and machine-gunned to death, after which the sheds were set on fire. How many Jews were killed in this way is not known exactly, but a figure of 20,000 was mentioned at Macici's trial. At his trial Macici denied that he was the person responsible for carrying out Antonescu's order, pointing to the fact that even the prosecution had recognised that he only arrived in Odessa on the morning of 23 October 1941. In answer to the charge that he had done nothing to stop the massacres, Macici replied that General Ion Iacobici, his superior as commander of the Romanian Fourth Army, was aware of what was happening in the city and had issued no orders to stop the reprisals. It was General Trestioreanu, Macici stated, who reported to Antonescu that he had carried out the order to take reprisals. *Cotidianul: Arhiva*, vol.5, no.3 (22 March 1996), p.3.

[4] *Universul*, 6 June 1945. Macici died in Aiud prison on 15 June 1950 of heart failure. *Cotidianul: Arhiva*, vol. 5, no.3 (22 March 1996), p.7.

plotted 'againt the unity of the Romanian nation'. Both groups included National Peasants.

The young king was greatly unnerved by these developments and appealed to Britain and the United States for help, invoking the principles of the Atlantic Charter and the Yalta Declaration. On 2 August at the end of the Potsdam Conference, both countries announced that they would sign peace treaties 'only with recognised democratic governments', a stipulation which gave some hope to the king and the opposition leaders, Maniu and Brătianu.[5] The latter discussed plans to remove the Groza government and on 20 August the king asked for Groza's resignation but the prime minister, with the backing of General Susaikov, refused. King Michael, in retaliation, boycotted the government; he declined to see any of its ministers and to sign decrees.

The stalemate lasted for over four months. It was broken at the Moscow conference of the foreign ministers of Britain, the United States and the Soviet Union, held between 16-26 December, where it was decided that a commission, composed of Ambassadors Clark Kerr and Harriman, and Deputy Foreign Minster Vyshinski, should go to Bucharest to advise King Michael on the inclusion in the government of one representative each from the NPP and NLP. After this reorganisation it was also agreed that free elections would be held 'as soon as possible on the basis of universal suffrage and secret ballot'.[6]

The Moscow Agreement was the final step for the Soviets in getting the West to recognise their dominance of Romania.[7] Had the agreement been respected to the letter, it would have represented a victory for King Michael's defiance, but as events were to prove, it merely allowed the Western Allies to disguise their impotence. Groza went through the motions of implementing the terms, accepting Emil Haţieganu of the Peasant Party and Mihai Romniceanu of the Liberals into his cabinet as ministers without portfolio, and undertaking on 8 January 1946 to hold early elections and to guarantee access to the radio and the media to all parties. On the basis of these assurances Britain and the United States expressed their willingness to recognise the Groza government at the begin-

5 Quinlan, *Clash over Romania*, p.140.

6 *Ibid.* p.151.

7 *Ibid.*

ning of February in the expectation that elections would be held at the end of April or early May. In the event Groza procrastinated. On 27 May both Britain and the United States protested to Groza at his failure to honour his pledges, and eventually his government produced an electoral law which was heavily weighted in its favour. All parties of the Left were to run on a common list, including the SDP which the Communists had succeeded in splitting.

A new wave of arrests took place in May 1946. Among those detained was General Aldea, the interior minister in the first Sănătescu government who was arrested on 27 May and charged with 'plotting to destroy the unity of the Romanian state' on the grounds that 'in the summer of 1945 he had brought together various subversive organisations under his own central command' in a 'National Resistance Movement' *(Mişcarea Naţională de Rezistenţă)*. The most important of these groups was *Haiducii lui Avram Iancu* (The Outlaws of Avram Iancu), which had been set up in Transylvania on 1 December 1944 by leading figures of the NPP, among them Iuliu Maniu's nephew. An off-shoot of this group was *Divizia Sumanelor Negre* (The Black Greatcoats' Division) which also had its centre of operations in Transylvania. Initially, these groups had acted independently, but in a declaration to the *Siguranţa* Aldea revealed that he had established links with them in autumn 1945 and brought them under his command. In fact, the National Resistance Movement was a paper tiger: its principal activity was the distribution of primitive anti-Communist propaganda; its actions largely consisted of attacks on Hungarians by members of *Haiducii lui Avram Iancu* in revenge for murders of Romanians by Hungarian policemen during the period of Hungarian rule of Northern Transylvania. It was these attacks which caused the greatest concern to the Soviet authorities for they raised the spectre of civil war in Transylvania. Aldea was tried along with fifty-five 'accomplices' on the eve of the polls in November and sentenced on 18 November to hard labour for life.[8]

[8] Aldea died in Aiud jail on 17 October 1949 of heart failure. The groups *Haiducii lui Avram Iancu* and *Divizia Sumanelor Negre* took their name from a Transylvanian Romanian Avram Iancu and the bands of men (*Cătanele Negre*) who raised a revolt against the Hungarian authorities in the 1848 Revolution. Reports on these opposition groups, together with examples of their manifestos, are preserved in Archive of the Romanian Security Service (henceforth abbreviated to ASRI), Fond 'D', file 9046, vols 1-4. A description of conditions in Aiud

Opposition meetings were frequently interrupted during the election campaign by gangs of hooligans and when the American political representative in Bucharest Burton Berry protested, Groza told him that

> [....] when the Anglo-Americans agreed to the Moscow decision they were thinking in terms of free elections such as were held in England or America, whereas the Russians were thinking in terms of free elections such as were held in Russia. In view of the presence of the Russian army in Romania, the coming elections would likely be held according to the Russian interpretation of free and unfettered.[9]

The results of the elections, held on 19 November, came as no surprise to the Foreign Office and to the State Department. The government bloc claimed almost five million votes (84%), while the National Peasants were awarded 800,000 and the Liberals less than 300,00. A total of 414 deputies were elected to a single chamber parliament, of whom 348 represented the government parties and 66 the opposition. In the view of Western diplomats and press correspondents the results were faked, and consequently Dean Acheson, the acting US secretary of state, declared that his government would not recognise them. In the House of Commons Hector McNeil, the under-secretary for foreign affairs said that the elections were neither free nor fair. During the campaign the opposition parties were, he argued, denied full freedom of speech, and the arrangements on polling day were such as to permit wholesale fabrication of the results. These assessments have been confirmed by recently-published documents from the RCP's own archives.[10] Yet despite this condemnation of the results the British

---

jail in 1947, written in English by an anonymous member of Antonescu's cabinet, was passed on to me in 1994. I have quoted from it in an annex to this chapter.

[9] *Ibid.*, p.154.

[10] These archives contained 'Confidential reports on the true results of the parliamentary elections'. The results in the counties of Cluj, Someş and Turda show a clear, but not overwhelming, victory for Maniu's NPP which obtained more than 40% of the votes. In Someş, for example, the Communists were officially credited with 67.9% of the votes, whereas in reality they polled only 22.8%. The NPP was awarded only 11.1% when it in fact won 51.6% (V. Ţârău, 'Campania electorală şi rezultatul real al alegerilor din 19 noiembrie 1946 în judeţele Cluj, Someş şi Turda', *Studii de Istorie a Transilvaniei*, ed. Sorin Mitu

government, on advice from the Foreign Office, decided not to support an American protest to the Russians calling for new elections, on the feeble grounds that Moscow would simply prevaricate.

King Michael threatened to postpone the opening of parliament but Burton Berry to whom he appealed for support, was unable to give him any encouragement. Yet more arrests followed the signing of the Peace Treaty with Romania on 10 February 1947. Its political clauses were so lacking in definition that the Ministry of the Interior could interpret the phrases 'organisation of a Fascist type' and 'war criminal' as arbitrarily as they wished. As one British observer pointed out, 'there was no mention of a judiciary body to try the cases against such organisations and war criminals [and] this enabled the Groza government to make war on individual National Peasants and National Liberals as 'Fascists' and 'war criminals'.[11] On 20 March 315 members of the opposition parties were arrested and on the night of 4 May, another 600. There was no legal basis for these arrests; those in May were made under the provisions of a top-secret order of the Ministry of the Interior and the persons detained were sent to the prisons in Gherla, Piteşti, Craiova and Miercurea Ciuc. Some of the 596 persons sent to Gherla were peasants who had opposed collectivisation, others were teachers, doctors and priests who had campaigned on behalf of the opposition parties in November 1946. Many did not know why they had been arrested. Several managed to escape and most were released after six months but the Communists authorities had acheived their aim: to intimidate the population and to prepare the ground for the liquidation of the opposition parties.

Such was the atmosphere of fear that even Tătărescu, the deputy prime minister, was moved in May to send a memorandum to the cabinet arguing that

> [....] preventive arrests must cease so that the atmosphere of insecurity may be dispelled. The security police should be continually on the alert, but it should act only against offenders. The guilty persons should be punished without mercy, but only within the letter of the law. All illegally detained persons should be released.[12]

---

and Florin Gogâltan, Cluj: Asociaţia Istoricilor din Transilvania şi Banat, 1994, pp.204-12).

11 A. Gibson MS.

12 A. Gibson MS. No copy of the top-secret order no. 50000 of 1947 under

Tătărescu's argument fell on deaf ears for the campaign to eliminate the opposition parties, approved by Stalin and coordinated by Vyshinski, had entered its final stage. Instructions were given to Pintilie Bondarenko, a senior NKGB agent in Bucharest who was made responsible for overseeing the *Siguranţa* to compromise the Peasant Party leadership. Bondarenko did this by getting an *agent provocateur* to persuade Maniu's deputy Ion Mihalache to attempt to flee the country in a plane provided by him.[13] The plan succeeded and on 14 July 1947 Mihalache and several prominent figures in the NPP were arrested as they were about to leave for Turkey from Tămădău airfield (about 50 km from Bucharest). A few days later Maniu was detained and the whole leadership of the party was put on trial on 30 October for plotting against the security of the state. Maniu and Mihalache were each sentenced to hard labour for life, commuted to life imprisonment, and neither man was ever seen in public again.[14]

The final obstacle to complete Soviet domination of Romania was King Michael. Even in 1945 the continuation of the Romanian kingdom within the Soviet orbit appeared, in the circumstances, to be an anomaly.[15] The young monarch had valiantly wrestled with the Soviet tentacles which were slowly throttling the country's independence, often with only half-hearted support from Britain and the United States, but the stage-managed trial of Maniu and the mockery of justice it represented were clear signs that his struggle was proving fruitless. Nevertheless, the Romanian people clung to him as the last symbol of hope for a sane and settled future. In September 1947 Foreign Minister Tătărescu had been compelled to dismiss several hundred members of his ministry who were regarded as pro-Western, and on 7 November he and other Liberal cabinet members were removed from their posts at Groza's insistence. The king felt obliged to accept the Communists

---

which the arrests were carried out has been found. The reasons for the arrests were many and have been reconstituted from local police reports by Dumitru Şandru in 'Detinuţii politici de la Gherla în 1947', *Anuarul Institutului de Istorie Cluj-Napoca*, vol.34, 1995, pp.271-82.

13 Ion Pacepa, 'Falsificarea istoriei', *Indiscret*, no.2, 1992, p.10.

14 Maniu died in Sighet prison on 2 February 1953, and Mihalache at Râmnicu Sărat on 5 March 1963.

15 Ionescu, *Communism in Rumania*, p.142.

Ana Pauker and Vasile Luca as respectively foreign minister and minister of finance, while on 23 December Emil Bodnăraş became minister of war. When the king went to London on 12 November with the queen mother for the marriage of Princess Elizabeth, Groza and Dej, now the first secretary of the Communist Party, hoped that he would renounce the throne and not return. Indeed Michael asked for American advice on this subject and the US ambassador in London considered that his return 'would serve no useful purpose'.[16] Nevertheless, the king, who while abroad had announced his engagement to Princess Anne of Bourbon-Parma, took the bold decision to return with the queen mother on 21 December. Nine days later the Communists acted. Groza and Dej asked the king to come to Bucharest from his mountain retreat at Sinaia and presented him with a ready-made abdication statement. When he refused the two men gave him half an hour to consider his position. In the mean time troops were brought in to surround the palace. Still the king declined to sign, whereupon Groza threatened civil war. Faced with the possibility of bloodshed Michael gave in. With his signature ended the Romanian kingdom and the country's possibilites of autonomous action. On that same day, 30 December 1947, the Romanian People's Republic was declared.

The threat of force used by the Communist leaders against the king was to typify the very nature of the People's Republic as one born not from the express will of the population, but from the dictates of a political group who were the puppets of a foreign master. Even the legality of the law establishing the Republic was suspect since the official record of the special session of the single chamber parliament, convened on the evening of 30 December, stated that it lasted only forty-five minutes. In this time the law was alleged to have been presented, a praesidium nominated, and both measures voted upon by the casting of white balls by 295 deputies. In addition there are said to have been nineteen ovations which interrupted the presentation. Doubts have been cast as to whether, in the first place, so many deputies could have been assembled so rapidly in Bucharest while parliament was in recess for the New Year, and secondly, proceedings could have been completed as rapidly as claimed.[17]

16 Quinlan, *Clash over Romania*, p.157.

17 E. Focşeneanu, 'O Descoperire Istorică', *România liberă*, 15 October 1991.

With the establishment of the Republic the foundations of the totalitarian state could be put in place.[18] The first step was to cement Romania into the Soviet bloc from a military point of view. This was done by the conclusion of a treaty of friendship, cooperation and mutual assistance between Romania and the Soviet Union which was signed on 4 February 1948.[19]

The second step was the consolidation of the single mass party composed of an elite and a dedicated membership. This was achieved by dissolving the major opposition parties, the NLP and NPP, in the summer of 1947, and by the merger of the SDP with the Communist Party on 12 November 1947.[20] The SDP's veteran secretary, Titel Petrescu had seen his authority gradually eroded after the war by Communist infiltration. This culminated with the party congress of 10 March 1946 which at the insistence of two leading members Lothar Rădăceanu and Ştefan Voitec, voted for collaboration with the Communist Party. Petrescu walked out of the congress and led the rump of the SDP under the name of the Independent Social Democratic Party. The official SDP held its last congress on 5 October 1947, attended by Groza, Gheorghiu-

[18] The imposition of the Soviet totalitarian model in Romania has been described in detail in Ionescu, *Communism in Rumania*, Fischer-Galaţi, *The New Rumania*, and briefly in Dennis Deletant, *Ceauşescu and the Securitate. Coercion and Dissent in Romania, 1965-1989* London: Hurst, 1995, pp.13-56.

[19] G. Ionescu, *op. cit.*, pp.147-9.

[20] Titel Petrescu's fate was emblematic of that of opposition leaders. He was arrested on 6 May 1948, held in the security police headquarters in Bucharest, sent to Jilava prison, and finally tried *in camera* in January 1952 for crimes against the state. He was sentenced to life imprisonment and served three years in Sighet jail before being transferred to the Calea Rahovei headquarters of the *Securitate* in Bucharest in December 1954 where he was told by the Minister of the Interior, Alexandru Drăghici, that a number of his colleagues in the former SDP would be released from prison if he signed a letter giving his support to the regime for publication in the Party daily *Scînteia* . He refused and was sent in August to Rîmnicu Sărat jail where he learned from fellow prisoners of the death in prison of numerous Socialists. He agreed to sign a text on 13 September on condition that all leading SDP members be released and he himself was freed but kept under virtual house arrest. The letter appeared in *Scînteia* on 18 December 1955 (see also *Cartea Albă,* vol.II, doc. 237, pp. 527-9) but only a small number of SDP colleagues were released. Petrescu complained to Petru Groza, the president of the Grand National Assembly, after which further releases were announced. Petrescu died in September 1957.

Dej and Pauker, where a resolution on merger with the Communist Party was passed by acclamation. According to figures presented at the Congress the SDP at that time had some half a million members, only half of whom appear to have joined the newly-fused party which was known as the Romanian Workers' Party (RWP) and had a combined membership of 1,060,000.[21]

The RWP held its first congress on 21-23 February 1948 and Gheorghiu-Dej was re-elected Secretary General, with Pauker, Luca and Teohari Georgescu as the other three members of the secretariat. Emphasis was now given to the elite character of the party and stricter membership requirements were introduced. No members of the 'former exploiting classes' were to be admitted, those applying for membership were to be carefully screened and a period of 'candidate' or trial membership was made compulsory.

A warning of these measures against perceived opponents of the regime was given in Dej's report to the congress. Here he categorised 'Iron Guardists, spies and diversionists' as 'the enemies of Romanian democracy'. Similarly attacks on the Catholic clergy who used the church 'as a means of propaganda directed against the democratic order', indicated what lay in store for them.[22] On 26 March this category of 'hostile elements' was augmented by 'the saboteurs' who in Dej's view, 'must be eradicated without mercy'. Thus the Stalinist method of abstract accusation, followed by the physical liquidation of the accused, found its way into the practice of the RCP. Virtually all of Dej's speeches in 1948 were a continuous tirade of incitement to persecution of actual or anticipated opponents of the regime and, at the same time, they represented an authorisation of Communist repression. They also gave the green light to informers and to thugs acting in the spirit of 'vigilance'.

The first step towards the legalisation of repression was the amendment on 27 February 1948 of the Penal Code which had been in force since 2 March 1940. The revised code borrowed a series of concepts from Soviet legislation which were alien to

21 King, *History of the RCP*, p.71.

22 *Cartea Albă a Securităţii*, vol.II, p.7. An analysis of the editorials in the party newspaper *Scînteia* charts the evolution of the language used to categorise the 'enemies of the state' during the years 1945 to 1953; see Liviu Ţirău, 'Ziarul "Scînteia" şi războiul rece. Atitudine politică şi limbaj, 1945-1953', *Revista Istorică*, vol.4 [1993], nos 7-8, pp.725-41.

Romanian law but useful for the consolidation of Communist political power. Novel notions such as 'counter-revolutionary sabotage', 'counter-revolutionary diversion', and 'counter-revolutionary agitation and propaganda' were introduced and were quickly applied to justify a round-up of Iron Guardists throughout the whole country during the night of 14–15 May 1948. By the end of the year some 4,500 arrests had been made, while a further 1,162 Guardists were placed under surveillance. It should be pointed out that the raids led to the discovery of 6,000 cartridges of ammunition, 649 grenades, thirty-two machine-guns, twenty-seven machine-pistols and 128 pistols, but the arrests merely steeled the determination of those who were prepared to transform their opposition into armed resistance, and in furtherance of their aims they took to the mountains.[23]

A further step in the legalisation of repression was a decree of 18 August which supplemented the Law on the Prosecution and Punishment of Those Guilty of War Crimes or of Crimes Against Peace and Security, introduced exactly one year earlier. Using this law, the Ministry of the Interior ordered the arrest of more than 1,000 officers of the SSI, the *Siguranţa,* and the *Jandarmerie.* Their place was taken by Communist Party appointees.

A verification campaign in the party was undertaken as a result of a Central Committee resolution of November 1948 by what was called 'a non-party *aktiv*' of some 200,000 investigators. This was a euphemism which covered the participation of the security police, the army, and officials of the Ministry of Justice.[24] The period of investigation lasted from November 1948 until May 1950 and was directed at the various waves of members who had been recruited into the party.

The first of these waves comprised politically-unaffiliated workers and young Iron Guardists who in 1945 had been given responsible positions in factories and trade unions as a reward for joining. This group included domestic servants who had been canvassed by the Communists for membership as useful instruments for report-

23 *Ibid.*, p.8.

24 Two army divisions, named 'Tudor Vladimirescu' and 'Horia, Cloşca and Crişan', had been formed respectively in October 1943 and April 1945 from Romanian prisoners of war in the Soviet Union. They were organised on the Soviet model in which political allegiance to the Communist Party was paramount. (see Chapter 2, n.24).

ing on the activities of their employers. The second wave had come in during 1946 and 1947 and was drawn from army units, such as the Tudor Vladmirescu division, which had been formed from Romanian prisoners of war in the Soviet Union.[25] It also included Romanian administrative personnel working for the Soviet army. A third wave had been generated by the merger of the SDP in 1948 and a fourth by those who had joined the new bureaucracy which staffed the institutions set up to effect the Communist revolution in all sectors of activity. The latter covered the personnel of the people's councils (the equivalent of the Western town hall), the peasants who had joined the collective and state farms and students and teachers in the reformed education system. Most of these recruits regarded party membership either as the key to advancement and privilege, or as insurance against being disadvantaged or even arrested, and there was a good deal of opportunism in their motivation.[26]

The verification process removed from the Communist Party 192,000 'exploiting and hostile elements' and their elimination augmented the sense of terror which permeated most of Romanian society. This purge which aimed at creating an elite, coincided with the party's programme of revolutionising agriculture, industrialising the economy and of transforming society. Implementing that programme required the institutionalisation of the new Communist system and to this end a party organisation was created to supervise every aspect of endeavour. Central Committee sections were set up for women, youth, peasants, trade unions, transport, supply, industry and commerce; these were paralleled at local level. Prime importance was attached to ideological training which not only helped to reinforce the sense of belonging to an elite, but also inculcated loyalty to the party and cocooned the member from insidious external influences. The A.A. Zhdanov School was set up by the party in October 1948 to prepare ideological cadres, and in July 1949 was transformed into a school of social sciences to train the teachers in the field, while the Ştefan Gheorghiu Academy was established to prepare party activists. The feeling of elitism and exclusivity and the privileges of rank also served to increase coherence and unity within the party.

25 Ionescu, *Communism in Rumania*, p.204.

26 *Ibid.*, p.206.

A third step in the imposition of the Soviet totalitarian model upon Romania was the introduction of a Soviet-based judicial system and the adoption in April 1948 of the constitution of the People's Republic. The purges initiated by Lucreţiu Pătrăşcanu in April 1945 continued throughout his term of office. The trimming of the judicial system to suit the political ends of the Communist Party was confirmed on 24 November 1947 with the passage of a bill reorganising the judiciary. It provided for the 'election' of magistrates, or 'people's assessors' who were party nominees. These 'assessors' sat alongside the judges and outnumbered them by two to one, thus ensuring that the party's will was in all cases paramount. In Pătrăşcanu's words: 'By including elected representatives of the working class among the judges sitting in the courts, justice has indeed become people's justice.'[27] Private legal practice was abolished by a decree of 31 March 1950. The constitution followed the pattern of the 1936 Soviet constitution. Parliament was called the Grand National Assembly, a single chamber which was described as 'the supreme organ of state authority'. A Praesidium, composed of a president, a secretary, and seventeen other members, acted on behalf of the assembly when it was not in session, which was quite often, while the Council of Ministers was the supreme executive body. All these bodies were, of course, subject to the power of the Communist Party. Guarantees of civil liberties were generously provided but meaningless, as Article 32 illustrated, 'Citizens have the right of association and organisation if the aims pursued are not directed against the democratic order established by the Constitution.'[28] That democratic order was defined by the Communist Party and buttressed by the security police.

The party moved swiftly to transform Romania on the lines of the Soviet model and by means of Stalinist norms and practices. The nationalisation in June 1948 of industrial, banking, insurance,

[27] M. Oprea, 'Cum a întinat Pătrăşcanu valorile comunismului', *Dilema*, no.177 (31 May-6 June) 1996, p.9. Under article 65 of the Constitution of the People's Republic, enacted in 1952, the role of the judiciary was defined 'to defend the regime of popular democracy and the conquests of the working people, to assure the respect of popular legality, of public property, and of the rights of citizens'. The courts, represented by the judges and assessors, also had the power to appoint defence attorneys whose role was largely limited to apologising for the defendant's alleged offences.

[28] Ionescu, *Communism in Rumania.*, p.157.

mining and transport enterprises not only allowed the introduction of centralised quantitative planning but destroyed the economic basis of those stigmatised as class enemies. Confiscating private share holdings and threatening their owners was relatively straightforward; agriculture posed more complex problems. On 2 March 1949 the ownership of land was completely removed from private hands. This permitted the liquidation of the remnants of the old landowning class and of the *chiaburi*, peasants who hired labour or let out machinery, irrespective of the size of their holding. The land, livestock and equipment of landowners who possessed property up to the maximum of 50 hectares permitted under the 1945 land law was expropriated without compensation. Virtually overnight the *Securitate* and the militia moved in, evicted 17,000 families from their homes and moved them to resettlement areas. The confiscated land, totalling almost 1 million hectares, was either amassed to create state farms *(Gospodăriile Agricole de Stat)* or was organised into collectives *(Gospodăriile Agricole Colective)* which were in theory collectively owned but in fact state run since the Ministry of Agriculture directed what crops were to be grown and fixed the prices. Members of the collective were allowed to keep small plots of land not exceeding just under half an acre.

The majority of peasants, ranging from the landless to *chiaburi* – those who worked their holdings using only family labour – were organised into state or collective farms. This required extensive coercion, despite Dej's assurance to villagers that 'under no circumstances should the peasantry be forced into collectives'.[29] Resistance to collectivisation resulted in some 80,000 peasants being imprisoned for their opposition, 30,000 of them being tried in public.[30] Collectivisation was completed in 1962 and its results put 60% of the total area of 15 million hectares of agricultural land in collective farms, 30% in state farms, and left 9% in private hands. (This last consisted of upland holdings whose inaccessibility made it impractical to collectivise them.)

The destruction of the opposition parties was followed by the liquidation of their press, as the media came under total state control. Libraries and bookshops were purged of politically incorrect

29 *Scînteia*, 22 January 1949.

30 *Scînteia*, 7 December 1961, quoted from Ionescu, *Communism in Rumania*, p.201.

titles, the activities of journalists, writers, artists and musicians were brought under the Agitprop section of the Central Committee of the party. Nothing could be published or performed without approval. By the end of 1954, almost 13 million copies of the works of Stalin and Lenin had been printed in Romanian.

Education was similarly dealt with. In August 1948 the Law for Educational Reform closed down all foreign schools, including those run by religious orders. A purge was conducted of the teaching profession and of university students. Eminent professors were removed from the faculties of history and philosophy and their places taken by Stalinist indoctrinators, the most notorious of whom in the history field was the Agitprop activist Mihai Roller. The Ministry of Education banned the use of certain teaching materials and authorised textbooks incorporating Marxist-Leninist precepts. Marxism-Leninism, in Stalin's interpretation, was made obligatory from secondary school upwards; the teaching of religion was totally banned.

The final major obstacle to the imposition of the Soviet model was the church. The *Securitate* was called upon to remove it. Yet in tackling this problem the RCP did not follow the Soviet solution to the letter. Both the Romanian Orthodox Church and the Uniate or Greek Catholic Church in Transylvania had been vital in preserving a sense of national cohesion and identity during the eighteenth and nineteenth centuries, and both retained the allegiance of millions of Romanians. If both churches could be manipulated to serve the regime's ends, then there was no point in destroying them. The Orthodox Church had been declared the dominant faith under the 1923 Constitution and had been given special privileges, such as the payment of its clergy's salaries by the state; the Communist Party was to use this dependence to bring the Orthodox hierarchy under its control. The Uniate Church presented a different problem: it had been created at the beginning of the seventeenth century as a result of the conversion by Jesuits of many Orthodox Romanians in Transylvania to accept certain articles of the Catholic faith, among them the primacy of the pope. As long as authority over the church resided in Rome, it would be difficult for the new regime to bring it to heel. Thus the RCP, while officially condemning religious worship, nevertheless tolerated it within certain bounds prescribed by law. In this respect it was more lenient than the Soviet regime. Tolerance of the recognised churches required their subservience to the party and their sonorous validation of the party's policies, whether domestic or foreign.

The new limits imposed on the churches' freedom of action were laid out in The Law on Religious Confessions, enacted on 4 August 1948, reducing the sixty religious denominations recognised under the previous law of 1928 to fourteen. Control of the affairs of all churches in the country was vested in the Ministry of Cults (reorganised in 1957 as the Department of Cults). While asserting from the very outset a guarantee of 'freedom of conscience and religion' (Article 1), it severely circumscribed that freedom by qualifying it with the open-ended provision that the religion practised was in harmony with the Constitution, internal security, public order, and general morality (Articles 6 and 7). Legal recognition of a denomination could be revoked at any time where considered justified (Article 13). Similar restrictions were implicit in Article 32 which stated that 'ministers of religious cults who express anti-democratic attitudes may be deprived temporarily or permanently of their salary, which is provided by the state'. All confessions were required to submit for approval to the Ministry of Cults a statute regulating their activities in accordance with the laws of the state; in return, the ministry would pay the stipends of clergy from recognised confessions.

Even before the introduction of the law, steps were taken by the Ministry of Cults in the Groza government to purge the hierarchy of the Orthodox Church (the principal confession with some 10.5 million members) of those considered to be opponents of the regime. This was done under a pretence of legality. A law introduced in 1947 provided an upper age limit of seventy for all clergy, and under its terms a number of incumbents of the five metropolitanates (Wallachia, Moldavia and Suceava, Transylvania, Crişana and Maramureş, Oltenia, and Banat) and twelve bishoprics were replaced: Metropolitan Irineu of Moldavia, Metropolitan Nifon of Oltenia, Bishop Lucian of Roman, Bishop Cosma of the Lower Danube and Bishop Gheronte of Constanţa were all forced to resign. A second law from the same year ensured the regime's control of the election of bishops. Previously episcopal assemblies had been composed of delegates elected by parishioners for a period of three years; under the new law they had to include members of parliament and ministers belonging to the diocese, thus guaranteeing a majority for government approved nominees.[31] In addition, the Orthodox Holy Synod and the National Church Council were stuffed with Communist Party members. Key positions in the church were thus entrusted to tools of the regime who were completely unknown to the population. The death of Patriarch Nicodim on 27 February 1948 allowed the election of Justinian (lay name Ioan Marina), installed only in the previous December as Metropolitan of Moldavia, as his successor on 24 May 1948. Justinian owed his rapid ascendance to the favour of Gheorghiu-Dej which he had gained by sheltering him in his parish church at Râmnicul Vâlcea for a few days in the summer of 1944, and to his own sudden enrolment in the party. In 1945 he was appointed episcopal vicar at Iaşi by Metropolitan Irineu of Moldavia, and after the enforced retirement of the latter in August 1947, Justinian was entrusted with the management of the archbishopric on the party's behalf.

The new statute of the Orthodox Church, drawn up under the personal direction of Justinian, gave the patriarch extensive control over the administration of the church and allowed him to intervene in the internal affairs of dioceses with or without the approval of the bishops. Such powers were in marked contrast to previous practice, which had permitted the bishops wide discretion. This provision was characteristic of the statute as a whole, since it created a highly centralised form of administration which allowed the regime to manipulate the church more easily.[32] As was the practice with party and state forums, obedience to the official line, unanimity of views and conformity with decisions made by higher party bodies were demanded. The new statute received the approval of the Ministry of Cults and became law on 23 February 1949.

By stripping the church of its assets, the regime removed its scope for independent action and made it reliant upon the favour of the state. Any church contribution to the creation of a civil society was thus stifled at a stroke. In consequence of the nationalisa-

[31] Raoul Bossy, 'Religious Persecutions in Captive Romania', *Journal of Central European Affairs*, vol.15, no.2 [July 1955], p.163.

[32] Keith Hitchins, 'The Romanian Orthodox Church and the State', in *Religion and Atheism in the USSR and Eastern Europe*, eds B.R. Bociurkiw, J.W. Strong, assisted by J. K. Laux, University of Toronto Press; London: Macmillan, 1975, p.317.

tion of its estates and funds the Orthodox Church vitally depended upon state support. Under the education law of 3 August 1948, its teaching institutions, 2,300 primary schools, twenty-four secondary schools, eight chapters' schools, thirteen seminaries and one academy of church music, were either taken over by the state or closed. Denied religious education in schools, the family, whatever its faith, played a vital role in transmitting it.

Two schools for priests were opened – in Predeal in 1948 and in Bucharest in 1951 – for students selected from Communist youth organisations, and in January 1949 a theological institute was opened in Bucharest University. The spirit in which students were trained can be assessed from the pronouncement in the party daily *Scînteia* on 22 February 1948 that 'the Romanian clergy has to follow the example of the Orthodox clergy in the Soviet Union, as the party of the working class cannot remain indifferent to the various prejudices and mystic views sowed in the ranks of the workers by the bourgeois landowning regime.'[33]

Religious worship, then, was not to be outlawed by the party, it was to be discouraged. Efforts made by the regime to inhibit religious practice included bans on the conduct of baptisms and church weddings and on the public celebration of Christmas and Easter. Party members were instructed not to attend church services, as were army officers and soldiers. Civil marriage ceremonies were the only ones recognised by the state, even after the ban on church weddings was removed. In the eyes of many who rejected the tenets of Orthodoxy about the necessary subservience of the church to the state, the prelates of the Orthodox Church, by compromising with the regime, ensured their survival at the expense of their moral authority.

Control by the Communist government of the Roman Catholic and Greek Catholic (Uniate) Churches met with greater resistance. This was partly because the close links they had with the West made them more resilient, but it is also the case that their bishops displayed remarkable dignity, courage, and fidelity to their creed. There was, however, a major difference in the treatment of the two churches at the hands of the regime: the Uniate Church was suppressed, the Roman Catholic was not, although it did not escape persecution. The explanation lies in the fact that most of

33 Bossy, 'Religious Persecutions in Romania', p.165.

the Roman Catholic faithful were Hungarians, and the Romanian regime was guided in its policy towards the church by the need to avoid actions which might be interpreted by its fraternal neighbour as directed specifically against the Hungarian minority. Consequently the Communist Party's policy towards the Roman Catholic Church was not to abolish it, but to manipulate it by replacing control from the Vatican with control from Bucharest. It was only a partial success. Although the regime severed the church's links with Rome, it was never able to impose its own authority on the church. Throughout the Communist era the Roman Catholic Church was held in the ambiguous position of being tolerated, but unrecognised. Agreement was never reached with the Ministry of Cults over the church's legal standing within the 1948 law on confessions and so the second largest surviving church in Romania remained effectively neither legal nor illegal.

The status of the Roman Catholic Church was governed by the Concordat between the Romanian government and the Vatican which was concluded on 10 May 1927. Under it five dioceses were established: Alba Iulia and Oradea-Satu Mare in Transylvania, which were largely Hungarian, Timişoara in the Banat, which was predominantly German, and Iaşi in Moldavia and Bucharest, which were mainly Romanian. Many of the Moldavian Catholics were Csangos, a people of Hungarian origin living near the town of Bacău, who had been largely assimilated. Of its estimated 1.3 million faithful approximately 450,000 belonged to the Alba Iulia diocese, 200,000 to Oradea-Satu Mare, 300,000 to Timişoara, 200,000 to Iaşi, and 80,000 to Bucharest. The five bishops in 1948 were Monsignor Aron Marton of Alba Iulia, Monsignor Ianoş Scheffler of Oradea-Satu Mare, Monsignor Augustin Pacha of Timişoara, Monsignor Alexandru Cisar of Bucharest and Monsignor Anton Durcovici of Iaşi. In the early months of that year the Concordat came under violent attack from the press and party leaders, with Dej denouncing it on 22 February 1948 as the sole obstacle to 'democracy'. The campaign culminated in the unilateral abrogation by the government of the Concordat on 17 July 1948. The Vatican's authority over the church was removed under the Law on Religious Confessions, which was introduced on 4 August 1948. Article 41 stipulated that 'foreign religious cults may not exercise jurisdiction over faithful on the territory of the Romanian state', a provision that was to have grave implications for the

Greek Catholics (Uniates) as well.[34] The government was able to reduce the number of Roman Catholic dioceses to two, Alba Iulia and Bucharest, by invoking article 22 of the law which stated quite arbitrarily that a diocese must have 750,000 faithful to warrant its existence. On this basis, three of the five bishops were deprived of their sees, with only Bishop Aron Marton of Alba Iulia and Bishop Alexandru Cisar of Bucharest remaining.

The law also required every denomination to present its own statute for the approval of the Ministry of Cults and the regime tried to draw the Catholic bishops into a compromise. Marton drew up an initial set of proposals but they were rejected by the government, and he was arrested in June 1949.[35] His fellow bishops shared the same fate. In March 1949, Bishop Ianoş Scheffler of Satu Mare was detained and held in the Franciscan monastery at Baia de Criş before being moved to the notorious Sighet prison in 1950 where he died. The former Bishop of Bucharest Alexandru Cisar was arrested in June 1949, as was his successor Augustin Pacha, together with Aron Marton, bishop of Alba Iulia, and Anton Durcovici, bishop of Iaşi. Pacha died shortly afterwards while Cisar was held in a monastery, Durcovici in the prisons of Gherla and Aiud, and Marton at the Ministry of the Interior in Bucharest; in 1950 all three were transferred to Sighet where Durcovici died on 10 December 1951.[36] Cisar was allowed to return to Bucharest shortly before his death in 1954.[37]

Failure to reach a *modus vivendi* led to the arrest of large numbers from among the 800 Roman Catholic priests and 250 monks and nuns. Under the education reform of 3 August 1948, confessional schools were abolished and the Catholic seminaries were closed. Roman Catholic newspapers and publications were suppressed, and by a decree of 29 July 1949 all Catholic orders and congregations were abolished. On 30 August 1949, an order was issued by which all monasteries and convents were to be completely evacuated

34 H. Stehle, *Eastern Politics of the Vatican, 1917-1979*, tr. by Sandra Smith, Athens, OH: Ohio University Press, 1981, p.265.

35 Janice Broun, 'The Latin-Rite Roman Catholic Church of Romania', *Religion in Communist Lands*, vol.12, no.2 (summer 1984), p.169.

36 *Persecuţia Bisericii din România sub Dictatura Comunistă*, Freiburg: Coresi, 1983, *passim.*

37 Stehle, *Eastern Politics of the Vatican*, p.422, n.5.

before midnight, and *Securitate* agents were charged with the speedy execution of this order.

To those Catholic clergy still at liberty the Ministry of Cults now applied intense pressure, via *Securitate* agents, to come to heel. The ruse chosen was the creation of the 'Catholic Committee for Action' whose task was to collect signatures for the Stockholm Peace Appeal and to advocate the placing of the Catholic Church in Romania under the ultimate authority of the People's Republic.[38] Support for the committee was given at an assembly of Catholic priests and laymen held on 27 April 1950 in Târgu Mureş which was also attended by a number of Orthodox headed by Petre Constantinescu-Iaşi, vice-president of the Romanian Academy. A prominent figure in the committee was Father Andrei Agota who was suspended by the Holy See and later excommunicated. Those who refused to endorse the committee's decisions were arrested, among them Monsignor Luigi Boga, vicar of the diocese of Alba Iulia, considered to be the head of the Roman Catholic hierarchy in the absence of the bishops, and Monsignor Glaser, administrator of the suppressed Iaşi diocese. Monsignor Glaser, as a result of brutal torture, died of heart failure on 25 May 1950; his body disappeared, apparently to forestall a religious funeral.[39]

Having removed the main opponents to the committee, the Ministry of Cults now entered negotiations with it to draft a new 'Statute for the Organisation, Direction, and Functioning of the Roman Catholic Confession in the Romanian People's Republic'. The agreed document recognised the pope as the supreme ecclesiastical authority of the church in matters of faith and dogma, but in all other respects the church was subject to the laws of the state. The right of the Holy See to appoint bishops was accepted but appointments were to be solely on the recommendation of the Catholic Church in Romania, and subject to the approval of the Romanian government. Communication with Rome was to be made exclusively through the Ministry of Cults and the Foreign Ministry, thus preventing any direct contacts with the Vatican. Before these proposals were presented on 28 July 1950 by the Committee for Action to all Catholics for acceptance, the pope instructed his nuncio O'Hara to veto them, thus ruling out any

[38] Bossy, *Religious Perecutions in Romania*, p.174.

[39] *Ibid.*

chance of reaching the kind of compromise with the government that was to be secured in Poland.

One subsequent commentator has been especially critical of the Vatican's behaviour towards the Romanian regime. Hansjakob Stehle claimed that the Romanian government was ready to procede with the new statutes and asked whether survival through the Stalinist period could not have been attempted on this basis. The Vatican, in Stehle's interpretation, saw these statutes only as a 'clever instrument for the subjugation of the church', which perhaps it was, but it should have taken the risk, 'as the Romanian Orthodox church did successfully, and so at least try to save the pastoral possibilities.'[40]

Stehle's appraisal of the Orthodox Church's compromise as 'successful' is highly questionable. Stehle was also critical of the decision to send an American bishop as nuncio to Bucharest at the height of the Cold War and of the Pope's readiness to prepare an underground church. Yet it was only *after* the arrest of the Roman Catholic bishops had begun that the Pope instructed O'Hara to consecrate secret bishops. In the first six months of 1950, the nuncio appointed twenty apostolic administrators, drawing up a list of replacements if one was arrested. O'Hara consecrated Joseph Schubert as bishop of Bucharest in the chapel of the Bucharest nunciature on 30 June 1950. Adalbert Boros was ordained as bishop of Timişoara and Ion Duma as bishop of Iaşi in a similar fashion. A week later O'Hara was ordered to leave Romania by the government. He had been accused of 'gathering military information' in a trial staged against his chauffeur, an accusation based on the fact that incidents of harassment of priests and faithful by Soviet troops based in Romania were reported to the nuncio who passed the information on to his American compatriots in the Allied Control Commission.[41] O'Hara, before his departure, also consecrated a number of Uniate bishops in secret but not one of them was ever able to officiate; all the Roman Catholic and Uniate bishops appointed in this way were under arrest by 1951. Bishop Duma, for example, was arrested on 5 December 1951 and held in the *Securitate* headquarters in Arad, and later in Cluj. He was then sent to Sighet prison where he served four

40 Stehle, *Eastern Politics of the Vatican*, p.266.

41 *Ibid.*, p.264.

years before being freed on 23 September 1955 into compulsory residence in the town of Tîrgu-Jiu.

In furtherance of their campaign to get the new statutes approved by a respectable number of Catholic priests, the Catholic Committee for Action convened a congress at Gheorgheni in Transylvania on 6 September 1950. The meeting, chaired by the excommunicated Andrei Agotha, was attended by 120 priests and 150 laymen and a final motion was passed calling for conclusion of legal relations between the Catholic Church and the state. A decision was taken to convene a second congress to confirm acceptance by the church of the new statues. A vast propaganda campaign was launched by the committee to persuade wavering clergy to accept. Regional assemblies were held in Oradea, Timişoara, Braşov and Bucharest, culminating in a congress at Cluj on 15 March 1951. Attended by 224 clergy and laymen allegedly representing the 683 parishes of Romania, the congress, under the presidency of Father Gregory Fodor, resolved to 'incorporate the Catholic Church within the legal order of the state, thus fulfilling the ardent wish of all peace-loving Roman Catholics of our country.'[42] An executive council, headed by Fodor and Dr Joseph Delner, was elected and drafted a declaration asking to be allowed to collaborate with the authorities in organising the work of the Roman Catholic Church. All priests were invited to sign this oath of loyalty and those that refused were arrested.

For some of those who had been on O' Hara's list for consecration and subsequently arrested, signature of the declaration meant release from prison. This was the case of Canon Franz Augustin and Canon Traian Iovanelli, who was appointed Vicar Capitular of the Bucharest Catholic diocese in place of Bishop Schubert on 5 April 1951. On 3 June, the Vatican declared Iovanelli's appointment invalid, as it did those of Agotha, Fodor, Joseph Torog, Mihai Kulcsar, and Joseph Pop who were all elevated by the government. The list of clergy arrested for refusing to serve the regime included Bishop Schubert of Bucharest and Bishop Boros of Timişoara, both detained on 17 February 1951. Other arrests followed in the same year.[43] Most of those arrested were brought before a

[42] Bossy, *Religious Persecutions in Romania*, p.177.

[43] Fathers Waltner, Heber and Schwartz from Timişoara, in February; on 8 March, Father Clementi Gatti, priest of the Italian church in Bucharest; on 10

military tribunal alongside Bishop Augustin Pacha in September 1951 in a show trial. Confessions were extorted from them and they were convicted of 'spying in favour of the Vatican and of the United States, and of having attempted to set up a Christian Social Party in order to overthrow the present regime with the help of the Americans'.[44] Schubert was sentenced to life imprisonment, Pacha and Boros to eighteen years' hard labour, and Father Gatti and Father Joseph Walther to fifteen years. Father Ion Heber to twelve years', and Father Schiopa to ten years'. To complete the mockery, Radio Bucharest transmitted a thirty-minute broadcast after the trial in which the accused repeated their confessions.

In a cynical attempt to deflect the embarrassment caused by deaths in jail, the Ministry of the Interior occasionally ordered the release of prominent prelates who were judged to be especially frail; Bishop Pacha went blind in prison and was released in 1954 into compulsory residence in Timişoara. He died two years later. Others served almost their full term before the general amnesties of 1963-64 gave them their freedom, although in some cases it was hedged with restrictions. Bishop Schubert, for example, was released in July 1964, after thirteen years in jail, into the compulsory residence of the mountain village of Timişul de Sus, just south of Braşov. The Vatican gave little support to its imprisoned bishops. 'The only attitude recognised in Rome is that of Monsignore Schubert', wrote Domenico Tardini (the secretary for extraordinary affairs in the Secretariat of State) as late as 10 May 1951, to the doubtful Bucharest cathedral chapter, when Schubert had already been in prison for three months and no other Romanian bishop remained free. That 'attitude', honourable and obedient, of course also gave those in the West who spoke of 'the silent church in the East with a pious shudder, an alibi for their own political sloth'.[45]

March, the curates Petz, Clofanda, Vamosin, Bachmeyer, and Mihoc from the diocese of Iaşi, Maghiar and Borz from the Oradea diocese; Imre Sandar, Czumbel, Bela Gajdaczi from the Alba Iulia diocese; on 24 April, three nuns: Mother Superior Hildegarde and sisters Judith and Christina; on 11 May Father Baltheiser from Bucharest.

44 *Procesul unui grup de spioni, trădători şi complotişti în slujba Vaticanului şi a centrului de spionaj italian, Bucureşti, 10-17 septembrie 1951*: Bucharest: Editura de stat pentru literatura ştiinţifică, 1952, p.102.

45 Some Western Catholics were highly critical of what they saw as the Vatican's lack of action on behalf of their imprisoned clergy in Romania. Stehle's own

Those clergy who were not 'honourable' and 'obedient' were treated with distrust by the Vatican. Franz Augustin, released from prison after signing a declaration of loyalty to the regime, was appointed administrator of the diocese of Bucharest in 1954 and served until his death in 1983. Although countenanced by the Vatican as '*ordinarius substitutus*' (provisional administrator) in 1961, the Holy See refused to promote him to the rank of apostolic administrator. Throughout the 1950s he served his Bucharest flock with dedication, providing religious instruction for children and attracting large congregations to the cathedral but this failed to impress Rome. Any credit he might have accrued in the Holy See was offset by his 'election' as a deputy in the Romanian parliament. His permission to visit Rome in 1964 to attend the Vatican Council, the first Catholic priest to be allowed to do so for sixteen years, was given as a reward for services deemed by the Ministry of Cults to have been rendered, as became evident from the refusal of the Romanian authorities to extend the same privilege to the bishops the Vatican *had* invited. As a result the Vatican refused Augustin entry to the council.

The Uniates' fidelity to their church resulted in a brutal campaign to destroy it. The last figures available before suppression indicated that there were one and a half million Uniates, with 1,725 churches served by 1,594 priests, thirty-four canons, and seventy-five prelates. Under the terms of the Concordat of 1927 five dioceses were recognised: Alba Iulia-Făgăraş, with its see at Blaj, Gherla, which in 1931 moved its see from Gherla to Cluj, Oradea Mare, Lugoj and Maramureş with its see at Baia Mare. In 1948 the incumbents were Metropolitan Bishop Ion Suciu, apostolic administrator of the see of Blaj, Iuliu Hossu, bishop of Cluj, Valeriu Traian Frenţiu, bishop of Oradea Mare, Ioan Bălan, bishop of Lugoj, and Bishop Alexandru Rusu of Baia Mare. There was also a vicar-general at Bucharest, Bishop Vasile Aftenie, who in 1940 had been consecrated

---

views are patently clear from this caustic conclusion to his chapter on the case of Schubert (*Eastern Politics of the Vatican*, p.268). According to Stehle, no attempt was made to free Schubert by the Vatican. It was only in early 1969, when he was already fatally ill, that he was permitted to leave Romania, arriving in Rome on 8 February. Then he had to wait two weeks before Pope Paul VI embraced him on 23 February 1969, just six weeks before his death in Munich on 4 April where he was buried in the Frauenkirche. Stehle, who first met Schubert in 1965, says that the bishop died an embittered man, unhonoured by his Church.

auxiliary bishop of Alba Iulia-Făgăraş while retaining his position in Bucharest. The Church had 143 religious houses, 377 educational institutes, and 111 charitable and welfare institutions.[46]

The same political reasons which had led to the creation of the Uniate Church in 1699 were invoked by the Communists to force it back into the fold of the Orthodox Church. The union with Rome was branded in official publications throughout the Communist period as 'anti-national and anti-historical' since it had split the unity of the Romanian people. The campaign to woo Uniates back to the Orthodox Church was part and parcel of the drive against the Concordat which was launched in February 1948. On 31 March 1948, the Grand National Assembly (parliament) took the decision to retire all priests over the age of sixty, a measure that was not recognised either by the Roman Catholic or by the Uniate hierarchy. A particular appeal to Uniates to 'return to the bosom of the Mother Church' was made on the occasion of the centenary of the meeting on the Field of Liberty near Blaj, where Transylvanian Romanians of both Orthodox and Uniate confessions had gathered on 15 May 1848 to demand recognition of their rights as a nation:

> Today, when the Romanian People's Republic guarantees equal rights, political, cultural, and religious, to all, no matter what their creed or race may be, to persist in the spiritual disunity which stemmed from the grave jeopardy in which the Romanians of Transylvania found themselves in 1700, means to desert the united front of the new destinies that our working people are creating for themselves in the dawn of the future.[47]

Patriarch Justinian, the newly elected head of the Orthodox Church, echoed the appeal on 6 June in his address to the Uniate clergy:

> 'What separates us at this time? Nothing but the faithful submission you still give to Rome. Give back this loyalty to the church of our nation, the church of our forefathers and of yours. [...] The widest prospects open before us and before our future activity, as soon as we no longer work in isolation.'[48]

46 Bossy, *Religious Persecutions in Romania*, p.167.

47 *Ibid.*, p.168.

48 *Ibid.*

With the example before them of the Uniates in Galicia who in April 1946 had been dragooned into merger with the Russian Orthodox Church, the authorities tried to infiltrate Communist party members into Uniate diocesan councils. Metropolitan Suciu preached resistance, issuing a pastoral letter on 29 June in which he called upon the faithful 'to remain steadfast in the confession of the faith which the Holy Fathers have defended with their blood and their suffering'.[49] His implacable opposition to the Communist Party had been demonstrated in innumerable sermons, examples being those he delivered in December 1947 in the Uniate church in Bucharest on Strada Polonă, and in the Catholic cathedral of St Joseph, in which he denounced Communism as the ideology of Satan and declared that Christians would never be afraid of such a creed.[50] When Suciu continued to urge defiance after the promulgation of the education law of 3 August banning religious instruction and closing confessional schools, it was only a matter of time before action would be taken against him. On 3 September an administrative decree suspended him from office. Bishop Hossu was confined to his residence and thirty priests and laymen who tried to call on him were arrested, as were Canons Tamaian, Barbu and Ghilea in Oradea.

The ground was now prepared by the Ministry of Cults for the manipulated merger of the Uniate and Orthodox Churches. Blank proxy forms were distributed throughout Transylvania for Uniate clergy to sign. These were to designate two priests from each district, possibly unknown to the signatories, who were to represent them at a meeting to be convened in Cluj on 1 October. The purpose of the meeting, according to the form, was 'the return of the Greek Catholic Church to the Orthodox Church'.[51] An indication of the methods used to extract signatures was provided by Nuncio O'Hara in a protest note handed to the Ministry of Foreign Affairs on 2 October:

> The priests were in many instances brought by force into the offices of the state security police, intimidated, threatened with imprisonment, with separation from their families, with deporta-

49 *Persecuţia Bisericii din România*, p.30.

50 Interview with Father Tertullian Langa, 31 May 1993.

51 Bossy, *Religious Persecutions in Romania*, p.168.

tion and even death. Those who resisted the initial acts of violence were thrown in underground cells, ill-treated, subjected to exhausting questioning, and finally set free only when, broken down by the inhuman treatment of their jailors, they consented to sign.[52]

By such means the *Securitate* managed to extort the signatures of 423 priests who thus delegated thirty-eight clergy, selected by the government, to represent them at the Cluj meeting. The meeting took place in the George Bariţiu school under the chairmanship of the protopope (archpriest or dean) Traian Balaşcu, who led the delegates in the signing of a resolution confirming their return 'into the bosom of our mother, the Orthodox Church'. On the following day the delegates travelled to Bucharest where they joined the patriarch who issued a synodal act acknowledging the passage to Orthodoxy, registering the breach with Rome, and accepting the new converts.

Monsignor O'Hara's protest note of 2 October was angrily rejected by the Romanian government two days later who considered it 'an act of provocation against the Romanian state and people'. The protest was 'a step in line with the campaign carried on by imperialist circles and their agents against the democratic achievements of the Romanian People's Republic'. On 21 October the 'reintegration' of the Uniate Church was celebrated in the Uniate cathedral of the Holy Trinity in Alba Iulia which was henceforth renamed the 'cathedral of the unification of the Romanian Church of Transylvania'. The ceremony ended with a speech by Dr Coriolan Tatar, in the name of former Uniate laymen. Six days later, the persecution of those opposed to the merger began.

During the nights of 27 and 28 October 1948 Metropolitan Suciu and all of his fellow bishops, together with some 600 Uniate priests, were systematically rounded up. The callousness of the security forces was illustrated by the fatal shooting of Father Ieronim Susman. He was gunned down while attempting to flee the village of Asinip near Blaj where he had been officiating. All six bishops (Suciu, Hossu, Frenţiu, Bălan, Rusu and Aftenie) were first taken to the summer residence of the Orthodox patriarch in the village of Dragoslavele near Cîmpulung in Wallachia, and placed under armed guard. Then on 27 February 1949, they were moved to the monastery of Căldăruşani north of Bucharest from where they

52 *Ibid.*, p.169.

could be more easily transferred to the Ministry of the Interior for interrogation. Many of the Uniate priests, such as Father Alexandru Raţiu, Father Augustin Olah, and Father Alexandru Ciudariu from Oradea, were sent to the monastery of Neamţu in Moldavia.[53] Just as the Vatican had acted in the circumstances of the arrested Roman Catholic bishops, so too in the case of the Uniates were instructions passed in 1950 to Nuncio O'Hara to consecrate secretly six auxiliary bishops on the recommendation of the six arrested ones. The secret bishops, whose names were soon discovered by the Communist authorities, but not listed in the *Annuario Pontificio,* were Ioan Ploscaru, appointed to the diocese of Lugoj, Ioan Chertes for Cluj-Gherla, Alexandru Todea for Alba Iulia-Făgăraş, Ioan Dragomir for Maramureş, Iuliu Hirţea for Oradea, and Liviu Chinezu for Bucharest.[54]

According to Father Alexandru Raţiu, Chinezu and Chertes were consecrated by Bishop Frenţiu on 3 December 1949 while they were all being held in confinement at Căldăruşani monastery; Dragomir, Hirţea, and Ploscaru were consecrated on 28 March 1949 by Nuncio O'Hara at the nunciature in Bucharest.[55] Todea was consecrated at the hands of the Roman Catholic Bishop Joseph Schubert on 19 November 1950 in St Joseph's cathedral in Bucharest. Father Gheorghe Guţiu was the only witness.[56] After the ceremony Todea returned to Reghin and went underground. The *Securitate* located the house in which he was staying and after surrounding it on 30 January 1951, forced Todea to give himself up. He was taken to Târgu-Mureş for interrogation, after which he was transferred to the Ministry of the Interior in Bucharest and then to Jilava and Uranus, one of the interrogation centres of the SSI, the intelligence service. Accused of being an enemy of the state, he was put on trial in Bucharest on 15 February 1952 and sentenced to hard labour for life. He began his sentence at Sighet prison on 28 February 1952.[57] By 1951, all the auxiliary bishops were under arrest; Chinezu died in Sighet prison on 15 January 1955.

53 Raţiu has written about his experiences in A. Ratiu and W. Virtue, *Stolen Church: Martyrdom in Communist Romania*, Huntington, Indiana: Our Sunday Visitor, 1978.

54 Stehle, *Eastern Politics of the Vatican*, p.422, n.4.

55 Ratiu, *Stolen Church*, p.169.

56 *Cartea Albă a Securităţii*, vol.II, August 1948-July 1958, doc.110, p.226.

Uniate churches were handed over to the Orthodox Church while their convents and monasteries were closed. Such was the fate of the Order of the Immaculate Virgin and the Institute of the Assumptionist Fathers in Blaj, of the Institute of the Basilian Order in Bixad, and the monastery of the Annunciation in Iedera near Moreni. In an unseemly gesture the Orthodox Metropolitan of Transylvania, Dr Nicolae Bălan, is reported to have entered the Uniate cathedral in Blaj on 31 October 1948 at the head of security troops in order to take possession of it.[58] Subservience was also displayed by some Uniate clergy: Teofil Herineanu was rewarded for his compliance with the regime's wishes by being promoted to the Orthodox see of Roman and Huşi on 8 June 1949. Only those Uniate priests who accepted Orthodoxy were paid a stipend by the state and the legal existence of the church was finally terminated by decree no. 358 of the Grand National Assembly issued on 1 December 1948 which abolished all dioceses and institutions of the Uniate Chruch and awarded all churches to the Orthodox Church.

An effort was made by their *Securitate* interrogators to link Suciu, Aftenie, and one of the clandestine bishops – Liviu Chinezu – with the groups of partisans who had set up centres of resistance to Communist authority in the Carpathian mountains in Transylvania. Aftenie was moved to Jilava jail where he shared a cell with Vasile Gârneţ. He told Gârneţ that he had been taken to the Ministry of the Interior for interrogation and from there to a villa in Sinaia to recuperate. While in Sinaia he was visited by Gheorghiu-Dej and Patriarch Justinian who tried to convince him to pass over to the Orthodox Church, offering as an inducement the metropolitan see of Iaşi. Aftenie reportedly replied to Justinian with the words 'nu am nici suflet, nici conştiinţă, nici credinţă, nici neam de vînzare' (I have neither a soul, conscience, faith, nor a people to sell). Aftenie was then taken back to Jilava and from there to the Ministry of the Interior where he was beaten so badly that he died on 10 May 1950. Details of his beating were passed on to Father Tertullian Langa by Father Johann Baltheiser, the parish priest of St Joseph's cathedral in Bucharest,

57 S.A. Prunduş, C. Plaianu, *Cardinalul Alexandru Todea*, Cluj: Ordinul Sfîntul Vasile cel Mare, 1992, p.28.

58 *Persecuţia Bisericii din România*, p.57.

who was ordered by two *Securitate* agents to officiate at a burial service in the capital's Bellu cemetery. Left for a few moments alone with the coffin at the cemetery, Baltheiser lifted the lid and saw that Aftenie had a badly beaten face and swollen eyes.[59]

Chinezu was transferred on 24 May 1950 to Sighet jail in Maramureş with Hossu, Rusu, and Bălan; they were joined there in September by Suciu, and later by Frenţiu. The latter died on 11 July 1952 at the age of seventy-seven. Less than a year later, Suciu died at the age of forty-three on 27 June 1953 and was buried near the jail, like Frenţiu. On 15 January 1955, Chinezu, who was in his late forties, died in the prison of hypothermia. Of the six imprisoned Uniate bishops – Iuliu Hossu, Vasile Aftenie, Alexandru Rusu, Ioan Bălan, Ioan Suciu and Valeriu Traian Frenţiu – only Bălan, Hossu and Rusu survived the five years of prison until their release on the orders of Dej in 1955.[60] None of the bishops had been brought to trial.

Bălan, Hossu and Rusu were released into compulsory residence at the monastery of Curtea de Argeş where they were visited by many Uniate faithful and this prompted them to request an audience with Petru Groza, president of the praesidium of the Grand National Assembly (parliament). When bishop Hossu requested permission to restore the Uniate Church, Groza is said to have retorted: 'But bishop, there are no Byzantine Catholics in Romania! Everyone is Orthodox, and there is no way to prove the existence of a Catholic Byzantine-rite Church.'[61] On 23 April 1956 the three bishops sent a memorandum to the government calling for the reestablishment of the Uniate Church. Petitions drawn up by the bishops attracted so many signatures that the Ministry of the Interior felt the need to act. It moved the bishops to the Orthodox monastery at Ciorogârla near Bucharest and then separated them; Bălan remained at Ciorogârla where he died, according to one source, on 4 August 1963 at the age of eighty-three,[62] and to another in 1969.[63] Rusu was exiled to the Cocoş monastery near Tulcea, while Hossu was

59 Interview with Father Langa on 31 May 1993.

60 Bălan was freed in January and Hossu and Rusu in June.

61 Ratiu, *Stolen Church*, p.48.

62 *Persecuţia Bisericii din România* p.73.

63 Prunduş, *Cardinalul Alexandru Todea*, p.102.

sent back to the monastery of Căldăruşani where he was left to languish in his confinement for a further fifteen years.

For Bishop Rusu the torment of prison was to return. The increasing number of calls made by Uniate priests for the restoration of their Church, exemplified by an open-air service in Cluj on 16 August 1956 at which Vasile Chindriş and Isidor Ghiurco officiated, made the regime especially nervous, particularly after the Hungarian uprising. In December 1956 Rusu was brought from the Cocoş monastery to Cluj where he was charged with having received an emissary from the Vatican who had allegedly discussed with the bishop his elevation to the vacant metropolitan see of Blaj. Sentenced with him in the same trial were Ludovic Vica, vicar general of the Baia Mare diocese, and Iosif Sângiorzan, vicar-general of Gherla. Rusu was found guilty and sentenced to twenty-five years' hard labour, even though he was seventy-two years old. He was sent to the prison of Gherla where for the following seven years he resisted the unheated cells and lack of medical care, comforting those in suffering by tapping out blessings in morse on his cell walls and distributing communion bread to those who requested it. He finally succumbed to the harsh conditions of his imprisonment on 9 May 1963.

Rusu had been joined at Gherla in 1963 by the auxiliary bishops Ioan Ploscaru, Ioan Chertes, Alexandru Todea, Ioan Dragomir, and Iuliu Hirţea. They had been transferred from Sighet in the spring of 1955 – one source gives an exact date, 9 April 1955 – to a succession of prisons.[64] Other Uniate priests were told at this time that they would be sent to their home towns for trial for 'instigating activity contrary to the welfare of the workers'.[65] In fact, they were released and told to get jobs. Father Alexandru Raţiu, one of those freed, described what had survived of the Church:

> In the five dioceses of Transylvania, there remained about seven hundred priests, two hundred nuns, and thousands of faithful. Meeting with these people was a joyful experience that gave us a surge of hope. The church was still there in these neglected souls, who after years of persecution and expectation, were now gathering in spirit and in truth. Who can ever know or tell their

64 Ratiu, *Stolen Church*, p.43.

65 *Ibid.*, p.45.

sufferings and hopes in those years of persecution? Throughout that time these good priests celebrated Holy Mass in the homes of the faithful, or in the still-open Latin-rite churches in the large cities. Of course, the security agents' informers tracked down these nests of resistance to the unification program.[66]

The freedom granted to the Uniate priests was short-lived for they were targeted in the waves of arrests which followed the Hungarian uprising. In October 1957 a group of priests, among them Alexandru Raţiu and Teofil Baliban, were tried in Bucharest on charges of 'plotting' to reinstitute the Uniate Church. After receiving sentences of fifteen years' hard labour, they were sent to Aiud jail and then transferred to Gherla. All were finally released in the general amnesty of 1964, as were the five surviving auxiliary bishops, Chertes, Dragomir, Hirţea, Ploscaru and Todea. Todea had been transferred from Sighet in March 1955 to Râmnicu Sărat, and then in 1957 to Piteşti. On 5 June 1960 he was moved to Dej, and then finally in February 1963 to Gherla. As was customary with these transfers, Jilava was used as a holding point for the prisoners. On his release from Gherla in 1964, Todea returned to Reghin.[67]

The persecution of the Uniate Church was the Orthodox Church's gain. Adjustment to their privileged position led the Orthodox Church hierarchy to seek a justification of its position. Patriarch Justinian gave expression to the role of the Orthodox Church under Communism in his 1948 New Year address as Metropolitan of Moldavia:

> 'This New Year finds Romania in new social conditions – the People's Republic of Romania. The Church is not bound by finite institutions, created by men for their needs of the moment. The Church is created by the Eternal God. In this present age she will support social justice, patriotism, and seek man's salvation. She must not remain closed, isolated within herself, but be permanently vibrant in order to revolutionise the religious life of her community.'[68]

66 *Ibid.* p.47.

67 Prunduş, *Cardinalul Alexandru Todea*, p.30.

68 A. Scarfe, 'Patriarch Justinian of Romania: His Early Social Thought', *Religion in Communist Lands*, vol.5, no.3 (autumn 1977), p.165.

Christianity's mission to defend the poor and needy provided the basis for Justinian's reconciliation of the church's role with dialectal materialism:

> 'Some consider materialism hostile to Christianity. We, however, judge men according to their deeds and achievements. We judge doctrine according to the order of society it produces. Can we not see in the present social order the most sacred principles of the Gospel being put into practice? Is not the sharing of goods, thus excluding them from the use of exploiters, better? [...] Let us therefore be loyal and recognise that the state leadership has brought peace to men by assuring them of an existence and by allowing them to live off the first-fruits of their own honourable labours.'[69]

There was nothing in Justinian's pronouncements of this period about the peace denied by the Communist regime to men, nor about its deprival of an existence to the tens of thousands of Romanians held in the prisons and labour camps, many of whom had been placed there simply for their fidelity to a particular religious faith. Instead, Justinian concentrated on preserving his own church by giving it goals consistent with the Communist revolution. To this end he proposed in 1949 the reorganisation of pastoral training, which would contain an emphasis on the education of villagers in new agricultural methods, assistance with the government's literacy programme and a reform of monastic life so that monks and nuns should be instructed in a useful trade. Justinian was anxious to point out that these 'new forms of life', as he called them, did not diminish the primacy of prayer.

Justinian's sympathies enabled the Orthodox Church to survive the early 1950s relatively unscathed. To his supporters he was regarded as a major reformer, whose encouragement of his clergy to take an interest in social work was a notable departure from Orthodox tradition. He improved theological training by requesting the professors of the two theological institutes to compile a number of manuals for use in seminaries throughout the country. As a result the Romanian clergy were, in the view of one Western observer, 'the best trained in the Orthodox Church', and after

[69] *Ibid.*, p.166.

1964 a number were sent to study in Western Europe.[70] Justinian's most successful reform involved monastic life. There were, in Justinian's first and only public admission of their numbers on 9 October 1955, 'more than two hundred monasteries'.[71] His requirement of monks and nuns to learn a trade enabled him to defend the monasteries by enabling them to register in 1951 as cooperatives and to set up workshops for weaving and other rural arts whose proceeds generated a useful income. Other monasteries set up farming cooperatives and in the process made themselves a vital part of a village community, employing labour from amongst the local peasantry.

To Justinian's detractors, this 'success' was seen as a reward for subservience to the Communist regime. Many Uniates dismissed Justinian as a Communist stooge and an opportunist, particularly because of his exuberant reaction to the suppression of their Church and its absorption into the Orthodox Church. Yet his attitude was one which was rooted in a widespread belief which identified the unity of the Orthodox Church with the unity of the Romanian people. Such an attitude was easily exploited by the regime's propagandists who translated diversity as a threat to national integrity. Many of those who were imprisoned by the Communists pointed with bitterness to Justinian's exhortations to his clergy to participate in the construction of the new People's Republic, but it was clear from the patriarch's writings, assembled in a series entitled '*Apostolat Social*' (Social Apostolate, 10 vols), that he saw forms of socialism as an integral part of Christian belief. What Justinian failed to do was to question the methods used to build the new republic, and in doing so he was following his conviction that the church should not engage in 'thoughtless' acts of opposition.[72]

70 T. Beeson, *Discretion and Valour: Religious Conditions in Russia and Eastern Europe*, London: Fontana, 1974, p.311. In 1973 there were 8,185 parishes and 11,722 places of worship served by 8,564 priests and 78 deacons. In Bucharest alone there were almost 250 churches and 400 priests. The church possessed two theological institutes of university standing, in Bucharest and Sibiu, with respectively 496 and 780 students in 1972-73. The majority of the clergy were trained in the seven cantors' schools and seminaries where 1,597 students were in residence over the same period (*Ibid.*, p.303).

71 Ioan Dură, *Monahismul românesc în anii 1948-1989*, Bucharest: Harisma, 1994, p.59.

72 K. Hitchins, '*Romanian Orthodox Church*', p.322.

Reconciliation of the church's transcendental mission to save souls through faith in the teachings of Christ with its perceived obligations to serve the best interests of the People's Republic can only be attempted if one denies that a political system can influence this spiritual mission. And this is precisely what Justinian argued, ascribing to the church a dual role as a spiritual body and a social institution. There is little evidence to suggest that many Orthodox faithful quibbled about this distinction, seeing in Justinian an effective leader and defender of their Church.

One price of Justinian's alignment with the regime was support for the regime's foreign policy which, until the late 1950s, meant Soviet foreign policy. In 1948 the Orthodox Church was dragooned, like its fellow churches in Eastern Europe, in the 'defence of peace', a movement initiated by the Communist inspired World Peace Council. Romanian theological journals engaged in ritual condemnation of the World Council of Churches and, in particular, the Roman Catholic Church, which were denounced as instruments of Anglo-American imperialism. In the early 1960s as Romanian foreign policy sought closer links with the West, so the Orthodox Church was encouraged to develop its own contacts beyond Eastern Europe and in 1961 it entered the ecumenical movement.[73]

Individual Orthodox priests did feel the hand of repression under Communism. In a report for 1949 drawn up by that department of the *Securitate*'s First Directorate responsible for overseeing the activity of the Orthodox Church, the writers concluded that 'the Orthodox problem has grown owing to the increase in the number of challenges to the regime which are the work of priests who own land.' This was clearly a reference to resistance from priests to the land reform of March 1949. However, the report went on to emphasise that 'the majority of the Orthodox clergy and faithful – there are 18,000 priests and monks – have elected to stand by the regime and to fight for peace.'[74] Such compliance by the Orthodox did not spare their church a measure of persecution. In a speech given on 12 May 1953, Justinian revealed that the Orthodox Church had 'more than 10,000' monks and nuns in 1951, but that this number had fallen two years later to 'almost

73 *Ibid.*, p.323.

74 Archive of the SRI (ASRI), Fond D, dosar 9051, vol.2. I am grateful to Marius Oprea for this information.

7,000'. Roughly half of these, he pointed out, worked in the monastery cooperatives. This figure of almost 7,000 remained stable until the strictures placed on the monastic life of the church were introduced in December 1958.[75]

Close supervision of Orthodox priests was among the string of drastic internal security measures adopted by Gheorghiu-Dej in order to preempt any anti-Communist agitation which he feared might arise after the withdrawal of Soviet troops from Romania in the summer of 1958, and to allay Khrushchev's fears that the withdrawal might undermine the Romanian party's control. Some priests had been associated with the Iron Guard. Priests were also involved in informal discussion groups and were among those arrested, tried and jailed in 1958 and 1959 on charges of belonging to 'clandestine reactionary and mystico-legionary associations'.[76] The monasteries were also identified as a source of potential opposition. In a report of October 1958, signed by Alexandru Drăghici, minister of the interior, Patriarch Justinian himself was accused of 'acting systematically since assuming the leadership of the Orthodox Church to remove progressive elements and to promote the most reactionary elements in the clergy, especially Iron Guardists'. After divulging to the party the large number 'of Iron Guard elements assembled in the monasteries', the interior minister proposed 'the removal from the monasteries of Iron Guardists [...]; the abolition of the monastic seminaries [...]; a fifty per cent reduction in the number of monasteries; and a minimum age-limit of fifty for entry into the monastic life.'[77] The principal points in Drăghici's plan of action were approved, as a *Securitate* report of 2 April 1960 indicates:

> During 1958, the party and state leadership analysed the position of monks in our country and reached the conclusion that the number of monasteries and monks in the Romanian People's

[75] Ioan Dură, *Monahismul românesc*, pp.56-7.

[76] Among these groups was the so-called *Rugul aprins al Maicii Domnului* (The Burning Stake of the Virgin Mary) which was accused of seeking to attract students from the theological institutes in Bucharest and Iaşi. Those arrested included the theologians Dumitru Stăniloae, Alexandru Mironescu, Sandu Tudor, Anania Valeriu Bartolomeu, Ghius Benedict, Braga Roman, and Antonie Plămădeală. (*Cartea Albă a Securităţii*, vol.III: *1958-1968*, p.56)

[77] *Ibid.*

Republic was inordinately high and that they had become centres of counter-revolutionary activity and immorality. In fact, on 15 December 1958 there were 224 monasteries and 6,214 monks in our country. In view of this situation, the Department of Cults persuaded the Synod of the Orthodox Church to take steps to restrict the number of monks and so, on 15 December 1958, the Synod decided to remove from the monasteries minors, those who had not completed elementary schooling, immoral persons and elements who were hostile to our regime.[78]

The report went on to say that according to this decision, 1,492 monks and nuns were to be dismissed from the monasteries, and that despite the opposition and machinations of some of the Orthodox Church leaders, 1,200 monks had been ejected by 1 November 1959. The main obstacle had been Patriarch Justinian Marina. Justinian's silence in the face of the persecution of the Roman Catholic Church, and his approbation of the Uniate Church's suppression in 1948, did not mean that he was prepared to stand aside when his own church was under threat. The *Securitate* reported that the Patriarch

> .... showed his opposition in the session [of 15 December] of the Synod, and then took a series of measures designed to compromise the decision, namely: he openly stated his intention not to recognise the Synod's decision in the presence of other Church leaders, describing it as a government measure and not a Church one and as contravening canonical laws; he urged some monks who were due to be expelled to put in requests to stay on in the monasteries, requests which he himself approved; under the pretext of setting up workshops in the monasteries, he sought to concentrate a group of nuns who were due to renounce orders at the Dealu monastery which at that time was no longer inhabited by monks [...][79]

Other prelates had shown solidarity with the patriarch and their common stance led some dismissed monks to return to the monasteries, prompting the intervention of the security forces who were called upon to eject them. Since the number of monasteries and monks failed to fall sufficiently, the Grand National Assembly issued a

78 *Cartea Albă a Securităţii*, vol.III: *1958-1968*, doc.74, p.243.

79 *Ibid.*

decree on 28 October 1959 stipulating that only monks over the age of fifty-five and nuns above the age of fifty could remain in the monasteries and that they should give up their state pension if they received one. The three monastic seminaries were closed, thus halting the flow of novices. In preparation for the application of the decree, the Department of Cults carried out a survey of monasteries and their populations and established that there were 132 monasteries and 3,239 monks and nuns. Under the terms of the decree, 1,456 monks and nuns were given orders to abandon the monastic life.[80]

Thus, in the space of ten months, almost 3,000 monks and nuns were compelled to leave the religious life and ninety-two monasteries closed. But the authorities were still concerned about the large number of Orthodox priests. In a paper of 1962, the *Securitate* calculated that the Orthodox Church had '9,853 priests for 6,000 posts', the excess being used for proselytising activities which were against the official policy of atheism. Among the methods used for reducing the figure was to restrict the number of students entering the theological institutes. In 1960, 701 priests were held in prison or under arrest; the majority were Orthodox accused of being former Iron Guardists.[81] In most cases their arrest had been prompted neither by any act of resistance to the regime, nor by their appartenance to the Orthodox faith, but because of the Communists' deep-seated fear of a movement which had drawn deeply in the 1930s upon the Orthodox priesthood for its support

80 *Ibid.*

81 *Ibid.*, p.57. The other priests were Uniates and Catholics. The last group of Uniate priests was arrested in February 1962 and they were all released two years later. In 1966, further strictures were placed on the monasteries with the introduction of a regulation stipulating that all nuns under forty and all lay brothers under fifty must leave their monasteries and take up 'more socially useful' work. (Beeson, *Discretion and Valour*, p.303). Discouragement of the monastic life continued throughout the Ceauşescu period but, as religious worship generally, toleration rather than suppression became the order of the day. On 25 June 1966 Justinian announced that there were 'over 2,500 souls living in the monasteries' of whom 'almost 2,000 were nuns.' (Dură, *Monahismul românesc*, p.59). The effect of the measures taken against the monasteries can be gauged from the decrease in the number of over 200 monasteries with almost 7,000 monks and nuns in 1956 to 114 monastic houses and 2,068 religious (1,493 nuns and 575 monks) in 1972 (Beeson, *Discretion and Valour*, p.303).

and validation and which was seen as the most serious potential threat to their rule.

Throughout the period of Communist power in Romania, Justinian's leadership was judged in terms of his effectiveness in preserving the church, in keeping Orthodox churches open as a sanctuary against the trials and torments of everyday existence, offering a place for private prayer and reflection for those deeply troubled by their ordeal under Communism. Ambiguity, as in other avenues of Romanian affairs, explains Justinian's achievement, for in harnessing the church to the social revolution, he was able to maintain throughout the twenty-nine years of his ministry – he died on 26 March 1977 – a church which provided a repository for the spiritual nourishment of his flock. Herein, the Orthodox will argue, lies the measure of his success.

6

THE *SECURITATE* AND THE USE OF TERROR

The security police was the blunt instrument of repression of the Communist Party. It was set up according to a Soviet blueprint and under Soviet direction. Broadly speaking, the role assigned by the Soviet authorities to the *Siguranţa* (the political police) after the 23 August coup was similar to that played by the *Siguranţa* under King Carol's dictatorship and that of Antonescu, but with one major difference: whereas the coercion between 1938 and 1944 was directed against one particular group in society, the Jews, and against the small number of individual opponents of the Antonescu regime, it was extended after the coup to the whole of Romanian society. Even during the war the landowner, the peasant, the banker, the lawyer and the priest carried on with their lives largely without the intrusion of the political police; now, in the building of the People's Democracy, the security police were called upon to eradicate existing political institutions and social structures. Police coercion and intrusion became part of everyday life and a feature of existence which generated a pervasive fear, a state of mind which revolutionised not just society's structures, but also personal behaviour. Animated conversation gave way to furtive whispers, or was expressed in parables, suggestion replaced open discussion, and the simplest of messages was wrapped in code.

Soviet penetration of the secret service, the SSI, and the security police, the *Siguranţa*, was undertaken by infiltrating them in autumn 1944 with Emil Bodnăraş's 'Patriotic Guards' and with NKVD/NKGB agents.[1] Control of both organisations was secured after the installation of the Groza government in March 1945. On 27 April Groza signed an order giving the secretary-general control of the SSI. The order stated that the SSI was constituted 'from

[1] See Chapter 4.

its own civilian personnel and from military personnel seconded from the Ministry of War on the recommendation of the secretary-general'. Another Soviet agent, Serghei Nikonov, was appointed to be the actual director of the SSI, under the supervision of Bodnăraş.

Nikonov's career is illustrative of the methods used by the NKGB to infiltrate their agents. Nikonov had been expelled from Iaşi University where he was a student of chemistry for participating in Communist meetings and was sent with funds from Communist coffers to Brussels to continue his studies. From there he moved to Marseilles where he was coopted into the local leadership of the French Communist Party. He was instructed by his controllers to return to Romania to run an espionage network but was caught, tried and imprisoned, first in Doftana jail, and then, after its destruction in the earthquake of November 1940, in Caransebeş where he joined Bodnăraş and Pintilie Bondarenko. Upon his release following the 23 August coup, he was reassigned duties by INU, the Foreign Intelligence Directorate of the NKGB, and these were institutionalised with his appointment as director general of the SSI on 7 December 1946. In 1951 Nikonov was made head of the anti-aircraft command, and in 1954 he transferred with the rank of lieutenant-general to head the Second Bureau of Military Intelligence of the Romanian General Staff, a post he retained until 1960 when he became head of the control directorate of the Ministry of Armed Forces.[2]

The SSI's remit covered 'the gathering of general intelligence which met the higher interests of the state'. It was organised in four sections and a secretariat. The first section was charged with 'obtaining intelligence from abroad of a political, economic, social and military nature' and 'control of all diplomatic offices abroad', and was subdivided into three departments, organised on a geographical

2 I am grateful to Claudiu Secaşiu for these details about Nikonov. Another example of the senior role given to NKVD agents in the security police was the appointment of Andrei Gluvacov as head of the *Siguranţa* in Braşov in 1947. He was born in Arad on 26 May 1914 and was a locksmith by trade. He was arrested for Communist activity in the 1930s and sentenced to six months' imprisonment which, according to his party file, he did not serve. He was suspected by the *Siguranţa* of having been trained in the Soviet Union as an NKVD agent. He joined the Ministry of the Interior on 1 October 1945 (*Cartea Alba a Securitaţii*, vol.I, doc.170, p.338).

basis, 'South', 'West' and 'North'. Section One also included the Office for Issuing Entry-Exit Visas and Passports to Romanian Citizens which was to be used 'as an auxiliary means of recruiting part-time informers'.[3] Here for the first time we find a policy statement of a government agency in Romania making the issuing of a passport conditional on collaboration with an organ of state security. It was a tactic that remained an integral part of the Communist regime's armoury of coercion until the overthrow of Ceauşescu.

Other sections of the SSI were responsible for obtaining intelligence from within the country and for mounting counter-espionage operations, both civilian and military. A Bessarabian-born Russian Pyotr Goncearuc was named head of the counter-espionage section. Born in 1911 in Chişinău, he joined the Communist Youth Movement in Bessarabia and in 1932 was sent to Moscow. Three years later he was infiltrated back into Romania across the Dniester with a mission but was quickly captured, tried and sentenced to ten years' imprisonment. After his release from Caransebeş jail in August 1944, he was given a post in the Administrative and Political Section of the Romanian Communist Party and in April 1945 transferred to the SSI.[4] According to Eduard Mezincescu who met him on several occasions in a professional capacity – Mezincescu was a senior Foreign Ministry official – Goncearuc was a 'cunning brute' who proved himself 'very efficient' with his interrogation methods. These were displayed in his treatment of Lucreţiu Pătrăşcanu (see Chapter 8).

Eavesdropping and shadowing of targets were carried out by Section Four of the SSI in collaboration with a parallel directorate in the *Siguranţa.* Military intelligence remained the task of the Second Bureau of the Army General Staff but this was also subordinated to a Soviet master, the GRU. The subservience of the Romanian security and intelligence services to the interests of the Soviet Union was completed by making the security police, still known by its pre-war title of *Direcţia Poliţiei de Siguranţă* (DPS), responsible in 1945 to Pantelimon Bondarenko, a Ukrainian-born Soviet agent, also known as Pantiusha, who had been imprisoned

3 *Organizarea şi funcţionarea Organelor Ministerului de Interne de la Infiinţare pînă în prezent*, Bucharest: Ministry of the Interior, 1978, p.87.

4 E. Mezincescu, 'Ecouri la Cazul Pătrăşcanu', *Magazin Istoric*, no.7 (July 1992), p.34.

for spying in Romania in the late 1930s. Bodnarenko assumed a Romanian name, Gheorghe Pintilie, as did Serghei Nikonov of the SSI (Serghei Nicolau) and a number of Soviet trained agents who later joined Bodnarenko at the apex of the *Siguranţa*, among them Boris Grunberg (who took the name of Alexandru Nicolski). Among the Soviet intelligence chiefs from whom instructions were channelled to Bodnăraş and Pintilie was Dmitri Georgievich Fedichkin, the chief Soviet adviser in Romania from 1944 to 1947 and principal representative of the External Intelligence Division (INU) of the NKGB.[5]

After the imposition of the Groza government the security police DPS, which remained subordinated to the General Directorate of Police within the Ministry of the Interior, was organised in four departments known as *servicii*. The first department followed the movements and activities of foreigners, the second covered suspected subversive figures, the third intercepted correspondence, and the fourth assured radio contact throughout the organisation. In 1946, a new 'special mobile brigade' was added to the DPS to carry out arrests and organise the transport of prisoners whose numbers had grown rapidly in the purge of 'Fascists' from public life which Prime Minister Groza announced on 7 March 1945.

Gheorghe Pintilie's promotion to membership of the Central Committee of the Romanian Workers' Party in February 1948, and the status of his wife Ana Toma as an agent of the Foreign Intelligence Directorate (INU) of the NKVD demonstrated the stranglehold which the Soviet security service had upon the Romanian leadership. Ana Toma's role was typical of that assigned by the NKVD to its female agents who were often described in Romanian party circles as 'amazons'. After being infiltrated into the party before the war, she seems to have acted as much as a custodian of her partners as a wife. Her first marriage to a veteran Communist Sorin Toma disintegrated following the latter's exile to the Soviet Union, and in 1942 she became the partner of Constantin Pîrvulescu, another senior figure in the embronic party. Four years later she married Pintilie who was a notorious drinker and over whom the NKVD deemed it prudent to have total supervision in view of the position he was given.[6]

5 Andrew, KGB: *Inside Story*, p.362.

6 Ana Toma was a close associate of Ana Pauker. When Pauker became foreign

In August 1948 Pintilie was moved from his post as head of the political and administrative section of the Central Committee to head the newly-reorganised *Siguranţa*. It was renamed *Direcţia Generală a Securităţii Poporului* (DGSP) or *Securitate* for short. The new name signalled a new mission for the security police. Formally, it remained a branch of the Ministry of the Interior. Its role, defined under its founding decree no. 221 of 30 August 1948, was 'to defend the democratic conquests and to ensure the security of the Romanian People's Republic against the plotting of internal and external enemies'.[7] Defence of the 'democratic conquests'

---

minister in November 1947, Toma was made secretary-general of the Foreign Ministry, and in 1950 she was appointed Pauker's deputy. Toma and Iosif Chişinevski worked closely together. In August 1951, Chişinevski instructed Toma to make the travel arrangements for a visit made by him, Gheorghiu-Dej and Miron Constantinescu to Moscow to obtain from Stalin backing for the purge of Pauker, Luca and Georgescu. Chişinevski ordered Toma not to tell Pauker a word about the trip; R. Levy, 'Did Ana Pauker Prevent a "Rajk Trial" in Romania?', *East European Politics and Societies*, vol.9, no.1, p.164, n.127. Pauker's son-in-law, Gheorghe Brătescu, accused Toma of betraying Pauker in 1952 and for this reason he never spoke to her from that date until her death in 1993 (author's interview with G. Brătescu, 30 July 1994). Soviet control was further illustrated by the composition in 1948 of Gheorghiu-Dej's immediate entourage. His private secretary was Nina Nikonova, wife of Serghei Nikonov, the head of the SSI, his *chef de cabinet* was Mikhail Gavrilovici, an NKGB agent, and the head of his personal guard was Valerian Bucicov, another NKGB officer. Bucicov (whose biography appeared in brief in a daily newspaper in 1995) was born on 8 December 1909 at Salabant in the district of Cetatea Albă in Bessarabia, at that time under Russian rule. According to his party file, he was a Romanian citizen of Russian nationality who was a carpenter by trade. In 1931 he deserted from the Romanian army to the Soviet Union from where he returned after several months to carry out espionage. He was arrested in September 1931, tried and sentenced by court martial in Chişinău to 15 years' hard labour. He served his sentence at Ocnele Mari, Doftana, Caransebeş and in the camp at Târgu Jiu, from where he was released on 23 August 1944. From 1948 until his retirement in 1963, he worked in the Romanian Ministry of the Interior (*Ziua*, 5 June 1995, p.3). Research by Claudiu Secaşiu, to whom I am grateful for these details about Bucicov's career, has shown that Bucicov was enrolled in the Communist Patriotic Guards after 23 August 1944. It is not clear exactly when he became head of Gheorghiu-Dej's bodyguard (Directorate Six); evidence points to the fact that he held this position in January 1949. (State Archives Bucharest, Archive of the Central Committee of the RCP, fond 1, dos.198/1944 [rola – 106-1-79-80], fila 173, cadrul 237; dos.205/1944 [rola – 106-1-79-81], f.207/c.572).

[7] *Cartea Albă a Securităţii*, vol.II, doc.33, p.157. The DGSP was organised in ten national or central directorates as follows: Information (I); Countersabotage (II); Counterespionage in the Prisons and Police (III); Counterespionage in the

meant the maintenance of the Communist Party in power and thus the new Romanian People's Republic officially certified itself a police state. Ninety per cent of the *Securitate* officers were party members and Pintilie's membership of the Central Committee was an implicit indication of nominal party control of the organisation.

Two weeks earlier, on 15 August, Lt.-Gen. Gheorghe Pintilie had been appointed by decree the *Securitate*'s director. Two assistant directors, with the rank of major-general, were appointed on 1 September; Alexandru Nicolski, a Russian-speaking Bessarabian Jew, and Vladimir Mazuru, a Ukrainian from Bessarabia (later Romanian ambassador to Poland).[8] All three were agents of the Soviet security service, known at this time as the MGB.[9] A body of Soviet counsellors from the MGB supervised the activity of the young *Securitate*. The MGB chief adviser in Bucharest from

---

Armed Forces (IV); Penal Investigation (V); Protection of Ministers (VI); Technical (VII); Cadres (VIII); Political (responsible for party purity) (IX); Administration (X). Auxiliary departments dealt with interception of mail, surveillance, and eavesdropping and further included a cipher section and a secretariat. Thirteen regional directorates, including that for the city of Bucharest, were established. The SSI, which was responsible for foreign espionage and counterespionage, worked in parallel with directorates I and IV of the DGSP between 1948 and 1951 when it was absorbed. Regional directorates *(direçii regionale)* were established to cover the capital Bucharest and the districts of Braşov, Cluj, Constanţa, Craiova, Galaţi, Iaşi, Oradea Mare, Piteşti, Ploieşti, Sibiu, Suceava, and Timişoara, and each of these directorates had its own organisation corresponding to that of the ten national directorates to which they were subordinated. Each regional directorate was further subdivided into county offices *(servicii judeţene)* which themselves encompassed town and communes bureaux *(birouri de securitate)*.

8 According to his party file, Mazuru had joined the Communist Party in 1944 after the 23 August coup. He was born in 1915 in Chişinău, then under Russian rule. By profession he was a medical instrument technician. He joined the Ministry of the Interior in 1947 when he was made director of cadres (personnel). A report on his character and work dated 26 April 1948 and signed by B. Fuchs as responsible for the personnel of the *Siguranţa*, described him as 'attentive to the needs of his colleagues, energetic, combative, courageous, vigilant, and harsh with his enemies. [...] He is liked by his subordinates, is authoritarian, but at the same time friendly.' *Cartea Albă a Securităţii*, vol.1, doc.170, p.338.

9 The NKGB (the People's Commissariat of State Security) had been raised in status in 1946 from a commissariat to a ministry, becoming the MGB, the Soviet Ministry of State Security. At the same time the NKVD (the People's Commissariat for Internal Affairs) became the MVD, the Soviet Ministry of Internal Affairs.

1949 to 1953 was Aleksandr Sakharovsky, who in 1956 became head of the First Chief Directorate of the KGB.[10]

It was Lavrenti Pavlovich Beria, head of the NKVD between 1939 and 1946, and since 1946 deputy chairman of the Soviet Council of Ministers, who oversaw the creation of the security framework with the satellite states. His power had grown enormously as a result of the war-time expansion of the security network, although Stalin had attempted to dilute it by replacing him as head of the NKVD in 1946. Beria remained the second most powerful figure in the Soviet Union, through his position as deputy chairman of the Council of Ministers, and through the deference shown to him by the new head of the MGB, Viktor Semyonovich Abakumov. Abakumov's management style in the MGB was, like that of Beria, brutal – a feature characteristic of the men chosen by the Soviets to head Romania's security police.[11] The conduct of both Pintilie and Nicolski speaks for itself. The former, as head of the Political and Administrative Section of the Central Committee whose function included party security, carried out the death sentence imposed on the former RCP General Secretary Ştefan Foriş in 1946.[12] He then gave instructions for Foriş's mother to be murdered. She was killed and her body, weighted with a millstone, was thrown into the Criş river in Transylvania.[13]

Pintilie's philosophy was outlined in an address he gave to *Securitate* chiefs on 1 March 1950: 'There is no place in our country for comrades who believe in God. [...] We need honest, dedicated party members so that we can carry out our tasks, there is no alternative. We are short on discipline. Why are we short on discipline? Because we consider ourselves the centre of things.' It

10 The Soviet ambassador to Bucharest, Serghei Kavtaradze, appointed in 1948, came under the authority of the newly formed KI (foreign intelligence service), headed by Vyacheslav Molotov and his deputy Fedotov, and was given control of the civilian (ex-MGB) and military (ex-GRU) residents in Bucharest. In 1949, Molotov was succeeded as foreign minister and chairman of the KI by Andrei Vyshinski, a client of Lavrenti Pavlovich Beria, head between 1939 and 1946 of the NKVD, and since 1946 deputy chairman of the Council of Ministers. (Andrew, *KGB: Inside story*, p.485).

11 *Ibid.*, p.349.

12 Mezincescu, 'Polemici', p.2. See also Chapter 7 of this book.

13 Ştefănescu, *Istoria Serviciilor Secrete*, p.250; see also Tismăneanu, 'Tragicomedy of Romanian Communism', p.350, n.47.

was this feeling of superiority which had led *Securitate* officers to be over-zealous in their beatings of the accused. Pintilie emphasised that prisoners should only be beaten on the orders and instructions of superior officers. Pintilie's manual background coloured his description of *Securitate* methods:

> Comrades, every craftsman, every doctor, everybody has an instrument and he looks after that instrument. In the *Securitate* what is our instrument? We too have an instrument. If the barber has his razor, if the carpenter has his lathe, I say that our informers are our instrument. Let us be conscious of our task and of our opponents. Just as the labourer takes care of his tools, so too must we take care of our informers. If the barber has his razor, we have people, and real people at that! That means that we have got to take care of them, give them instructions, indicate the party line and not, just like that, to beat them till they are black and blue! If a carpenter destroys his lathe, what will he eat the next day? Is that what the party teaches us?[14]

Yet Pintilie did not follow his own advice. He offered clear signs of megalomania after attending a concert given by the Ministry of the Interior choir and orchestra on 8 May 1949:

> I order the artists not to be so glum! An artist is an artist, irrespective of his feelings, and he should not forget that he is on the stage! And why is the symphony orchestra in the pit and the chorus on the stage? The orchestra should immediately mount the stage, because together with the chorus it forms an ensemble and they should support each other. Accordeons should be added forthwith to the symphony orchestra so that vigorous and mobilisatory marches can be played.[15]

Pintilie's deputy, Alexandru Nicolski, was born on 2 June 1915 in Chişinău, the principal town of Bessarabia which at that time was under Russian rule. In 1932 he joined the Union of Communist Youth in his native town and in the following year was detained for two weeks by the *Siguranţa*. Between 1937 and 1939 he did

14 M. Oprea, 'Zeii de lut ai Securităţii Române', *Dilema*, III, no.133, p.11. Pintilie was appointed a deputy minister of the interior in 1950, a position he held until 1962.

15 *Ibid.*

his military service in a signals regiment in Iaşi and after being demobilised he obtained a job in the telephone exchange in Chişinău. In December 1940, six months after the Soviet annexation of Bessarabia, he was recruited by the NKVD and moved to Cernăuţi where he underwent training as an agent of the Foreign Intelligence Directorate (INU) of the NKVD. Supplied with false Romanian identity papers in the name of Vasile Ştefănescu, he was sent across the frontier on 26 May 1941 to gather information on Romanian troop movements. Within two hours he was arrested by Romanian frontier guards. According to the record of his interrogation, his rudimentary knowledge of Romanian betrayed his foreign identity and he passed himself off as an ethnic Russian with the name of Alexandru Sergheevici Nicolski. He was tried for espionage in July 1941 and sentenced to forced labour for life. The first part of his sentence was served in Ploieşti jail from where he was moved to Aiud to join other imprisoned Soviet spies, among them Vladimir Gribici, Simion Zeigner and Afanasie Şişman, all of whom stayed in Romania after their release in August 1944. After the imposition of the Groza government in March 1945, Nicolski was named deputy to the head of the police Corps of Detectives, Gheorghe (Guţa) Petrovici.[16] On 17 April 1947 he was appointed inspector-general of the *Siguranţa (Poliţia de Siguranţă)* and when the DGSP was established in the following year, he was made one of Pintilie's deputies. In 1953 he was given the post of secretary-general of the Ministry of the Interior.

Despite the veil of secrecy which was cast over the personnel of the *Securitate*, Nicolski's reputation for brutality earned him the dubious distinction of becoming the first senior officer to achieve notoriety outside Romania. In a statement made in Paris in January 1949, Adriana Georgescu Cosmovici, a twenty-eight-year-old woman arrested in Bucharest in July 1945 on the grounds of having belonged to a resistance movement, recounted how the 'Communist secret police investigators' beat her repeatedly with a sand-filled leather hose, struck her head against a .wall, and hit her face and chin until she was left with only six teeth in her lower jaw. She named three investigators as having threatened her with guns: Stroescu, Bulz and Nicolski.[17] Documents published after Nicolski's death

16 I am grateful to Claudiu Secaşiu for this information.

17 *Suppression of Human Rights in Romania*, Washington, DC: Rumanian National

on 16 April 1992 suggested that in July 1949 he ordered the murder of seven prisoners, allegedly leaders of an anti-Communist resistance movement, in transit from Gherla jail.[18]

Consultation of rudimentary figures surviving in the Ministry of Interior archives relating to the strength of the DGSP indicates that the number of officers serving in the ten national directorates shortly after its constitution was 1,151 of whom 848 were listed as secretarial and manual staff (the latter all carried military rank, such as sergeant-major, even if they were typists, chauffeurs, plumbers or waitresses).[19] The thirteen regional directorates employed 2,822 officers, roughly two-thirds of whom were manual or ancillary staff.[20] These figures may appear abnormally low, given the popular conception of the DGSP as a ubiquitous and all-pervasive instrument of coercion. But they do not include the network of informers who enabled the *Securitate* to function as efficiently as it did.

Soviet advisers were attached to each of the national directorates

---

Committee, 1949, p.65.

18 *Cuvîntul*, no. 119 (May), 1992, p.6.

19 The structure of the *Securitate* is laid out in Deletant, *Ceauşescu and the Securitate*, pp.57-62. Recently released documents from the personnel files of the *Securitate* shed light on the social background and competence of the new force. The head of Directorate I was Colonel Gavril Birtaş. He was born in 1905 in Baia Mare and was a carpenter by trade. He joined the Ministry of the Interior in 1946 and in April 1948 was head of the *Siguranţa* in Oradea. A character reference in his party file noted 'an occasional inability to link theory to practice'. (*Cartea Albă a Securităţii*, vol.I, doc.168, p.337. Major Nicolae Briceag, chief of the Someş county office in the Regional Directorate of Cluj, was born in Negreni in Olt county in 1916 into a peasant family. A tailor by trade, he joined the Ministry of the Interior in 1945 and in April 1948 is recorded as being head of the *Siguranţa* in Dej. A character reference in his party file describes him as being 'of mediocre intelligence'. (*Cartea Albă a Securităţii*, vol.I, doc.164, p.335. Lt.-Col. Mauriciu Strul, head of the Regional Directorate of Galaţi, was born 1911 in the commune of Sarmoş in the county of Mureş. He had a doctorate in law and practised as a lawyer before the war. He joined the Ministry of the Interior in 1945 and in April 1948 his party file records him as being head of the *Siguranţa* in Târgu-Mureş (*Cartea Albă a Securităţii*, vol.I, doc.158, p.332). Lt.-Col. Ludovic Czeller, head of the Regional Directorate of Oradea, was born on 24 July 1896 in Kismarja, Hungary. He was a lathe-operator by trade and joined the Romanian Ministry of the Interior in May 1945. He was described in his party file as having 'a short temper'. (*Cartea Albă a Securităţii*, vol.I, doc.163, p.334)

20 ASRI, Fond 'D', file 10,970, p.107 and Deletant, *Ceauşescu and the Securitate*, p.63.

to supervise the training of the Romanian recruits and to monitor their activity, and communication was carried out through interpreters, many of whom were from Bessarabia. Emphasis was placed on trustworthy cadres. In the eyes of the Soviet advisers many educated Romanians were considered unreliable and compromised because of the Antonescu regime's alliance with Germany. A second reason for caution derived from the fact that very few Romanians had willingly shown any enthusiasm for the RCP before its propulsion to power, whereas conversely, some members of the ethnic minorities had. Hence we should not be surprised to find several recruits for the senior positions in the *Securitate* drawn from two categories of person: from the ethnic minorities; and from unskilled manual workers.

Contrary to claims made by ultranationalists, the numbers drawn from ethnic minorities, although disproportionate, do not appear to be excessive. I stress 'appear' because it is clear from the *Securitate*'s own listings of the ethnic identity of its senior officers that it wished to obscure the Russian provenance of its three principal commanders, Pintilie, Nicolski and Mazuru, by entering them as Romanians. However, there is no evidence to suggest the 'Romanianisation' of officers of other ethnic origins.[21] As far as professional

[21] An examination of the ethnic and professional background of senior officers in the DGSP, (i.e. with the rank of major and above) shows that out of a total of sixty, thirty-eight were Romanians, fourteen were Jews, three Hungarians, three Russians (Pintilie, Nicolski and Mazuru), one Czech and one Armenian. These figures hardly bear out the claim made in the extreme nationalist weekly *România Mare* of 25 October 1991 by its editor Corneliu Vadim Tudor, a notorious sycophant of Ceauşescu, that the DGSP was staffed largely by Hungarians and Russian-speaking Jews. Both the latter minorities were well-represented in the DGSP, but not abnormally so. Of the total number of 3,973 employees listed in 1950, 247 were Hungarians and 338 were Jews. Most of the former were employed in those regional directorates which covered the major concentrations of Hungarian population such as Braşov (seventy-two Hungarians), Cluj (fifty-one), Oradea (sixty), Sibiu (twenty-six), and Timişoara (twenty-seven). This same observation is valid also for the Jews: of the 1,151 personnel in the central directorates based in Bucharest 148 were Jews. Regional directorates with the largest numbers of Jewish staff were Bucharest (sixteen), Cluj (thirty-six), Iaşi (thirty-five), Oradea (thirty-four) and Suceava (thirty-four). The composition of the *Securitate* by ethnic background in 1948 was as follows:

Total number of personnel of all ranks of whom –	3,973
–Jews (J)	338
–Hungarians (H)	247

background is concerned, the information available limits us to the national directorates and the secretariat; among twenty-five persons appointed to senior officer rank, there were two electricians, two carpenters, a locksmith, a blacksmith, a lathe operator, a craftsman, a tailor, a chemist, a schoolteacher, a doctor, an accountant, a lawyer, one person without a higher education, five with degree studies and five whose background was not given.[22] Compared to the population of some 17 million, the number of *Securitate* officers seems very small and the evidence provided by consultation of *Securitate* files shows that they relied heavily for information upon informers, numbering 42,187 in 1948 – the first year of the Republic. In the local bureaux, where there were often no more than a handful of staff, the officers were overworked. Their principal brief was to identify and monitor the activities of former members of outlawed opposition parties and organisations, such as the Iron Guard, and to provide monthly reports to the directorates responsible for information and counter-sabotage in Bucharest. These reports represent an invaluable survey of political allegiances and their relation to social background in Romania of the early 1950s.[23]

A major task of the *Securitate* was 'to unmask imperialist espionage activity'. Its main opponents in the Dej era, judging from the *Securitate*'s archives, were the American, British, Yugoslav and Israeli intelligence agencies. At the beginning of 1949, the Central Intelligence Agency, through its Office of Political Coordination under the direction of Frank Wisner, began to recruit Romanians

– Russians (Rus)	24
– Germans (G)	5
– Armenians (Ar)	3
– Czechs (Cz)	5
– Italians (It)	1
– Bulgarians (B)	3
– Yugoslavs (Y)	13
– Romanians (R)	3,334

For further details see Deletant, *Ceauşescu and the Securitate*, pp.63-4.

22 The heavy recruitment of manual workers into the *Securitate* is mentioned in the annual report for 1949 of Section Three of the First Directorate which dealt with the Orthodox Church. 32% of its personnel was made up of factory workers while only 40% had some professional training or experience in security matters (ASRI, fond D, file 9051, vol.2, p.10.

23 Some of these reports are reproduced in *Cartea Albă a Securităţii*, vol.II.

from refugee camps in southern Germany, Austria and Yugoslavia. Preference was shown for young men who knew those regions in which partisan activity had been reported. These men were trained for secret missions whose objectives were either to obtain information about Romania's defences, or to link up with the anti-Communist resistance groups in the mountains. The Yugoslavs either infiltrated their agents across the border or used Romanian citizens of Serbian nationality. To combat border inflitration, a counter-intelligence section of the frontier troops was set up and subordinated to the Ministry of the Interior. Israeli intelligence activities focused on the situation of the Jews in Romania. According to *Securitate* files, 45,299 persons were suspected of espionage in Romania in 1951. They were monitored by networks made up of 904 agents, of whom five were resident *Securitate* officers, 306 qualified informers and 593 unqualified informers. As a result of the information gathered, 267 persons were arrested for spying.[24]

A second principal aim of the *Securitate* was to seek out and destroy any form of internal resistance to the regime. This was described in *Securitate* jargon as 'subversive anti-democratic activity by enemies of the people'. The main targets were former factory owners and landowners, members of the outlawed democratic parties and of the Iron Guard, priests, students and teachers, and retired army officers and policemen.[25] In 1951, 417,916 persons

24 ASRI, fond 'D', file 9189, p.7.

25 To ensure the obedience of the army it was purged and a People's Army created under the supervision of a party-controlled body called 'The Higher Political Directorate of the Army' (*Direçia Superioară Politică a Armatei).* The DSPA was set up on 28 March 1948 and was staffed by officers known as 'political educators'. It was organised in five directorates responsible for planning and organisation, administration and accounting, education in the military schools and colleges, propaganda, and cadres or personnel In addition it managed the Army Central Club, the Centre for Physical Education, the Military Institute, and Army publications. An indication of the importance attached by the regime to the DSPA was the elevation of the civilian designated to be its head in March 1950 to the post of deputy minister of the Armed Forces with the rank of lieutenant-general; the civilian in question was Nicolae Ceauşescu.

The DSPA exercised party control in all army units. At the level of the division it was organised through a political council composed of a party secretary, and secretaries for propaganda, for organisation, for culture and sport, and for the Communist Youth Organisation, the UTM, to which all conscripts belonged. All such secretaries held senior military rank, and virtually all army officers were party members. At the regimental level there was a party committee with secretaries

were kept under surveillance of whom 5,401 were arrested for 'hostile activity'.[26] Information on them, as in the case of those suspected of espionage, was gathered by informers working under the control of a *Securitate* officer. Details were collated at the local bureaux and a daily bulletin on the situation in each area was transmitted by telephone to the regional offices between 5 and 5.30 p.m.

Eavesdropping and monitoring of suspects' movements were auxiliary means used by the *Securitate* to gather evidence against their targets. The latter was particularly labour-intensive and for this reason informers were often employed to supplement the shadowing carried out by the departments of the *Securitate* charged with surveillance. It was not only perceived enemies of the regime who received such attention; senior party members were also targeted. Among those whose telephone calls were monitored from 1948 by what came to be called 'Unit T' of the *Securitate* were Ana Pauker, Vasile Luca, Teohari Georgescu, Ion Gheorghe Maurer, Alexandru Bîrlădeanu and Valter Roman. Between 1953 and 1961 further names were added to this list: Iosif Chişinevski and his wife Liuba, Constantin Doncea, and Nicolae Ceauşescu. In 1963 Miron Constantinescu became a target, and in 1964 Gheorghe Pintilie, the former head of the *Securitate*. In charge of this eavesdropping was, up to 1954, Alexandru Nicolski. Not even Dej was

---

corresponding to the divisional ones, while in the battalions there was usually a single 'political commander' who held the rank of major and was responsible for organising regular lectures on party policy. The political commander authorised the posting of wall newspapers (*gazete de perete*) which contained anonymous criticism and, sometimes, denunciation of troops and officers. Reciprocal spying was encouraged under the euphemism of 'revolutionary vigilence' and reports were passed on either to Section II for military intelligence of the General Staff, or to the Fourth Directorate of the DGSP which dealt with military counter-intelligence. Ever since the imposition of the Groza government in March 1945 the activity of Section II of the General Staff had been closely monitored by Soviet officers and in 1948 a number were formally attached as counsellors to train young pro-Soviet Romanian officers in the work of counter-espionage. On 15 February 1951 Section II of the General Staff was renamed the Directorate for Intelligence of the General Staff and on 2 April was transferred from the Ministry of National Defence to the Ministry of the Interior. Throughout the period of Communist rule control of the frontier guards (*trupele de grăniceri*) alternated between the Ministry of National Defence and the Ministry of the Interior.

26 *Cartea Albă a Securităţii, vol.II, p.45.*

spared. Colonel Andrei Arghiropol, who worked in Unit T of the Technical Directorate, revealed in 1968 that his first job in 1949 was to intercept the telephone calls made by Dej.[27] The only other persons who knew about this operation, which was carried out on orders from Moscow channelled through the Soviet counsellors, were Pintilie, Nicolski, and Colonel Alexandru Neacşu, head of Unit T.[28]

Securitate files indicate that more than 70,000 people were arrested in the decade from 1948 to 1958, 60,428 of whom between 1948 and 1953 alone. These figures presumably relate to a particular set of categories since, on Gheorghiu-Dej's own admission in 1961, 80,000 peasants alone had been arrested to enforce collectivisation of agriculture.[29] Many of the arrests were illegal for they were carried out by *Securitate* officers acting purely on telephoned instructions from their superiors without an arrest warrant issued by the procurator's office. Cases of mistaken identity led to the arrest of the wrong person. In 1955, the Ministry of Interior gave instructions to *Securitate* officers to carry out arrests only on the basis of an arrest warrant issued by a procurator, yet in September 1958, Alexandru Drăghici, Minister of the Interior, was still complaining of cases in which arrests had been made 'without foundation and prematurely'.[30]

In the early years of the *Securitate*'s existence emphasis was placed on the quantity of informers rather than upon their quality. Many were small-time crooks and delinquents and their number included the casual informants and busybodies which, as Walter Bacon has remarked, all totalitarian regimes produce in parasitic abundance.[31] These categories boosted the number of informers to the levels reported as being used at the close of 1951 by the

[27] ASRI, Fond 9604, vol.IV, published in *Sfera Politicii*, no.44, 1996, p.44.

[28] The officers in charge of all surveillance were Alexandru Nicolski (1948-54), Tănase Evghenie (1954-7), Vasile Negrea (1957-65), and Cornel Onescu (1965-67). The heads of Unit T were Alexandru Neacşu (1948-52), Nicolae Panaitescu (1952-3), Alexandru Szacsko (1953-61), and Ovidiu Diaconescu (1961-89). (ASRI, Fond 9604, vol.IV, published in *Sfera Politicii*, no.44, 1996, pp.44-5).

[29] *Ibid.*, p.44 and Ionescu, *Communism in Rumania*, p.201.

[30] *Cartea Albă a Securităţii*, vol.II, p.64.

[31] W. Bacon, 'Romanian Secret Police' in *Terror and Communist Politics: The Role of the Secret Police*, ed. J.R. Adelman, Boulder and London: Westview Press, 1984, p.135.

Directorate of Counter-Sabotage and the Directorate of Internal Intelligence, namely 30,585 and 10,698 respectively.[32]

Informers were often blackmailed into collaborating with the *Securitate*. Charges against them for offences committed were dropped in return for collaboration. They were often roughly treated by their controllers, as Pintilie's speech quoted above shows, and threats were levelled at them. Documents reveal that at the regional *Securitate* headquarters in Cluj and Constanţa, informers were brought in wearing blacked-out spectacles so that they could not recognise the place and 'thrown into a room'.[33] The unreliability of many of them led to a major purge of 70% of their numbers in March 1956 with fresh informers being recruited from amongst intellectuals.

Informers were also used by two other organs of internal security, both of which were established early in 1949. On 23 January, the militia (*Direcţia Generală a Miliţiei*) was set up to replace the police, and on 7 February, the security troops (*Trupele de Securitate*) were created to take over the duties of the gendarmerie.[34] Both bodies were placed under the authority of the Ministry of the Interior. Among the militia's duties was that of issuing residence permits, one which facilitated its task of regulating the movement of population, of monitoring suspects and of preparing for deportations.[35] The principal duties of the security troops were to guard public buildings and foreign legations, and to maintain public order in the major industrial centres, but they were often deployed to quell any resistance to government measures such as collectivisation or confiscation of goods and property. Throughout the 1950s they were used to eradicate partisan resistance in mountain areas and, in a more passive role, were employed to guard the labour camps (*colonii de muncă*) which in 1950 had been placed

32 *Cartea Albă a Securităţii*, vol.II, p.47.

33 *Ibid.*

34 V. Mihalache and I.P. Suciu, *Jandarmeria Română. Pagini dintr-o istorie nescrisă, 1850-1949*, Bucharest: Editura Ministerului de Interne, 1993, p.171.

35 The militia was estimated to have a strength in 1953 of 40,000 while the number of security troops was put at 55,000 officers and men, organised in brigades and equipped with artillery and tanks: 'The Armed Forces' in *Captive Rumania: A Decade of Soviet Rule*, London: Atlantic Press, 1956, p.363.

under a special department of the Ministry of Interior known as *Direcţia Unităţilor de Muncă*.

A legal framework for the actions of the *Securitate*, the militia and the security troops was provided by the introduction of new laws which made opposition to the regime a criminal offence. The death penalty for treason and economic sabotage was introduced on 12 January 1949, and a decree promulgated in the same year punishing acts 'considered as dangerous to society', even if these were 'not specifically provided for in the law as crimes'. A law of 12 August 1950 imposed the death penalty for crimes against national independence and sovereignty, for negligence by workers 'leading to public disaster', for theft and destruction of military equipment, and for plotting against the state, spying and economic sabotage. The death penalty was applicable for the betrayal of 'state secrets' to a foreign power but the nature of these state secrets was not defined. 'Plotting against the internal and external security of the RPR' also attracted the death penalty, but once again 'plotting' was not defined. The open-endedness of this legislation permitted its arbitrary application by the authorities. The category of 'counter-revolutionary crimes' made its appearance in decree no. 83 of 1949. This provided for punishments of up to fifteen years' hard labour for those who resisted the expropriation of land under the land reforms of 1945 and 1949.

The party body charged with initiating arrests and criminal proceedings was an institution specific to Communist regimes and was known in Romanian as the *Procuratura*. It was vested with 'supreme supervisory power to ensure the observance of the law by the ministries and other central organs, by the local organs of state power and administration, as well as by officials and other citizens'.[36] The *Procuratura* was divided into twelve directorates whose powers included the direction of military, state security and criminal prosecutions, the supervision of court activities and of militia criminal investigations, the fixing of penal sentences and inspection of prisons. Like the *Securitate*, the *Procuratura* relied heavily upon informers whose activities were encouraged and rewarded, in the spirit of the procedures laid down by the Soviet prosecutor-general of the show trials of the 1930s, Andrei Vyshinski, who

[36] Ionescu, *Communism in Rumania*, p.217.

boasted that 'thousands of informers ensure that the *Procuratura* can react swiftly'.[37]

An idea of the 'principles' adopted by the Communist authorities in determining the guilt of citizens was given by an interrogator to George Tomaziu, an artist arrested in 1949 on the charge of being a spy in the pay of France and Britain. To Tomaziu's affirmation that at university he had learned that it was preferable to let one guilty man go free rather than imprison ten innocent suspects, his interrogator replied: 'That was bourgeois justice and the reason why the bourgeois system collapsed. In the Communist case the reverse is true. To avoid the risk of letting one guilty person slip through our hands, it is preferable to imprison him along with the other nine suspects.'[38]

In the political trials conducted after the imposition of the Groza government the defendant was often found guilty not because he or she had committed an offence, but because they stood accused.[39] And because they were accused, they had to be removed. This was the perversion of justice which Communism practised. It was not just the actions of the person which were on trial, but the person himself, his family and his background. This was most graphically illustrated by the public trials of alleged saboteurs of the Danube-Black Sea canal project in 1952, and it was equally true of the trial of Lucreţiu Pătrăşcanu in 1954. Many of the trials between 1948 and 1964 had a preventive character, with the accused being held guilty of potential crimes. This principle had been feverishly applied by Andrei Vyshinski as public prosecutor in the Moscow trials between 1936 and 1938, and it was under his supervision that it was introduced in Romania.

[37] V. Veniamin, 'The Judiciary' in *Captive Rumania*, p.313.

[38] G. Tomaziu, *Jurnalul unui Figurant*, Bucharest: Univers, 1995, p.173.

[39] The question put by Mircea Vulcănescu to the court, after studying the case brought against him in January 1948 as an alleged war criminal, was whether his accusers 'were seeking the punishment of a guilty man or the sacrifice of a victim' (M. Vulcănescu, *Ultimul Cuvînt*, Bucharest: Humanitas, 1992, p.23). Vulcănescu, a university teacher of sociology, served as under-secretary of state in the Ministry of Finance (January 1941-August 1944) in the Antonescu government. Like all ministers who had served under Antonescu, irrespective of their portfolios, Vulcănescu was arrested under the Law for the Prosecution and Punishment of Those Guilty of War Crimes or Crimes against Peace or Humanity, gazetted on 18 August 1947. He was found guilty and sentenced to eight years' hard labour. He died in Aiud prison on 28 October 1952 aged forty-eight.

In the conduct of political trials particular importance was attached to confession.[40] The means of extracting this was torture, be it psychological, physical, or both. The insistence upon confession and the use of torture to extract it were alien to the Romanian legal system and it is tempting to speculate what impression it left on the senior Romanian Communists who had experienced the less ruthless regime of interwar Romania. Some Romanians have argued that the rituals of liquidation imported from the Soviet Union after 1945 required the hand of Bessarabian or Ukrainian-born NKVD agents such as Nicolski and Gonceariuc, but this would be to overlook the brutality of a number of ethnically Romanian *Securitate* officers, for example, Ion Şoltuţiu, under whose directions Belu Zilber, Lucreţiu Pătrăşcanu and Remus Kofler were beaten.[41]

Beatings were usually administered at the direction of senior officers of Directorate Five for Penal Investigation. It was this directorate of the *Securitate* which gave the latter the character of a political police. Confidential instructions issued by the Ministry of the Interior empowered the *Securitate* to detain a person for twenty-four hours without the need of an arrest warrant from a procurator. During this period the detainee was asked to give a declaration.[42] Arrest warrants were then issued for the *Securitate* by military procurators on instructions from the Ministry of Justice. After the issue of an arrest warrant, interrogation of the prisoner began in the presence of a stenographer. The Fifth Directorate's first head was Colonel Mişu Dulgheru who was himself arrested in November 1952 on the charge of having delayed the investigation into Pătrăşcanu's activities.[43] *Securitate* documents indicate that Dulgheru approved the use of beatings, threats, the falsification of prisoner's statements, and extension of interrogation beyond the physical endurance of the prisoner. Even Alexandru Drăghici, appointed minister of the interior in May 1952, recognised that

[40] The role of the confession in the Moscow trials is examined in *Ritual of Liquidation: The Case of the Moscow Trials*, Glencoe, IL: The Free Press, 1954, pp.81-276.

[41] See Chapter 9.

[42] This was given the Orwellian term in Romanian of giving a declaration *în fază de libertate* (in a state of freedom).

[43] Dulgheru was dismissed from the Ministry of the Interior on 5 May 1955.

interrogation officers in this directorate 'had a fairly low level of training and general knowledge', but that these shortcomings were compensated for by 'their powerful revolutionary enthusiasm, their healthy [i.e. 'non-bourgeois] background and their work capacity which was placed at the service of the proletarian revolution'.[44]

The low level of knowledge was often illustrated by the interrogations recorded in the *Securitate* files. One officer asked a prisoner: 'When did you meet Cowles who is from Uruguay in the United States?'; another was unaware that the National Peasant Party was outlawed by the Antonescu regime; a third was unable to write the figure 309, confusing it with 3,009, 30,009, and 300,009. To surmount these difficulties, the Soviet counsellors drew up a list a questions and the desired replies, and in order to extract them, the interrogators resorted to psychological or physical pressure, denying the prisoner cigarettes, cutting his food ration, or beating him. Some *Securitate* interrogators broke the legs of prisoners by stamping on them, others threw water on the concrete floors of a cell so that the prisoner would freeze, or would force a prisoner to stand upright until he dropped unconscious. In October 1954, at a meeting at the headquarters of the Penal Investigation Directorate, Drăghici ordered a halt to the use of such pressure by officers except in cases where he personally gave approval. The cynical explanation given for the brutal treatment meted out to some prisoners was because the directorate 'had not organised a meeting with all heads of penal investigative sections in the country where they could exchange information and be given precise instructions for action'.[45] Nevertheless, a *Securitate* report of September 1958 admitted that some officers continued to beat prisoners, thereby 'breaking the most elementary rules of interrogation'.[46]

It is difficult to give precise figures for the numbers of persons arrested and jailed in the Dej era for the simple reason that the *Securitate*'s own statistics are contradictory. One Ministry of the Interior report states the following: in the ten years from 1948 to 1958, 58,733 persons were convicted of a multitude of crimes, all of which were of a political nature: conspiring against social

44 *Cartea Albă a Securităţii*, vol.II, p.57.

45 *Ibid.*, p.58.

46 *Ibid.*, p.60.

order, belonging to subversive or terrorist organisations – these included the former democratic political parties and the Iron Guard –'hostile instigation against the regime', illegally crossing the frontier, failing to report a crime against the state, crimes 'against humanity and activity against the working class', treason, espionage, distributing forbidden leaflets, sabotage, and 'hostile religious activity'. Most of those convicted received sentences ranging from one to ten years' imprisonment. A total of 73,310 persons were sentenced to imprisonment in the period 1945 to 1964, of whom 335 received the death penalty (for several it was commuted). A further 24,905 were acquitted or had the cases dropped against them. In addition, 21,068 people were sent to labour camps in the same period. The numbers of those who died in detention is given as 3,847, of whom 2,851 died while serving their sentence, 203 under interrogation, 137 as a result of the execution of the death sentence, and 656 in the labour camps.[47] Yet another set of statistics shows that in the period from 1950 to 31 March 1958, 75,808 persons were arrested, of whom 73,636 were convicted. In the same period, 22,007 persons were sent to labour camps and between 1949 and 1958, about 60,000 put under house arrest.[48] Independent sources

[47] These figures were compiled by Service 'C' of the Ministry of the Interior and were communicated to me privately. I have no date for their compilation. The editors of the official history of the *Securitate, Cartea Albă a Securităţii*, appear not to be aware of these figures for they claim that a lack of documentation makes it impossible to give an exact figure for the numbers of persons who died while in the custody of the *Securitate* during the period of terror under Dej (vol.II, p.73). Corneliu Coposu, the secretary of Peasant Party leader Maniu and himself an inmate of Romanian prisons for 17 years, put the numbers of those arrested after 1947 as 282,000 of whom he estimated 190,000 to have died in detention. (Coposu, *Vartan Arachelian*, p.95). His figures appear to be exaggerated. The exact number of those who died in detention will probably never be known.

[48] The use of house arrest in 1949 was illegal since there was no legislation in place to authorise it. The breakdown by year of the figure of 75,808 persons arrested is as follows:

1950: 6,636
1951: 19,236
1952: 24,826
1953: 4,730
1954: 5,073
1955: 3,332
1956: 2,357
1957: 3,257
1958: 6,362

Cartea Albă a Securităţii, vol.III, p.159.

have produced quite a different set of figures; an examination of court records of the period indicates that in the period 1949 to 1960, 134,150 political trials took place involving at least 549,400 accused.[49]

The majority of those sent to labour camps were not tried or sentenced. They were sent there on the orders of the Ministry of the Interior which itself was acting on instructions from Gheorghiu-Dej and the Soviet counsellors. The euphemism 'administratively sentenced' (*condamnat administrativ*), which disguised the illegality of their plight, was used to justify their detention. Not even this fiction was employed to justify the arrest between 1948 and 1950 of the ministers of the pre-Communist regime, the bishops of the Greek and Roman Catholic Churches, and former policemen. There was no offence in the Penal Code to cover their arrest and they were imprisoned on the basis of orders issued by the Ministry of the Interior. This was the fate of Dumitru Caracostea, minister of education in the Gigurtu government of July 1940, and several hundred others who had held ministerial office in the pre-Communist period. Caracostea was arrested in September 1950 and taken overnight to Sighet jail. On his certificate of release, issued on 6 July 1955, there are blank spaces against the number of the arrest warrant and the reason for his detention, proof from the authorities themselves that there was no legal basis for his arrest or for the five years of his imprisonment. Many of those detained in the labour camps were peasants who resisted the introduction of collectivisation through the land reform of 2 March 1949. Their fate offers a graphic example of the use of terror by the *Securitate* to implement the Communist revolution.

The chance discovery in the summer of 1992 of 316 skeletons in a common grave in the grounds of a 19th-century manor house in the village of Căciulaţi, some 20 km north of Bucharest, led to claims that they belonged to victims of *Securitate* executions. Several of the skulls unearthed were said to bear the marks of bullet holes (*România liberă*, 24/25 October 1992, p.1). An inquiry by a team of Argentinian pathologists was inconclusive. The local *Securitate* headquarters was established in the house concerned in 1948 and moved to another building within the grounds in 1951 when the manor house was given to the Romanian Academy. Whether the skeletons are of persons murdered on the spot or, as local belief has it, of families who resisted collectivisation in the 1950s and whose bodies were brought for burial in this remote spot, remains unclear.

[49] M. Lupu, C. Nicoară, G. Onişor, *Cu unanimate de voturi*, Bucharest: Fundaţia Academia Civică, 1997, p.22.

The ideological premise upon which collectivisation was based was contained in the Communist Party resolution of 3-5 March 1949. The main and most difficult task in the construction of socialism, it claimed, was the solution of the peasant problem. According to the party there were five categories of people on the land: the first was the agricultural proletariat, that is landless peasants who numbered some 265,000 families and worked for the *chiabur* or rich peasant; poor peasants made up the second category. They had holdings of up to 5 hectares, which represented over 57% of the total area held by individuals. The resolution considered their plots unproductive as they were scattered in many places over more than one lot, and concluded that these poor peasants would prefer a different form of production. The middle peasants formed the third category and produced 60% of the country's agricultural production. They used only family labour, had holdings of between 5-20 hectares which represented 34% of the total area of cultivated land, and were to provide the nucleus of the collective farms. The fourth category consisted of rich peasants *(chiaburi)* who were so defined because they hired labour or charged rent for machinery, and not because of the size of their holdings. The fifth category had been what remained of the landowning class, whose estates had been broken up by the 1945 land reform and distributed to peasants.[50]

Outlining the task facing the party in imposing collectivisation, Gheorghiu-Dej identified the first as 'the complete liquidation of *chiaburi* property in the village'.[51] The *chiaburi* were not to be admitted to the collective farms. The second objective was to persuade the poor and middle peasants to unite in the collectives. The emphasis was upon persuasion and not coercion and as a preliminary step tillage associations (*întovărăşiri*) were set up. Nevertheless, harsh penalties were introduced for failure to deliver mandatory cereal quotas to the state and it was in opposition to these that the first incidents of peasant resistance were reported. This was in May in the village of Roma in the county of Botoşani when *Securitate* troops fired on demonstrators.[52] Large-scale dis-

50 Ionescu, *Communism in Rumania*, pp.187-9.

51 O. Roske, 'Colectivizarea agriculturii în România, 1949-1962', *Arhivele Totalitarismului*, vol.1 no.1 (1993), p.151, and Roberts, Rumania, p.324.

52 A chronology of collectivisation is to be found in Roske, 'Colectivizarea

turbances occurred in July in Bihor which resulted in the execution by the *Securitate* of sixteen peasants and the deportation of a further 200. There was more violence in August, this time in Arad county where twelve peasants were shot by *Securitate* troops and more than 100 arrested.

Fear of peasant discontent led Ana Pauker, who was entrusted with directing the Agrarian Commission which had been established with the express aim of supervising the creation of the collectives, to proceed cautiously. Her strategy was in direct contradiction to the views of Veretenicov, one of the Soviet advisors to the commission.[53] At a meeting of the commission on 1 September 1949, she approved only four out of twelve proposals to set up collectives; of the remaining eight, she postponed the inauguration of half of them until certain conditions were met, and she rejected the other half outright. She displayed similar reserve at a session of the Council of Ministers on 13 September, when the proposed expropriation of peasant property was discussed:

> 'Purely and simply, there are to be no expropriations from poor and middle peasants for several thousand lei, because they're going to drink away the money and afterwards won't have anything to work with. They must receive other land in return. [...] It's great to have a new railway, but it's not at all great to have peasant discontent.'[54]

Only fifty-six collectives were set up in 1949 in the face of isolated resistance from the peasantry. But in January 1950, the Party Central Committee replaced the Agrarian Commission with an Agrarian Section and gave it increased resources to step up the campaign of collectivisation. Despite this, Pauker rejected 655 of the 900 proposals for collectivisation that were submitted to the Section in April. Her prudence did not carry the day for

---

agriculturii', pp.146-68.

53 The other Soviet advisors were listed as Sevcenco, Potimkin, Zubcov, Bobovnicov, Homeacov and Tomoshenco; see R. Levy, 'The "Right Deviation" of Ana Pauker', *Communist and Post-Communist Studies*, vol.28, no.2, p.251, n.90. A study of Central Committee papers reveals that Pauker, contrary to popular belief generated by Dej and his acolytes, was not an ardent advocate of rapid collectivisation and was indeed guilty of the charge, levelled against her in 1952 after her purge, of 'disregarding Soviet experience and the assistance given by Soviet advisors... and not taking measures that put their advice into practice' (*ibid.*, p.251).

54 *Ibid.*, p.242.

long. In the summer, while Pauker was in Moscow receiving treatment for breast cancer, the pace of collectivisation was suddenly stepped up and in July and August approval was granted for the creation of 1,012 new collectives, regardless of the conditions in the areas concerned. As a consequence resistance from the peasants was country-wide.

The *Securitate* and militia were brought in, often in the middle of the night, to force peasants to register in the collectives. They were threatened with forced labour, or the expulsion of their children from school. Those that refused were arrested and taken to the People's Council headquarters where they were beaten and tortured. In the Cluj region some were given the choice of either paying a huge fine and spending ten years in jail, or joining a collective. Many families were expelled from their homes when their land was absorbed into the collective and received either poor quality land elsewhere in compensation or no land at all.

In a number of regions including Arad, Argeş, Dolj, Bihor, the Apuseni mountains, Vlaşca, Hunedoara and Timişoara, the peasants, sometimes aided by 'partisan groups', were engaged in violent skirmishes with the *Securitate* troops and militia. Peasant opposition to the reform was such that, in some areas buildings on the newly-created collective farms were set on fire. This was the case in the county of Arad where *Securitate* documents show that after a state farm had been destroyed on 31 July 1949, frontier troops were summoned from Radna and restored order on 3 August after arresting ninety-eight persons and shooting twelve peasants from the villages of Apateu, Somoşches, Berechiu and Sepreuş on the spot. Reports signed by the head of the *Securitate* office in Timişoara, Colonel Coloman Ambruş, and his deputy Major Aurel Moiş, give details of what they called 'this rebellion' and mentioned that two other peasants were shot dead 'while trying to escape while under arrest'.[55]

An open rebellion took place in the north of Vlaşca county at the beginning of July. Peasants from more than a dozen villages armed themselves with pitchforks and axes and ransacked the local party offices, destroying photographs of the party leaders and cutting the telephone lines. Communist officials were beaten and driven from the buildings. The security forces were called in and fired

55 *România liberă*, 2 October 1993, p.16.

on the protesters, killing ten of them and wounding many more. These events were repeated in several areas across the country.[56]

The accelerated process of collectivisation coincided with increased pressure applied to the *chiaburi*. After the introduction of land reform, the *chiaburi* had been permitted by the party to rid themselves of the stigma of their class by 'donating' land to the collectives. This practice contributed considerably to the consolidation of the farms since the poorer peasants had little or no land to give. But in the summer of 1950, the Agrarian Section was told by the Party leadership that henceforth '*guilty* [my italics] *chiaburi* should be sent to trial and their land confiscated'.[57] The authorities in some counties dispensed with even this fig-leaf of legality by confiscating the land and sending the *kulaks* and their families to the Danube-Black Sea canal without trial. Thousands suffered this fate. As Gheorghiu-Dej later admitted, 'In the name of the struggle against the *chiaburi* more than 80,000 peasants were sent for trial, the majority of them hard-working peasants, and of them more than 30,000 were tried in public trials.'[58]

Dej claimed that these arrests were made on the orders of Ana Pauker[59] but, as mentioned above, she was in Moscow for six weeks in June and July 1950 receiving medical treatment. She returned there in September and was unable to resume work until December. In her place, Alexandru Moghioroş, a close associate of Dej, issued instructions to the Agrarian Section, including the order of the arrest of *chiaburi*.[60] Furthermore, her statements to the Agrarian Section after she resumed her duties indicate clearly that she regarded her gradual approach to collectivisation as the best one and the use of force against the peasantry as a grave error. In January 1951, she proposed that the Central Committee pass a measure to put on trial those who forced peasants into collectives, declaring that 'those who acted in this fashion are not humans'. Shortly afterwards, she halted the consolidation of the

56 Roske, 'Colectivizarea agriculturii', p.156.

57 Levy, 'Ana Pauker', p.244.

58 Gheorghe Gheorghiu-Dej, *Articole şi cuvântări, iunie 1961-decembrie 1962*, Bucharest: Editura Politiă, 1962, p. 206.

59 Ionescu, *Communism in Rumania*, p.201.

60 Levy, 'Ana Pauker', p.245.

state farms' (GOSTATS), a process that was due to be completed, according to the land reform, by 1952.

Pauker recognised the error of the policy of coercion in collectivisation when addressing the Agrarian Section of the Central Committee on 28 April 1951:

> Instead of continuing on this path [the gradual one], a path that proved to be the best one, a path where things went more slowly and carefully – instead of this path, we began to use methods of forcefully pressuring the peasants to enter the collective farms. [...] Starting in last summer, we proceeded with actions that are absolutely opposed to the line of our party and absolutely opposed to any serious Communist thought. Only someone irresponsible, only an adventurer, only a person cut off from the masses and from our party, only a person who imagines himself as here today and gone tomorrow can think that it is possible to establish collective farms with people who are forced, and that such collective farms can possibly be viable.[61]

An internal party report makes it plain that Pauker halted the creation of new collective farms during the winter of 1950-1951. 'Our first concern', she argued, 'must be the existing collectives, to strengthen them and transform them into examples for the individual peasants.' As a consequence, not one new collective farm was set up in 1951; the sixty-two that were officially established that year (as compared with 971 in 1950) had actually been created and consolidated during the summer and autumn of 1950, but had not yet been formally inaugurated.[62]

Dej, too, showed himself critical of the abuses committed during collectivisation. In a speech delivered on 11 May 1951, he criticised the 'methods of constraint used' which, he said, 'had led to flagrant deviations from the party line'. Some regional committees had organised competitions for the creation of the largest number of collectives, and this had resulted 'in a forced rate of growth in the number of collectives'.[63] But such displays of regret can only strike the reader as cynical, since the Central Committee archives show quite clearly that the party leadership knew full well what

61 *Ibid.*, p.246.

62 *Ibid.*, pp.246-7.

63 Roske, 'Colectivizarea agriculturii', p.158.

'methods of constraint' were being used and did nothing to put a stop to them when they were mercilessy applied.

Indeed, on 3 July 1952 Dej called for the intensification of the campaign against the *chiaburi*, calling on the press 'to mobilise the mass of the working peasantry in the unremitting struggle against the *chiaburi*'.[64] They continued to be arrested in their thousands, often for the most petty oversights such as failing to tie up their dogs. A *Securitate* report of 1953 showed that 34,738 peasants had been arrested in 1951 and 1952, of whom 22,000 were *chiaburi*.[65] Nevertheless, peasant opposition slowed down the progress of collectivisation. By 1955, only 26% of arable land had been collectivised or made over to state farms. In January 1958, there were numerous incidents in the county of Galaţi involving peasants who demanded that they be allowed to withdraw from the collectives, while on 12 January 1958, none other than Nicolae Ceauşescu, as a party secretary for agriculture, is alleged to have given the militia orders to open fire on the villagers of Răstoaca in Vrancea, Moldavia who were against collectivisation.[66] Throughout the following year, collective farms in various districts in Moldavia were attacked by peasants demanding their dissolution, and these actions were repeated across the country over the next three years, right up to the eve of Dej's announcement to a plenary meeting of the Central Committee on 27 April 1962 that collectivisation had been completed.

Its results put 60% of the total area of 15 million hectares of agricultural land in collective farms, 30% in state farms, and left 9% in private hands (this last was upland whose inaccessibility made it impractical to collectivise).[67] The small peasant plots allowed to members of the collectives under the 1949 law represented 6% of the collectivised area, thus giving a total of 15% of land in private ownership after 1962. The cost of collectivisation in human lives and misery is impossible to calculate.

The machinery of terror used against the peasantry to force

64 *Ibid.*, p.160.

65 *Cartea Albă a Securităţii*, vol.II, doc.189, p.426.

66 *România liberă*, 22 April 1996, p.1.

67 In the upland region of Maramureş, for example, only Ieud commune and Săpânţa were collectivised by 1962. The *kulaks* in these two villages who resisted were arrested, tried and sent to prison.

through collectivisation was set in motion by the party to carry out the mass deportations of Serbs and Germans living in the western area of the Banat. These groups were considered a security risk when tension between Yugoslavia and Romania grew following the former's expulsion from the Cominform in June 1948. Stalin coined a new heresy – 'Titoism' – and the satellite states were forced to conduct witch-hunts of senior cadres. Those who were purged served as an example to any who might have placed loyalty to their country before fidelity to Moscow. Following the Soviet lead, Romania and the other Cominform states expelled Yugoslav diplomats in 1949. The Romanian government stopped all rail and postal links with Yugoslavia in January 1950 on the grounds that Yugoslav espionage was taking advantage of them, and in the summer of that year put on trial a group of twelve Romanians of Serbian descent, among them two former employees of the Yugoslav embassy in Bucharest, accused of being 'in the service of the espionage of Tito's Fascist clique'. Three of the defendants were sentenced to death and the others received prison terms ranging from three to twenty-five years.[68]

The deportations from the Banat region began in the summer of 1951. On 14 November 1950 the *Securitate* finalised the deportation plan under the title 'Evacuation plan of the frontier zone with Yugoslavia over a belt of 25 km. of elements who present a danger through their presence in the area'. The operation was expected 'not to exceed three months';[69] 40,320 persons were targeted for deportation from the area of Timişoara, Sînnicolau Mare, Oraviţa, Moldova Nouă, Reşiţa, Almaş, Turnu Severin, Baia de Aramă, Strehaia, Vînju Mare and Pleniţa. The *Securitate* classified the deportees as follows: 1,330 foreign citizens, 8,477 Bessarabians, 3,557 Macedonians, 2,344 persons who had collaborated with the German army during the war, 257 Germans, 1,054 'Titoists', 1,218 people with relatives who had fled abroad, 367 persons who had helped the 'anti-Communist resistance', 731 'enemies of the socialist order', 19,034 kulaks and inn-keepers, 162 former landowners and industrialists, and 341 convicted criminals.

[68] *Trial of the Group of Spies and Traitors in the Service of the Espionage of Tito's Fascist Clique*, Bucharest, 1950.

[69] A register of the numbers deported from the Banat and from which villages is contained in *Rusalii '51 Fragmente din deportarea în Bărăgan*, Timişoara: Editura Marineasa, 1994, pp.217-31. See also *România liberă*, 2 July 1993, p.11.

Many of the adult males had been enrolled in the Communist Party but this did not spare them their fate. Included in the number of deportees were 590 persons who lived outside the frontier zones. Under the plan they were all to be moved to the regions of Ialomiţa in the Bărăgan and Galaţi, more specifically to the villages of Bîlga, Ciulniţa, Călăraşi, Mărculeşti, Feteşti, Andrăşeşti, Perieţi, Bucu, Cioara, Lunca Dunării, Vădeni, Frumuşiţa, Dudeşti and Urleasca.[70]

The deportations themselves began on 16 June 1951 and were carried out by 10,229 officers and men from the Frontier Guards Academy at Oradea and from the Firemen's Training School. The whole operation was carried out under the strict supervision of Major-General Mihai Burcă, the deputy minister of the interior, and Major-General Eremia Popescu, the commander of the Ministry of Interior troops (*trupele de securitate*).[71] For transporting the deportees 2,656 railways carraiges were used and 6,211 lorries. Documents from the *Securitate* show that rumour of the impending deportations had led many people to attempt to cross the frontier secretly into Yugoslavia, while others placed their children with friends and relatives outside the designated zone.

The first trains left between 16 and 20 June 1951. The deportees were only allowed to take what belongings they could carry, the rest of their property being purchased by specially constituted commissions who paid only a fraction of the true value. A shortage of trains meant that many of the deportees had to wait in the burning heat for two or three days in the fields. The special trains were guarded by troops and avoided stops in the main railway stations to prevent any communication with ordinary citizens. Upon arrival fortunate deportees were allocated makeshift clay-walled huts with straw roofs in special settlements, some of which had been given Soviet names, such as 'Iosif Clisitch' in the region of Galaţi where 859 people were placed. Others, even on the *Securitate*'s own admission, were literally 'dumped in the middle of nowhere in the full glare of the sun without the necessary

70 *Rusalii '51*, p.228.

71 Burcă was a mechanic who had joined the Communist Party in his twenties and was one of a group of young Romanians who volunteered to fight in the Spanish Civil War. Like several of his colleagues, he was withdrawn to the Soviet Union after the war and interned for a period. He returned to Romania in October 1944. He died in Bucharest on 21 December 1994.

means of shelter'.[72] The same reports talk of a lack of drinking water and irregular supplies of bread, and many cases of children suffering from over-exposure to the sun. Despite their privations the deportees erected simple houses out of clay and wood and toiled ceaselessly to coax the soil into supporting crops.

A task of the *Securitate* equally as vital as that of removing alleged opponents of the regime was that of 'defending the achievements of socialism' in Romania. For the *Securitate* and the militia May Day, like the other red-letter days in the Communist calendar, was not a holiday as it was for most other citizens. On such a hallowed day, the destruction of a placard or of a poster presented a great danger to the regime through the example it offered and was therefore regarded as a crime against the state. Consequently, the party leadership charged the *Securitate* with keeping a close eye on the crowds and with the careful stage-management of the parades. The first directive in this respect was issued in 1952 by Gheorghe Pintilie and was renewed with only minor modifications up until the overthrow of the regime in 1989.[73]

The *Securitate* was required to 'guarantee the personal security and homes of leading members of the party and to ensure the orderly and peaceful conduct of the festivities throughout the country'. Precise measures included the supervision by *Securitate* officers of the construction of official stands which were guarded day and night by the militia. Officers were ordered to make background checks on every person involved in the construction, and to inspect all the drains and sewers around the stands and on the route taken by the parade. Five days before May Day, all persons who had access to the stands and those instructed by the party to be in charge of the rows and columns of marchers-by were to be verified. Similar checks were made on those serving drinks in the stands and on those who prepared the floats – an officer disguised in overalls would ride on each one.

Major-General Alexandru Drăghici, deputy minister of the interior and head of its political directorate, issued instructions that festooning with flags, ribbons and banners should begin on 28 April and the decorations be removed on 3 May. On official

72 *România liberă*, 2 July 1993, p.11.

73 'Directiva în vederea măsurilor de ordine, pază şi securitate cu ocazia zilei de I MAI 1952', ASRI, Fond 'D', vol.9897, pp.416-27.

buildings flags were to be flown in the proportion of three-quarters red party flags to one quarter the national *tricolore*.[74] As national Communism took the place of Stalinism, so the proportion of national flags increased. The *Securitate* was also given the job of making sure that there were stalls selling fried sausages and soft drinks along the parade route, and that bouquets of flowers were made up for handing to party leaders in the stands.

May Day, the international day of labour, was celebrated in a different fashion in the labour camps and in the prisons. A directive of the Ministry of the Interior, dated 8 April 1953, ordered normal working and a doubling of the guard. The only change for the prisoners was that no food parcels or mail would be delivered.[75]

74 Order no. SO111713 of 18 April 1952.

75 Details of this directive were given to me by Marius Oprea.

7

DEJ'S STRUGGLE FOR DOMINANCE

Neither Dej's struggle for dominance within the Romanian Communist Party, nor his success in maintaining himself at its helm until his death in March 1965, can be understood without consideration of the party's relationship to the Soviet Union. This relationship was, throughout the late 1940s and early '50s, one of total dependence. Unflinching subservience to Stalin characterised the deeds of Dej throughout the years 1944-53 as he acted out scenarios provided by the Soviet dictator, and in 1952 it was Dej alone who, when the order to purge alleged Zionists came, found himself in the position of being offered by Stalin the opportunity to assign the roles.

The purge had an honoured place in Communist practice.[1] Stalin provided the models and sharpened the instruments: Dej knew this and indeed conducted his own purge in the murder of Foriş; but Foriş's fate was settled before the RCP was securely in the saddle and relations with the Soviet Union regularised. After 1948, however, the Soviet context becomes vital in explaining the behaviour of the RCP leadership, including Dej. All of them knew who cracked the whip – but 'Moscow' meant different things to different members: their likelihood of tenure in Bucharest depended on decisions arrived at in Moscow, and in order to influence the decision-making processes, a 'protector' in the upper echelons of the Communist Party of the Soviet Union was necessary. Even then, the Romanian member had to hope that his or her 'protector' would not step out of line and be purged himself.

It is, indeed, relationships with the Soviet Union that defined some interpretations in Western scholarship of the purges in Romania in the early 1950s. These were seen in terms of a conflict between so-called 'local Communists' led by Gheorghiu-Dej, who were

[1] G. Hodoş, *Show Trials: Stalinist Purges in Eastern Europe, 1948-1954*, New York: Praeger, 1987.

interned during the war in Romania, and the 'Muscovites' under Pauker and Luca, who spent the war years in Moscow.[2] But this dichotomy is misleading and incorrect. It was precisely because of Dej's loyalty to Moscow that he was able to eclipse his 'Muscovite' rivals. Newly-available evidence confirms that it was a personal conflict between Dej on the one hand, and Ana Pauker and Vasile Luca on the other, rather than a conflict of ideology, that fuelled the struggle for power.[3]

The release since 1989 in Romania of documents relating to the arrest, interrogation and trial of Lucreţiu Pătrăşcanu, have in particular shed light on the struggle for dominance within the party which spanned the years 1944-54. Within the space of this decade Gheorghe Gheorghiu-Dej oversaw the removal of three comrades whom he regarded as potential rivals for power: two of them, Ştefan Foriş and Lucreţiu Pătrăşcanu, were executed, and the third, Ana Pauker, was reduced to the state of a political corpse.

That Dej should have reached this position was, in part, testimony to his own abilities, as a patient tactician and consummate manipulator. But his consolidation of power depended on his avoidance of giving his Soviet master any reason to question his loyalty. His vulnerability to Stalin's suspicions was all the greater because he alone among the leading figures in the RCP had not been schooled in Moscow and was therefore something of an unknown quantity, as Georgi Dimitrov, Comintern secretary, admitted to Ana Pauker in September 1944.[4] To overcome this disadvantage Dej did two things. First, he surrounded himself with a number of NKVD agents who had been held in prison during the war, and appointed

[2] See Fischer-Galati, *New Rumania*, p.31. Victor Frunză, in his study *Istoria Stalinismului în România*, Bucharest: Humanitas, 1990, p.219, makes a similar division, calling the 'Muscovites' the 'externals' *(exteriori)*, and the 'local Communists' the 'internals' *(interiori)*.

[3] Three scholars in particular pointed out that neither of the two groups, 'local Communists' and 'Muscovites', was so rigidly defined since personal allegiance often cut across this artificial division. Thus Leonte Răutu, who had spent the war in Moscow close to Pauker, aligned himself with Dej, while Miron Constantinescu, a fellow inmate of the internment camp at Tîrgu-Jiu with Dej, associated himself initially with Pauker; see B. Vago, 'Romania' in *Communist Power in Europe, 1944-1949*, London: Macmillan, 1977, p.113; Shafir, *Romania* p.35; and Fischer, *Nicolae Ceauşescu*, p.42.

[4] See below and n.36.

them to senior positions in the security services and the Ministry of the Interior, thereby offering Stalin a guarantee of his loyalty. Among them were Pantelimon Bondarenko, Sergei Nikonov, Pyotr Goncearuc, Misha Postanski and Vania Didenko. The latter was one of Dej's closest friends and had escaped with him in August 1944 from Tîrgu-Jiu.[5] Secondly, Dej used every opportunity to exploit the potential flaws in the actions of his rivals, thereby giving Stalin grounds for doubting their reliability, while at the same time reinforcing his own credentials as a faithful servant. If Stalin was the only person who could call Dej to account, then Dej could get away with anything subject to his master's agreement.

Although Dej was not directly involved in the planning of the coup on 23 August 1944, his victory in the contest for party control secured for him the credit in Communist historiography of playing a leading role not only in the preparations, but also in the events of the day. After the arrest of Lucreţiu Pătrăşcanu in 1948 there was, predictably, no mention till the early 1960s of his part as representative of the Communist Party in the discussions of the National Democratic Bloc preceding the coup. Typical of the regime's version of the coup was the view, enunciated by Dej in a speech in May 1961, that King Michael 'was forced to accept the plan of action established by the Communist Party, the only genuine political force active in the toppling of Antonescu's government'.[6] The magnification of Dej's part in the coup was

[5] Some 50 NKVD agents served time in Romanian prisons during the war; interview with Eduard Mezincescu, 16 June 1994.

[6] G. Gheorghiu-Dej, *Articole şi cuvîntări 1959-1961*, Bucharest: Editura Politică, 1961, pp.438-40; quoted from Shafir, *Romania*, p.32. An interesting sidelight on Dej's interest in the presentation of the coup at this time was given by Ion Mocsonyi-Styrcea, the former marshal of the royal court, who played a key role in the preparations for the coup and was at the palace at the time of Antonesu's arrest. In a letter in English to this author, dated 4 August 1984, he revealed that he was brought from Dej prison 'by train to Braşov on the night of 18 October 1961 and by Black Maria the next night to the brand new Malmaison annex for highly secret unicellular reclusion, to write "the whole truth about the unknown preliminary set-up and final realization of the 23 August 1944 coup d'état": *conditio sine qua non* of my survival, release, amnesty, rehabilitation and justified, though so far neglected, decoration for my well-known important contribution to the successful issue of that historic act, not without hinting that I would be granted the highest possible pension and restitution of the legally recuperable part of my totally confiscated fortune if my wife (who had resumed her Swiss citizenship) returned to Romania instead of claiming for

facilitated by the fact that his rivals for the leadership, Ana Pauker and Vasile Luca, were still in the Soviet Union on 23 August 1944 and could therefore claim no credit at all.

The coup, and the use made of it by Dej, was but one of two events from which we can trace the origins of the internal party struggle for supremacy. The second, which also took place in the summer of 1944 *before* the entry of Soviet troops into Bucharest, was the decision to remove Ştefan Foriş as general secretary of the party in April 1944. The circumstances in which this decision was taken are not entirely clear, for the mists of politically-engineered distortion still linger over the matter. According to the version propagated during the period of Dej's supremacy within the party, a meeting was held on 4 April in the hospital of the Tîrgu-Jiu internment camp involving Dej, Emil Bodnăraş, Constantin Pîrvulescu, Iosif Rangheţ and Chivu Stoica at which Dej demanded the removal of Foriş on the grounds that he was a police informer.[7] In his place a provisional secretariat of Bodnăraş,

---

our reunion abroad. These proposals were made by Drăghici in his *Securitate* director's office and presence, and accepted by me on the only condition that not a word of my text would be censored, altered nor the meaning of a sentence distorted by any part of its omission, which both "comrades" hastened to promise solemnly, eagerly adding that I should therefore sign the typed copies of my eventually illegible handwriting. Yet, after three days, I stopped writing, refused signing nine-tenths of their cleverly "summarized" i.e. tendentiously mutilated versions of my perfectly legible pages, which the respective wardens pretended to have sent in for filing, whence they couldn't be returned. After a week on my last hunger-strike, the prison doctor menancing me with force-pump feeding, I was hurriedly jeep-motored towards midnight 30 or 31 October to a new or restored building of the town's centre, where Gheorghiu-Dej and Bodnăraş received me alone in a pompously decorated huge congress hall and managed to convince me that what had happened was due to a mistake and a wrong interpretation of their sincere desire to get the genuine record of my 1940-1945 memoirs, "including even everything I knew about his [Gheorghiu-Dej's] first Royal audience, with Pătrăşcanu, when I had forced him, namely Dej, to put on *my* black tie... since there was nothing to fear and hide any more from Moscow", whereupon Bodnăraş called for Drăghici who was told to have their dentist put a dental prothesis into my toothless mouth, let me eat, drink and smoke whatever I wanted, and see to prevent anybody interfere with my task! This ended with almost 2,000 typed pages and lasted till the eve of my release, Gara de Nord, Wednesday 28 November 1962 at 4 pm with a second-class ticket for Cîmpulung-Muscel in my torn London jodhpurs' hind pocket, but no cash left to buy a pack of *Plugari* gaspers or an apple to try my third dentition on!'

7 Author's interview with Eduard Mezincescu, 16 June 1994. In an undated

Pîrvulescu and Rangheţ was appointed by those present who also instructed Bodnăraş, Pătrăşcanu and Ion Gheorge Maurer to join the other political parties in an effort to extract Romania from the war with the Soviet Union. Both these decisions were instrumental in establishing the authority of Dej and his associates over the party, and in presenting Stalin with an effective party leadership which played a significant part in the overthrow of Antonescu and in the new government. The latter role provided the basis for the party's claim for broader support within the country and Dej exploited this to the full in the party's propaganda after 23 August 1944.

It is important, however, in the light of the subsequent ascent of Dej, to remember that he was not appointed party leader at this meeting. Nevertheless, in the course of time, Dej came to be portrayed in the Communist media as having been the architect of the decision to exclude Foriş, for it served both as a stick with which to beat rivals such as Pauker who had allegedly questioned his removal, and as a banner of Dej's defence of Romanian interests when the rift with Moscow occurred in the early 1960s.[8] Yet the merit to be gained from Foriş's removal depended on his being proved a 'traitor'. Without that proof his dismissal and, more importantly, his murder had no justification. Barely three years after Dej's death, the accusation of being a 'traitor' made against Foriş was dropped: in April 1968, at the Party Plenary

declaration signed while under interrogation between 1949 and 1954 Foriş's deputy, Remus Kofler, maintained that on 3 April 1944, Foriş revealed to party members that Bodnăraş had recently succeeded in re-establishing contact with the Soviet Union using espionage channels *(pe linie de spionaj)* through the agency of a recently-arrived agent from the Soviet Union (Levy, 'Power Struggles', p.79). One must, of course, handle with caution information extracted from prisoners under torture.

[8] Fischer, *New Romania*, pp.38 and 276, n.10. When Ana Pauker met Pătrăşcanu in Moscow at the time of the armistice negotiations in September 1944 she asked him why Foriş had been removed. Pătrăşcanu replied that he had little knowledge of the affair. Pauker is said to have put the same question to Dej when they met shortly after her arrival in Bucharest on 16 September 1944, being particularly anxious to know the reason because Foriş had been confirmed in his position by the Comintern in 1940. (Author's interview with Eduard Mezincescu, 16 June 1994. Mezincescu, who during the war had been secretary of the Romanian branch of the MOPR, the Comintern-controlled aid organisation, was a protégé of Pauker and was brought into the Foreign Ministry by her in 1948.)

Meeting, Nicolae Ceauşescu condemned Dej for the 'assassination' of Foriş, who was considered 'innocent' of being an enemy agent. Nevertheless, Foriş was still branded as guilty of 'grave shortcomings' in his work which had made his dismissal necessary.[9]

Responsibility for the decision to remove Foriş was consistently attributed to Dej throughout the Communist era, but there are suspicions that it was a decision taken in Moscow. This is because of the key part in its implementation played by Emil Bodnăraş and the involvement of Dej's closest friend, Vania Didenko, an NKVD agent.[10] After Foriş and his assistant Victoria Sârbu were taken into custody by Bodnăraş on 4 April and moved to a safe house,[11] they were instructed by Bodnăraş to write material for the underground party newspaper *România liberă*. This requirement lapsed within a month, causing Foriş and Sârbu to demand 'clarification of their situation'.

In the light of these demands Bodnăraş and Didenko separated Foriş from Sârbu, taking the former away to another safe house until 24 December 1944 when he was reunited with his partner. At the beginning of January 1945, Bodnăraş and Didenko returned, telling the couple that they had been found innocent and that they were free to go to Cluj where the party had found work for them. But it seems that Foriş was not satisfied with this decision and he threatened to go to Hungary and serve the Communists

[9] *Ibid.*, p.131.

[10] Eduard Mezincescu, who had occasion later to discuss in detail the career of Emil Bodnăraş with Serghei Nikonov (Sergiu Nicolau), appointed head of the SSI, the Intelligence Service, under Bodnăraş on 7 December 1946, learned from Nikonov that the replacement of Foriş had been first discussed in the prison hospital at Tîrgu-Jiu in June 1943. Dej's view was that Foriş should simply be ousted. The decision to place Foriş under house arrest was apparently a Soviet one, carried out by Bodnăraş (author's interview with Mezincescu, 16 June 1994). According to a declaration of Victoria Sârbu, given under interrogation on 7 February 1950, Bodnăraş handed Foriş a type-written note ordering him to surrender all party materials and authorising his house-arrest. Bodnăraş told Foriş that the order had come from the Soviet Union (Levy, 'Power struggles', p.79, n.3).

[11] See Chapter 2. According to Ilie Zaharia, a veteran Communist interviewed by Robert Levy, Foriş was only detained for two or three months and was seen looking for work at the party headquarters in August 1944. He was re-arrested in 1945 when Dej and Bodnăraş produced 'proof' that he was working for the *Siguranţa* (Levy, 'Ana Pauker', p.6. I am grateful to the author for providing me with a copy of this unpublished research paper).

there. This would explain why, according to Sârbu, two security agents appeared on 23 March 1945 and took Foriş to the Ministry of the Interior where he was held for several days for questioning about his activities.

Foriş seemed to sense his end was approaching for he made his will on 7 April.[12] At the end of that month, Sârbu gave birth to a daughter whom she named Vera-Victoria. During the following month, Foriş and Sârbu were able to spend a few days together. On 9 June, he went into town to buy food for a trip he intended to make to see one of Sârbu's brothers who lived in the country. That was the last time that a member of Foriş's circle saw him. Later that summer, Foriş's mother came to see Eduard Mezincescu, head of the Patriotic Defence organisation which provided food and money for former Communist detainees, with a request for help in tracing her son but he was unable to help.[13]

Just as the decision to remove Foriş was used as a political expedient, first by Dej and then by Ceauşescu, so too was the order to murder him. The possibility that the order came from Moscow, and that it suited Dej by denying Foriş the chance of a comeback as party leader, should not be overlooked. Some have attributed the decision solely to Dej; others – basing themselves on Ceauşescu's account given at the April 1968 Central Committee plenum at which Foriş was rehabilitated – to a collective decision by Dej, Pauker, Luca, and Teohari Georgescu.[14] It is difficult to

[12] He expressed his pride in his achievements and those of the RCP while admitting also his mistakes and shortcomings. He left most of his modest possessions to Sârbu and his books in German to Remus Kofler. (Betea, 'Foriş', p.44).

[13] Author's interview with E. Mezincescu, 16 June 1994.

[14] See the articles by E. Mezincescu and V. Tismăneanu in *România literară,* nos 21, 27 and 41, 1992 and Shafir, *Romania*, p.34. Pauker's son-in-law, Gheorghe Brătescu, concedes that while his mother-in-law was a party to the order to arrest Foriş, she was not consulted about the decision to murder him which, he alleges, was taken one evening at a secret meeting of Dej, Bodnăraş, and Pintilie. Indeed, after Pauker learned of Foriş's death, she told Dej that Foriş should have been put on trial. Dej replied that the Romanian courts were not competent to handle such a trial. Pauker then said that, in that case, Foriş should have been handed over to the Soviets (interview with G. Brătescu, 30 July 1994). Dej's apparent failure to consult Pauker over the decision to murder Foriş lends weight to the view that Dej, supported by Bodnăraş, had Stalin's authority for the move. In another explanation for the murder, the claim has been made that Foriş had Moscow's backing in autumn 1943 to conclude a

believe that such a move would have been taken without at least the acquiescence of Stalin, especially as it required the liquidation of a former party leader without trial. The fact that according to documents produced at the Party Plenary Meeting of 22-25 April 1968, the assassination was entrusted to Pintilie Bondarenko (Gheorghe Pintilie), an NKVD agent, is similarly not without significance. He, as head of the Political and Administrative Section of the Central Committee whose attributes included party security, admitted to having carried out the death sentence imposed on Foriş. Foriş was seized in the street by Pintilie on Dej's orders and held in cells in the Ministry of the Interior. In the summer of 1946, he was taken by officers under the command of Petre Bulgaru to party headquarters on Aleea Alexandru on the pretext of being questioned there. Upon arrival he had a final discussion with Alexander Nicolski, who asked him about a notebook found in the safe house in which he gave details of his activity during the war. He was then taken to an annexe where he was bludgeoned to death with an iron bar by Gheorghe Pintilie and his chauffeur, Dumitru Mitea (Necin). His body was buried in the grounds of the building.[15]

Persistant inquiries from Foriş's mother about her son's whereabouts led Pintilie to summon her to his office in the summer of 1947. He failed to convince her that no one in the party had any information about him. Pintilie then ordered Gavril Birtaş, head of the security police in Oradea, a town in western Transylvania, to take the old woman and 'silence her'. Pintilie persuaded

deal with Antonescu which involved the sacrifice of the Communists in Romania (Fischer-Galaţi, *New Rumania*, p.21). With plenty of examples of Soviet cynicism from the interwar period to point to, Dej and his interned colleagues decided to preempt this move by removing Foriş and taking over the party before the arrival of the Red Army and the Moscow bureau, which of course included Pauker. The murder of Foriş may well have suited Stalin, for any public revelations about attempts to forge a deal with Antonescu, not to mention one made at the expense of the interned Communists, would have exposed them to charges of duplicity before the Romanian public, have severely embarrassed the Gheorghiu-Dej faction in the party, and damaged Stalin's relations with the Western Allies.

15 Pintilie's admission came in a statement signed on 15 May 1967 and presented to the party commission charged with investigating the death of Foriş. Since this statement offers further testimony to the suspicion held by Dej about Foriş's activity, I have translated it in full in Appendix 3.

Foriş's mother to get into Birtaş's car by saying that her son was in the Oradea area and that Birtaş knew exactly where. Asked later what he had done with her, Birtaş said that he had handed Foriş's mother over to two policemen in Oradea who had thrown her into the Criş river with a millstone hung around her neck.[16]

Dej's internment came to an end on 12 August 1944 when a group of Communists, under instructions from Ion Gheorghe Maurer, managed to extract him from Tîrgu-Jiu. They found shelter for several days with a series of sympathisers in Oltenia, among them an Orthodox priest, Ioan Marina, who put them up in his parish house in Rîmnicul Vâlcea; they then went on to Bucharest.[17] Again, Communist mystification has clouded the truth of subsequent developments regarding the party's leadership. Although Dej was credited throughout the era of his dominance and the Ceauşescu period with being general secretary of the party after the dismissal of Foriş, a study of the party newspaper *Scînteia* reveals otherwise. In its first non-clandestine issue of 21 September 1944, a communiqué signed by Constantin Pîrvulescu was published. Pîrvulescu was styled 'general secretary of the Romanian Communist Party'. The following day's edition printed his photograph with the same title. Over the next few weeks, Pîrvulescu was given titular precedence in the paper when party documents were reproduced, but two other ethnic Romanians, Dej and Pătrăşcanu, were given the most column inches.[18]

16 Ştefănescu, *Istoria Serviciilor Secrete*, p.250; see also Betea, 'Foriş', p.45.

17 The officially sanctioned account of Dej's escape, written by one of the group instructed by Maurer, was published at the height of Dej's power within the Party in 1964; see M. Roşianu, 'Cum a fost organizată evadarea tovarăşului Gheorghe Gheorghiu-Dej din lagărul de la Tîrgu-Jiu în august 1944', *Scînteia*, 18 August 1964, pp.2-3. Marina's part earned him elevation, on Dej's recommendation, to the position of Patriarch in May 1948. Further light is shed on the initiative for the escape by Eduard Mezincescu who told this author that although Bodnăraş, Pîrvulescu and Rangheţ were all in favour of Dej's escape from the camp, Dej himself was reluctant to leave because he felt safer inside than out. He agreed to be released only on condition that Maurer make arrangements that would ensure that Dej would not be hurt during the escape. Maurer therefore contacted the lawyer Grigore Geamănu, a cousin of a senior official in the Inspectorate of Gendarmes in Bucharest, who paid a suitable sum of money to the official to persuade Colonel Şerban Lioveanu, the camp director, to relax security on the perimeter fence on the day planned for the escape.

18 Pîrvulescu's name continued to appear with this title. However, by July 1945

In the first few weeks after the 23 August coup, Pătrăşcanu overshadowed Dej as the most prominent Communist; his gradual eclipse from his leading position illustrated perfectly how Dej exploited Soviet suspicion of a potential rival to his own advantage. In Pătrăşcanu's case there was an added keenness to Dej's motivation; he resented Pătrăşcanu's seniority over him in terms of party membership – he had joined well over a decade before Dej, who was suspicious of his background. Born in the Moldavian town of Bacău in 1900, Pătrăşcanu came from a middle-class family quite removed from the working-class origins of Dej. His father was a writer and professor and he himself achieved distinction in his academic studies, graduating in law at Bucharest University in 1922 and completing a doctorate at Leipzig on the agrarian reform of 1918-21 in Romania. He continued his studies in France, was one of five Communists elected to the Romanian parliament in 1931 although he never took his seat because the elections were declared invalid, and from the autumn of 1933 until the spring of 1934 was the permanent representative of the RCP to the Comintern. On his return to Romania, he worked in the propaganda section of the party in Iaşi. During this period he acted as defence counsel for a number of Communists and was himself arrested six times between 1924 and 1941, although the longest period he was held for questioning was two months.[19]

The contrast between Dej and Pătrăşcanu was even highlighted in their treatment by the authorities. While Dej and associates such as Apostol, Moghioros and Stoica were sentenced to long prison terms, Pătrăşcanu was simply placed under surveillance by the *Siguranţa* and his home frequently searched. This apparent leniency on the part of the police towards Pătrăşcanu was to be used later by Dej to support the accusation that he was a police informer, and after Pătrăşcanu's arrest in 1948 Dej instructed his interrogators to extract confessions from Pătrăşcanu's friends to this effect.[20] Pătrăşcanu's relatively gentle treatment at the hands

---

Scînteia styled him simply as a 'member of the Central Commitee of the RCP' (H. Nestorescu-Bălceşti, 'Structura Conducerii Superioare a Partidului Comunist Român', *Arhivele Totalitarianismului*, vol.2, nos 1-2 [1994], p.334).

19 Fischer, *Nicolae Ceauşesau*, p.40. Pătrăşcanu's own account of these arrests was given in a signed declaration to the *Securitate* dated 7 February 1950; see *Cartea Albă a Securităţii*, vol.II, doc.89, pp. 222-5.

20 In the report of the party commission, set up in November 1965 to clarify

of the Antonescu regime was exemplified by the fact that he was briefly interned on only two occasions during the war, for five months in 1940, and for eight months in Tîrgu-Jiu in 1943,[21] while the rest of the time he was confined to the family villa at the mountain resort of Poiana Ţapului where he wrote two major political studies. In December 1943 he obtained permission to spend twenty days in the capital on medical grounds and extended his stay until May 1944. He was able to do this with the help of his cousins Colonel Ştefan Stoica, who worked at the Ministry of Military Procurement, and Colonel Octav Ulea, who was on the staff of the marshal of the palace. During his stay in the capital Pătrăşcanu was able to meet the king as well as opposition leaders. According to *Siguranţa* records, he was unable to get permission to remain in the capital after May and therefore went into hiding, but this did not prevent him from continuing to negotiate on behalf of the party with the other parties in the NDB between April and August 1944. Pătrăşcanu's subsequent appointment as the only Communist minister in the Sănătescu government, and then as minister of justice from November 1944 until February 1948, enhanced his standing both within some circles in the party and within the country.

Coupled with Dej's resentment of Pătrăşcanu's growing public stature was an envy of his intellectual powers. Dej, by contrast, had little formal education and published nothing. In 1944 and 1945, Pătrăşcanu published two major political studies and was the author of several articles in *Scînteia* on industrialisation in Romania.[22] His analytical publications on the inter-war period had already given him prestige among the intellectuals of the RCP and Dej

---

the circumstances of Pătrăşcanu's arrest, interrogation and execution, this accusation was deemed to be without foundation. See 'Raportul Comisiei de partid, constituită în vederea clarificării situaţiei lui Lucreţiu Pătrăşcanu', *Cuvîntul*, no.35 (1-7 September), 1992, p.9. The report was made public for the first time in September 1992.

21 Pătrăşcanu's release from Tîrgu-Jiu in 1943 came as a result of the intervention of Colonel Magistrate V. Gelep, the secretary-general of the Ministry of Internal Affairs, who had been paid a large sum of money by Pătrăşcanu's wife to secure her husband's release. See 'Raportul Comisiei de partid, constituita în vederea clarificării situaţiei lui Lucreţiu Pătrăşcanu', *Cuvîntul*, no.36 (8-14 September), 1992, p.6.

22 *Sub trei dictaturi*, 1944 and *Un veac de frămîntări sociale*, 1945.

came to fear that he was seeking to capitalise upon this in order to make himself the centre of a popular movement rivalling the Dej-Bodnăraş leadership of the party.[23] This attempt had become manifest in the propagation of the slogan '*Pătrăşcanu la putere*' (Power to Pătrăşcanu!) which was chanted at several Communist-organised meetings held in September and October 1944. It has been suggested that Pătrăşcanu had the support of 'a small group of genuinely revolutionary intellectuals, mostly young and of Jewish extraction, who, like him, were already sickened by the ease with which opportunists, politicians and intellectuals alike, were given full rights in the Communist Party under the new leadership'.[24] A manifestation of Dej's displeasure at Pătrăşcanu's popularity was recalled by Gheorghe Pintilie who related that when a column of supporters shouted out Pătrăşcanu's name at a demonstration in early 1945, Dej tugged his arm and whispered 'Bugger that Pătrăşcanu.'[25]

But while Pătrăşcanu with his neatly groomed appearance and his suit and tie offered a reassuring face of the party to the population, the smoothness of his public image obscured a distrust which the Russians were beginning to feel about him. Pătrăşcanu had aroused the suspicion of the Russians at the armistice negotiations in September 1944 with his close questioning of Molotov over some of the conditions.[26] Bodnăraş, aware of these suspicions, had him

[23] Personal communication to author from Eduard Mezincescu, 30 Dec. 1992.

[24] Ionescu, *Communism in Rumania,* p.95.

[25] Cristian Popişteanu, 'Cazul Grupului Pătrăşcanu (V)', *Magazin Istoric,* no.11 (November) 1991, p.44. Silviu Brucan, a deputy editor of *Scînteia* at the time, also recalled how Pătrăşcanu was want to remark to foreign diplomats at receptions that he should have been party leader. Reports of these remarks undoubtedly reached Dej's ears (conversation with S. Brucan, 15 June 1994). Pătrăşcanu's behaviour at a New Year's Eve party, thrown by Ana Pauker in 1944, shows how little he had in common with some of the party leadership. Pătrăşcanu left before midnight, offering his apologies to Pauker and thanking her for the invitation. When Pauker said that his departure would not look good to Dej, Bodnăraş and others, Pătrăşcanu said that he preferred to see the New Year in with his students at the Faculty of Law (interview with Tatiana Brătescu, 30 July 1994). Several years later Pauker told her son-in-law, Gheorghe Brătescu, that she had a great admiration for Pătrăşcanu as a person but did not agree with his anti-Soviet views (interview with G. Brătescu, 30 July 1994).

[26] On his return from the armistice negotiations in Moscow on 14 September 1944, Pătrăşcanu told Corneliu Coposu, who had an office adjacent to his in

placed under close surveillance following his return from Moscow in September, as he revealed under interrogation in 1949.[27]

Soviet suspicions about him can only have been confirmed by comments made by Vasile Luca in a conversation with V. Morev, the TASS correspondent in Romania, in December 1944. Luca is reported to have said that Pătrăşcanu's words 'did not always reflect the point of view of the Communist Party'. Pătrăşcanu, Luca continued, 'is not even a member of the Central Committee, he entered by chance into history, and found himself at the helm of events. He is not a consistent Communist.'[28]

---

the council of ministers where he (Coposu) was secretary-general, that an audience with Zhdanov on 11 September had depressed him and made him pessimistic about Romania's future. Zhdanov, whom Pătrăşcanu had known since he served as Romanian delegate to the Comintern, met him with the reproach: 'What are you doing here *Mr* [i.e. not Comrade] Pătrăşcanu?' 'Well, we overturned the dictatorship and brought Romania onto the side of the Allies, and we've come to sign the armistice.' To which Zhdanov replied: 'You've done wrong, for you've upset all our plans.' These plans were for the Soviets to capture Bucharest, overthrow Antonescu, and to treat Romania as a conquered enemy, without the impediment of a Romanian government to deal with ('Exilul Românesc: Identitate şi Conştiinţă istorică,' *Lupta*, no.232 [7 Oct. 1994], p.5).

27 'Immediately after my return from Moscow in September 1944, I discovered that...Emil Bodnăraş had ordered Comrade [Vania] Didenko to tail me by car at the time when I was minister without portfolio. I never discussed with Bodnăraş why he had taken this step, but I did, however, get an explanation from Bodnăraş himself who told me in a conversation at that very time that in two weeks, exactly the period which I had spent in Moscow, anyone can become a traitor or a spy. He then explained to me the step he had taken. In December 1944 Emil Bodnăraş summoned me to the Central Committee and took out a file – my file – and asked me a series of questions, from which it clearly emerged that I was under surveillance.' (Undated declaration of L. Pătrăşcanu, ASRI, Fond Y, File 40002, vol.1, p.23, translated from Levy, 'Power Struggles', p.85.)

28 The Archive of The Ministry of Foreign Affairs of the Russian Federation, fond 0125, opis 33, folio 127, file (box) 6, pp.128-34. (I am grateful to Prof. Florin Constantiniu for drawing my attention to this note.) Copies of Morev's note, dated 10 January 1945, were sent in the following order: (1) Stalin, (2) Molotov, (3) Malenkov, (4) Beria, (5) Vyshinski, (6) Dekanozov, (7) to the file. Vladimir Georgievich Dekanozov, a Georgian, was a close associate of Beria who brought him to Moscow in 1938 to serve as head of INU, the foreign intelligence department of the NKGB/NKVD. In 1940 he was appointed Soviet minister to Berlin, and in 1941 became a deputy people's commissar for foreign affairs alongside Andrei Vyshinski. He was arrested in July 1953 at the same

Moscow's knowledge of Pătrăşcanu's secret meetings with members of the National Peasant and National Liberal parties with a view to finding a way out of the *impasse* created by King Michael's demand on 20 August 1945 for the Groza government's resignation hardened those suspicions, as the party inquiry into the Pătrăşcanu case reported in 1968. Although Pătrăşcanu later declared under interrogation that he had informed the party about these discussions with Grigore Niculescu-Buzeşti, Victor Rădulescu-Pogoneanu, Constantin Vişoianu, and Ion Mocsony-Styrcea, all confidants of the king, he admitted concealing the proposal made to him that he should become prime minister.[29] Their deliberations, in any case, were rendered pointless in the face of the Russians' firm rejection of Michael's demand and his eventual submission.[30]

Dej was to play on this Soviet distrust to block Pătrăşcanu's election to the Politburo at the first National Conference of the Party which opened on 17 October 1945.[31] While Pătrăşcanu was elected to the Central Committee, he did not find a seat on the seven-member Politburo, four of whom – Dej, Pauker, Luca, and Georgescu – were declared secretaries. According to Dumitru Petrescu, the political head of the army and a fellow member of the Central Committee (although his military position prevented this from being made public), Pauker supported Pătrăşcanu's inclusion in the Politburo over the objections of Dej and the matter was allegedly raised by all four secretaries with Stalin during a visit to Moscow.[32] Petrescu claimed that Stalin came down on the side of Pauker, which would explain why, according to the 1968 report of the Party Commission set up to look into the Pătrăşcanu case, he was coopted into the Politburo in July 1946.[33]

time as Beria and executed alongside him in December.

29 'Raportul Comisiei de partid, constituită în vederea clarificării situaţiei lui Lucreţiu Pătrăşcanu', *Cuvîntul*, no.38 (22-28 September), 1992, p.6.

30 A. Şerbulescu [Belu Zilber], *Monarhia de Drept Dialectic*, Bucharest: Humanitas, 1991, p.68.

31 Ionescu, *Communism in Rumania*, p.118.

32 'Declaration of Dumitru Petrescu to the Party Commission of Inquiry into the Pătrăşcanu case, dated 2 November 1967' quoted in C. Popişteanu, 'Un epilog neaşteptat: Malenkov aprobă lichidarea lui Lucreţiu Pătrăşcanu', *Magazin Istoric*, no.3 (March) 1992, p.38.

33 'Raportul Comisiei de partid, constituită în vederea clarificării situaţiei lui Lucreţiu Pătrăşcanu', *Cuvîntul*, no.35 (1-7 September), 1992, p.8. The first mention

Yet there were those among the Soviets who were prepared to back Pătrăşcanu. He revealed under interrogation in 1949 that General Susaikov, the head of the Allied (Soviet) Control Commission, had appealed to him not to resign as minister of justice following an attack on him by Gheorghe Apostol, an ally of Dej, at the National Conference. Such encouragement led Pătrăşcanu to feel that he was regarded as a key figure by the Soviets and that he could hope to continue to play a major role in Romania's future.[34]

At the same time, his reservations about Soviet intentions led him to see in the Americans and British a potential counterweight. Through his colleague Belu Zilber, he maintained close contact with American and British officials in Bucharest and confided in them. His most regular links were with officers of the Western Allies' intelligence services. The two Communists had their first meeting with officers of the American Office of Strategic Services on 21 October 1944 and opened an association which lasted until 1946. Both Pătrăşcanu and Zilber impressed the Americans with an honesty which the latter considered rare in Romanian political circles.[35] To one of his American contacts, the historian and OSS officer Henry Roberts, Pătrăşcanu explained that 'the working class movement [in Romania] was just getting under way and represented a potential rather than actual strength'. The Communists, therefore, should not seek power through force but should act as a loyal opposition during the period of economic reconstruction until such time as they could assume political authority through popularity.[36]

---

of Pătrăşcanu as a member of the Politburo of the RCP is in *Scînteia* in its edition of 24 July 1946, p.1; see Nestorescu-Bălceşti, 'Structura Conducerii a PCR', p.357.

34 Levy, 'Power Struggles', p.87.

35 The views of Pătrăşcanu and Zilber about developments in Romania are recorded in OSS reports which have been analysed by Eduard Mark, 'The OSS in Romania, 1944-45: An Intelligence Operation of the Early Cold War,' *Intelligence and National Security*, vol.9, no.2 (April 1994), pp.320-44.

36 Both Pătrăşcanu and Zilber revealed themselves as true Marxists *and* as opponents to Soviet Communism. Their ideological opposition soon came to be bolstered by patriotic indignation: Soviet reparation demands were described by Zilber as 'ridiculous and impossible'. This anti-Russian feeling sometimes clouded their judgement. Zilber, for example, confidently predicted that Stalin would not

Until the return of Pauker and Luca from the Soviet Union in mid-September 1944, the leadership of the RCP was composed principally of ethnic Romanians who had spent the war years in Romania: Dej, Pătrăşcanu, Pîrvulescu, Georgescu, and Apostol. Included in this group was Bodnăraş, a Romanian of Ukrainian and German parents. But this group was, with the exception of Bodnăraş, unknown to the Soviets and it was precisely because Stalin and Dimitrov, the head of the post-1943 'frozen' Comintern, had little idea of what was happening among the Communists in Romania, that Dimitrov ordered Ana Pauker to assume the leadership of the party.[37] During an interrogation by a party commission in June 1956, Pauker said that she was ordered by Dimitrov to return to Romania in September 1944 with two radio-transmission specialists. Pauker was apparently reluctant to do this: 'Comrade Dimitrov', she explained, 'I am a woman, I haven't been in Romania during the war, I was in prison [in Romania] and I've no idea what the situation is; ten years have passed and it is a difficult

---

back the Romanian Communists after Rădescu opened his attacks on them in February 1945 (*ibid.*, p.333).

37 Although the Comintern was officially dissolved at the beginning of June 1943, it continued to operate in a reorganised fashion till the autumn of 1945. Its central organisation and relations with the Communist parties was subordinated to the Section for International Information of the Central Committee of the Communist (Bolshevik) Party of the Soviet Union. Officially, its head was Sherbakov, candidate member of the politburo and secretary of the Central Committee, but in reality, it was directed by Georgi Dimitrov who, in June 1944, received the formal position of head. A resolution of the politburo confirmed the section's place in the organisational structure of the Central Committee of the Soviet Communist Party. Documents from the Central Committee and those of other Communist parties show that long-term objectives and current problems of the satellite Communist parties played an important part in the section's work. After the return at the end of the war of many of the activists who worked in the Section for International Information to their countries of origin (e.g. Dimitrov to Bulgaria), the section operated as a foreign policy arm of the Central Committee of the Soviet Communist party under the direction of Mihail Suslov. It was an important instrument of supervision of the East European Communist parties and was responsible for drawing up and transmitting Soviet directives. To this end coded radio messages were sent and meetings held with party activists who regularly visited Moscow. Another means used was the frequent visits of section members to the East European countries. Those whose reported on Romania, apart from Suslov, included L. Baronov, M. Burtsev, A. Kuznetzov and I. Medvedev (see L. Ghibianski, 'URSS şi câteva aspecte ale formării blocului sovietic în Europa Orientală' in *6 Martie 1945*, pp.254-61.

thing you are asking me to do. I am a woman, a Jewess, and an intellectual.' She then claimed to have told Dimitrov that Dej should be the party leader: 'We don't know too much about him, I saw him for a couple of hours at Caransebeş [jail], but I knew that he was a very popular comrade, a railwayman and a tried and trusted figure.' Dimitrov disagreed: 'We haven't had any information for the last five years from Romania. We don't know any one, but you we do know.'[38] Dimitrov also probably had in the back of his mind the fact that, unlike Pauker and indeed, Pătrăşcanu, Dej had not been exposed to the discipline of Comintern instructors, either in Moscow or elsewhere.

Thus the predominance of the Dej group in the RCP leadership changed with the arrival of Ana Pauker. She was flown to Bucharest on 16 September 1944 in a Soviet military aircraft with her daughter Tatiana and upon arrival at Popeşti-Leordeni airfield was whisked away to a RCP safe house. A day or so later, she was visited by Dej and immediately found herself at odds with him. In the very first meeting she attended of the provisional party leadership, Pauker is said to have ridiculed Pîrvulescu and to have given Dej, Bodnăraş and the others present the feeling that she had come from Moscow

38 Levy, 'Power Struggles', pp. 79-80. Levy quotes from a transcript of Pauker's interrogation by Alexandru Moghioroş, Constantin Pîrvulescu and Ion Vinţe dated 18 June 1956. Pauker's cover was an order from the Political Directorate of the Red Army to join the 'Political Directorate of the Second Ukrainian Front' in Bucharest in order to supervise the publication of the Romanian-language Red Army newspaper *Graiul Nou.* (E. Mezincescu, 'Punct', *România literară*, no.9 [9-15 March 1994], p.14). In reality, she had two missions: the first, to assume leadership of the party and second, to make regular reports to Moscow using the two radio operators about what was happening within it. Eduard Mezincescu effectively torpedoes assertions that Pauker was met at the airport by Dej, on which occasion she allegedly berated him for removing Foriş. She had, in fact, been seen in the northern Moldavian town of Botoşani on 7 April 1944 with the advancing Soviet forces. She was dressed in Soviet military uniform and was a political officer of the Second Soviet Army. She took charge of the reorganisation of the local authorities in which Communists were given the leading positions (Şlomo Leibovici, 'Cum au apărut fruntaşii comunişti Ana Pauker şi Vasile Luca la Botoşani în preajma lui 23 August 1944', *Magazin Istoric*, vol.29, no.12 [December 1995], pp.26-7). Soviet agents worked in conjunction with a radio-operator to communicate details to Moscow of German troop movements and of political developments in Romania throughout the war. One such team, run by an agent called Lowin, was caught in the Vatra Luminoasă district of Bucharest; its Russian radio operator shot himself (C. Troncota, *Eugen Cristescu*, Bucharest: Roza Vanturilor, 1994, pp.438-9).

with precise instructions to reorganise the party. 'She waved around a piece of paper which she kept taking out and putting back in her handbag, to give us the impression that these were the orders which she had received', recalled Bodnăraş in a politburo meeting of March 1961.[39]

Pauker was particularly critical of the party's involvement in the 23 August coup, leaving Dej perplexed. 'Now I don't know what to believe. Comrade Ana might have discussed this matter with the Soviet comrades and if it is their view that it would have been better for them to have entered Bucharest as a conquering army, thereby ridding themselves of the king and of the bourgeois parties, there might be something in that', Dej admitted to Silviu Brucan, a young journalist on *Scînteia.*[40] She expressed a similar view to Lucreţiu Pătrăşcanu, saying that it would have been better if they (i.e. Pauker and the Soviets) had come and the Communists in Romania had not carried out the coup.[41] The convenience of collective leadership masked the struggle for control of the party.

Pauker's deputy in taking over the leadership of the party was Vasile Luca. He returned to Romania in October 1944.[42] Within a month, Luca had joined Pauker and Dej to form the leading triumvirate of the party, with the latter two appearing to have equal prominence with each other. However, according to Pauker's daughter and to Pătrăşcanu, Ana Pauker was, in effect, general secretary till the RCP National Conference of October 1945.[43]

39 Stenogram of the Politburo meeting of 13-14 March 1961, p.158. I am grateful to Vladimir Tismăneanu, Robert Levy and Marius Oprea for a sight of this document.

40 S. Brucan, *Generaţia Irosită*, Bucharest: Univers & Calistrat Hogaş, 1992, p.56.

41 Deposition of Elena Pătrăşcanu, Lucreţiu's wife, made in 1967 in preparation for the Plenum of April 1968 at which Lucreţiu was rehabilitated (Archive of the Executive Committee of the CC of the RCP, no.264/18.Feb.1972). My thanks to Marius Oprea for showing me this document.

42 Recently published testimony has placed him in the northern Moldavian town of Botoşani in June 1944, when he was allegedly seen in the uniform of a Soviet officer at the time of the Red Army's entry (M. Stoian, 'Punctul pe i', *România literară*, no.9 (9-15 March), 1994, p.15) but according to his own testimony, given under interrogation in March 1954, he returned in October (Levy, 'Power Struggles', p.81, n.1).

43 Author's interview with Tatiana Brătescu, 30 July 1994. Pătrăşcanu made the same claim in a declaration under interrogation dated 2 November 1949 (*ibid.*, p.80, n.4).

Their evidence contradicts the account given by Silviu Brucan of Dej's elevation to the position of general secretary. Brucan, who at the time was a deputy editor of *Scînteia* but still a junior member of the party, has claimed that Stalin anointed Gheorghiu-Dej general secretary during the latter's visit to Moscow in January 1945. Dej did, indeed, pay a visit to Moscow from 31 December 1944 to 16 January 1945,[44] the official purpose of which was for Dej, in his capacity as minister of communications in the Rădescu government, to discuss economic and transport problems with Stalin. The real aim was, Brucan alleges, to allow the Soviet leader to size up Dej for himself.[45] Dej gave Brucan an account of his meeting with Stalin, at which Vyacheslav Molotov, the Soviet prime minister, was also present. Stalin came straight to the point by telling Dej that he had invited him in order to discuss the leadership of the RCP. In response to Stalin's question as to the most urgent question facing the party, Dej replied that there were two such tasks: the first, to defeat the Germans; the second, to revive the Romanian economy. Stalin agreed, at which point Molotov, a close friend of Ana Pauker, intervened to say that he had spoken to her the day before and that she had underlined the priority of the military front.[46] After reflection Stalin addressed Molotov: 'My dear Vyacheslav Mikhailovich, Ana is a good, reliable comrade, but you see, she is a Jewess of bourgeois origin, and the party in Romania needs a leader from the ranks of the working class, a true-born Romanian.' Stalin then came up to Dej and held out his hand with the words: 'I have decided. I wish you every success, comrade secretary-general.'[47]

[44] ASRI, Fond D, Dosar 7432, p.172.

[45] S. Brucan, *The Wasted Generation*, Boulder, CO: Westview Press, 1993, p.42.

[46] Pauker's connection to Molotov was through her close friendship with his wife, Polyana Zhemchuzhina, who was later arrested in 1949 as part of Stalin's anti-Semitic witch-hunt and sent into internal exile.

[47] S. Brucan, *The Wasted Generation*, p.42. Doubts about Dej even meeting Stalin during his visit to Moscow are conveyed in a telegram from Lord Halifax, British ambassador in Washington, to the Foreign Office, dated 3 February 1945. Burton Berry, the senior US political representative on the Allied Control Commission in Romania, had reported on 30 January a conversation with the marshal of the court in which the latter stated that King Michael 'had talked with Gheorghiu-Dej who confessed that he had not (repeat not) had interviews with Soviet leaders but had "gained the general impression" that the Romanians'

If we believe Brucan's account, we have difficulty in explaining why, in the light of Stalin's alleged decision, the question of the party leadership should have come up again in a meeting between Molotov and Pauker held in Moscow in early summer 1945. According to her family, the question was raised by Stalin and Pauker ruled herself out as leader on the grounds that she was Jewish, that she was a woman, that she was an intellectual and not a worker, and that she had spent the war years in Moscow. She herself recommended Dej. Molotov expressed pleasure with her answer, declaring her 'a clever woman', but her son-in-law suspected that Pauker secretly wished that Molotov had shown regret at her self-effacement.[48]

If Pauker and Dej shared the public stage as the principal figures in the Communist Party at this time, there is no doubt that behind the scenes Emil Bodnăraş was a pivotal, if ambiguous, figure. Even now it is far from clear where his ultimate loyalties lay. He commanded considerable authority as Moscow's most trusted agent and his credentials as an NKVD officer made him the obvious choice for the position of secretary-general to Prime Minister Petru Groza, to which he was appointed on 17 March 1945. On 27 April, Groza signed an order giving Bodnăraş control of the SSI, the Foreign Intelligence Service.

Bodnăraş had developed a close personal bond with Dej, which went back to their days together in the prison of Doftana. This relationship served Dej well in offering his Soviet masters, through the person of Bodnăraş, a guarantee of his obedience, and helped to offset any claim that Pauker could advance of a close relationship with the Kremlin. But Bodnăraş was a master of deviousness and was prepared to file negative reports equally upon Dej, as well as upon Pauker and Luca, to senior Soviet officials. In a written statement given immediately after being purged in 1953, Pauker declared: 'Between 1945 and 1946 comrade Bodnăraş submitted reports against Luca and me and emphasised the fact that reactionary

---

position *vis-à-vis* the Russians would be improved if a Communist government were installed.' Commenting on the telegram, a Foreign Office hand notes, 'Dej's confession suggests that he and Pauker have claimed Russian support for their programme without having really received it' (FO 371/48547. R2516/28/37).

48 Mircu, *Dosar Ana Pauker*, p.141, and author's interview with Dr G. Brătescu, 30 July 1994.

circles were talking too often about us both as party leaders. It was then proposed that we should be removed from Romania.'[49] The idea to remove Pauker and Luca, came, Pauker claimed later, from Andrei Vyshinski.[50] Vyshinski strongly disapproved of the formal pact made in August 1945 between Teohari Georgescu, acting for Pauker, and Nicolae Pătraşcu, a leader of the Iron Guard, which admitted into the ranks of the Communist Party a considerable part of the membership of the Fascist organisation.

Vyshinski put the proposal to remove Pauker to Dej and the latter brought up the matter with Stalin during a visit to Moscow in February 1947. Pauker was urgently summoned to join them. At a meeting of all three Stalin asked rhetorically whether nationalism existed in the Romanian Party – a reference to the ethnic origin of Pauker and Luca – and then stated: 'we are a party of class, not of race'.[51] In his own account of the meeting Dej responded to Stalin: 'We are not aware of such matters, you are probably thinking of the Pătrăşcanu case. It is a well-known one.' Stalin replied, 'No, it is not well-known.' Whilst hinting at a reprimand for Dej, this incident is indicative not only of Dej's rivalry with Pauker and Luca, but also of Vyshinski's preference for Dej over Pauker and Luca. As long as Molotov remained in office, Pauker could rely upon the support of the foreign minister to carry her over the obstacle of his deputy.

She could also take solace from Bodnăraş's servility as an agent of the Soviets. In a confrontation with Pauker, Luca and Bodnăraş in early summer 1947, Dej was accused by Bodnăraş of leaning too much towards the British and Americans. Bodnăraş repeated his complaint to General Susaikov, deputy head of the Allied

49 Levy, 'Power Struggles', p.83.

50 Pauker revealed this on 18 June 1956 to a party commission, set up to interrogate her, which was composed of Alexandru Moghioroş, Constantin Pîrvulescu and Ion Vinţe (*ibid.*, p.83, n.3). Dej confirmed in a meeting of the Romanian Politburo on 29 November 1961 that the idea to remove Pauker was planted in his mind in January 1946 by Vyshinski; see 'Stenograma Şedinţei Biroului Politic al CC al PMR din ziua 29 noiembrie 1961', pp.12–13, reproduced in *Sfera Politicii*, no.48, 1997, p.36. The relevant extract from the Politburo minutes is reproduced in Appendix 4 of this book.

51 *Ibid.* According to Tatiana Pokivailova, Dej's proposal to Stalin to oust Pauker and Luca was put in February 1947; 'Tragica greşeală a lui Lucreţiu Pătrăşcanu', *Magazin Istoric*, vol.30, no.8 [August 1996], p.49.

Control Commission, adding that 'radical steps should be taken'. Susaikov communicated this denunciation on 10 June to Mikhail Suslov, secretary of the Soviet Party Central Committee, but added his own comments to the effect that its author was wide of the mark; Dej had made an appeal to the British and Americans for some economic assistance but only because he felt that the Soviet Union was itself experiencing economic difficulties.[52]

These divisions in the party leadership were echoed in a detailed report on the political situation in Romania compiled by a senior official in the Section for International Relations of the Soviet Communist Party. V. Lesakov visited Romania from 7-20 August 1947, and six days after his return to Moscow submitted his findings to his chief, L.S. Baranov (see Appendix 2). He relayed General Susaikov's view that Dej was seeking to oust Pauker and Luca from the party leadership.[53]

Ostensibly, collective leadership of the party continued throughout the period from 1945 until 1948. At the first post-war National Party Conference of October 1945 no new general secretary was named by *Scînteia* and four of the seven-member Politburo, namely Gheorghiu-Dej, Pauker, Luca, and Teohari Georgescu, were declared secretaries. Gheorghiu-Dej presented the political report to the conference, while Pauker gave the report on the party statutes; the precedence given to these two in the party newspaper, with Dej's name being listed first in alphabetical order, was maintained for the next three years.[54] Gheorghiu-Dej was appointed 'political' secretary i.e. general secretary by the secretariat[55] although a record of this meeting has only recently entered the public domain.[56] Dej's public role had been enhanced by his inclusion in November 1944 in the second Sănătescu government as minister of transport

52 G. P. Muraschko, A.F. Noskowa, T.Wolokitina, 'Das Zentralkomitee der WKP(B) und das Ende der "nationalen Wege zum Sozialismus"', *Jahrbuch für Historische Kommunismusforschung*, 1994, p.17.

53 The notes of Lesakov's discussions with Susaikov, Luca, Pauker and Dej, which were annexed to his report for Baranov, were published by Ioan Chiper *Dosarele Istoriei*, no.3(8) 1997, pp.61-3. As they shed an invaluable light upon the divergences within the leadership of the RCP, they are translated in full in Appendix 2.

54 Fischer, *Nicolae Ceauşescu*, p.44.

55 Ionescu, *Communism in Rumania*, p.188.

56 Levy, 'Power Struggles', p.82, n.1.

and communications, and was consolidated in the Groza government of March 1945 when his portfolio was enlarged to include public works. Joining fellow Communists Dej and Pătrăşcanu in the government was Georgescu, who was promoted from under secretary to head the Ministry of the Interior. In November 1946 Dej took over as minister of national economy (renamed the following year as industry and trade), and in this capacity he ensured that Romania's economic obligations to Russia under the Armistice Agreement were met while at the same time taking stock of national resources and wealth in preparation for nationalisation. This particular ministerial responsibility required several visits to Moscow which Dej doubtless used to impress upon the Soviet leadership his obedience.

Pauker's grand leap into the public arena came on 7 November 1947 when she was appointed foreign minister.[57] She was joined by Vasile Luca, who was named minister of finance on the same day. Ana's leading position within the party was translated into a senior position of state, one which was guaranteed to bring her the greatest international exposure, albeit of a notorious kind.[58] A top-level delegation led by Prime Minister Groza, Dej, and Pauker left for Moscow on 4 February 1948. There they signed a Treaty of Friendship, Cooperation and Mutual Assistance. But the photograph of the delegation's departure from Moscow on 11 February, published in *Scînteia,* indicated the Soviet view of precedence in the RCP, even if the caption beneath it, entered in Bucharest, did not reflect this. The line-up for the photograph, dictated by the Soviet authorities, showed Groza, Molotov, Dej,

[57] Major changes of personnel had already taken place in the Romanian Foreign Ministry. See Appendix 5.

[58] Since Pauker was minister of foreign affairs she became better known to the West than her colleagues. The reactions were frequently unfavourable. In a lengthy article in *Time* (20 September 1948) she was described thus: 'Now she is fat and ugly; but once she was slim and (her friends remember) beautiful. Once she was warmhearted, shy and full of pity for the oppressed, of whom she was one. Now she is cold as the frozen Danube, bold as a boyar on his rich land and pitiless as a scythe in the Moldavian grain.' Her fidelity to Moscow attracted a number of jokes. In June 1952, when Pauker was purged, *Time* recounted one of them: 'One sunny day in Bucharest, as the story goes, a friend stopped Ana Pauker in the street and asked: "Ana, why are you carrying an umbrella? It's not raining." Replied Romania's no.1 Communist: "It's raining in Moscow. I heard it on the radio."'

and Vyshinski in the front row. Pauker and Luca were relegated to the second row. Dej, second only to Prime Minister Groza in the Romanian delegation in the photograph, was identified as head of the RCP. However, because of her position on the far left of the photograph, Pauker was listed in the caption first, followed by Groza, Luca, Molotov, Dej and the others.[59]

Stalin's preference for Dej was confirmed at the First Congress of the new Romanian Workers' Party, formed from the union of the RCP and the Social Democratic Party, and held on 21-23 February. Dej was elected general secretary while Pauker and Luca were appointed to the party secretariat and the Politburo. Dej's elevation to a position of *primus inter pares* in the party was complemented by the final eclipse of his earlier rival Pătrăşcanu. Although the latter had been pictured in *Scînteia* only ten days earlier greeting the Romanian delegation upon its return from Moscow, he was suddenly accused in a speech given at the congress by Teohari Georgescu, the minister of the interior, on 22 February of 'becoming an exponent of bourgeois ideology' and of 'over-estimating the forces of the class-enemy, potentially helped by the Western imperialist powers'.[60] Pătrăşcanu was not elected to any of the RWP bodies and shortly afterwards he was dismissed from the ministry of justice. The final sanction upon him came after a few weeks when he was banned from giving his lectures at the Bucharest law faculty.[61]

59 Fischer, *Nicolae Ceauşescu*, p.46.

60 Ionescu, *Communism in Rumania*, p.152.

61 Pressure was brought to bear on George Fotino, a private secretary to Georgescu, to 'unmask' Pătrăşcanu in front of the students but Fotino alerted Pătrăşcanu to this and as he entered the classroom the first words of his lecture were already on his lips, thereby denying Fotino the opportunity to denounce him (interview with G. Fotino, 9 April 1994).

8

THE DOWNFALL OF LUCREŢIU PĂTRĂŞCANU

Pătrăşcanu's downfall cannot be attributed solely to Dej. While it is clear that Dej disliked Pătrăşcanu, and that his behaviour had angered other senior Party members,[1] there is strong evidence to indicate that Moscow was the source of the order for his demise.[2] In Soviet eyes, a catalogue of 'errors' had been committed by him since the coup of 23 August. Their distrust of him had been

[1] Most importantly, Bodnăraş. In a memorandum addressed to Nicolae Ceauşescu, secretary-general of the Communist Party, at the time when the latter had ordered an inquiry into the abuses committed by the *Securitate* (1967-8), Anton Raţiu, a former commander of the 'Patriotic Guards', claimed to have been present at a discussion at the beginning of November between Bodnăraş and Vania Didenko, an agent of the NKVD in Romania who had been released after 23 August 1944. Bodnăraş commented on the fact that, at a meeting on 7 November 1944 in the 'ANEF' stadium in Bucharest, the slogan 'Pătrăşcanu as prime minister' had been chanted. Bodnăraş remarked: 'That man is getting too big for his boots. We've got to get something on him! Pantiusha, Serghei, Vania and Misha should tail him!' (State Archives, Bucharest, Archive of the Central Committee of the Romanian Communist Party, fond 95, file 122.420, p.4). I am grateful to Claudiu Secaşiu for this information. His paper 'Serviciul de Informaţii al PCR; Secţia a II-a informaţii şi contrainformaţii din cadrul Comandamenţului formaţiunilor de luptă patriotică (FLP)', *6 Martie 1945*, p.153, is also noteworthy. The four men designated by Bodnăraş were Pintilie Bondarenko, known as Pantiusha (he later called himself Gheorghe Pintilie), Seghei Nikonov, Ivan/Vania Didenko (known later as Ioan Vidraşcu) and Misha Postanski (later Vasile Posteucă). They were among a group of about forty NKVD agents who had been sent to Romania in the inter-war period and captured. Their shared experience of prison with Dej made them his faithful servants and with Bodnăraş, they could vouch for Dej's *bona fides* to Moscow.

[2] Charlotte Gruia, a senior official in the Party's Control Comission, and Eugen Szabo, a *Securitate* officer, both interviewed by Robert Levy, maintain that the Romanian politburo received orders from Stalin late in 1947 to link Pătrăşcanu with the arrested leaders of the National Peasant and National Liberal parties, Iuliu Maniu and Constantin Brătianu (see Levy, 'Ana Pauker', p.153).

fuelled in particular by his rash display of patriotism in a speech delivered in Cluj on 13 June 1945 in which he announced the establishment there of a People's Tribunal for the trial of war criminals. Taking a line which contrasted sharply with the conciliatory approach of Groza, Pătrăşcanu denounced 'chauvinist elements' who were, he said, conducting a whispering campaign designed to convince the Hungarian population of Northern Transylvania that the return of this province to Romania was not final. After paying tribute to the Red Army's part in the liberation of this region, he appealed to the Hungarian population to accept the idea of a single Romanian state and its national symbols. The appearance of the Soviet flag side by side with the Romanian had been hailed with enthusiasm, but the juxtaposition of Soviet and Hungarian colours had not always been made in good faith and at times it was intended as an incitement to chauvinism and Fascism. The official language of the whole country was Romanian and in all branches of the administration, including justice, the Romanian language alone was valid. In conclusion Pătrăşcanu stated that he was not prepared to consider as reactionary the opposition of a 'small part' of the Romanian population to the Groza government which was largely due to ignorance.[3]

Pătrăşcanu's comments provoked an animated debate within the Communist Party leadership and the speech was released for publication in the face of strong opposition from Luca and Moghioros – both Hungarians – and Chişinevski. A year later almost to the day, Pătrăşcanu returned to Cluj in the wake of clashes between Hungarian and Romanian students in the city over the proposals in the Paris Peace Treaty to ratify the return of Northern Transylvania to Romania. Speaking in the name of the government and the RCP Central Committee, Pătrăşcanu claimed that the tension in Northern Transylvania had been fuelled by Hungarians from the region who had left Romania before August 1940, the time of its award to Hungary, and had returned during the Hungarian occupation. Measures would be taken, he said, against Hungarians and Romanians alike who stirred up hatred and tried to disturb the peace in Transylvania.[4]

[3] Despatch from I. Le Rougetel, British political representative in Bucharest, to Foreign Office, 22 June 1945, Public Record Office, FO 371/48645/ XC 5498.

[4] *Roumania: Annual Review for 1946*, Mr A. Holman to Mr Bevin, 12 March

Although well received by pro-government and opposition newspapers, this speech had attracted the wrath of Dej who, in an address to the Central Committee on 'the position of the RCP regarding chauvinist and revisionist trends' delivered on 7 July 1946, criticised Pătrăşcanu for allegedly not mentioning the role of the National Peasant and National Liberal parties in fomenting hatred among Romanians towards the Hungarian minority.[5] But in the back of Dej's mind was the forthcoming Peace Conference in Paris where charges of fomenting ethnic tension were the last thing Romania needed if her possession of Northern Transylvania was to be confirmed. Indeed, Pătrăşcanu's presence at the conference in Paris was later exploited by his interrogators to bring accusations of his attempting to foment a split in the RCP and of assisting Foreign Minister Constantin Vişoianu's flight to the United States.[6]

'Chauvinism', a cardinal sin in Stalin's catechism of the late 1940s, was served up in 1948 as a euphemism for the alleged anti-Russian postures of Tito in Yugoslavia, Kostov in Bulgaria,

---

1947, PRO, FO 371/67233/114052. A text of Pătrăşcanu's speech was printed in *Scînteia* on 14 June 1946. Among the declarations made by Pătrăşcanu during his interrogation by the *Securitate* and written up by Lt.-Maj. Simion Siegler on 7 January 1952 was an 'admission' that 'he concealed a part of his Cluj speech from the Central Commitee because he feared that he would not receive the party's permission to use it since it addressed the problem of Northern Transylvania'. It is not clear to which of the two Cluj speeches, that in June 1945 or that in June 1946, Siegler is referring. Pătrăşcanu is also alleged to have recognised that 'his nationalist deviations and manifestions placed him in the position of a traitor, exacerbating the conflict between Hungarians and Romanians in his Cluj speeches of June 1945 and July (sic!) 1946' (C. Popişteanu, ' "Cazul" Grupului Pătrăşcanu (V)', *Magazin Istoric*, no.11, [November 1991], p.41).

[5] Ionescu, *Communism in Rumania*, p.154 and *Scînteia*, 8 July 1946, p.3.

[6] In a declaration signed while under interrogation on 11 June 1951 Pătrăşcanu stated that before his departure for Paris at the end of July 1946 Vişoianu had sought an audience with him at the Ministry of Justice and passed on to him an invitation from Brigadier-General Cortland Van Rensselaer Schuyler, the US military representative on the Allied Control Commission, to go to the United States 'on whatever terms he wanted'. Pătrăşcanu adamantly turned down the invitation. Because he failed to divulge this invitation to the party, Pătrăşcanu 'admitted' his complicity in Vişoianu's defection (Vişoianu left Romania secretly in an American aircraft in October 1946 and settled in the United States). Pătrăşcanu also admitted to having had a conversation with Richard Franassovici, a member of the Romanian delegation in Paris, who proposed to him that he set up a breakaway Communist Party, and that he had failed to disclose this to the Party (C. Popişteanu, 'Pătrăşcanu', pp.40-1).

Gomulka in Poland, and Rajk in Hungary. In Pătrăşcanu's case it had been used by Dej in 1946 to refer to the latter's anti-Hungarian attitude. Dej had not been alone in the party in his anger at Pătrăşcanu's intemperate pronouncements: Pauker, Luca, Rangheţ, and other senior Central Committee members such as Iosif Chişinevski, the propaganda secretary, and Miron Constantinescu, had all expressed criticism at party gatherings over the summer and autumn of 1946 of Pătrăşcanu's 'self-importance' and his failure to follow an agreed party line but it had not led to any sanction against him.[7]

Pătrăşcanu's vulnerability had been increased by the arrest of Iuliu Maniu, the Peasant Party leader, and his colleagues in the party in July 1947.[8] Among the latter was Victor Rădulescu-Pogoneanu.[9] Pătrăşcanu must have been concerned that Rădulescu-Pogoneanu might reveal their secret meetings in August and September 1945 over the king's demand for the Groza government's resignation, and that the Soviets might order his own arrest. It would be later alleged, at his own trial in April 1954, that after the arrest of Maniu, Pătrăşcanu decided to flee the country. He was said to have instructed a trusted assistant, Nicolae Betea, to find a pilot who would fly them to Istanbul and Betea was put in touch with a captain Zaharia. Unfortunately, Zaharia was also an SSI informer. When Betea told Pătrăşcanu the pilot's name, the latter recognised it and realised that his plans were compromised.[10] There is, however, no reliable independent evidence to back these claims.

7 Author's interview with E. Mezincescu, 30 December 1992.

8 Declarations made to the security police by those involved in the escape attempt are published in *Cartea Albă a Securităţii*, vol.I, Anexă, Manifestaţia de la 8 Noiembrie 1945. Capcana de la Tămădau, 14 July 1947, pp.51-92.

9 According to Ion Pacepa, in the winter of 1947 Pintilie informed Pyotr Vasilyevich Fedotov, the new head of the foreign intelligence service of the KI, the Committee of Information (formed from the merger of INU and GRU (Soviet Military Intelligence) in the autumn of that year) that Pătrăşcanu was sabotaging 'Romania's march towards Communism' and furnished proof that the minister of justice was using his position to protect opposition party leaders (*Moştenirea Kremlinului*, Bucharest: Editura Venus, p.108). It would go against the pattern of relations between local security heads and their Soviet advisors for the former to have had a direct channel of communication with the head of a Soviet intelligence body in Moscow.

10 Şerbulescu, *Monarhia de Drept Dialectic*, p. 69. These details were confirmed by George Fotino in an interview with the author on 9 April 1994. However,

The expulsion from the party of Herbert (Belu) Zilber in March 1947 for not following the 'party line' and on suspicion of being an 'Anglo-American spy' had provided a clear warning to Pătrăşcanu. Zilber was a close friend who had seconded Pătrăşcanu in the talks conducted with the opposition parties to plan the 23 August coup. Abandoned now by his own friends and colleagues Zilber was driven to pen a letter to Ana Pauker in November 1947 requesting his own arrest and interrogation so that his innocence be established. His request was granted for on 6 February 1948 he was arrested by order of the Central Committee.[11]

Pătrăşcanu's concerns about his position drove him to seek advice from Serghei Ivanovici Kavtaradze, the Soviet ambassador to Romania. On 29 January 1948 the two men meet at the embassy. The Soviet record of their discussion records that Pătrăşcanu wished to speak to the ambassador 'who was a comrade with greater experience, in a very delicate matter related to his position in the party'. According to Kavtaradze, 'Pătrăşcanu began with a brief reference to the fact that he had been a member of the RCP for twenty-nine years, being alongside Ana Pauker one of its founders.' Despite making a few mistakes during this period, he said, he had remained a disciplined party member. During the war, he had played an important role in planning the 23 August coup, which had earned him some popularity. This had increased considerably after the coup but was looked upon with suspicion by some leading party members and had led to various accusations being levelled against him, among them that of being a nationalist. This was based on two things: his speech on the question of Translyvania, given in Cluj in 1946, and his position over the return of Jewish property.[12]

Pătrăşcanu considered the charge to be unfounded. In his speech at Cluj, he argued, he had criticised the Hungarian prime minister for his 'chauvinist stance towards Romania over the problem of Transylvania', not the Hungarian people. In the matter of Jewish

---

the Party Commission of Inquiry set up to examine the Pătrăşcanu affair, concluded that 'Pătrăşcanu did not intend to leave the country permanently, even though he had many opportunities to do so' ('Raportul Comisiei de partid, constituită in vederea clarificării situaţiei lui Lucreţiu Pătrăşcanu', *Cuvîntul,* no.43 (27 October-2 November 1992), p.6.

11 Şerbulescu, *Monarhia de Drept Dialectic,* p.46.

12 Pokivailova, 'Lucreţiu Pătrăşcanu', p.49.

property, Jews had been evicted from their property by a decree of Antonescu and he – Pătrăşcanu – had been unable, as minister of justice, to right that wrong because many of the flats involved were now occupied by state officials upon whom the new Groza government relied for the smooth running of the country; Jews were to be given back their property, with the exception of those dwellings in which civil servants resided.

The hostility towards him, Pătrăşcanu said, emerged immediately after the arrival of Pauker and Luca in Bucharest in September 1944. It was then that the word was put around that he played no role in the party. Moreover, in December 1944 and January 1945, *Scînteia*, the party daily, received instructions that Pătrăşcanu's activity as a senior party figure and the sole Communist minister in the Government should receive no mention in its columns. What angered Pătrăşcanu most of all, he confessed to the ambassador, was the refusal of the party to assign him any party role, despite the numerous requests he had made over the previous eighteen months. He had discussed these problems with Dej and Pauker, but his talk with Pauker had not gone well. 'He knows', Kavtaradze wrote, 'that his main enemy in the Politburo is Ana Pauker, but he does not know the reasons behind this because up to now, no direct accusation has been brought against him.'[13]

Pătrăşcanu repeatedly told the ambassador that he was not asking him to intervene on his behalf with the RCP, but sought only advice. He insisted upon the confidential nature of the discussion. Kavtaradze said that he could only give him one piece of advice: that the Politburo discuss his position and take a decision. 'Pătrăşcanu', the Ambassador concluded, 'accepted this advice.' On 19 February, he transmitted the following report on his talk with Pătrăşcanu to Moscow:

> For some years now, an atmosphere of only marginal trust and caution has surrounded the person of Pătrăşcanu. Matters have reached the point of suspicion that he is in contact with Anglo-American espionage. But firm, convincing evidence has not been produced. [...] The discussion related above represents a mixture of tendentiousness, lies, and ambition. Pătrăşcanu gave me the impression of a man without a very clear conscience. Recently, the minister of the interior, namely Teohari Georgescu, passed

13 *Ibid.*, p.52.

on secret information relayed to him from a reliable source. It is lethal to Pătrăşcanu. According to this information, Pătrăşcanu has adopted an anti-Communist and anti-Soviet position and has contacts with reactionary circles of émigrés who have asked him to join their organisation.

In view of the fact that Pătrăşcanu could become a member of the Romanian Workers' Party, and that its congress opens on 21 February 1948, I immediately placed the question of Pătrăşcanu before the secretariat of the Central Committee (Dej, Pauker and Georgescu), and proposed that light should be finally shed on this sombre affair and a decision taken.

The secretariat was in total agreement with me and decided to resolve the Pătrăşcanu problem by the time the congress began. I shall inform you of what follows.[14]

Pătrăşcanu's downfall may well have been sealed by plans to establish a Balkan federation embracing Yugoslavia, Bulgaria and Romania, and Stalin's reaction to them. On 17 January 1948, Georgi Dimitrov, the Bulgarian Communist leader, had hinted at the creation of a Balkan federation in a statement made in Bucharest. Both Dej and Pauker were careful to refrain from backing it. A month earlier Tito had visited the Romanian capital for the signing of a Yugoslav-Romanian Treaty. Dimitrov was forced to retract his statement following a violent attack on him in *Pravda* on 28 January and on 10 February was summoned to Moscow by Stalin who instructed him to cease all talk about a federation; his death in Moscow shortly afterwards ensured just that. At the same time Stalin is said to have told Ana Pauker, during the visit of the top-level Romanian delegation, to distance Romania from Tito and on 12 February the Romanian government ordered that all pictures of Marshal Tito be removed from shop windows. A further instruction then followed from Moscow: 'chauvinistic' elements were to be purged from the party.[15]

Pătrăşcanu was the obvious victim. He had, moreover, been among those who had received Tito in the previous December and could easily be implicated in charges of a pro-Tito conspiracy. Failure to act promptly might invite a charge of 'chauvinism', this time with an anti-Russian meaning, against other party leaders.

14 *Ibid.*

15 Hodoş, *Show Trials*, p.96.

In line with Soviet ambassador Kavtaradze's recommendation that a decision be taken on 'the Pătrăşcanu problem', Teohari Georgescu, as minister of the interior, was called upon by Dej, to make the public denunciation of Pătrăşcanu at the opening congress of the Romanian Workers' Party, which was held from 21-23 February.[16] With his target sitting close by, Georgescu named Pătrăşcanu as one of those who had become 'exponents of bourgeois ideology in various respects, were breaking away from the masses, and were distancing themselves completely from the ideology and principles of the party of the working class.'[17] Four months passed before the charges were made more explicit. In a resolution of the Central Committee plenary meeting of 10-11 June it was alleged that

> .... several weeks before March 1945 Pătrăşcanu, in complete contradiction to the party line, resuscitated the slogan of collaboration 'with the whole bourgeoisie or with an important part of it'. In 1946 he defended the thesis of an alliance with the 'whole' peasantry, therefore also with the exploiting elements hostile to the working peasantry. [...] In his practical activity he followed the policy of appeasement towards the exponents of bourgeois-landlord reaction when the party was fully engaged in the struggle against reaction. He followed the line of nationalist-chauvinist policy.[18]

Indications that a Soviet hand was behind these accusations was the claim that Pătrăşcanu wanted to work with 'the whole peasantry, including the exploiting elements hostile to the working peasantry'. This charge echoed one made at the same time by the Soviet Communist Party against the Yugoslav one, namely that the Yugoslav Communist Party (YCP) failed to distinguish between kulaks and other peasants and that it had ceded the leading role in the country's affairs to the Yugoslav People's Front composed of 'kulaks, merchants, small manufacturers, bourgeois intelligentsia,

[16] On 12 November 1947, the Social Democrat Party agreed to merge with the Communist Party, thereby creating the Romanian Workers' Party.

[17] *Congresul Partidului Muncitoresc Român. Bucureşti, 21-23 februarie 1948,* Bucharest: Editura PMR, 1948, p.156.

[18] *Scînteia*, 21 June 1948, p.1. These charges are analysed by Ionescu, *Communism in Rumania*, pp.152-4.

various political groups, including some bourgeois parties'.[19] The link between the charges against Pătrăşcanu and the Soviet-Yugoslav crisis became clearer two weeks later when the YCP sent a letter on 20 June announcing its decision not to attend the Cominform Conference, due to be held at the end of the month in Bucharest. In retaliation, the Cominform expelled the YCP, making its decision public on 28 June, and moved its headquarters from Belgrade to the Romanian capital.

The chronology of the steps taken against Pătrăşcanu shows Dej's need to follow a scenario whose script was prepared by Stalin or Beria, or both. The interval between Georgescu's attack, on 23 February, Pătrăşcanu's detention, on 28 April, the explicit charges, on 10 June, and the fact that he was only formally arrested two months later, on 24 August, indicate that there was some hesitation as to how to proceed against him. The delay can probably be attributed to two things: Pătrăşcanu's stubborn refusal to subscribe to all the charges against him, and Dej's need to await further instructions from Moscow which were slow in coming.

The five month interval between Pătrăşcanu's arrest in August 1948 and his interrogation at the hands of the police (as opposed to the party) in January 1949 probably resulted from Moscow's wish to coordinate his purge with those of Titoist heretics in other satellite states that culminated in the trials and executions of Laszlo Rajk in Hungary and Traicho Kostov in Bulgaria in September and December 1949 respectively. In testimony given on 11 May 1967 before the Committee of inquiry set up by the party's Central Committee to prepare the rehabilitation of Pătrăşcanu, Foriş and others, Gheorghe Pintilie claimed that he had been ordered (he did not say by whom) in 1949 to contact three Soviet counsellors based in Bucharest over the Pătrăşcanu case. Pintilie could only recall the names of two of them, Aleksandr Mikhailovich Sakharovsky, and Patriki. From the latter Pintilie learned that all three had been involved in preparations for the trial of Rajk. Throughout 1949 both Pătrăşcanu and his wife were interrogated at length in the DGSP (*Securitate*) headquarters on Calea Plevnei, and during this period the interrogation was guided by the Soviet

[19] 'Letter from the Central Committee of the Communist Party of the Soviet Union to the Central Committee of the Communist Party of Yugoslavia, 4 May 1948', *The Soviet-Yugoslav Dispute*, London: Royal Institute of International Affairs, 1948, p.45.

counsellors in an unofficial capacity. They were assisted by a second secretary from the Soviet Embassy who communicated information about the progress of the interrogation to Moscow. Later in the year, Sakharovsky was appointed chief MGB adviser to the Ministry of the Interior while the other two counsellors returned to Moscow.[20] Dej, Pauker and Chişinevski were kept informed by Sakharovsky about the Pătrăşcanu case and occasionally Pintilie was summoned to Dej's home to discuss it with him and Chişinevski.[21]

Several stages can be established in the evolution of Pătrăşcanu's interrogation and that of his friends. In March 1948, the SSI arrested Nicolae Betea, Anton Raţiu, Constantin Pavel, and Remus Micşa, all of whom were friends of Pătrăşcanu with posts in public institutions. In the following month Pătrăşcanu and his wife were detained and questioned by members of the party Central Committee. In June Betea, Raţiu and Pavel were handed over to the *Securitate.* Between January and October 1949, Pătrăşcanu and his wife were interrogated by the *Securitate.* In October 1949 the SSI took over the interrogation of Pătrăşcanu and twenty-five other persons which lasted until May 1950. On 24 January 1950, thirty-six other persons, led by Alexandru Ştefănescu, were examined by the *Securitate.* Then in February 1951 another stage of the inquiry began, with the interrogation by the *Securitate* of the groups associated with Pătrăşcanu, Ştefănescu and Remus Kofler, a veteran party colleague of Foriş, in an attempt to link them in a grand plot against the regime.[22]

On 28 April 1948, Pătrăşcanu was summoned by Dej to party headquarters and detained; this was two months after his denunciation at the party congress.[23] This lapse in time was probably due to a delay in receiving further instructions from Stalin as to

[20] The MGB (Soviet Ministry of State Security) 1946-54 was the successor to the NKGB (People's Commissariat of State Security) which had existed in 1941 and 1943-6. The NKVD (People's Commissariat for Internal Affairs) 1922-46 incorporated the OGPU (Soviet Security service) between 1922-3 and 1934-3. In 1946 the NKVD became the MVD (Soviet Ministry of Internal Affairs).

[21] Popişteanu, *Magazin Istoric*, no.11 (November) 1991, p.43.

[22] Popişteanu, *Magazin Istoric*, no.9 (September) 1991, p.48.

[23] The Report of the party commission on the Pătrăşcanu case stated that he was detained on this date on the basis of 'an instruction given by Dej'; 'Raportul Comisiei de partid, constituită în vederea clarificării situaţiei lui Lucreţiu Pătrăşcanu', *Cuvîntul*, no.35 (1-7 September, 1992), p.8.

how to procede with 'national chauvinists'. Pătrăşcanu was told by Dej in the presence of Alexandru Drăghici that he would have to appear before a party commission charged with investigating his activity during the period in which the party was outlawed (1924–44). He was escorted by Dej from the headquarters to a secret house for interrogation at Băneasa belonging to the political and administrative section of the Central Committee where a commission, composed of Teohari Georgescu, the minister of the interior, Iosif Rangheţ, deputy member of the Politburo and secretary responsible for the party cadres, and Alexandru Drăghici, deputy head of the political and administrative section, awaited him.

The commission began its enquiries by asking Pătrăşcanu about his alleged intention to flee the country, an intention which the former minister of justice resolutely denied. For several weeks its members sought to get Pătrăşcanu to admit to plotting against the party leadership but its efforts were frustrated because Georgescu himself, or so Drăghici suspected, had advised Pătrăşcanu to keep his mouth shut.[24] Pătrăşcanu was not at the time technically under arrest, an indication, perhaps, that Dej was waiting for further signals from Moscow, but Georgescu's advice to Pătrăşcanu was ambiguous. He recalled, almost thirty years later: 'I went to see Pătrăşcanu and said, among other things: "Look here Andrei [Pătrăşcanu's code-name], what's wrong with you? Help the party clear up this matter." He was very depressed and cried the whole time. "Why won't you be honest?" He told me that he was terrified of the SSI and of Goncearuc, who was a sadist and he was afraid of ending up in his hands.'[25]

The failure of the commission's investigations 'along the party line', as party jargon put it, to get the former minister of justice to admit to any 'mistakes' necessitated the adoption of more coercive measures. A warrant for Pătrăşcanu's arrest was issued on 24 August 1948; he was accused of being a police informer and an agent of British espionage who 'carried out a criminal activity to paralyse the actions of the Romanian Communist Party and to destroy the party from within, thereby contributing to the cause, maintenance

24 E. Mezincescu, 'Detenţie fără mandat de arestare', *Magazin Istoric*, no.6 (June 1992), p.58.

25 Archive of the Central Committee Executive Committee, 264, vol.21, p.15.

and continuation of the war against the USSR.'[26] He was ordered to be taken to Jilava jail. However, Eduard Mezincescu maintains that after the issue of the warrant Pătrăşcanu was driven the few kilometres from the house in Băneasa to his villa by lake Snagov some 35 km to the north of Bucharest where he rejoined his wife Elena. Both were held in confinement there under armed guard for the following five months.[27]

On 19 January 1949, the next stage in their ordeal began. On that date they were visited by Gheorghe Pintilie, Colonel Valerian Bucicov, a Soviet adviser to the Sixth Directorate, responsible for Dej's bodyguard,[28] and Iosif Ranghet, a deputy member of the Politburo charged with counter-espionage in the party, who brought them to the DGSP's headquarters on Calea Rahovei in Bucharest where they were placed in separate cells in the basement.[29] They were not to see each other again. Their interrogation followed Beria's blueprint for the purges of 'Titoist heretics' which were being prepared in Hungary, Bulgaria, and Czechoslovakia. Synchronisation with these trials required that charges that Pătrăşcanu was a traitor and police informer be proved, and it be shown that he was not working alone, but as the head of a group of conspirators with links to Tito and the 'western imperialists'. To give the semblance of a plot, Remus Kofler was arrested several months later on 13 December 1949. Under torture a 'confession' was extracted from Kofler admitting that he and Foriş had been 'agents of the bourgeois-landowning Fascist police', and that in 1941 they had recruited Pătrăşcanu. The latter, it was alleged, had given information to the police which had led to the arrest of a number of Communists, including Teohari Georgescu.[30]

The links to Tito and the imperialists were provided by the inclusion in the 'plot' of several representatives of Yugoslav minority organisations in Romania and of a number of Pătrăşcanu's friends, among them Herbert (Belu) Zilber, Ion Mocsonyi-Styrcea, former

26 Popişteanu, *Magazin Istoric*, no.7 (July 1991), p.62.

27 Mezincescu, 'Detenţie fără mandat', p.58.

28 Bucicov also supervised the search of Ana Pauker's house after her arrest (author's interview with Tatiana Brătescu, 30 July 1994).

29 Mezincescu, 'Pătrăşcanu', p.33.

30 Hodoş, *Show Trials*, p.99.

marshal of the royal court,[31] Alexandru Ştefănescu, an industrialist, Jac Berman and Emil Calmanovici, both construction engineers, Victoria Sârbu, Harry Brauner, a musician and former director of the Institute of Folklore, Herant Torossian, a Romanian-born Armenian businessman who had served as consul in Paris,[32] and

[31] Baron Ion de Mocsony-Styrcea was born at Cernăuţi on 16 May 1909. He graduated from Cambridge with a degree in modern languages in 1932 and joined the Romanian Foreign Ministry two years later. Between 1 April and 11 August 1942 he was private secretary to King Michael and head of the royal chancery, and from the latter date until 1 April 1944 served as acting marshal of the royal court. On 23 August 1944 he was made marshal of the court, a position from which he resigned on 4 November 1944 for health reasons, but he remained on the roll of the Foreign Ministry until the purge of non-Communist employees on 6 March 1946. He was arrested on his estate at Bulci in the Banat on 6 September 1947 and forced to become a prosecution witness in the trial of Maniu and others in which he was a co-defendant (29 October-11 November 1947). Sentenced to two years' imprisonment for concealing the so-called Maniu 'plot' to overthrow the regime, he served his time in Craiova jail from 12 December 1947 until 22 October 1949. He was charged a month after his release with being 'a wartime profiteer' because of his ownership of large estates in the Banat, and although acquitted before a tribunal in Timişoara, continued to be held in custody, first in Timişoara jail (23 November 1949-25 September 1950), and then at Casa Verde, a former royal hunting lodge 10 km. from the city (25 September 1950-16 May 1951). On 16 May 1951 he was taken, first to Timişoara *Securitate* headquarters for interrogation in connection with the Pătrăşcanu 'plot' and afterwards to the Ministry of the Interior in Bucharest where he remained until 18 March 1952. He was then transferred to the SSI's interrogation centre at Malmaison on Calea Plevnei in Bucharest where he was held until the trial of Pătrăşcanu on 6 April 1954 in which he was also a defendant. He was sentenced on 14 April to fifteen years' hard labour which he served in a succession of jails, Aiud (8 April 1954-15 February 1955), Jilava prison (15 February-4 April 1955), Aiud (4 April 1955-13 August 1956), Jilava (13 August 1956-20 July 1957), Piteşti (20 July 1957-1 June 1959). On 1 June 1959 he was transferred, together with other prisoners from the Pătrăşcanu trial, to Dej prison. On 18 October 1961 he was brought to Malmaison and was offered a deal by Drăghici: that he should write his eye-witness account of the 23 August coup on condition for his release from prison into house arrest. Styrcea accepted and on completion of his text, which he was forced to re-write several times, he was sent to the town of Câmpulung-Muscel on 28 November 1962 to which he was confined until he was allowed to leave Romania on 4 September 1964. He settled in Switzerland (letter from Mocsony-Styrcea to the author, 4 August 1984).

[32] Torosian was caught trying to leave Romania secretly in March 1948 in order to rejoin his wife in Paris who was ill. He was sentenced to five years in jail.

Lena Constante, an icon painter.[33] The Yugoslav officials were portrayed as agents of Tito while Pătrăşcanu and his friends were alleged to have set up a spy network under orders from the British and American intelligence services.

These allegations against Pătrăşcanu mirrored the charges against Laszlo Rajk. Rajk had served in the Spanish Civil War as a Com-

[33] Lena Constante has given an account of her ordeal in her book *The Silent Escape*, Berkeley: University of California Press, 1995. In this autobiography she recounts the 3,000 days which she spent, between 1950 and 1957, in solitary confinement as a political prisoner in Romanian jails. Lena was first arrested in April 1948 and was accused of involvement in an espionage ring run by Lucreţiu Pătrăşcanu. She was released six months later, re-arrested in January 1950, and finally brought to trial in April 1954 when she was sentenced to twelve years' imprisonment. By the time of her conviction she had served more than four years in solitary confinement and she spent a further three and a half years in the same conditions before being moved, in October 1957, into a communal cell. With the distinction of being the only woman in Romania to endure a total of eight years of total isolation, she was finally released in July 1961.

Constante's link to Pătrăşcanu was through his wife Elena. Constante had studied fine arts and had a particular fondness for dolls, puppets and the puppet-theatre. In 1945 she joined Elena Pătrăşcanu in a project to establish the first puppet theatre in Bucharest and as a result of this collaboration the Pătrăşcanus became firm friends of Constante and her partner, Harry Brauner, an ethnomusicologist (they eventually married after their release from prison). Both Constante and Brauner were, together with other friends of the Pătrăşcanus, to become scapegoats for a Stalinist show-trial in Romania whose principal victim was Lucreţiu Pătrăşcanu.

The 'silent escape' of the title is Constante's flight into self-examination during incarceration. She combines this examination with a meticulous account of prison ritual and routine, and of the boredom which accompanies it. The despair in the face of the endless passage of minutes, hours and days is punctuated only by the lingering pain from torture used against her during interrogation. Her literary style mirrors this trickle of time, which is itself an excruciating form of torture for the prisoner in solitary confinement. To give her illusions the reality of words she slips slowly, without pencil, without paper, into a world that had not been part of her, of poetry. Recalling, for example, the first two lines of Baudelaire's 'La Beauté' she discovers the secret of rhythm, the importance of stressed syllables. When these lines lost all meaning for her through repetition, she created her own lines, in French.

French is the original language of the memoir. Constante began writing it in Paris in 1977, during one of her visits there after she and her husband, Harry Brauner, were allowed to travel by the Romanian authorities. Publication in Ceauşescu's Romania was out of the question, while publication abroad would have led to exile. So she ended up, in her own words, 'writing this book with no hope of ever seeing it published' (p.257).

munist 'volunteer' and was interned in the south of France when it ended. He was released from internment in 1941 with the help of the American Noel Haviland Field, an NKVD agent working as a relief worker, and returned to Hungary, but Field's subsequent eccentric behaviour, which included contact with Allen Dulles, head of the Office of Strategic Services (the forerunner of the CIA) in Switzerland, aroused Soviet suspicions about his motives in helping with Rajk's release. In the summer of 1948 Matyas Rakosi, the Hungarian party first secretary, was summoned to Moscow to be informed that Rajk, his minister of the interior, was an American agent infiltrated into the leadership of the Hungarian party. General Fyodor Belkin, chief Soviet adviser of the MGB for South-East Europe, sent two generals, Likhachov and Makarov, to Budapest, to supervise preparations for Rajk's arrest and show trial. Some thirty other MGB officers joined them later. On 30 May 1949, Rajk was arrested and his interrogation overseen by Belkin.[34] His trial, which opened on 16 September, implicated Pătrăşcanu: Lazar Brankov, one of Rajk's co-defendants, alleged that Pătrăşcanu supported Tito's plans to create a Balkan federation of 'bourgeois democratic states' which would include Romania.[35]

Shortly afterwards in October 1949 Pătrăşcanu and his wife were handed over to the SSI, the foreign and counter-espionage service, for questioning on the personal order of Dej – himself acting on instructions from Sakharovsky. Lt.-Gen. Serghei Nikonov (Sergiu Nicolau), the head of the SSI, explained that the reason for this was to establish his connection with foreign espionage agencies through the intermediary of Lena Constante.[36] Charged with Pătrăşcanu's interrogation was Petre (Pyotr) Gonceariuc, head of the Counter-espionage Directorate of the SSI. In a deposition made to the 1967 inquiry, Gonceariuc declared that in 1950 he had received verbal orders from Nikonov, head of the SSI, to interrogate the Pătrăşcanus and that they were brought to him at the headquarters of the SSI Second Directorate in Maxim Gorki street from a villa near Băneasa airport by Colonel Valerian Bucicov. Nikonov gave Gonceariuc a list of questions for clarification in the course of interrogation; these included the following: which

34 Andrew, *KGB: Inside Story*, pp.413-15.

35 Hodoş, *Show Trial*, p.63.

36 Popişteanu, *Magazin Istoric*, no.12 (December) 1991, p.72.

of the enemy intelligence agencies had recruited Pătrăşcanu as an agent? What undertakings had Pătrăşcanu given to a *Siguranţa* chief upon his release from prison? How did he prepare his own flight and that of Anton and Betty Raţiu? What links did he and his wife Elena have with foreigners?

Gonceariuc's declaration gave nothing away about his conduct of the interrogation and he maintained that neither Pătrăşcanu nor his wife was tortured. He did admit, however, that after one session in which Pătrăşcanu's relations with the palace were raised, the latter tried to commit suicide by slashing his wrists with a razor blade. In order to prevent detection of the source of the razor blade Pătrăşcanu broke it into small pieces and then swallowed it. What Gonceariuc did not add was that SSI officers were instructed to give laxatives to Pătrăşcanu in an effort to retrieve the fragments and closely examined his bowel movements. Although they managed to piece together the object the gastric juices had removed any traces of finger prints.[37] After recovering, Pătrăşcanu was moved to another building of the SSI where he took an overdose of sleeping tablets in a further unsuccessful attempt at suicide. Pătrăşcanu's actions are the signs of a man driven to despair and hardly fit in with the sanitised account given by Gonceariuc.

According to Eduard Mezincescu, a senior official in the Romanian Foreign Ministry at the time and an acquaintance of Gonceariuc, the latter was a 'cunning brute' who proved himself 'very efficient' with his interrogation methods.[38] Mezincescu has recently recounted details of conversations with Gonceariuc which add details to the latter's 1967 declaration. Questions were put to Pătrăşcanu about alleged hard currency dealings with Herant Torossian but Gonceariuc's main objective was to discover what links Pătrăşcanu had with the British Secret Intelligence Service which were maintained, allegedly, through the intermediary of a folklorist Harry Brauner and his wife Lena Constante who had been arrested shortly after the Pătrăşcanus.[39] According to Gonceariuc, Brauner admitted that he had accepted the proposal of a foreign intelligence agency that he should flee the country in order to take up a post at the BBC dealing with folk music and he had decided to avail himself of

37 Mezincescu, 'Ecouri la "Cazul" Pătrăşcanu', p.35.

38 *Ibid.*

39 *Ibid.*

the earliest opportunity to do so. Gonceariuc was convinced that Brauner was a British spy but Brauner had given no information which could implicate Pătrăşcanu with British intelligence.[40]

Gonceariuc described Pătrăşcanu's attitude throughout his interrogation of him as 'completely insincere and arrogant'. He denied 'absolutely everything which seemed to be an accusation against him, demanding continually a reinstatement of the party investigation and an audience with Dej and Teohari Georgescu'. He declined to give any written declaration or explanation of his own actions, or those of Anton and Betty Raţiu, Harry Brauner and Lena Constante. The methods of interrogation were discussed with Sergiu Nicolau and George Firescu (real name Filipescu), head of the Interrogation Section of the SSI, but whether they involved torture is not disclosed. In 1952, after Goncеariuc's transfer to the DGSP, following its gradual absorption of the SSI, he passed on the Pătrăşcanu dossier, on Pintilie's orders, to Lt.-Col. Ioan Şoltuţiu.[41]

In specific terms Pătrăşcanu was accused of working for British intelligence, the links with it being allegedly provided by Harry Brauner, Lena Constante, Kofler, and Ştefănescu. The contacts they had with British officials on the Allied Control Commission were now adduced as proof of Pătrăşcanu's complicity in espionage, even though at the time the British were allies of the Soviets. At the same time as confessions were extracted through beatings from the accused to support these charges, the accusations of 'Titoist heresy' were not forgotten. An item in the official Yugoslav daily

[40] Popişteanu, *Magazin Istoric*, no.1 (January) 1992, p.86.

[41] Goncеariuc added that during his investigation of Pătrăşcanu the SSI was absorbed into the DGSP and he was made head of Directorate B for Counter-espionage with the rank of Colonel (Popişteanu, *Magazin Istoric*, no.1 (January) 1992, p.86). According to the records of the Ministry of the Interior, the SSI was absorbed into the *Direcţia Generală a Securităţii Statului* (which the *Direcţia Generală a Securităţii Poporului* had been rechristened in 1949) on 2 April 1951. Preparations for the merger had been under way during the preceding months under the supervision of Sakharovsky; these involved the transfer of staff from the SSI into the DGSS directorates and, in some cases, their allocation to other duties. Thus the SSI head, Sergei Nikonov, was appointed head of the anti-aircraft command, and transferred in 1954 from this post to become head of military intelligence (DIMSM). In 1960, he was appointed head of the Control Directorate of the Ministry of Armed Forces (details taken from Nikonov's party file and communicated to me by Claudiu Secaşiu).

Borba on 4 March 1950 announced that Pătrăşcanu was shortly to be tried with a number of Yugoslav citizens for a pro-Tito conspiracy,[42] but for reasons that are still unclear Beria allegedly ordered a postponement. One explanation given is that in comparison with the Rajk and Kostov trials, which led to extensive government purges in Hungary and Bulgaria, the Pătrăşcanu version could only appear lame and therefore Beria demanded a wider and deeper purge.[43] The reason for its lameness was the failure to extract from Pătrăşcanu a confession to his 'crimes', and the absence of any corroborating evidence from his friends.[44]

Another possible reason for the delay in bringing Pătrăşcanu to trial was the opposition of Ana Pauker and Teohari Georgescu.[45] Recent research has suggested that Pauker and her protégé Georgescu resisted attempts to prosecute Pătrăşcanu on trumped-up charges and that their protection of him was a significant factor behind the accusation of 'right-wing deviationism' launched against them in May 1952.

The difficulty in finding credible evidence against Pătrăşcanu was highlighted by Pintilie in his statement given on 11 May 1967 to the Committee of Inquiry into the Pătrăşcanu and Foriş cases. He admitted that it was only after persistent 'hard' questioning that the interrogators managed, in the first place, to link all the members of the so-called Pătrăşcanu group to the same charges. For two or three months after the Pătrăşcanus were handed over to the *Securitate* (in January 1949), the three Soviet counsellors led by Sakharovsky guided the lines of interrogation, although they had no official status. It was only later in the year that Sakharovsky was named principal counsellor to Teohari Georgescu. There was also a second secretary in the Soviet embassy who reported to Moscow on the progress of the interrogations. These Soviet officials kept Dej, Pauker and Chişinevski informed about the Pătrăşcanu case but Pintilie provided no evidence of any opposition from them to its conduct,[46] even though Dej's rebuke of Georgescu at the May 1952 plenary meeting of the Central

42 Ionescu, *Communism in Rumania*, p.155.

43 Hodoş, *Show Trial*, p.99.

44 This was not through want of trying on the part of Goncеariuc; see above.

45 This has been plausibly argued by Levy in 'Ana Pauker', pp.143-78.

46 Popişteanu, *Magazin Istoric*, no.11 (November) 1991, p.43.

Committee for not pursuing the Pătrăşcanu enquiry rigorously enough – revealed by the party commission – might have been interpreted as evidence of vacillation on the part of the minister of the interior.[47]

There is no evidence to ascribe the delay in bringing Pătrăşcanu to trial to deliberate obstruction by Dej.[48] Against such a claim one must set the atmosphere of terror that reigned in the satellite parties during and immediately after the show trials of 1949. Self-preservation would have dictated prudence and a respect for Soviet dictates. Dej followed instructions from Moscow, which probably originated from Beria who was now ably abetted by Vyshinski, Molotov's replacement as foreign minister. The master-servant relationship between Vyshinski and Dej – forged in the prelude to the establishment of the Groza government – was renewed in applying purge scenarios, which changed according to the prevailing political mood of Stalin. The leading role played by Soviet counsellors in establishing the thrust of the Pătrăşcanu group's interrogation between October 1949 and 1952 bears this out.

That Dej was anxious to remove any trace of suspicion over his loyalty to Stalin and to follow Soviet instructions to the letter is clear from his address to the third Cominform Conference, held in Bucharest in November 1949.[49] He used the occasion to attack Tito's heresies and identified Rajk, Brankov, Kostov and Pătrăşcanu as agents of the Anglo-American imperialist espionage agencies alongside the Yugoslav leader. Yet there was still no confession to back up this charge against Pătrăşcanu.[50] Dej's address was, according to Khrushchev, prepared in Moscow by Pavel Iudin,

[47] At the plenary meeting of the Central Committee held on 26 May 1952 Georgescu was removed from all his party and government positions.

[48] As maintained by George Hodoş, *Show Trials*, p.100.

[49] Dej's anxiety was well-founded. In April 1968 Colonel Andrei Arghiropol, a former member of the eavesdropping directorate of the *Securitate*, revealed to a Communist Party committee that his first assignment in 1949 had been to intercept Dej's telephone calls on the orders of Pintilie and Nicolski. The latter were doubtless acting on orders from Moscow (Archive of the Executive Committee of the Central Committee, 264, vol.23, p.45). My thanks to Marius Oprea for providing me with this reference.

[50] *Scînteia*, 6 December 1949, p.1.

Mihai Suslov, and Georgi Malenkov.[51] At the same time, Dej's delivery of the address served to confirm his seniority in the RCP.

The Stalinist script was clear: proof of the 'anti-state and anti-communist activities' of those under arrest was to be produced *after* official party judgement had been passed on them. But proof, in the form of a confession from Pătrăşcanu, could not be extracted from him. Renewed efforts were made by the interrogators to 'prove' the existence of a grand plot involving Pătrăşcanu, Kofler and Ştefănescu and linking them with Rajk, Kostov and others. These efforts were made on the instructions of Sakharovsky and his two Soviet colleagues who had examined the lack of progress in the case during the winter of 1950. They recommended the abolition of the SSI and the transfer of its officers to the DGSS (*Securitate*). The restructuring took place in January and February 1951 and Directorate G (Penal Investigation) was given responsibility for the Pătrăşcanu case.[52] Further evidence that their course was plotted by Moscow was an attack by Gheorghiu-Dej published in *Pravda* on 4 September 1951 under the title 'The Revolutionary Vigilence of the Peoples in the Struggle for Socialism' in which he listed Pătrăşcanu among those 'inveterate traitors and paid provocateurs and agents of the bourgeois class like Rajk, Kostov,

51 *Khrushchev Remembers: The Glasnost Tapes*, translated and edited by J.L. Schecter with V.V. Luchkov, Boston, 1990, p.103. I am grateful to Robert Levy for this reference. Iudin is more likely to have been consulted in Bucharest since he was the representative of the Comintern when it was based in Yugoslavia and moved with it when its headquarters were transferred to Bucharest in June 1948. Pavel Fedorovich Iudin (1899-1968) was a leading theorist of the Soviet Communist Party. Director of the Institute of Philosophy of the Soviet Academy of Sciences from 1938 to 1944, he was appointed editor-in-chief of the journal *Sovetskaya kniga* in 1946 and elected a member of the Central Committee at the Nineteenth and Twentieth Party Congresses. He was succeeded as Comintern representative in Bucharest by Mark Borisovich Mitin. Mikhail Andreevich Suslov was appointed secretary of the Central Committee of the Soviet Communist Party in 1947 and between 1947 and 1950 was editor-in-chief of *Pravda*. In 1950 he became a member of the Praesidium of the Supreme Soviet. Georgi Malenkov was a trusted servant of Stalin. In the 1930s he helped to evaluate intelligence provided by the NKVD for the Politburo and became a member of the five-man State Defence Committee in 1941. He briefly succeeded Stalin as First Secretary.

52 The *Securitate* documents optimistically refer to this period as 'the final stage in the inquiry' (Popişteanu, *Magazin Istoric*, no.9 (September) 1991, p.48.

Koçi, Dzodze and others who were led by the Belgrade agency of American espionage, the band of Tito and Rankovici'.[53]

This second stage of the Pătrăşcanu investigation was initially entrusted to Colonel Mişu Dulgheru, head of the penal investigation directorate, who received instructions from Sakharovsky and Tiganov, the Soviet counsellor for this directorate.[54] Still no satisfactory progress was made. The frustration of Dej, and no doubt of the Soviet counsellors, was translated into the decision to replace Teohari Georgescu as minister of the interior with his deputy Alexandru Drăghici at a plenary meeting of the Central Committee on 26 May 1952. Among the accusations levelled at Georgescu was that 'even after four years he had failed to bring to a conclusion the

53 Nestorescu-Bălceşti, 'Structura Conducerii Superioare a PCR', p.361.

54 Mişu Dulbergher (Dulgheru) was born in Tecuci on 16 January 1909. He started his professional life as a bank clerk in Galaţi in 1927. Shortly afterwards he left to take up positions as an accountant, first with his uncle's firm of wholesale cereals merchants, then at his cousin's shop. In 1938, he married and in the following year he and his wife opened a workshop for making men's underwear. Poor sales led them to seek other employment and in 1940 his wife Liza secured a post at the Soviet commercial legation in Bucharest. Through her intervention Mişu was taken on at the legation as a chauffeur. On 22 June 1941, the day after Romania's attack on the Soviet Union, the Dulberghers were arrested and interned at Tîrgu-Jiu where they were 'adopted' by the Communist internees. Mişu was sent out on work parties while Liza spent her time in a workshop in the camp wrapping soap in cellophane. After the 23 August 1944 coup, Mişu was assisted by fellow-inmate Vania Didenko (Ion Vidraşcu), an NKVD agent who played a leading role in setting up a Communist secret police. After a brief period in the 'Patriotic Guards', the Communist paramilitary group run by Bodnăraş, Dulbergher was made an inspector in the *Siguranţa* on 15 March 1945. It was at this time that, in order to provide himself with a cover, he changed his name to Dulgheru. When the DGSS was established in 1948, he was made head of the Directorate for Penal Investigation.

In internal evaluations Dulgheru was praised for his 'vigilence'. Lena Constante, one of the political prisoners who encountered him (in 1951), described him as follows: 'He was tall, about 40 to 50 years old, in a light grey suit. He received me in a spacious and elegant office. The furniture was upholstered in bright-red velvet. [...] I sat down on a chair which had been placed for me some distance from his desk. He told me that if I told the truth he would give me some American cigarettes. He opened the door at the back of the office, which opened onto a sort of cupboard, took a packet of Chesterfield cigarettes, and gave me one. But I said nothing.' (Marius Oprea, 'Micul funcţionar şi capcanele memoriei', *Dilema*, no.126 (9-15 June), 1995, p.9 and *Cartea Alba a Securităţii*, vol.I, doc.159, p.332).

investigation regarding the espionage and counter-revolutionary activity of Pătrăşcanu and Kofler.'[55]

A fresh team of interrogators was constituted under Colonel Ioan Şoltuţiu who undertook to expedite matters.[56] To help him in his task he was sent to Prague where he sat in for a while on the Slansky trial. According to Victor Vânătoru, one of the inter-

[55] Nestorescu-Bălceşti, 'Structura Conducerii Superiorae a PCR', p.362.

[56] Şoltuţiu was a railwayman who became party secretary for Cluj county after the war and was recruited into the SSI in 1949 by Ranghet. The rest of Şoltuţiu's team was composed of Maj. Toma Drăghici, Maj. Gheran Moraru, Maj. Victor Vânătoru, Maj. Teodor Staicu, Maj. Mircea Anghel, Maj. Teodor Micle, Gheorghe Rujan, and Alexandru Gorun, who acted as secretaries. Recently published transcripts of some of the interrogations conducted in the marathon Pătrăşcanu investigation show the resilience and dignity of this veteran Communist whose resolve and commitment had been steeled in the prison camps of King Carol's governments and who was now forced to call upon those resources to withstand an immeasurably greater ordeal at the hands of those acting in the name of erstwhile colleagues and the party he had served. Here, by way of an example, is an extract from the transcript of the interrogation conducted by Lt.-Col. Ioan Şoltuţiu between 0825 and 1300 hrs on 23 October 1952 which was countersigned as a correct record by Pătrăşcanu:

Question: Why did you oppose the extension of the law regarding war criminals?

Answer: I opposed it because I considered that Romania had fulfilled her obligations under the Armistice Convention.

Question: What did the party demand of you in connection with the extension of the law regarding war criminals?

Answer. The Party demanded nothing of me in this respect. In March or April 1947 the president of the Allied (Soviet) Control Commission sent a letter to the Romanian government presenting a series of cases requiring the extension of the law on war criminals. Since I considered these cases inconclusive, I maintained my initial point of view.

Question: Whose interests were you serving by adopting this point of view?

Answer: By not extending the law on war criminals I served the interests of the Romanian state.

Question: What discussions and with whom from Palace circles did you discuss the problem of the war criminals.

Answer: I discussed this problem with the former King Michael. King Michael was against the extension of this law. On this matter the king had the same view as I did.

Question: Do you admit that you sabotaged the extension of the law on war criminals?

Answer: I do not recognise this because it cannot be a question of sabotage.

(Popişteanu', *Magazin Istoric*, no.1 (January) 1992, p.86).

rogators, Şoltuţiu reported to Sakharovsky and Chişinevski and repeatedly urged the team to establish Pătrăşcanu's guilt as a traitor. Beatings were administered to Kofler, Calmanovici and Berman, but they consistently denied the allegations made against them. Dej followed this phase of the investigations closely, annotating the statements of the accused and offering advice on what direction the interrogations should take. The coordination proper of the interrogations was carried out by Sakharovsky and his subordinate, Tiganov, the Soviet counsellor of the Penal Investigation Directorate of the *Securitate*, thereby indicating the direct interest of Moscow in staging a sensational show-trial in Romania that would rival those held elsewhere in the Eastern Bloc. The frustration felt by Sakharovsky eventually led him to order the arrest on 26 November 1952 of Colonel Dulgheru on the grounds of having delayed the investigation.[57]

At the same time, increased psychological pressure and beatings

[57] Popişteanu,' *Magazin Istoric*, no.12 (December) 1991, p.74. Dulgheru was interrogated for two years and three months but no charges were brought against him and he was released. Unlike the victims of his directorate he was not tortured during his detention and was well fed, given medicines when he required them and clean clothing.

In 1967 Dulgheru recounted details of his arrest and interrogation to the party commission on rehabilitation. On 26 November 1952 he was ordered by Pintilie to go to the *Securitate* detention centre on Strada Uranus in Bucharest to receive an important prisoner. Upon arrival there he was placed under arrest for carrying out 'an identified criminal activity'. His interrogators lacked experience, according to Dulgheru, but they received guidance from Sakharovsky and Tiganov, the counsellor of the directorate for penal investigation. 'Various methods were used to destroy my morale, culminating in interrogation in shifts. I was taken for interrogation on Wednesday morning and held without food or sleep until 2 p.m. on Saturday, that is for eighty hours, while the interrogators were replaced every eight hours'. After nine months he was handed over to the interrogator Teodor Micle who repeatedly uttered threats against Dulgheru's life and that of his wife and children. Addressing the Party commission on rehabilitation in 1967 Dulgheru exclaimed:

> 'Comrades, I do not want to be misunderstood. I maintain, however, that from 1941 until 1944, the period in which I was held in the Tîrgu-Jiu internment camp, I did not experience by a long way such maltreatment as that applied to me by my own people. [...] Sakharovsky showed a particular interest in my interrogation since he sought at any price to prove the guilt of Pătrăşcanu and of those arrested in connection with the Pătrăşcanu inquiry. I felt this personally during my own interrogation when he wanted to prove that I was a spy.' (Popişteanu, *Magazin Istoric*, no.12 (December) 1991, p.74).

were administered to the prisoners up till the time of their trial in April 1954 in order to extract confessions. These illegal methods were the subject in 1967 of a voluminous secret report drawn up by the Central Committee which noted 'the use of beatings, of torture, of the tearing out of hair, and of prolonged starvation of the prisoners'.[58] These abuses forced the accused to tell lies,

[58] Sakharovsky's leading role was emphasised in Şoltuţiu's declaration to the Party committee in 1967:

> 'In 1952 the interrogation of the Pătrăşcanu group was under my direction, but this was a mere formality since the enquiry was directed by the two Soviet counsellors, Sakharovsky and Tiganov, and by comrade Minister Draghici. [...] The process of interrogation was as follows: one copy of all the declarations of Pătrăşcanu, or of others in the group which were of some importance in respect of Pătrăşcanu, was given to Sakharovsky, and another to Drăghici.[...] After this I was summoned either to Sakharovsky's office, or to that of Drăghici, where I received instructions on how to proceed. [...]
>
> The declarations which I handed over to Drăghici were returned to me personally by him [...] and on them were notes in the margin written by Gheorghiu-Dej, while comrade Minister Drăghici told me how to carry on the interrogation. When these declarations were given back to me counsellor Sakharovsky, who was Drăghici's personal adviser, was in most cases present Throughout the interrogations I realised that the counsellor was in permanent contact with Gheorghiu-Dej and Chişinevski. [...]
>
> I recall a moment when, in the presence of either comrade Minister Pintilie, or of comrade Minister Drăghici, Counsellor Sakharovsky said that all that the interrogation had established at that point were Pătrăşcanu's mistakes, but that here it was not a question of mistakes, but of hostile and treacherous actions on the part of Pătrăşcanu. We interrogators had to understand this, for they, the Soviets, have all the details in connection with the hostile and treacherous attitude of Pătrăşcanu right from the time when he was in Moscow as a representative of the Romanian Communist Party at the Comintern.
>
> I emphasise that the questions put by me to Pătrăşcanu were formulated by counsellor Sakharovsky on the basis of the material he had from the other interrogations.
>
> (Popişteanu, *Magazin Istoric*, no.12 (December) 1991, p.74).

Şoltuţiu also admitted that some of the Pătrăşcanu group had been beaten, namely Kofler, Calmanovici, and Zilber, but disclaimed any knowledge of torture administered to Lena Constante. He alleged that Sakharovsky had suggested the use of force against the prisoners and denied that he had played any part in it. Two footnotes are worth providing to illustrate the cynicism of the regime in the Pătrăşcanu affair: Major Toma Drăghici, one of the interrogators, was given Pătrăşcanu's flat on Strada Vasile Lascăr no.100; and Drăghici and his fellow *Securitate* interrogators Alexandru Gorun, Victor Vînătoru, Gheran Moraru, Teodor Micle, Gheorghe Rujan, Ludovic Weiss, and Ioan Şoltuţiu, were all decorated

as Gheorghe Pintilie himself acknowledged in the report, and these lies were to lead to the death, in April 1954, of Lucreţiu Pătrăşcanu and Remus Kofler.

The conduct of investigations against Pătrăşcanu between 1948 and 1952 clearly confirm the back-seat role to which Dej and others in the RCP leadership were confined by their Soviet masters in the conduct of Romania's affairs, and that Dej thought it prudent – and useful – to accept it. The interrogation of Pătrăşcanu and his associates lay firmly in the hands of Aleksandr Mihailovici Sakharovsky, the MGB adviser to Georgescu, the minister of the interior, and the sequence of different accusations levelled against Pătrăşcanu followed a scenario established in Moscow.[59] Dej's behaviour, and that of the Romanian Party leadership, during the interrogations indicate men and women anxious, not unnaturally, to protect themselves from the whims of Stalin and to demonstrate their fidelity to Moscow.[60] Holding on to power required anticipation of Stalin's next move and preemptive action in accordance with one's instincts. This explains the caution with which Dej proceded over Pătrăşcanu and why he was anxious to be kept informed at every stage of the progress, or lack of it, in respect of his interrogation. Either could be implicated as an imagined enemy in the absurd game of roulette which was played out in Stalin's mind. It was Dej who weighted the wheel in his own favour.

'for their important contribution to the struggle for the defence of the fatherland and the working people' on 22 May 1954, thirty-six days after the execution of Lucreţiu Pătrăşcanu (*ibid.*, p.75).

59 Archive of the Executive Committee of the Central Comittee, 264, vol.20, pp.309-63. My thanks to Marius Oprea for sharing this report with me.

60 For this reason Dej and Pauker compiled questionnaires which were put to Belu Zilber by his SSI interrogator George Firescu (real name Filipescu) in the winter of 1949. Dej could not hide signs of an inferiority complex in the questions he had transmitted, being particularly insistent as to why Zilber had allegedly described him as a 'zombie' and uneducated. Pauker, on the other hand, was more interested in the 'capitalist' literature Zilber had read (Şerbulescu, *Monarhia de Drept Dialectic*, p.75).

9

THE ROMANIAN GULAG

Senior members of the Communist Party in Romania were no strangers to jail. Alongside members of the Iron Guard, the Communists had been the principal targets of the the *Siguranţa.* Dej himself had spent more than ten years in jail for political activity hostile to the regime. With this experience fresh in their minds, the Communists probably lost little sleep over the incarceration of those whom they regarded as their political enemies. Their victims were preordained: whether they were guilty of their alleged crimes was irrelevant: Communist theory said they had to be. The party system of 'law' was outside the formal legal system and the latter only served as the public explanation of the measures taken. The Communists abandoned pre-war Romanian penology, and practice, which was largely of French inspiration, and introduced the Soviet system which depended on self-incrimination and in which, accordingly, defence pleas could only be for mitigation.

Dej was directly involved in the application of terror. His principal instrument throughout his rule was Alexandru Drăghici. Born on 27 September 1913 in Tisău in Buzău county, Drăghici was Dej's junior by twelve years. He followed in Dej's footsteps first, as a railway worker, being employed as a locksmith in the railways yards in Buzău and Bucharest, and then as a participant in the Griviţa strike in 1933. He joined the Communist Party in the following year. In 1936, he was sentenced to nine years and nine months – later reduced to seven years and five months – imprisonment as a 'notorious Communist' with Ana Pauker and others and served his time in Jilava, Doftana, Caransebeş and Văcăreşti. Released on 25 April 1944, he was then interned in Tîrgu-Jiu where he joined Dej.

After his release in August 1944, Drăghici who had left school at the age of eleven, became a public prosecutor. He took part in the trials of alleged war criminals in summer 1945, and in October 1945 was co-opted on to the Central Committee of the

Party at its National Conference. In February 1948 he was promoted to full member. Two months later, he joined Teohari Georgescu and Iosif Rangheţ in the initial investigation of Pătrăşcanu. On 30 December 1950, he was appointed head of the Political Directorate of the Ministry of the Interior, replacing General Mihai Burcă. His career ended abruptly in April 1968, when he was removed for 'crimes and abuses' from all his party and state positions and reduced from general to the ranks.

As one of Dej's most trusted associates, Drăghici thus became a senior figure in the Ministry of the Interior at the height of Soviet control. The Pătrăşcanu case became an obsession with Dej and the Soviet counsellors, and Drăghici, on becoming minister of the interior in May 1952 in place of Teohari Georgescu, and then head of the newly-created Ministry of State Security in September 1952, was ordered by the party secretary to provide him with a 'blow by blow' account of the progress in the interrogations. Dej's frustration at the lack of results boiled over in his comments – written in macabre red ink – in the margins of Drăghici's reports. Dej vented his spleen on Pătrăşcanu, aware that failure to deliver a 'traitor' into Stalin's hands could possibly signal his own demise.

Drăghici too was conscious of the need to follow the Soviet blueprint of terror. A reasoned estimate would put the number of his victims, held in the seventy-five prisons and labour colonies used by the regime during the early years of the 1950s at about 100,000[1] Certain prisons were earmarked for certain categories of prisoner. Sighet, because of its proximity to the Soviet Union in the northern province of Maramureş, was chosen as the centre

[1] *Securitate* files show that more than 70,000 persons were arrested in the decade from 1948 tó 1958. (*Cartea Albă a Securităţii*, vol.II, p.45). This figure must be treated with caution since, on Gheorghiu-Dej's own admission in 1961, 80,000 peasants alone had been arrested in the collectivisation drive. Moreover, the number of detainees in the labour colonies on the Danube-Black Sea canal project alone was more than 20,000 in 1951. Many of these had not been 'arrested' but merely rounded up and did not figure in *Securitate* figures. Alexandru Drăghici was transferred from the Ministry of the Interior on 20 September 1952 to head the new ministry. The Ministry of State Security was reincorporated into the Ministry of the Interior on 7 September 1953. Drăghici retained his status as the most senior party member directly responsible for state security by being made first vice-president of the Council of Ministers on 20 August 1954. He resumed his former post as minister of the interior on 20 March 1957. The minister of the interior from September 1952 until March 1957 was Pavel Ştefan.

for incarceration of what the regime considered to be its most dangerous opponents, the heads of the major democratic parties, former ministers and leading churchmen. Built as a jail in 1896 by the Hungarian authorities when Transylvania was part of the Austro-Hungarian Empire, its first political prisoners entered its gates on 22 August 1948. Between that date and 1956, its seventy-two cells held four former prime ministers, notably Iuliu Maniu; Constantin Brătianu, the head of the National Liberal Party; and the bishops of the Roman Catholic and Greek Catholic Churches. About 180 members of Romania's pre-war ruling elite were held in the prison, more than two-thirds of them being over the age of sixty, and several, as in Maniu's case, over the age of seventy. Many of them had never been tried for any crime but had merely been arrested on orders issued by the Ministry of the Interior and taken straight to Sighet. Such was the fate of Constantin Giurescu, professor of history at Bucharest University, who served as minister of propaganda in the Tătărescu government of May and June 1940.

Giurescu was arrested at his home on 6 May 1950 at 4 a.m. and driven straight to Sighet in a prison van with several other former ministers of the period, among them Dumitru Caracostea, a member of the Romanian Academy, who was for a brief spell minister of education in the Gigurtu government of August 1940. He arrived at Sighet on the following evening. He was released on 5 July 1955 but given mandatory residence in a village near Brăila, close to the Danube delta. He was allowed to return to his family in Bucharest in November. During his period of mandatory domicile, he recalled his experiences in Sighet in a manuscript which his family kept carefully concealed until the fall of Communism.[2]

Prisoners were usually placed two in a cell and were required to carry out menial duties, such as chopping wood, cleaning the

[2] This manuscript was entrusted by Giurescu's son, Dinu, to the care of Paul Michelson, an American history professor in the 1980s and after Dinu was allowed to emigrate to the United States in 1988, Michelson sent him a photocopy of the MS., which was published in Romania in 1994 under Constantin Giurescu's name as *Cinci Ani şi Două Luni în Penitenciarul de la Sighet* (Bucharest: Editura Fundaţiei Culturale Române, 1994). An English edition appeared in the same year as *Five Years and Two Months in the Sighet Penitenciary* (Boulder, CO: East European Monographs).

corridors, carrying tubs of food, collecting water from a hand-pump in the courtyard and carrying it to the higher levels, and taking containers of human waste from the cells to the toilet. The toilet was, in Giurescu's words, 'a hole cut in the dirty cement of the floor'. There was no running water. The cleaning of the toilets was done by prisoners.

Some of the warders were sadists and known by the initial 'B' for beast – namely B-1, B-2 etc. Others were designated by the letter 'C', from Romanian *cur* ('ass-hole'). With a few exceptions, the names of the warders were unknown to the prisoners. 'B-1 was also called "the Mongoloid". He stunk so bad that you felt ill around him. Arba, formerly imprisoned for murder, cursed like B-1 and had taken a sadistic pleasure in tormenting and humiliating the prisoners.' But there were also warders who showed compassion and helped prisoners by bearing messages and by giving extra food.[3]

The prisoners' duties, while not onerous in themselves, became so by reason of the ferocious discipline with which they were enforced. Prisoners were punished for the slightest deviation from prison rules, such as the ban on speaking during exercise. Transgressors were flogged and made to act as a 'horse' while jailers vaulted over them,[4] or placed in solitary confinement in the *neagra*, a cell without windows. Those who were punished in this way were put inside wearing only a shirt and underwear, or even completely naked. Shortly after his arrival, Giurescu got up on his bed to look at at the prisoners in the yard, but he got down before the warder Arba entered the cell unexpectedly. He asked Giurescu three times whether he wanted to look out of the window, promising that he would not punish him if he answered honestly. Giurescu admitted that he did and for that he was sent to the *neagra*.[5]

A feature of incarceration was the permanent sensation of hunger. In the morning prisoners received a mug of water with a 'vague smell of lime'.

From 8 May 1950 to 3 July 1953 barley was the main meal in

[3] Giurescu, *Sighet Penitenciary*, pp.xiii-xiv.

[4] Details related by my mother-in-law, Dumitru Caracostea's own daughter-in-law.

[5] *Ibid.*, p.xv.

prison, and there were periods, like between 20 December 1950 and 5 January 1951 when we were given it all the time for lunch and dinner. The dinner consisted of barley soup, in reality a sort of leftover dish water. [...] A half an hour after you finish your lunch, you are hungry again; this sensation becomes more and more intense and reaches its extreme at half past five in the evening when, usually, the bell for dinner rings. After the watery soup in the evening, you don't even have half an hour's respite as with lunch; you are hungry the moment you finish eating.[6]

Giurescu's experience was matched by that of the inmates of Romania's other jails – in Aiud (see Appendix 6), where former members of the Iron Guard were concentrated,[7] in Galaţi, the prison to which NPP members were sent; in Gherla, where many schoolteachers and lawyers ended up; and in Făgăraş, the jail chosen for the detention of former policemen.[8]

The acme of deliberate degradation was practised in the prison at Piteşti, situated some 120 km. north-west of Bucharest. It became notorious for an experiment of a grotesque originality which began there on 6 December 1949. Termed 're-education', the experiment employed techniques of psychiatric abuse designed not only to inculcate terror into opponents of the regime, but also to destroy the personality of the individual. Details of the nature and enormity of this experiment, conducted by prison officers under the direction of Alexandru Nicolski of the *Securitate*, are still largely unknown in the West. The 're-education' experiment lasted until August

[6] Giurescu, *Penitenciarul de la Sighet*, p.11. The prison was finally closed in 1974. ('Memoria şi istoria', *România liberă*, 22-23 May 1993).

[7] Its commandants were Lt-Col. Mihai Dorobanţu (1950-51), Lt. Ludovic Czegledi (1952-53), Col. Ştefan Koller (1954-58), and Col. Gheorghe Crăciun (1958-64). (*Ministerul Justiţiei. Direcţia Generală a Penitenciarelor*, document no. 35.372, dated 19 February 1992) According to his party file, Crăciun was born on 24 July 1913 in the commune of Mintiul Gherlei in the county of Someş in Transylvania. He worked as a maintenance man on the railways and joined the Communist Party in 1945 when he was recruited into the Ministry of the Interior. By spring 1948, he had been given the rank of inspector in the *Siguranţa* in Sibiu (*Cartea Albă a Securităţii*, vol.I, doc.166, p.336).

[8] The commandants of Galaţi were Lt-Maj. Tiberiu Lazar (1948-51), Lt-Col. Nicolae Moromete (1952-53), Capt. Ioan Stănescu (1954-56), Col. Dumitru Voda (1957-59), and Col. Marian Petrescu (1960-65); those of Făgăraş were Maj. Iosif Maraviov (1954) and Lt-Col. Aron Trîmbiţaş (1955-59).

1952 and was conducted in other prisons as well, including Gherla, albeit on a smaller scale, but the process became synonymous with Piteşti.[9]

Physical torture was commonly applied by the *Securitate* during interrogation both in *Securitate* centres and in prisons, but in the process of 're-education' the prisoner, after interrogation, was placed in a cell with his torturer who was a fellow prisoner, and torture continued. The programme was implemented by Alexandru Nicolski, the assistant director of the *Securitate* with special responsibility for interrogation of prisoners, who used as his principal instrument Eugen Ţurcanu. Ţurcanu was himself a prisoner in Piteşti and was instructed by Nicolski in the autumn of 1949 to form a team of torturers from among his fellow prisoners.[10] The majority of these were students from the university centres of Bucharest, Iaşi and Cluj, 1,000 of whom had been rounded up in 1948 on charges of belonging either to the Iron Guard, NPP or to the Zionist movement.

Piteşti was chosen for the experiment because of its location. The prison there was a maximum security one, built early in the century. Outside the town, far from any dwelling, the place was well suited for torture because no one could hear the screams from within its walls. In this ideal centre for experiments all the students arrested up till 1948, roughly a thousand, were assembled. The students were divided into four groups. The first comprised those imprisoned without trial, which did not prevent them from serving six to seven years, the second those convicted of minor

[9] I have described the prison regime at Piteşti in my *Ceauşescu and the Securitate*, pp. 29-42. It is based on D. Bacu, *The Anti-Humans*, Monticello, IL: TLC, 1977 and Virgil Ierunca, *Piteşti*, Paris: Limite, 1981. The effects of the extension of the re-education programme to Gherla prison in Transylvania in autumn 1951 are described by Aristide Ionescu, a former prisoner there, in his recently published memoir, *Dacă vine ora H pe cine putem conta*, Piteşti, 1992, pp.46-55.

[10] Transcripts of Ţurcanu's interrogation and extracts from the proceedings of his and his associates' trial, which began on 20 September 1954, are reproduced in *Memorialul Ororii. Documente ale Procesului Reeducării din închisorile Piteşti, Gherla*, Bucharest: Editura Vremea, 1995. Despite its wealth of documents, this volume lacks a critical introduction and apparatus. The material is the *Securitate*'s version of the re-education experiment, therefore it is not surprising that there is no mention of Alexandru Nicolski's role. Nor does the volume refer to the books by Bacu and Ierunca.

offences, such as aiding political opponents of the regime, with sentences of three to five years, the third, and largest, those accused of 'plotting against the social order', with sentences of eight to fifteen years; the last group contained those sentenced from ten to twenty-five years' hard labour and comprised the leaders of student associations. It was from this later group, considered the most resilient, that in the middle of November 1949 a group of fifteen students, led by Sandu Angelescu, were moved into hospital ward no. 4 of the prison where they found Ţurcanu's group, also made up of fifteen prisoners, already installed. Befriending each other they confessed their intimate thoughts until 6 December when one of the warders ordered Angelescu to give him his pullover. Angelescu was left in the unheated ward in mid-winter in just his shirt and cursed the warder as he left. This prompted his best friend in the cell Ţurcanu to strike him without warning in the face and to chide Angelescu for cursing the warden. At this signal the other members of the Ţurcanu group pounced on their 'friends' and a general brawl ensued. It was broken up by the entrance of warders, the prison director Captain Dumitrescu, and the political officer Lieutenant Marina. Angelescu explained what had happened and Dumitrescu, pretending to be furious with Ţurcanu, demanded a reply. The latter then revealed that he was the head of the ODCC, the Organisation of Prisoners with Communist Convictions, and that their attempts to persuade Angelescu's group to join them had resulted in their being attacked.

Things had obviously been pre-arranged. Angelescu was accused of resisting 're-education' and was ordered, together with his friends, to strip naked and to lie down on the bare concrete floor. Then they were beaten for half an hour by the wardens armed with iron bars and clubs and left with Ţurcanu and his colleagues. For several days afterwards the beatings were repeated, this time by Ţurcanu and his cronies. In between the beatings Ţurcanu applied the programme of 're-education'. It progressed in four stages. The first was known as 'external unmasking' by which the prisoner had to show his loyalty to the ODCC by revealing everything he had hidden from the *Securitate* interrogators. The results were written down by Ţurcanu, signed by the prisoner, and forwarded to the Ministry of the Interior. In the second phase, called 'internal unmasking', the tortured student had to reveal the names of those who had behaved more kindly or leniently towards him in prison, be it a fellow inmate or a member of staff. The third and fourth stages had another purpose: the destruction of the prisoner's personality and moral fibre. Thus the third stage, known as 'public moral unmasking', required the student to denounce everything he held most dear, his family, his faith, his friends and finally himself. Only when his moral collapse seemed to Ţurcanu to be complete, and when he was thus worthy of admission into the ODCC, was the student subjected to the final stage, the one which guaranteed no return: the re-educated figure was forced to conduct the process of re-education of his best friend, torturing him with his own hands and thus becoming one of Ţurcanu's disciples.

The confessions were regularly interrupted by physical violence. Over a period of weeks the student was subjected to an exhausting programme of labour. Sometimes he was made to clean the floor of a cell with a rag clenched between his teeth and to goad him on one of the re-educated students would ride on his back. At night the students slept on pallets. Other students, who had already been through the experiment, sat at the foot of each pallet and at the moment when a student fell into a deep sleep, the one at the end of the pallet was required to strike him hard on the soles of his bare feet with a rubber hose. Each night thus became a torment during which the student tried *not* to fall asleep. Weary, and in constant fear of pain, the student soon reached a state of helplessness and desperation.[11]

In this first stage of brainwashing the treatment required the victims to experience sensations of intense pain when eating and drinking. Students were made to kneel on the floor with their hands behind their backs and lap up scalding-hot food from bowls as fast as they could. Their excrement was sometimes placed in these same bowls and they were forced to eat it. Eating thus became a source of humiliation as well as of pain, and the senses of taste, smell, and touch were repeatedly associated with pain. Ţurcanu was particularly sadistic towards theology students. Some were 'baptised' in the mornings by having their heads plunged into a bucket of urine while others chanted the baptism rites. One student had been tortured in this way so often that he 'baptised' himself automatically in this way every morning. On Easter morning

11 Raţiu, *Stolen Church*, p.101.

1950 a student was made to play the role of priest. He was dressed in an excrement-covered sheet and given a roll of DDT in the shape of a phallus which his colleagues had to kiss. Many doubtless contemplated escape by suicide but there were no means of effecting it. Cutlery was only given to the re-educated, and the students were watched permanently. One succeeded: Şerban Gheorghe threw himself down the stairwell from the fifth floor of the prison.

Ţurcanu's special victim was Alexandru Bogdanovici, his former friend whom he held responsible for his own arrest. In March 1950, he subjected him to three days of uninterrupted torture by jumping on his stomach and chest until his internal organs were crushed. Bogdanovici went into a coma and died on Maundy Thursday.[12] During his interrogation at Piteşti on 4 April 1953, Ţurcanu said that he had killed Bogdanovici because he had been a member of the SSI (the Secret Intelligence Service) during the war against the Soviet Union.[13] At least fourteen others died in Piteşti during the re-education process.[14]

Eventually, 'tortured, starved, sleepless, terrified, trapped, alone, at the edge of death but not allowed to die, the student at last reached a point at which he would plead to give incriminating evidence against himself.'[15] It was at this point, after six weeks of torment, that the 'unmasking' began. It took the form of a written confession of the student's 'crimes'. He was made to dwell on every misdeed he had ever done prior to his arrest, even things he intended to do. Ţurcanu and his assistants sought systematically to destroy everything that anchored the personality of the prisoner so that they could control him at will. Each student who was an active Christian had to deny his faith by blaspheming the Eucharist and singing hymns into which obscene words had been inserted. Each family member's past was distorted and invested with aberrant features. A father, for example, had to appear as a crook. As many of the students were from country areas and were sons of priests,

12 Ierunca, *Piteşti*, p.46.

13 C. Aioanei, C. Troncotă, 'Arhipelagul Ororii (II)', *Magazin Istoric*, vol.27, no.4 (April 1993), p.11, n.1.

14 At the trial, the prosecution identified the following as victims and mentioned an unspecified number of others: Alexandru Bogdanovici, Corneliu Nita, Eugen Gavrilescu, Gheorghe Şerban and Gheorghe Vatajoiu. *Memorialul Ororii*, p. 644.

15 Raţiu *Stolen Church*, p.101.

they were forced to describe erotic deeds ascribed to their fathers, while their mothers were made out to be prostitutes.

Next, the student was made to deny his own identity (his mask) by writing a false autobiography for which he concocted a history of sexual deviance. This was meant to inculcate in him a sense of moral decadence and to destroy his value system. Through torture lies were turned into truth and truth into lies. The student, as Bacu writes, 'would see the world as a god with two faces; the first, which he had thought was real, had now become unreal; the second, fantastic and ugly beyond any previous imaginings, had now become real. [...] The lie was accepted as a biological necessity for survival.'[16]

Stripped of his old persona the student was now dependent on Ţurcanu's lies and a slave to his commands. Crazed with fear and reduced to an infantile state of reliance, the student became Ţurcanu's puppet, ready to be jerked into action. As a final act of self-destruction he was ordered to prove his loyalty to his new master by inflicting on the next group of students the same treatment that he himself had undergone. If he was regarded as too lenient in the beatings he gave, or less than zealous in depriving his victims of sleep, he was seen as a failure and subjected a second time to the 'umasking' process. When the students were forced to inflict torture on others, or simply to witness it, their imagination exaggerated the pain felt; this had a stronger psychological effect than if they themselves were being struck. One student described this to Bacu:

> 'Watching others being tortured, I had the impression that I had been bound and placed on a powder keg, and that a madman constantly circled the keg with a lighted candle. I expected the flame to touch the powder at any moment, and that the keg with me on it would be blown up. That could have happened at anytime; in other words, if a re-educator suddenly took the notion that I had been given too light a punishment for my suspected guilt, he could have transferred me from "spectator" to "sufferer" on the spot – the equivalent of setting off the powder with the candle flame.'[17]

[16] *Ibid.*, p.104.

[17] *Ibid.*, p.106.

Gaining the confidence of those to be subjected to the process was a prerequisite for the brainwashing. Those freshly re-educated befriended or renewed old friendships with their intended victims. Then, at a given signal, they would pull out concealed cudgels and ferociously beat them. One can imagine the mental collapse this produced in the victim. As the programme was applied throughout 1950 and 1951 in Piteşti teams of re-educated students were unleashed and sent to other prisons, notably to Gherla and the Danube-Black Sea Canal labour camp at the peninsular colony. At the latter the students were responsible for seeing that each day's work norm was done, and they pushed many prisoners so hard that they died of exhaustion. Re-education was carried out in huts 13 and 14, the group in the former being led by by a Cluj medical student named Bogdănescu, and that in hut 14 by Enăchescu, a student of medicine at Bucharest. The most notorious torturers in these two groups were Laitin, the Grama brothers, Cojocaru, Climescu, Stoicescu, Lupaşcu and Morărescu.

It was Bogdănescu's manslaughter of an eminent doctor, Professor Simionescu, while undergoing re-education in hut 13 that precipitated the termination of the programme at the canal. Simionescu's beatings at the hands of Bogdănescu led him to throw himself on the barbed wire perimeter fence where he was shot by the camp guards. News of the doctor's death reached his wife who protested to the Ministry of the Interior, and foreign radio stations broadcasting in Romanian such as Voice of America, Radio Free Europe and the BBC. Their reports prompted a Ministry of the Interior inquiry at the peninsular camp. Here is a vivid illustration of the iniquity of the Communist regime's machinery of repression: the very body which, in the person of Nicolski, implemented the programme, on realising that its details could no longer be kept secret, set up an inquiry to absolve itself of responsibility. As a result of the inquiry some ten 're-educators' were transferred from the canal camp, and its director Georgescu was replaced by a certain Lazăr. Conditions in the camp improved; better food was served to the prisoners and standards of hygiene raised. Such were the circumstances in which the programme was stopped at the canal.[18]

The selection of students sent to the canal camps had been made at Piteşti by Colonel Zeller, an officer in the Penitentiary

[18] Ierunca, *Piteşti*, pp.70-1.

Directorate of the Ministry of the Interior. In the winter of 1951, he also despatched a group of thirty to forty 're-educators', led by Ţurcanu and including the Livinski brothers and Ion Popescu, to Gherla, to test the programme on older victims. Another group was sent to the Ocnele Mari prison near Rîmnicu Vîlcea, and a third one to the prison sanatorium for tuberculosis sufferers at Tîrgu Ocna in Moldavia where the programme was supervised by Nuţi Pătrăşcanu. It was at these last two institutions that the programme ran into difficulties. In the sanatorium the patients, being sick, could not be subjected to its full force. One patient, a student called Virgil Ionescu, tried to commit suicide and other students went on hunger strike. One Sunday, while a football match was being played on ground adjacent to the sanatorium, the patients screamed for help and word reached the town. The local *Securitate* bureau chief Captain Bălan ordered an inquiry. Not one of the re-educators was punished, but the programme was halted.[19] At Ocnele Mari the prison regime was less severe than at Piteşti since it also held common criminals and it was easier for prisoners to communicate amongst each other. Some prisoners were ex-ministers and university professors who threatened mass-suicide when attempts were made to apply the programme. Fears that word would get out about the programme led to its suspension there.

Threats of disclosure did not always work. Bacu relates a visit to Gherla made, it seems, by Nicolski during the re-education drive in the prison and mentions the complaints made by a prisoner to the assistant director of the *Securitate*. The prison commandant Gheorghiu denied any knowledge of the programme. Subsequently the prisoner was tortured by Ţurcanu who pulled out his toe-nails with a pair of pliers. Former prisoners at Gherla testified to Bacu about the direct involvement of the prison commandant, his political officer Avădanei and the prison doctor Bărbosu in the re-education process. Aristide Ionescu, a Gherla inmate and one of the few unsuccessful targets of re-education, recalls the names of some of Ţurcanu's assistants: the Livinski brothers, Mărtinuş and Popa Ţanu.[20] These had not been through the programme themselves. Other torturers at Gherla who had done so were Paul Caravia,

19 *Ibid.*, p.59.

20 Ionescu, *Dacă vine*, p.46.

later an archivist at the architecture faculty of the University of Bucharest, Aristotel Popescu, Cornel Pop, Danil Dumitreasa, Morărescu and Măgirescu. Another Gherla torturer named by Bacu was Ludovic Rek, a Transylvanian Hungarian, who clubbed to death Ion Fluieraş, a leading member of the Social Democratic Party, with a sack of sand in 1953.

Gherla, it appears, was the last bastion of the re-education programme. It was here that the veteran re-educators were active until the summer of 1952 when they were told to pack their belongings. Ţurcanu, Popa Ţanu, Livinski and others were moved to Bucharest and the prisoners at Gherla could breathe a little more easily. There is no published record of what happened next to Ţurcanu and his colleagues; word-of-mouth testimony indicates that they were ordered to write a report on the programme, its methods, and its effectiveness, for the *Securitate*. On its completion they were asked to make a declaration stating that the programme had been carried out without authority from the party and even without that of the prison authorities. They then realised that a trap had been laid for them and refused. It was now their turn to be tortured.

The re-education experiment was brought to an end in 1952. Its termination was linked to the purge of Pauker, Luca and Georgescu, and was possibly part of Dej's strategy to demonstrate the validity of his claims to have ended a regime of terror initiated by the troika. The fact that Colonel Zeller, an officer in the Penitentiary Directorate of the Ministry of the Interior directly involved in the programme and a friend of Pauker, shot himself shortly after her dismissal, supports this explanation. But just as Pauker's friendship with Stalin and Molotov spared her a trial, so Nicolski's connection with the NKGB ensured his immunity from prosecution. Marin Jianu, a deputy minister of the interior under Georgescu, directly implicated Nicolski in the re-education programme carried out in Gherla, during his interrogation shortly after Georgescu's arrest on 18 February 1953.[21] Preparations for the trial of Ţurcanu

21 ASRI, dosar 40009, vol.21, p.111. The relevant part of the transcript of Jianu's interrogation reads:

Question How and in what circumstances were a number of self-denunciations made by the prisoners in the prisons?

Answer I know from Colonel Teodor Sepeanu, Colonel Dulgheru and General

and his accomplicies lasted two years with only Gheorghe Calciu and Măgirescu resisting and refusing to make the required declarations; and they were, in fact, tried separately. In order to absolve the regime of any blame in the re-education programme, the re-educators were to be portrayed as agents of Horia Sima, the former Iron Guard leader. This scenario required that all the torturers who had no Iron Guard connections be tried separately (i.e. Titus Leonida, Fuchs, Steiner, Bogdănescu, Dan Diaca, and Cori Gherman). Thus only the former guardists Ţurcanu, Popa Alexandru (Ţanu), Nuţi Pătrăşcanu, Livinski, and eighteen others stood trial together.

At the secret trial of Ţurcanu and his associates, which opened on 20 September 1954, it was alleged that Horia Sima, from his place of exile in Spain, had given Ţurcanu orders in 1949 to carry out a programme of torture in Piteşti in order to compromise the Communist regime.[22] The prosecution indictment stated that twenty-two prisoners, led by Ţurcanu, were being sent for trial 'for the murder of over thirty prisoners, and the abuse and torture of over 780 prisoners, of whom 100 had been left with severe injuries. Some of them had committed suicide to avoid torture, while others had gone mad owing to the psychological and physical pressures to which they had been subjected.'[23] Nothing was said about the involvement of the Soviets or of Nicolski, but the collusion of certain prison staff in the actions of Ţurcanu's group was recognised. In the words of the indictment: 'At Suceava prison the Iron Guardist Eugen Ţurcanu worked with the governor Tiron

---

> Nicolski that in the prisons, as a positive result of the work of the newly-introduced department of inspections, the Iron Guardists held in prison began to make self-denunciations of their own accord, making fresh disclosures which had not emerged during their interrogation before trial. I asked Colonel Sepeanu how he achieved these results. He replied that by using the 'enlightenment methods' employed by the officers in this department and the information which they extracted, they succeeded in persuading the imprisoned Iron Guardists to denounce themselves. I was not told that other methods or physical pressures were used in this respect.

(Declaration of Marin Jianu, from ASRI, *Dosarul de anchetă al lotului de la* Interne, Ministerul de *Interne* [Interrogation file of the group from the Ministry of the Interior], dosar 40009, vol.26, f.141).

22 Ierunca, *Piteşti*, p.80.

23 Aioanei, 'Arhipelagul Ororii (II)', p.16.

and Second-Lieutenant Marici in the re-education of the prisoners, and later he arranged with the latter his transfer to Bucharest jail to organise the so-called re-education there. Both the inspector general of prisons Farcaş and his political advisor Stanga were aware of this transfer.' In the case of Piteşti prison, the indictment accused the governor Alexandru Dumitrescu, the political adviser Marina, the inspector general Iosif Nemeş, and Lieutenants Mihai Mircea and Nicolae of helping Ţurcanu.[24]

The most senior figure in the Ministry of the Interior to be implicated in the experiment in evidence presented under interrogation by some of the accused was Marin Jianu, a deputy minister of the interior. He was alleged by Gheorghe Popescu to have told prison officials at Piteşti to 'use beatings for intimidation... and then he chose five of us and told us that we would receive extra food if we administered the beatings as well.'[25] But it was the smaller-fry in the ministry who were used as scape-goats. Colonel Tudor Sepeanu of the Prison Directorate of the Ministry of the Interior, Alexandru Dumitrescu, director of Piteşti prison, and three officers who had worked at Gherla, Gheorghe Sucigan, Constantin Avadanei and Viorel Bărbosu, were tried in April 1957 for 'encouraging criminal acts of terror' to take place, code for their part in the re-education programme at Piteşti and Gherla. They were sentenced to terms of imprisonment ranging from five to eight years, to be calculated from the time of their detention for questioning in spring 1953.[26]

No distinction was made at the trial, presided over by Colonel Alexandru Petrescu – who had officiated at the trial of Iuliu Maniu in 1947 – between the two categories of accused: those who had not been subjected to the programme (Ţurcanu, Popa, Nuţi Pătrăşcanu, and Livinski) and those who had become torturers because they had (Gheorghe Popescu, Cornel Pop, Dan Dumitrescu, and Octavian Voinea). On 10 November 1954 the Bucharest Military Tribunal found the accused guilty and sentenced them all to death. The twenty-two were Eugen Ţurcanu, Alexandru Popa (Ţanu), Nuţi Pătrăşcanu, Mihai Livinski, Gheorghe Popescu, Cornel Pop, Dan Dumitrescu, Octavian Voinea, Vasile Puşcaşu,

[24] *Ibid.*

[25] *Ibid.*

[26] *Memorialul Ororii*, pp.781-2.

Vasile Păvăloaie, Ion Stoian, Grigore Romanescu, Aristotel Popescu, Maximilian Sobolevschi, Constantin Juberian, Cornel Popovici, Ion Voiu, Ion Cerbu, Cristian Paul Şerbănescu, Constantin Ionescu, Octavian Zrbanca and Nicolae Colibaş. The youngest was twenty-five and the oldest thirty-four (Ţurcanu was twenty-nine). Six of the condemned, Alexandru Popa, Nuţi Pătrăşcanu, Dan Dumitrescu, Octavian Voinea, Vasile Puşcaşu, and Aristotel Popescu, were spared execution for they were to be tried on other charges connected with the programme. They benefited from an amnesty in 1955 which commuted all death sentences into ones of forced labour for life. Ţurcanu and the fifteen others were executed at Jilava by firing squad on 17 December 1954.[27]

Nothing illustrates more graphically the coercive nature of the centralising policies pursued by the Communist regime than its use of forced labour. Just as the Ministry of State Security was, at Stalin's death in 1953, the second largest employer of labour in the Soviet Union, so too the Ministry of the Interior in Romania was effectively charged with managing part of the economy. Cosmetically obscured by the euphemism 'temporary labour service', forced labour was used as an instrument of punishment for the thousands charged with 'economic sabotage' and 'absenteeism'. Included among their number were the tens of thousands of peasants who resisted the forced collectivisation of agriculture. The list of others liable to internment in the camps was compendious: those who spread 'alarmist, tendentious and hostile rumours', who slandered the Romanian Workers' Party, its leaders, the Soviet government and its leaders, and the other People's Democracies, Romanian citizens who visited 'imperialist' embassies or who had contacts with the diplomats or families of such embassies, those who urged resistance to government policies, 'elements with a well-known reactionary past', active members of the former democratic opposition parties and of the Iron Guard, members of the former SSI, the *Siguranţa*, and of the former police, those convicted of trying to cross the frontier illegally since 1945, convicted speculators and saboteurs, the father and adult sons of those who had fled the country after 1945, and of Iron Guardists who had fled before 1944.

Forced labour was officially introduced under the labour code

27 *Cartea Albă a Securităţii*, vol.II, doc.219, pp.487-8.

of 8 June 1950 although it had been practised for more than a year in the construction of the Danube-Black Sea Canal. The labour camps themselves, initially known as 'labour units' (*unităţi de muncă*), were similarly legalised retrospectively on 13 January 1950 by a decree of the Grand National Assembly since they had been established for the canal project in May 1949. The decree stipulated the setting up of units for 'the re-education through labour of elements hostile to the RPR'.[28] It placed the running of the camps under the authority of the Council of Ministers, an authority which was transferred to the Ministry of the Interior by a further decree of 10 March 1950. Persons liable to be interned in the camps were defined in an order issued on 3 April 1950 by Gheorghe Pintilie, head of the *Securitate*.[29]

On 22 August 1952, the Council of Ministers adopted Resolution 1554 by which the camps were renamed 'work colonies' (*colonii de muncă*). It was signed by Dej as president of the council. Ten new categories of persons liable for internment were added to

[28] *Organizarea şi funcţionarea Organelor Ministerului de Interne de la Infiinţare pîna în prezent*, Bucharest; Ministry of the Interior, 1978 (mimeographed), p.112. Article 1 of the decree of 13 January 1950 read: 'Labour camps are to be established for the re-education of elements hostile to the Romanian People's Republic and for the preparation and integration of these elements into the social life of a People's democracy where socialism is being constructed.' Persons liable to be sent to the camps were defined in article 2 as

(*a*) 'those who through their actions or attitudes, directly or indirectly, threaten or attempt to threaten the People's democracy, who hamper or try to hamper the construction of socialism in the RPR, as well as those who slander the state or its bodies, [even] if these deeds do not constitute, or cannot constitute by analogy, crimes; and

(*b*) those convicted of crimes against the security of the RPR who, on the expiry of their sentence, show themselves not to have been re-educated.'

The re-education term was stipulated to be from six months to two years, but the same article 4 provided for its extension up to five years. Anyone leaving the camps without written authority was subject to a imprisonment for a period from six months to five years.

[29] They included 'all those who launch or spread alarmist, tendentious or hostile rumours, or listen or spread the shameless propaganda of the imperialist radio stations: all those who slander the Romanian Workers' Party or its leaders, or the Soviet Union and its leaders; all those Romanian citizens who have frequented or frequent the libraries and embassies of the capitalist powers in Romania', and those who instigated resistance to collectivisation or conducted religious proselytisation; see Cristian Troncota, 'Colonia de munca', *Arhivele Totalitarismului*, vol.1, no.1 (1993), p.170.

those in the order of April 1950. The resolution also introduced the penalty of fixed domicile, or internal exile, *(domiciliu obligatoriu)* which was aimed at those who had not been 're-educated' in prison or in the labour camps and were still deemed to represent a threat to state security. Within its remit also fell former landowners, bankers and wholesale merchants, the close female relatives of those who fled the country before 1944 (Iron Guardists) and those who left since 1945 and were opponents of the regime in exile. Exempted from these provisions – as long as they were not relatives of Iron Guardists – were artists, sculptors, composers and academicians 'who work honestly and are useful to society'.[30]

Identifying those to be sent to the labour camps – and later, into internal exile – was entrusted to a commission of the Ministry of the Interior, set up on 25 August 1952 by Drăghici, and put under the chairmanship of his deputy, Gheorghe Pintilie, who was also chief of the *Securitate*.[31] The numbers of inmates were swelled by the victims of mass deportations from the major cities carried out by the militia. These had begun in 1952 to make room for the workers drafted in to provide manpower for new urban-based factories created in the drive to industrialise. Under a decree of 16 February 1952, several categories of person were to be removed from Bucharest. The families of war criminals, persons in prison, and of those who had fled abroad, purged army officers, former judges, lawyers, industrialists, and those who owned more than 10 hectares of land, were to be deported on twelve to twenty-four hours notice, and were allowed to take with them 50 kilos of luggage. Many of them were in fact taken to the labour camps.

The largest concentration of labour camps – fourteen in all – was for construction work on the Danube-Black Sea Canal project.

[30] Resolution 1554 of 22 August 1952 of the council of ministers. The conditions under which internal exile was to be served were revised in March 1954 when the period of detention was fixed at between six months and five years. Certain localities in the Bărăgan plain to the west of Bucharest were designated for internal exile (Resolution 337 of 11 March 1954 of the council of ministers). The designated villages or communes were Drepia, Pelican, Ezerul, Olaru, Măzăreni, Zagna, Rubla, Schei, Bumbăcari, Brateş, Salcîmi, Valea Viilor, Răchitoasa, Movila Goidoului, Lădeşti, Fundata, Viişoara, Dolga Noua.

[31] The six other members were Maj.-Gen. Alexandru Nicolschi, Col. Aurel Corin, Lt.-Col. Iosif Erdei, and Majors Francisc Butica, Marin Vintilă and Wilhelm Einhorn.

In them were packed prisoners from every walk of life: members of the professional classes rubbed shoulders with dispossessed farmers, Orthodox and Uniate priests with Zionist leaders, Yugoslavs from the Banat with Saxons from Transylvania, all were victims of the total denial of human rights which accompanied the Romanian regime's programme of political and economic revolution. The construction of the canal was undertaken on the initiative of Comecon and approved by the Romanian Politburo on 25 May 1949. Its official purpose, according to decree no. 75 of the Grand National Assembly of 23 March 1950, was to provide the cheapest and most direct means of transport by river to the Black Sea by building a canal cutting the Danube's passage to the sea by 260 km. Construction of the canal would also help to industrialise the southeastern corner of the country, would improve the irrigation of the Dobrogea province, thereby increasing agricultural yields, and would provide training in new engineering techniques to those involved in its construction.[32]

But the canal may also have had a broader economic purpose as well as a military significance: in respect of the former, it could have served as part of a wider Soviet scheme to create an 'Eastern Ruhr' for which Soviet iron ore was to be shipped through a double canal: Black Sea-Danube and Danube-Oder-Rhine; its military rationale lay in the ability it offered Stalin to send many small Soviet vessels up the Danube in the event of a deterioration of relations with Yugoslavia. Support for both scenarios was found in the Soviet decision to give financial backing to the project, backing which would not have been given to other Romanian economic plans.

Work on the canal began at the end of the summer of 1949 on the basis of construction plans drawn up by a special Soviet-Romanian commission in May. The plans were approved by the Council of Ministers on 22 June under resolution 613 and a board called the *Direcţia Generală a Lucrărilor Canalul Dunăre-Marea Neagră* (The General Directorate of the Danube-Black Sea Canal Works) was set up to run the project. In September, Gheorghe Hossu was appointed director and Mayer Grunberg first assistant-director

32 Doina Jela, *Cazul Nichita Dumitru. Incercare de reconstituire a unui proces comunist*, Bucharest: Humanitas, 1995, p.28.

and chief engineer.[33] Before excavation proper could be undertaken, a great deal of preparatory work was necessary. This involved the erection of barrack-like wooden shacks to house workers and of canteens; the construction of access-roads to the sites; modifications to the railways; installing electrical generators; and of particular importance, measures to remove the mosquitoes that infested the area. Medical care was to be provided by one doctor, a health-worker, and two nurses for every 1,500 workers.

The workforce was to be supplied from three sources: volunteer paid labour, forced labour, and army conscripts. On 29 June 1949 the Canal Directorate (DGC) requested all ministries to instruct every factory under their control to recruit manpower for the canal. There was an urgent need for surveyors, mechanical and building engineers, and technicians. Administrative personnel were also required such as managers and accountants, together with support staff such as typists. Among the skilled labourers sought were welders, blacksmiths, carpenters, locksmiths, plumbers, car mechanics and bricklayers. Recruiting offices were set up in Bucharest and in the major towns. It was reported that by September 8,960 persons had been recruited.[34]

Both the planning and execution of the canal were supervised by Soviet counsellors. The whimpering tone of some of the requests sent by Gheorghe Hossu, the director-general of the canal, to Shaposhnikov, the head of the Soviet commission for planning the canal, indicates that relations between the two parties were far from smooth, and to judge from a stenogram of a meeting in May 1952 between Hossu and another Soviet specialist called Vorobiov about the payment of bonuses, Vorobiov considered himself to be a master rather than a partner.[35]

A special newspaper called *Canalul Dunăre-Marea Neagră* was printed to instil enthusiasm into the work-force. Initially it appeared as an eight-page weekly, but later appeared two or three times a week. In its first edition of 3 September 1949, it took up a speech of Ana Pauker, given on the eve of 23 August, the national

33 *Ibid.*, p.26.

34 On 9 August 1949, the DGC sent in a request to the Ministry of Trade and Food for 28,500 kg. of salted bacon for the workforce. At the same time, a large number of Ziss lorries were ordered from the State Planning Committee.

35 *Ibid.*, p.31.

holiday, in which she saluted the plan for the canal which 'we will build without the bourgeoisie and against it'. In fact, this slogan was hung from a pole in front of the canteen on the site at Cernavodă. Pauker's threatening tones constrasted with the idyllic, exalted character of the other articles in this issue, one of which reported the ceremonial handing-over of a library and a radio to the workers on the sites at Poarta Albă and Canara. The library, it said, numbered almost a thousand volumes, 'many of which were works of Soviet literature'. The festive occasion was crowned by the singing of the *Internationale* and the showing of a Soviet film.

Another article laid down the tasks of the 'agitator', who was to read aloud the party newspaper *Scînteia* in the evening in the dormitory, to get the labourers to listen to the radio in a group, to concoct suitable slogans to inspire the work-force, to encourage workers in the surrounding villages to give support to the canal labourers, and last, but probably not least, to unmask saboteurs. The charge of 'sabotage' against unfortunate scapegoats came to be used with increasing frequency in an attempt to cover-up a lack of planning which became all too evident in most areas.

Most of the employees of the prison system were poorly educated. Collaboration by selected inmates brought privilege. Without spies and stool-pigeons, and opportunists, the labour camps would have become unmanageable. Terror cowed the mass of prisoners; petty status – and the fear of its loss – drove the gaolers.

The canal files are revealing: insufficient on-site accomodation meant that many workers were forced to sleep either in or under carts; the unasphalted tracks exacted a heavy toll on lorry tyres which continually exploded and there was a shortage of facilities for reparing inner-tubes, medical care was administered from peasant houses due to a lack of clinics. Feeding the huge force of voluntary workers not only posed logistical problems but placed an enormous strain on the resources of the Dobrogea region. A report from the Ministry of Industry dated 26 September 1949 expressed alarm that between 600 and 800 sheep were being slaughtered daily to feed the workers on the canal. These sheep were prized for their wool and the ministry recommended that sheep from other parts of the country that gave poorer-quality wool should be slaughtered in their place.[36]

[36] *Ibid.*, p.38.

It is now possible to give more exact figures about the number of political prisoners exploited on this project since some 2,400 files on the scheme, held in the State Archives in Constanţa, have been opened for research.[37] These prisoners were euphemistically termed *forţe MAI* (labour resources of the Ministry of the Interior) and were held in fourteen camps. By spring 1952, their numbers had reached 19,000. In addition, 20,000 voluntary civilian workers were employed together with 18,000 conscript soldiers.[38] Once they had arrived at the canal, the political prisoners were subjected to the process of 're-education through labour'. The methods used were described in an internal report of the military procurature, drawn up for the Ministry of the Interior on 27 February 1954:

> Many prisoners were beaten without justification with iron bars, shovels, spades and whips. Many died as a result of the blows received while others remained crippled for the rest of their lives. A number of prisoners were shot dead, others were denied medical treatment when sick and forced to work against medical advice and consequently several died. Prisoners were put naked or skimpily dressed in isolation cells in winter. Prisoners were punished by making them stand in frozen water until lunchtime. Prisoners were tied by the hands and exposed naked in the summer to be bitten by mosquitos.[39]

The camp officers most frequently mentioned by prisoners as perpetrators of these excesses were Ioan Pavel, the commandant of the Salcia camp, and his fellow officers Ion Popa, Petre Manciulea and Tudor Ilinca, and Liviu Borcea from the Capul Midia camp. On Drăghici's orders, the deaths of prisoners were covered up and not reported to the registrar of deaths. It is therefore impossible to calculate accurately how many prisoners died in the camps. A *Securitate* investigation in 1967 into deaths in the labour camps revealed that 'no documents were drawn up for the deaths of 1,304 prisoners who had died in the camps, and the deaths were not notified to the local council registrars.'[40]

[37] These have been studied by Doina Jela and the results of her research have been published in her study cited above.

[38] *Ibid.*, pp.21, 148.

[39] Troncotă, 'Colonia de muncă', p.174.

[40] *Ibid.*, p.176. Not all camp commandants turned a blind eye to excesses. On

Labour-camp memoir literature offers much detail about the conditions in which the political prisoners toiled. Eloquent in this sense are the views of no less a figure than Gheorghe Cristescu, the general secretary of the outlawed Romanian Communist Party from 1921 to 1924, who spent periods in prison in the inter-war period as a member of an illegal organisation. In 1949, he was re-arrested for 'rightist deviation'. Asked by a fellow prisoner at the Capul Midia penal colony – one of the fourteen camps supplying labour for the Danube-Black Sea canal – to compare the penal regime under King Carol with that under the Communists, Cristescu replied that treatment at the hands of the 'bourgeois' *Siguranţa* and their prisons was 'luxurious' in comparison with that meted out by his comrades.[41]

The fellow-prisoner in question was Şerban Papacostea. In the spring of 1950, as part of its campaign to break contacts with the West, the regime clamped down on Romanians who frequented Western institutes and libraries. Many students were arrested, among them Papacostea, who was detained on 3 March 1950 for using the French library in Bucharest. After being taken to *Securitate* headquarters on Rahova street, he was moved to Jilava jail and then to a screening centre at Ghencea on the outskirts of Bucharest, from where he was transported by train to the Capul Midia labour camp on the Black Sea. On arrival, the prisoners were lined up before the camp commandant who called out their names and assigned them their tasks. Papacostea noticed that the commandant had a file for each prisoner and that a coloured diagonal stripe on it indicated the regime to be appplied to him. Although suffering from a muscular disability, Papacostea was put to the daily task of digging 4m^3 of earth a day and carting it up a mound with a wheelbarrow. Unable to fulfil this quota he expected severe punishment, but in fact he was shielded by one of the guards, a Lieutenant Filip, who often helped the prisoners.[42] Other prisoners were less

---

23 August 1950 a prisoner at the Poarta Albă camp on the canal was shot by a guard while trying to escape. Captain Domşa, the commandant, who was the son of a priest from the Banat, ordered the arrest of the guard. The latter was tried and sentenced to five years' detention in the same camp where the prisoners regularly beat him. (Communication from Alexandru Salca, AFDP, Braşov, 30 March 1997.

41 Communication from Dr Şerban Papacostea, 5 March 1995.

42 Interview with Dr Şerban Papacostea, 24 April 1996. The food at Capul

fortunate; many were driven to exhaustion in their attempts to meet this daily quota of earth and died of tuberculosis or heart failure. According to *Securitate* figures, in the month of January 1953 alone, 133 prisoners died at the Canal.[43]

In the Capul Midia penal colony, which Papacostea estimated to house some 4,000 detainees – twenty huts each containing about 200 men – there was only one small hut designated as a 'medical centre'. It had no medicines and the only doctors available were those who were themselves prisoners. The terms of imprisonment for those held ranged from six months to two years. The detainees were not issued with fresh clothing and not being entitled to parcels of food or clothing sent from home, they remained in the same clothes in which they had been arrested and these soon become threadbare and tattered. They were awoken at 5 a.m., they washed perfunctorily from standpipes, then had a cup of chicory and a piece of bread or *mămăligă* (polenta), before being summoned to parade for the count before they left for the construction site. The counting of several thousand prisoners lasted more than an hour. The prisoners were ordered to march off and return to the construction site singing a Communist song so as not to appear downcast. A break for lunch was taken at 1 p.m. on the site. It consisted of a mug of water and bean mush. Labour continued until the early evening. Upon their return to the colony, the prisoners were again counted in and only after the count had been completed were they allowed to wash and have their evening meal which usually consisted of potato soup.

The conditions under which even the conscript soldiers were expected to work drove them to protest. Their low morale was the subject of a *Securitate* report dated 1 October 1949. They complained that they had no underwear, boots or trousers, which conditions led them to coin the slogan '*Armata democrată, desculţă*

Midia was, in Papacostea's opinion, more consistent than in Jilava jail where breakfast consisted of a cup of chicory, lunch a piece of bread and cabbage or beans, and the evening meal a pearl barely soup. At the end of July 1949, Papacostea and other students held on the same charge were released and brought by train to Bucharest.

43 *Cartea Albă a Securităţii*, vol.II, Anexă, doc.22. This figure leads us to question the accuracy of a Ministry of the Interior document when it states that the *total* number of deaths in *all* labour camps between 1945 and 1964 was 656.

şi dezbrăcata' (A people's army [is one which is] unshod and undressed). Insufficient food and space in the military canteens, unfinished billets, no washing facilities or soap added to their misery. They therefore washed in the Danube.[44] A report of the following day registered workers' dissatisfaction that they had not received their wages. Other reports signalled soldiers' complaints about their officers who struck them when they criticised the working conditions.

The true reasons for the abandonment of the canal project were never made public but the documents in the Constanţa archives reveal that bad planning played a major part. Work began long before the plans were completed and when they finally arrived, it was discovered that the original estimates in scale and cost of the construction were 50% below the true costs. The geological studies made by Soviet specialists were found to be inaccurate, and the machinery imported from the Soviet Union was either in poor condition or did not work at all since much of it was brought from the construction sites for the Volga-Don Canal and that linking the White Sea and the Caspian Sea. Facing huge losses and robbed of a major propaganda victory, Dej sought scapegoats and the *Securitate* was ordered to organise show-trials of workers who were accused of sabotage.

In the summer of 1952, Colonel Mişu Dulgheru, head of the penal investigations directorate of the *Securitate*, was summoned to a meeting at the Ministry of the Interior. The principal persons present were the minister, Alexandru Drăghici, politburo member Iosif Chişinevski, *Securitate* generals Gheorghe Pintilie, Alexandru Nicolski, Vladimir Mazuru, a Soviet official Agop Garabedian, and the Soviet security counsellors, Alexsandr Sakharovsky, Tiganov, and Maximov. Chişinevski ordered Dulgheru to organise a show trial of saboteurs at the canal and told him that 'comrade Gheorghiu-Dej wants this trial over quickly'.[45]

The first of these trials opened on 29 August 1952 in the workers' club at Poarta Albă, some 20 km. west of Constanţa. Eight engineers and two mechanics were charged with carrying out premeditated acts designed to sabotage the construction of the canal. One of the charges was that they had neglected the

[44] *Ibid.*, doc.6, p.13.

[45] *Ibid.*, doc.31, p.96.

maintenance of machinery, including locomotives, which had consequently broken down. The accused, having undergone long hours of interrogation, confessed to their 'crimes'. Thirty-one witnesses were produced for the prosecution and none for the defence. On 1 September, the military prosecutor, Major Ovidiu Teodorescu, read out the indictment. The proceedings had, he argued, 'removed the mask from the hideous face of the criminals in the dock; this small number of worthless individuals, the scum of society, aided by the British and Americans, those cavaliers of crime and the gun, those propagators of death and destruction, have shown here their true face'.[46]

After the defendants expressed regret for their 'crimes' to the court, sentence was passed immediately: five received the death penalty and the other five were condemned to hard labour for periods ranging from twenty years to life. The party newspaper reported that 'the working people greeted the just sentence with stormy applause'. Upon appeal, two of the death sentences were commuted to hard labour for life; the other three were upheld. On 14 October 1952, Nicolae Vasilescu, Aurel Rozei-Rozemberg, and Dumitru Nichita were executed by firing-squad somewhere in the Dobrogea.

In a move that was apparently linked to the Politburo's decision of 14 March 1954 to put Lucreţiu Pătrăşcanu and his associates on trial, a review of all internees in labour camps was ordered by the Council of Ministers.[47] All former Iron Guardists, senior members of the opposition parties, and officers of the pre-Communist SSI and *Siguranţa* were to be interrogated, presumably in an attempt to glean fresh evidence against the Pătrăşcanu group. By the same resolution of the Council of Ministers, the release was ordered of most of the other internees i.e. those categorised in resolution 1554 of August 1952.

The deployment of conscript soldiers in the construction of the canal presented another dimension to the practice of forced labour. In effect, the Romanian soldier was used as a navvy on major construction projects throughout the entire period of Communist rule and his conditions of labour were often little better

46 Jela, *Cazul Nichita Dumitru*, p.193.

47 Nestorescu-Bălceşti, 'Structura Conducerii Superioare a PCR', p.363. The Council's resolution was dated 11 March.

than those of the political detainees. In some cases, on security-sensitive sites, these conditions posed major health risks, as in the uranium mines in the Apuseni mountains. In the mine at Băiţa-Plai, some 20km. east of the town of Ştei, several thousand conscript soldiers – one source puts the number at 10,000 – worked under the command of Soviet officers in the extraction of uranium ore. The ore was then crushed and the dust shipped in 50-kilo drums to Kharkov in the USSR. The Soviet officers lived in purpose-built blocks of flats with their families while the conscripts were quartered in wooden huts. Many of the soldiers working underground and in the open-cast mines suffered hair-loss because of the high levels of radioactivity and in 1956 the mine was allegedly closed and the Russians withdrew from the site.[48]

Under a resolution of the Council of Ministers of February 1958 the conditions under which forced labour was used as a punishment were extended to those who 'endanger public order, even if they do not commit any crime'. Persons were still sent to perform it until 1963, by which time *Securitate* documents show that 25,735 people had been subjected to it since 1950.[49] This figure includes only those considered 'political detainees', for the common law offenders sent to the labour camps are listed separately in the archives of the militia. Even so, we must treat this figure with caution since the party investigation into the abuses committed against former activists showed in 1968 that tens of thousands were sent to the labour camps without trial and without any record of their detention being compiled.

Here is what Ilie Bădică, former deputy director of the *securitate* directorate for labour camps, had to say on the subject on 16 March 1968:

> 'The camp authorities had no means of knowing what each detainee had done since they had no arrest warrant. [...] Very many of the prisoners did not know the reason for their arrest, and some were released after a year or two without ever knowing

[48] See the interview given by Constantin Andrieş, who was posted to the mine in 1955, to Vasile Iancu under the title 'Un fost ofiţer aduce mărturii revelatoare', *România liberă*, 23 April 1996, p.4. According to Andrieş, there was another uranium mine under Soviet command at Ciudanoviţa, 20 km. north of the town of Oraviţa, in the Banat.

[49] C. Troncotă, '*Colonia de muncă*', p.172.

why they had been arrested. [...] At the Canal there were many prisoners who were held simply on the orders of the Ministry of the Interior, in breach of the constitution and of any law.'[50]

The arrests were made, in fact, on other criteria, as Bădică admitted:

'These detainees had been arrested to meet the labour required for the construction of the Danube-Black Sea canal. If they needed 5,000 men at the canal, comrade Hossu, the director general there, telephoned comrade Teohari [Georgescu] and then Colonel Dulgheru's machinery, at the Penal Investigation Directorate [of the *Securitate*], went into action and established the numbers of people to be rounded up by each county.'

This practice of the *Securitate* of arresting people at the whim of the Interior Ministry was confirmed by Pavel Ştefan, himself minister of the interior from 1952 to 1957,[51] in a declaration also given in March 1968:

'There was a lawyer called Calotă who helped us a great deal in 1945. They arrested him because he was a National Peasant Party member and they took his house. I asked him why he had been arrested, perhaps he had said something. He replied that he hadn't. Then I rang Pintilie and asked him, because he knew Calotă well. Pintilie retorted: "How many are there whom we haven't arrested just because we needed their houses!"'[52]

Pintilie's actions typified the regime's violation of human rights. This had given rise to vigorous protests by the Western governments and the United Nations in 1949. On 3 November 1950, the General Assembly had passed a resolution condemning Romania, Hungary and Bulgaria for the disregard shown by their governments for the rights and liberties of the persons under their jurisdiction. The effect was nil. In 1954, however, the Soviet Union now sought international acceptance of its satellites by proposing their admittance to the United Nations. On 25 September 1954, the Romanian government submitted a request for UN membership

50 *Ibid.*

51 Ştefan was appointed minister after responsibility for the *Securitate* was moved to the newly-created Ministry of State Security in September 1952.

52 *Ibid.*, p.173.

to the General Assembly. Dej, aware of the sensitivity of the United States and Britain to his regime's human rights' record, gave the signal in the summer of the following year for the release of thousands of political prisoners, including many of the former ministers imprisoned without trial in Sighet. At the same time, in order to show that he was not turning his back on his faithful lieutenant, Dej promoted Drăghici to the rank of Colonel-General on 20 August 1955. Exactly one month later, all those who had received sentences of up to ten years' imprisonment were pardoned. Excluded from the pardon were ministers in the 'Fascist' governments in the period 6 September 1940 to 23 August 1944.

In a package deal of 14 December 1955, Romania, Hungary and Bulgaria were among sixteen nations admitted to the United Nations. Italy, Spain and Finland were the most significant admissions gained by the West in return. Respect for the principles of the UN charter required the Communist satellites to release all political prisoners, Dej making further concessions in this respect by issuing a series of pardons to so-called 'Zionists', 'Titoists', 'saboteurs' and 'deviators' in 1956 and 1957. Among those released, on 26 May 1956, was Elena Pătrăşcanu, wife of Dej's most notable victim.

This 'clean-up' of the regime's image also led to the arrest of several labour-camp officers. On 10 June 1955 a military court sentenced thirty-two persons – twenty-one officers of the Ministry of the Interior and eleven prisoners in charge of work details – to prison terms ranging from five years to hard labour for life. But at the intervention of Drăghici, decrees were issued between August and November 1957 giving a pardon to more than fifty convicted torturers, among them camp commandants. On top of this, Pintilie, Drăghici's deputy, sent them away to the ministry's rest homes for a month, after which they were reassigned to other duties in the ministry. An edifying example of this cynicism on the part of Drăghici was the case of Liviu Borcea, a camp commandant on the Black Sea canal, who was arrested on 1 December 1954 and sentenced to twenty-five years' hard labour. Drăghici had him released within eighteen months and he was assigned the post of a deputy commandant of Cluj jail.

The records show that those convicted were merely subordinates who had carried out orders from the party and the Ministry of the Interior. By treating them in this way, Drăghici and Pintilie bought their silence, but not for long. The party inquiry of 1967 and 1968 into abuses against former activists uncovered their responsibility and led to Drăghici's final removal from all positions of authority in 1968.

10

ARMED RESISTANCE

Overt challenges to Communist rule under Dej were uncommon and none threatened to overthrow the regime, but it is unfair to accuse the Romanians on that account of being 'weak' and 'timorous'. Such accusations were based on what *appeared* to be a complete absence of challenge to the Communist regime in Romania when compared with the riots in Poland and East Germany in the early 1950s, and the uprising in Hungary in 1956. The unchallenged acceptance of these accusations is precisely a measure of the success of the *Securitate* in preventing information about resistance to the regime from leaking out. Virtually nothing was known in the West of the courageous struggle in the Carpathian mountains of small bands of partisans, led by Gheorghe Arsenescu, Toma Arnăuţoiu, and Ion Gavrilă-Ogoranu.

Armed opposition to the Communist role in the government surfaced in the winter of 1944 and had been coordinated by General Aurel Aldea (interior minister in the first Sănătescu government) in the summer of 1945.[1] This so-called 'National Resistance Movement' posed little direct threat to the Groza government, its principal activities being the distribution of primitive anti-Communist propaganda. After Aldea's arrest in May 1946, this opposition crumbled but the attacks it had carried out during the winter of 1944 on Hungarians in revenge for murders of Romanians by Hungarian policemen during the period of Hungarian rule of Northern Transylvania, had raised the spectre of civil strife in Transylvania behind the Soviet front line and showed that it offered a potential nucleus of armed resistance to Communist rule.

A number of Aldea's supporters escaped arrest by taking to the mountains. They were nearly always on the defensive, fending off regular attempts by the security forces to round them up. A

[1] See Chapter 5.

letter from J.E. Hartley, a British consular official in Cluj to the British Legation in Bucharest, dated 1 May 1949, retold stories he had heard of partisan exploits and misadventures in the Carpathians. Though he discounted many of them on the score of distortion and exaggeration, he was convinced that the partisans had come to stay. Their leader was General Dragalina. They were all Romanians, a point Hartley regarded as being in their favour should the question of Transylvania raise its head once more in the future. The partisans enjoyed the sympathy of the peasantry and appeared to have sufficient small arms and ammunition for their defensive tactics. They were not short of money either. He went on:

> I am told, however, that clothing and medicines are short and this is probably true as their numbers have been increased by a considerable proportion of women and children since the March 1st land expropriation. I have been given a figure as high as 20,000 as the number who have joined since the expropriation. [...] The increase in the number of women and children will create problems of survival next winter. [...] I am told now and again of lorries of army supplies going over to the partisans, sometimes by capture and sometimes by desertion, but I cannot say to what extent this is happening.[2]

Such was the number of similar tales in circulation that the legation in Bucharest commented that it was 'fairly confident that there must be a growing number of men in the hills who are outside the law and in armed opposition to the established authority of Romania.' The Legation was cautious in attaching much importance to this resistance: 'We doubt if it would be right to describe these dissidents as more than outlaws. Nor are they likely to be able to influence the course of events in any foreseeable circumstances'.[3]

Partisan activity was sufficiently serious for the CIA to try to exploit it. At the beginning of 1949, the Office of Political Coordination (OPC) under the direction of Frank Wisner, began to recruit Romanians from refugee camps in southern Germany, Austria and Yugoslavia. Preference was shown for young men who knew

2 Public Record Office (PRO), FO.371/78603 15584.

3 *Ibid.*

those regions in which partisan activity had been reported. Gordon Mason, the CIA station chief in Bucharest from 1949 to 1951, revealed that these agents were instructed to contact the resistance groups and to deliver light weapons, ammunition, radio transmitters and medicines to them. The agents were given three objectives. First, to encourage the partisans to carry out acts of sabotage on railways and factories; this would also offer proof of their existence and of their activity. Second, the agents were to monitor troop movements, especially those which might indicate preparations for an attack on Yugoslavia or on Western Europe. Finally, they were to encourage the partisans to harass Soviet troops should a war break out.[4]

The OPC set up training schools in France, Italy and Greece. Recruits were instructed in parachute drops and in the use of radio transmitters. Gratien Yatsevich, who directed CIA covert operations in the Balkans at the time, disclosed that in terms of resources allocated and agents recruited, the operations in Romania came second only to those in Albania. Among the Romanians recruited at the beginning of 1951 were Constantin Săplăcan, Wilhelm Spindler, Gheorghe Bârsan, Matias Bohm, and Ilie Puiu. Their interrogation by the *Securitate* after their capture revealed that they had been recruited in Italy by a former Romanian pilot and introduced to two American agents code-named Charles and Gunter. They were given their training in enciphering at a Franciscan convent in Rome and were then taken first to the Netherlands and then to Frankfurt where they were given parachute training at an American air-base. After completing this, they were flown to Athens from where they took off for Romania. They were dropped on the Negoiu mountain in the Făgăraş range on the night of 18/19 October at a pre-arranged spot. They tried to make radio-contact but their sets failed to work and they were caught within a month. Bârsan committed suicide on being arrested and his colleagues were executed in 1952.[5] A protest note was delivered by the Romanian Government to the Americans on the basis of an admission by the two men that they had been

[4] E.W. Hazard, *Cold War Crucible: United States Foreign Policy and the Conflict in Romania, 1943-1953*, Boulder, CO: East European Monographs, 1996, p.207.

[5] ASRI, Fond D, dosar 10716. I am grateful to Marius Oprea for this reference.

'sent to carry out acts of terrorism and espionage against the Romanian army'. The US Government denied any connection with Spindler and Săplăcan, but former CIA officers have since admitted that the group were American agents.[6]

After the overthrow of Ceauşescu details emerged of how several small bands of self-styled 'partisans' took to the Carpathian mountains in the late 1940s and resisted arrest by the authorities.[7] The last member of the longest-surviving group was not rounded up until 1960. This 'armed anti-Communist resistance', as it has been called, was a spontaneous phenomenon and there were no links between the different groups, but they were driven by a common aim, namely not to submit themselves to the consequences of communisation of their country. The groups were composed on average of between twenty and forty persons and yet, as long as they remained at liberty, they undermined the regime's claim to have total control of the country.

The groups were formed in the villages in the mountain foothills and were composed of peasants, former army officers, lawyers, doctors, and students. Ill-equipped, they relied on an assortment of rifles, revolvers and machine-pistols left over from the war and were always faced by an acute shortage of ammunition. They received support from villagers who brought them food and clothing and often gave them shelter. The Communist propaganda of the period dubbed these anti-Communist partisans 'legionaries', that is, members of the Iron Guard, and indeed several of them had belonged to it. However, the partisans were by no means exclusively 'legionaries', as the *Securitate's* very own statistics show. A report of the *Direcţia Generală a Securităţii Poporului* of 1951 states that the political affiliation of 804 persons arrested for either belonging to, or aiding seventeen *bande din munţi*, was as follows: eighty-eight

[6] E. Hazard, Războiul Rece a Inceput în România', *Magazin Istoric,* vol. 30, no.8 (August 1996), pp. 58-9.

[7] For a useful sketch of the activity of these partisan groups, together with a bibliography, see Ştefan Andreescu, 'A Little-Known Issue in the History of Romania: The Armed Anti-Communist Resistance', *Revue Roumaine d'Histoire,* vol.33, nos 1-2, 1994, pp.191-7. This article can be supplemented by first-hand accounts from survivors of groups which have appeared in the review *Memoria,* published by Fundaţia Culturală Memoria since 1990. See also *Cartea Albă a Securităţii,* vol.II, *passim.* For an account of the partisan group, led by a forester Nicolae Pop, in the Ţibleş mountains in Maramureş see Ştefan Bellu, *Pădurea răzvrătită,* Baia Mare: Editura Gutinul, 1993.

former members of Iuliu Maniu's National Peasant Party, seventy-nine members of the Ploughmen's Front, seventy-three former legionaries, forty-two former members of the Communist Party, fifteen members of the National Liberal Party and others.[8] According to another *Securitate* report, dated September 1949, there were 'terrorist bands' active in the regions of Craiova, Braşov, Sibiu, Ploieşti, Suceava, Galaţi, Oradea, Cluj, Timişoara and Constanţa. None of these groups was more than twenty-five strong, and most of them had less than ten members.[9]

The longest-surviving group was the *Haiducii Muscelului* (Outlaws of Muscel). Elisabeta Rizea, the only surviving member of the group, has given us an account of the early months of its activity but her arrest shortly afterwards means that for the remainder of the story we have to rely upon the second-hand versions by relatives of the participants. Many of the dates and incidents are confirmed by the *Securitate* records, but not surprisingly, the latter give a different interpretation to them. For example, these records allege that innocent civilians were murdered by the 'partisans' who are constantly vilified, being termed 'fascist terrorists'. What is reasonably clear from both sides is that the group, which at

[8] *Cartea Albă a Securităţii*, vol.II, p.82. Most of the members of the partisan group led by Major Nicolae Dabija in the Apuseni mountains between 1947 and 1949 were peasants who were not, as the Communist authorities claimed, *chiaburi* or owners of land. Thirty-two persons were tried as members or sympathisers of the group at the end of September 1949 in Sibiu, and seven were sentenced to death and executed on 28 October. Their unmarked graves were identified in the Communal Cemetery of Sibiu in January 1994 (see Andreescu, 'Armed Anti-Communist Resistance', p.191); see also *Cartea Albă a Securităţii*, vol.II, doc.55, pp.180-2, doc.65, p.190. The memoirs of a former Iron Guardist (or legionary) show that caution is required in applying the label 'Guardist' indiscriminately to the resistance groups. Filon Verca acknowledges that one of two main partisan groups in the Banat mountains in 1948 was led by Spiru Blănaru, a former Guardist, but points out that one of the commanders of the second group was Colonel Ioan Uţă, a prefect of Lugoj county, who had acted against the Guardists in 1939 (Filon Verca, *Paraşutaţi în România vândută. Mişcarea de rezistenţă 1944-1948*, Timişoara: Editura Gordian, 1993). Blănaru and the bulk of his small group were caught and executed near Timişoara on 16 July 1949. Uţă's band of thirty partisans fought off a company of *Securitate* troops near the village of Teregova on 22 February 1949, only to be caught on 8 March in a skirmish in which Uţă died. See also *Cartea Albă a Securităţii*, vol.II, doc.58, pp.184-5.

[9] *Cartea Albă a Securităţii*, vol.II, doc.75, pp.198-204.

one time never numbered more than thirty or forty persons, was formed by two ex-army officers, Gheorghe Arsenescu (1907-62) and Toma Arnăuţoiu (1921-59), in their native district of Muscel in the foothills of the Carpathians. According to the *Securitate* records Arsenescu had hidden weapons at a hermitage in the village of Cetăţeni in the summer of 1947 and in the following spring had set up a 'terrorist group' comprising Gheorghe Hachenzelner, Petre Cojocaru, Longhin Predoiu, Ion Mica, and Ion and Gheorghe Purnichescu. Arsenescu spent the autumn and winter in Bucharest and it was there, at the end of 1948, that Toma Arnăuţoiu contacted Arsenescu with a view to setting up a resistance group in the district around Nucşoara. From the recent accounts given by contemporaries, Arsenescu seems to have put his faith in a general armed insurrection which was to be led by other former army officers in the west of the country but which never materialised. He agreed to provide Arnăuţoiu with small arms and the latter then returned to Nucşoara with Nicolae Nitu and recruited his brother Petre Arnăuţoiu, Ion Chirca, and the village priest Ion Drăgoi. In March 1949, Arsenescu came to Nucşoara to join the group and in the ensuing months it expanded to include several more villagers.

The Ministry of the Interior was clearly worried that the symbol of resistance posed by the band might be contagious, and for this reason poured troops and *Securitate* officers into the region. Helped by their local knowledge of the difficult mountain terrain and by several families in the commune of Nucşoara, notably Gheorghe and Elisabeta Rizea, Ion Săndoiu and Ion Sorescu, the group secured provisions and escaped arrest. On the night of 18 June 1949, members of the group were ambushed as they came to collect supplies and in the ensuing gun-fight two *Securitate* officers, Constantin Apavaloaiei and Florea Lungu were killed. The group's escape under cover of darkness through a security cordon thrown around the area resulted in a massive search being carried out for them by two army batallions and units of the *Securitate* troops, and the arrest of families suspected of aiding them.[10]

Among those arrested was Elisabeta Rizea. She recounted how she was taken to the mayor's office in Nucşoara where she was

[10] A. Marinescu, 'Pagini din rezistenţa armată anticomunistă', *Memoria*, no.7 (1992), pp.47-51.

beaten with a heavy stick by 2nd-Lt. Constantinescu of the *Securitate*.[11] She was then held in the cellar of a peasant house for four days after which she was transported to the prison in Piteşti. Eighteen months passed before she was put on trial. In the meantime she was beaten on several occasions by warrant officers Zamfirescu and Mecu. She was finally tried and sentenced in December 1950 to seven years' imprisonment for helping the partisan group.[12]

After the ambush of 18-19 June 1949, Arsenescu decided to split his men into two bands, one under his command, the other under the leadership of Arnăuţoiu. The first band, which included Ion Chirca, Titi Mămăligă, Benone Milea, Constantin Popescu, and Nae Ciolan, based itself in the Rîul Doamnei valley, and the Arnăuţoiu band, made up of his brother Petre, Titu, Maria and Constantin Jubleanu, and Maria Plop, in the Vîlsan valley. Arsenescu's band did not survive for long. Milea was captured on 1 November 1949 and Popescu and Ciolan suffered the same fate three days later. Chirca disappeared without trace. Arsenescu and Mămăligă were caught in a trap by the security troops, the latter being wounded in a shoot-out while Arsenescu fled from the area, and led a hermit-like existence in the hills for ten years until he was finally caught in 1960. Mămăligă managed to make his way to the Arnăuţoiu group.

Shortly afterwards, in the spring of 1950, this group too was forced to split up to avoid detection. One band, made up of the husband and wife Titu and Maria Jubleanu, their son Tică, and a young doctor Ion Marinescu were tracked down and in the resulting gunfight Maria was shot dead. Titu Jubleanu was arrested but the two young men managed to escape, joining the second band, composed of the two Arnăuţoiu brothers, Toma and Petre, Maria Plop, and Mămăligă. Marinescu and Mămăligă were killed in skirmishes with the *Securitate* in 1952 and the remaining four hid out in a cave near the village of Poenărei for several years. On 20 May 1958, the brothers were deceived by a local man into drinking drugged spirits, and after falling into a comatose state were arrested. Plop, who two years earlier had given birth to a daughter as a result of her love for Toma Arnăuţoiu, surrendered

[11] I had the privilege of talking with Mrs Rizea about her exploits in her home on 9 February 1992.

[12] *Povestea Elisabetei Rizea din Nucşoara*, Bucharest: Humanitas, 1993, pp.118-25.

with the child, but Tică Jubleanu refused and shot himself.[13] A sweep of the surrounding villages in the district was made and scores of families detained for assisting the Arnăuţoiu brothers. The two brothers and Maria Plop were taken to Piteşti jail. There, together with others who were rounded up and accused of aiding the group, they were interrogated over a period of twelve months.[14]

The trial of the brothers took place in the following year. Toma and Petre Arnăuţoiu were sentenced to death and executed at Jilava prison by firing squad, on 18 October 1959, as were the following persons accused of rendering them assistance: Nicolae Andreescu and Ion Constantinescu, Orthodox priests in Poenărei, Ion Drăgoi, the Orthodox priest of Nucşoara; Nicolae Băşoiu, Titu Jubleanu, Constantin Popescu, Ion Săndoiu, Nicolae Sorescu and Gheorghe Tomeci, all peasant farmers, and the teachers Alexandru Moldoveanu, Nicolae Niţu and Gheorghe Popescu. Benone Milea was also sentenced to death and executed but Maria Plop received life imprisonment and died in jail in 1962[15] Others also tried with this group were, according to the *Securitate* records, Ilie Dragomirescu and Ion Grigore, arrested on 22 June 1958, Nicolae Vasilescu, arrested on 4 July 1958, and Ion Dumitrescu, arrested on 6 February 1959. All received long jail terms.[16] Arsenescu's trial took place in February 1962, two years after his capture. He was sentenced to death and executed at Jilava on 29 May 1962. His wife Maria and his father Gheorghe were also tried for assisting him and were given prison terms of ten and fifteen years respectively.[17]

13 Ioana-Raluca, the daughter of Toma Arnăuţoiu and Maria Plop, was taken into care and brought up in an orphanage in Câmpulung. She was only able to discover who her mother was after the overthrow of Ceauşescu.

14 A comprehensive record of Arnăuţoiu's interrogation and trial has been published by his daughter, Ioana Raluca, in *Luptătorii din munţi. Toma Arnăuţoiu. Grupul de la Nucşoara. Documente ale anchetei, procesului, detenţiei*, Bucharest: Vremea, 1997. Toma Arnăuţoiu was interrogated on forty-two separate occasions; twenty-one of the sessions lasted from three to six hours, eleven from six to ten hours, and one from ten to fifteen hours (five of the interrogation transcripts do not show their duration). His brother Petre faced thirty-seven sessions, eleven of which lasted between ten to fifteen hours. I am grateful to Ioana-Raluca Voicu-Arnăuţoiu for passing on her compilation of these figures which are based on files in the Ministry of Justice.

15 Marinescu, 'Pagini din rezistenta', pp.57–8.

16 ASRI, Fond D, File 9585, UM 0336 Piteşti, pp.44–66.

17 M. Arsenescu-Buduluca, 'Sunt soţia 'teroristului' Gheorghe Arsenescu',

A second notable resistance group was that led by Ion Gavrilă-Ogoranu in the Făgăraş mountains. Gavrilă-Ogoranu, a twenty-five-year-old student at Cluj university, formed his group of eleven from his university colleagues in 1948. For seven years they tied up several companies of security troops before being captured and sentenced to death in 1957. Gavrilă-Ogoranu was enterprising enough to escape arrest and with the help of friends escaped detection until June 1976, when he was finally picked up in Cluj.[18]

Unlike Arnăuţiou and Arsenescu, Gavrilă-Ogoranu was spared the death penalty and survived the Communist era to offer a unique personal view in his autobiography of the reaction of the population to his small band of 'partisans':

> When we took to the mountains, we knew enough about that unknown part of [Romanian] history. We never fooled ourselves. We did not count on the fact that everyone in the district of Făgăraş would join us or understand us. When I said that the mountain villages might have risen up in 1949 and in 1950, or that we were received and helped by the local people, I was not

---

Memoria, no.8, 1993, p.59. The unwillingness of the post-1989 Romanian authorities to recognise that opponents of the Communist regime were the victims of political assassinations is illustrated by the following case. In December 1951, Traian Murariu, a peasant from the commune of Pădureni in the county of Timiş, was sentenced to death for sheltering Nicolae Mazilu and Ion Mogoş, two members of the anti-Communist group in the Făgăraş mountains. He was executed a year later at Jilava jail for 'plotting against the social order'. In 1992, his daughter appealed to the Supreme Court for the sentence to be rescinded. After three years, the court informed her that the sentence was 'well-founded and legal'. (*Ziua,* 18 July 1995)

18 Ion Gavrilă-Ogoranu, *Brazii se frîng, dar nu se îndoiesc,* vol.2 Timişoara: Editura Marineasa, 1995, p.264. Gavrilă-Ogoranu's arrest in Cluj is tersely reported in a *Securitate* note of 30 June 1976 (*Cartea Albă a Securităţii,* vol.IV, doc.136, p.372. Gavrilă-Ogoranu recounts an episode in 1952 which illustrates the motivation of the resistance groups. In order to distract the pursuing forces of the *securitate,* Gavrilă-Ogoranu took part of his group to a tourist chalet near lake Bâlea. After forcing the tourists from the chalet Gavrilă-Ogoranu addressed them as follows: Tell everyone that there is still a place in the kingdom of Romania which has not bowed to Communism. As long as our heads are on our shoulders, this corner of the country will be free. Tell the people not to lose faith, for the day will come when the whole of Romania will be free. Pray God for it, so help us God' (Gavrilă-Ogoranu, *Brazii se Plâng,* vol.1, p.304).

> referring to a particularly large number of people. [...] There might have been a hundred, two hundred, maybe a thousand. But the rest of the inhabitants? Some did not come out of fear. And they have to be understood. Others were only concerned with their own interests. Any step you take in life is a calculated one. Regimes change, the profiteers remain. One side exits the scene, and that very same side returns. They never have principles or pangs of conscience. Regimes and ideologies cannot be changed as long as they are able to adapt themselves so quickly. [...] You are then left with the great mass of the labourers, whose life is reduced to work and food, in an eternal cycle, and whose consciences do not rise above the bowl of food in front of their noses. They are so down-trodden and so well-conditioned to be down-trodden that they cannot, would not and do not think of looking beyond. Their eyes are those of a mole's. They hate anyone who wants to deliver them from their existence as slaves. With them the authorities can do what they want; in the first place, to do their thinking for them.[19]

This appraisal, coming from such a venerable figure in the resistance to Communist rule as Gavrilă-Ogoranu has a more convincing ring about the attitude of much of the local population to resistance groups than the tendency towards hyperbole which characterises some of the writing about the 'armed resistance' which has appeared since the revolution. It is as though some authors feel embarassment at the fact that challenges to Communist authority in Romania under Dej were not as widespread or as serious as in some of the other Soviet satellites and seek to overcompensate by exaggerating the scale of resistance in Romania. The publication of *memoir* literature and the opening of the *Securitate* files have dispelled the general impression that there was no opposition to Communist rule, but at the same time, they have revealed the true dimension of resistance. It was not widespread, as Gavrilă-Ogoranu points out, and never threatened to overthrow the regime. In consequence, his activity, like that of Arnăutoiu and Arsenescu and others, appears all the more valiant and poignant.

19 Gavrilă-Ogoranu, *Brazii se frâng*, pp.267-8.

11

DEJ EMERGES SUPREME, 1952-1956

If Dej had played his part in scenarios provided by Stalin since the imposition of Communist rule in Romania, from 1952 he was offered the opportunity to direct. This was amply demonstrated when the order came from Stalin to purge alleged Zionists. Apart from its political impact the purge had a further significance, in that it continued the pattern of internecine struggles which characterised the history of the RCP; and in so doing it reinforced a culture of violence and fear that permeated Romanian society.

At this stage, Dej had two major rivals in the Romanian leadership – Ana Pauker and Vasile Luca – but even Dej could not simply have them removed. There had to be ostensibly doctrinal reasons. By 1950, 'Zionism' had replaced 'Titoism' as the heresy of the day and by this token Pauker fell into the suspect category. In May 1951, at the celebration of the thirtieth anniversary of the RCP, Dej recognised Pauker and Luca as the oldest serving members of the party leadership while they acknowledged Dej as the sole leader. Barely four months later, Dej was in Moscow, accompanied by fellow Politburo members Iosif Chişinevski and Miron Constantinescu, seeking Stalin's approval for the purge of Ana Pauker, Vasile Luca and Teohari Georgescu. One reason for Dej's eagerness was the opposition shown by Pauker and Georgescu to the bringing to trial of Lucreţiu Pătrăşcanu, who had been arrested six years before. Recent research has argued strongly that Pauker and her protégé Georgescu resisted attempts to prosecute Pătrăşcanu on trumped-up charges and that their protection of him was a significant factor in the delay in bringing him to trial. This obstruction contributed to the charge of 'right-wing deviationism' launched against them both in May 1952.[1]

The origins of Pauker's downfall are to be found in the 'verification'

[1] Levy, 'Ana Pauker', pp.143-78.

findings relating to party membership. This 'verification' had been based on a Central Committee decision of November 1948 aimed at eliminating 'careerist and opportunist' elements and the investigation had lasted until May 1950. It resulted in a purge which removed 192,000 'exploiting and hostile elements' from the party who had been granted membership following a formal pact made in August 1945 between Teohari Georgescu, acting for Pauker, and the leader of the Iron Guard. Andrei Vyshinski, the Soviet deputy foreign minister, was particularly critical of Pauker in this regard and it was he who first suggested to Dej in January 1946 that he remove Pauker.[2] On 23 June 1950, an article by Dej had appeared in the Cominform journal *For a Lasting Peace, for a People's Democracy* condemning this recruitment policy which had led to the admittance into the party of 'careerists...Fascists, bourgeois nationalists, exploiters, etc'.[3] These comprehensive categories could include Pauker.

In September 1951 the campaign was stepped up and in Moscow an article signed by Dej appeared in *Pravda* on 4 September which resumed the Soviet-inspired drive to put Pătrăşcanu on trial:

> In the spring of 1948, when Pătrăşcanu and his accomplices were unmasked, it was proved that they constituted a secret enemy conclave in the leadership of our party. The penetration of enemy agents into our party leadership is explained by the fact that during the war and immediately afterwards our vigilance was weak. [...][4]

The arrest of Rudolf Slansky, the secretary-general of the Czechoslovak Communist Party, on 24 November 1951 as part of a Zionist 'conspiracy', provided another signal to Pauker that despite her close relations with Stalin and Molotov she was not immune, and

[2] *Ibid.*, p.165.

[3] See Chapter 7, n.50, and Ionescu, *Communism in Rumania*, p.209.

[4] *Ibid.* An epigram popular at the time in party circles echoed the ubiquity of Iron Guardists in the party:

> *Ţine minte trei cuvinte,*
> *Camarade: 'Nu fi trist!'*
> *Garda merge înainte*
> *Prin Partidul Comunist.*

(Remember three words, comrade: 'Don't be sad!' The Guard goes forward via the Communist Party.)

yet another to Dej that she was not untouchable. Dej acted upon the signal to remove his only serious rivals for power. At a Central Committee plenary meeting held on 29 February and 1 March 1952 attacks were launched against Luca, and by implication Pauker and Georgescu, which presaged their eventual purge.

Several interpretations of the purge have been offered and require discussion. Firstly, the purge was not *simply* a manifestation of a struggle between a 'native' Dej faction and the Pauker 'Moscow' faction. Teohari Georgescu, an ethnic Romanian who had spent the war years with Dej, was included among those accused of 'right-wing deviation'. His inclusion may have resulted from Dej's fear that Stalin might use him against him since the Cominform had in 1940 suggested Georgescu as general secretary of the party, an elevation that Georgescu is said to have refused.[5]

Secondly, the attack on Pauker should not be seen in itself as evidence of anti-Semitism. When the order came from Stalin to purge alleged Zionists throughout the Soviet bloc, Pauker's Jewishness was a fortunate accident for Dej; he used the opportunity to dismiss not just Pauker but Luca who was gentile and a Transylvanian Hungarian. Moreover, two of Dej's associates in his move to take advantage of Stalin's paranoid delusions about a Zionist 'conspiracy' were themselves Jews, namely Iosif Chişinevski, who became a leading figure in the party secretariat and Leonte Răutu, head of the party propaganda body.[6]

Thirdly, the purge should not be interpreted as the embryo of Dej's autonomous policies of the early 1960s. Dej had shown himself to be no less Stalinist than Pauker and Luca. It was Dej who carried out Stalin's brief of denouncing Tito at the Cominform conference in Bucharest in July 1949, and in the following year he ordered the deportation of the Serb minorities living on Romania's border with Yugoslavia to an area east of Bucharest.[7] While the signal for the purge came from Stalin, the identity of the victims suggested itself and Dej went ahead with advice from his Soviet advisors. The charges against the 'deviators', as Pauker, Luca and

5 See Tismăneanu, 'Tragicomedy of Romanian Communism', p.361.

6 Pauker may have contributed to her own downfall by her alleged support of Romanian Jews. This theory is advanced by Ion Calafeteanu, 'Schimbări în aparatul diplomatic românesc după 6 martie 1945' in *6 Martie 1945*, p. 168.

7 Hodoş, *Show Trials*, p. 101.

Georgescu were dubbed, were prepared by Constantinescu, Chişinevski and Alexandru Moghioroş under strict supervision from Soviet counsellors, the principal one of whom was Alexandr Mihailovich Sakharovsky, the Soviet security adviser to the Ministry of the Interior. A second counsellor who is alleged to have been consulted was Mark Borisovich Mitin, a member of the Central Committee of the CPSU and editor-in-chief of *For a Lasting Peace, for a People's Democracy*.[8]

Luca was vulnerable. Several months earlier, in September 1951, the *Securitate* had begun to report an increase in violent criticism of the government and of the Russians as a result of persistant rumours of a currency reform. These rumours regarding what would be, in effect, a second confiscation of people's savings – following on the currency reform of August 1947 – had been reinforced by the issue of instructions by the Ministry of Finance and the State Bank to speed up tax collection. Popular dissatisfaction with the reform continued after its introduction and Dej called upon Luca, as minister of finance, to pay the price for it, even though the reform had been drawn up with the approval of the Politburo at the insistence of the relevant Soviet counsellors. In Dej's reckoning Luca had to go in order to create a breach in the Pauker group. Increasingly prey to fits of anger – he suffered from chronic asthma, chronic laryngitis and problems with the liver, which forced him to follow a special diet – Luca offered the easiest target. Furthermore, Luca's personal behaviour had lost him several of his friends in the Politburo and he was therefore less difficult to remove.

The attack was mounted at the Central Committee plenary meeting held on 29 February and 1 March 1952. Luca was criticised for allowing 'grave' mistakes and 'frauds' to be committed by the Finance Ministry and the National Bank when applying the currency reform of 28 January. In a meeting of the Politburo before the plenary meeting, Pauker and Georgescu had come to the defence of Luca, but without success. They were to pay for their action. By taking a 'conciliatory line' and shielding Luca, they could be implicated in these errors.[9] On 9 March, the party commission set up by the Central Committee to investigate Luca and the

[8] Tismăneanu, *Tragicomedy of Romanian Communism*, p.382.

[9] Ionescu, *Communism in Rumania*, p.210.

'rightist deviation' denounced the activity of 'a large number of hostile, counter-revolutionary elements, grouped around comrade V. Luca, who have extensively undermined the regime of the people's democracy'. The report recommended Luca's dismissal as minister of finance, which was announced in *Scînteia* the same day. The charges were formally presented to the Central Committee at a meeting held on 13 March. They consisted of aiding 'capitalist elements in the villages and towns' through fiscal measures and increasing prices of agricultural products, of undermining the progess of industrialisation by 'putting a brake on investment', and betraying Party secrets in respect of the currency reform.'[10]

The March report of the party commission concluded that Luca should be sent for investigation by the Party Control Commission for having sabotaged the currency reform and undermined the development of collective farms.[11] It demanded, in addition, 'the mobilisation of the entire party in the fight against opportunism and conciliatoriness and the unmasking of Vasile Luca's and T. Georgescu's waywardness'.[12] The term 'waywardness' *(împăciuitorism)* was soon to be replaced in party accusations against both men by the more dreaded 'deviation' *(deviere)*.

Luca's expulsion from the party followed at a second plenary meeting on 26-27 May. Pauker was strongly criticised at the same plenary meeting for having 'helped and encouraged the rightist deviations of Luca and Georgescu', and was not re-elected to the Politburo, but since she had 'acknowledged some of her errors' she was allowed to retain her post as foreign minister.[13] The next day, *Scînteia* reported that Georgescu, minister of the interior since November 1944, whose defence of Luca Dej had never forgiven, had been replaced by Alexandru Drăghici.[14]

10 ASRI, Fond 'P', file 40009, vol.32, pp.308-9.

11 A senior officer in the *Securitate* alleged that Luca was also accused by Dej of not honouring the reparations agreement with the Soviet Union by failing to hand over sufficient material confiscated from the Germans (Private information). Confiscated property was administered by an agency called *Casa Bunurilor Inamice*.

12 ASRI, Fond P, file 40009, vol.32, p.312. Information supplied by Marius Oprea.

13 Ionescu, *Communism in Rumania*, p.211.

14 Drăghici had served as Pintilie's deputy in the political and administrative section of the Central Committee. The section's duties included counter-espionage monitoring of CC members, and when Pintilie left to assume the direction of

Dej's pre-eminence in the Romanian party was sealed by his appointment, on 2 June 1952, as president of the council of ministers (prime minister), a post which he combined with that of secretary-general of the party held since October 1945. He promptly intensified the attack on Luca, Pauker and Georgescu. In a speech delivered on 29 June, he blamed Luca for 'retarding the development of heavy industry', for protecting thousands of kulaks by disguising them as middle peasants and for encouraging capitalism and profiteering. Pauker was condemned for obstructing the organisation of cooperative farms and Georgescu for allowing the abuses committed by Luca and Pauker to take place.[15]

Luca was arrested on 16 August 1952 and placed under interrogation. It lasted until the autumn of 1954 when he was put on trial. Arrested alongside him were twenty-eight persons. The interrogation of Luca and his associates was coordinated by the Soviet counsellors to the Ministry of the Interior. Colonel Francisc Butyka, charged with leading the interrogation of Luca later recalled: 'At that time we had Soviet counsellors who took the initiative from the very start. And as usual, as in other cases, nothing was done without their guidance. The entire strategy of the inquiry, including the questions, was translated into Russian and monitored by the counsellors.'[16] Butyka's contact with the Soviet counsellor in question, Tiganov, was through General Vladimir Mazuru, one

the DGSP in August 1948, Drăghici succeeded him. On 30 December 1950, Drăghici was named first deputy to Teohari Georgescu and head of the General Political Directorate of the Ministry of the Interior in place of Mihail Burcă. He was given the rank of Major-General. On 20 September 1952, the DGSP, now renamed the DGSS, was separated from the Ministry of the Interior and incorporated in a new distinct body, the Ministry of State Security *(Ministerul Securității Statului)* of which Drăghici was made the head. On 2 October, Drăghici was given the rank of Lieutenant-General. The DGSS structure remained unchanged, except for the addition of a general inspectorate and section K for counterintelligence in the militia and prison service. This reorganisation was short-lived; perhaps the conflict with Beria and his arrest in June 1953 warned the new Soviet leadership under Khrushchev of the dangers of giving a state security service too long a leash, and it was for this reason that instructions were given to the Soviet advisors in Bucharest to recommend the merger of the MSS with the Ministry of the Interior. On 7 September 1953, the amalgamation of the two bodies was decreed (*Organizarea Ministerului de Interne*, p.113).

15 Ionescu, *Communism in Rumania*, p.213.

16 Archive of the Central Committee's Executive Committee, 264, vol.19, pp.90-5. Documents shown to me by Marius Oprea.

of the deputies of Gheorghe Pintilie, head of the *Securitate*. Brute force, involving beatings with an iron rod, was also applied, as one of the interrogators himself admitted to the party inquiry in March 1968. Alexandru Jacob, the deputy finance minister and one of the prisoners, told his interrogator: 'If I am badly beaten with an iron rod, as has been threatened, I shall try to tell the truth, but if I cannot stand the beatings, I shall invent lies.'[17] Ion Craiu, another prisoner in the Luca group, was 'beaten and held forty days and nights without sleep, being forced in this way to sign statements which did not contain what I had declared.'[18]

Using these methods the *Securitate*, under Soviet supervision, extracted from the twenty-nine prisoners one lie after another. These formed the charges upon which three were sent for trial along with Luca; twenty-four were released, and one died while in custody. The other three to be put on trial were Alexandru Jacob, and two senior trade and finance officials, Ivan Solymos and Dumitru Cernicica. Jacob was sentenced to twenty years' hard labour, Solymos to fifteen, and Cernicica to three. Whether this group was to be placed on trial with Pătrăşcanu remains a matter of speculation but any such plans were probably buried with Stalin's death.[19]

Pauker and Georgescu were initially spared arrest but the political assassination of the former proceeded rapidly. A rumour campaign was launched by the *Securitate* that she had contacts with Western intelligence agencies through her brother who lived in Israel, and that she had money deposited in a personal bank account in Switzerland. On 5 July 1952 she was dismissed as foreign minister but held on to her post as vice-premier of the council of ministers until 24 November when she was stripped of that as well. Her association with Stalin and Molotov may well explain why her elimination from public life was gradual, in contrast to Luca's abrupt arrest. The manner of her exit from politics, as well as the fact that she was succeeded as foreign minister by Simion Bughici, also a Jew, shows that her demise had little to do with the anti-Semitic drive which was at its height at the time in the rest of Eastern Europe.

17 *Ibid.*, p.74.

18 *Ibid.*

19 Hodoş, *Show Trials*, p.105.

Pauker was arrested on 20 February 1953. Like Luca, she denied the accusations of 'rightist deviation'. She was interrogated about her activity in Moscow during the war and her contacts with the Comintern, but she was spared the tribulations of Luca and Georgescu. Stalin's death proved her salvation. As a result of several telephone calls from Molotov to Dej, she was released exactly two months after her arrest (on 20 April). She was effectively a political corpse; she lived a secluded existence in Bucharest until her death on 3 June 1960.

With the purge of Pauker, Dej had removed his most formidable political rival. Their rivalry was fuelled by intense personal dislike of each other, which Dej later tried to obscure in periodic bouts of nostalgia in Politburo meetings when he fondly reminisced about his 'friendship' with 'our Ana'. What Pauker lacked in proletarian credentials, she more than made up with her experience in the Comintern and her contacts in Moscow. For Dej, the position was reversed. Each played on their respective strengths in their struggle for Stalin's favour, with Dej emerging the victor.[20]

Georgescu and his deputy at the Interior Ministry, Marin Jianu, had been arrested two days before Pauker.[21] The inquiry into Georgescu's activities lasted two and a half years and set itself two objectives: first, 'the verification in detail of the entire activity of Teohari Georgescu up to 23 August 1944'; and second, 'to ascertain the nature of the counter-revolutionary activity of Teohari Georgescu during the time he was minister of the interior and of his hostile and anti-state activity alongside Vasile Luca and Ana Pauker'.[22]

20 Pauker's views on Dej were reflected in her discussion with the Soviet emissary Lesakov in August 1947 (see Appendix 2); she often attempted to outmanoeuvre Dej by emphasising her loyalty to Moscow while suggesting that Dej was inclined to look to the West. But such arguments proved unconvincing. Vyshinski held her responsible for the admission of thousands of Iron Guardists into the RCP and it was ultimately this charge which provided Dej with a convenient pretext for her purge.

21 ASRI, Fond 'P', file 40009, vol.21, p.112.

22 *Ibid.*, Dej's report to the plenum of the Central Committee, held from 28 November to 5 December 1961, provided a gospel according to Dej of party history. Dej sought to lay the blame for Stalinism in Romania on others, notably on Ana Pauker and Vasile Luca, the '*émigrés* from Moscow'. Dej claimed that it was the Pauker-Luca alliance who actually ran the party until their purge in 1952. On orders given by Pauker 'the organs of the Ministry of the Interior, which were not under the control of the party leadership, began to put party

In the first matter, the *Securitate* investigators could find no reliable evidence that Georgescu had prejudiced the party in any way and they concluded that 'we have no precise proof that Teohari Georgescu was an informer of the *Siguranţa*, as some indirect evidence suggested'.[23] Following the second line of enquiry, they found that 'in the period in which Teohari Georgescu was minister of the interior, he conducted himself against the interests of the party and the state. Losing his sense of class, he formed relations with corrupt and hostile elements'. These included former Iron Guardists for whom Georgescu was alleged, under the influence of Pauker, to have facilitated contacts with members of the democratic opposition in order to sabotage the regime between 1945 and 1947. Georgescu was also found to have had extra-marital relations over a long period with a considerable number of woman – forty-one on his own admission – most of whom were 'dubious elements' belonging to the 'bourgeois class'. These relations were largely sexual favours demanded by Georgescu from the wives and daughters of political detainees in return for their release. He was also found to have accepted large sums of money and jewellery from businessmen seeking passport to emigrate.[24] Jianu was accused of selling a passport, in one case, for a set of cutlery!

---

and state cadres under surveillance, to tap telephone conversations, measures from which not even the secretary general of the party's Central Committee was excepted' (Ionescu, *Communism in Rumania*, p.334). Dej maintained that Pauker and Luca terrorised the senior party members, especially those who had fought with the International Brigade in Spain and in France in the resistance during the Second World War, and these accusations were borne out in 1950 by several such figures, among them Petre Borilă and Valter Roman, respectively chief of the Army Political Directorate and minister of posts and telegraphs. While insisting on Pătrăşcanu's crimes, these two alleged that without Dej's intervention, they too would have been arrested and placed on trial, and they praised Dej for having protected them and for saving their lives (*Ibid.*, p.53, n. 36). In the stage-managed context of the 1961 plenum a question-mark hangs over the veracity of their statements, supportive as they are of Dej. It is true that Stalin saw 'potential Rajks' in all the former volunteers in Spain, but according to one veteran Romanian Communist, Stalin was principally concerned about those Communists who on his orders had moved to France after the Spanish Civil War and had worked in the French resistance (Interview with Eduard Mezincescu, 7 April 1993).

23 *Ibid.*, p.137.

24 After Georgescu's arrest his wife burned the hard currency and threw the gold he had received into Lake Snagov (*ibid.*, pp.138-41, 153).

In spite of the evidence which had been amassed against them, neither Georgescu nor Jianu were brought to trial. In contrast to thousands of others, they passed through the hands of the *Securitate* and emerged shaken but relatively unscathed. After his release in 1956, Georgescu was sent to work as a proof-reader at the 13 December printing press (formerly *Cartea Românească*) and in a rare sign of apparent magnanimity from Dej was made director of this same press in which he had secured his first job in 1923 as a typesetter.[25]

Stalin's death on 5 March 1953, and the trial and execution of Beria in December of the same year, released a power struggle in the Kremlin; it also removed the pressure on Dej for a major show trial. The Moscow struggle confused the party leaderships in the satellite states but did not affect the master-servant relationship. In internal and external policies Romania, like the other East European satellite states, continued to imitate the Soviet Union. Dej showed himself to be both cunning and cautious in handling the repercussions of the Soviet political succession. By continuing with the trials of 'spies' and 'terrorists' he could arm himself against possible criticism of relaxing 'vigilance' against 'imperialist' enemies and earned himself some time to see which way the wind was blowing in Moscow. It became clear that separation of power was to be the order of the day when Khrushchev became first secretary of the CPSU in September 1953 and Georgi Malenkov was made prime minister. Yet this very separation of power in the Soviet Union gave Dej more room to manoeuvre and weave, and until April 1954 he resisted Soviet pressure to separate his own powers as general secretary and premier by introducing collective leadership.

Before doing so he took perhaps the most cynical decision of a career littered with shameful deeds of repression. In order to eliminate the most important rival to his personal power whom he feared might receive the support of the 'reformist' Soviet leadership, he ordered that Lucreţiu Pătrăşcanu, who had been held in custody since 1948, be brought to trial. It was not staged as a Soviet initiative but was, rather, a manoeuvre by Dej to hold on to power in the face of de-Stalinisation. The absence of any proof of the 'guilt' of the defendant showed that Dej was merely using

[25] He died in 1976.

the cover of legality to remove his most serious rival. This required a reprise of the previous six years, conducted in the categories of Communist social theory.

The charges against Pătrăşcanu had first been presented on 22 February 1948 at the First Congress of the Romanian Workers' Party. Teohari Georgescu, the minister of the interior, had denounced Pătrăşcanu as 'an exponent of bourgeois ideology' who had 'overestimated the forces of the enemy, that is, of the class-enemy, potentially helped by the Western imperialist powers'.[26] These accusations had been expanded in a resolution of the Central Committee plenary meeting of 10-11 June:

> Several weeks before March 1945 Pătrăşcanu, in complete contradiction to the party line, resuscitated the slogan of collaboration with the whole bourgeoisie or with an important part of it. In 1946 he defended the thesis of an alliance with the whole peasantry, including the exploiting elements hostile to the working peasantry. [...] In his practical activity he followed the policy of appeasement towards the exponents of bourgeois-landlord reaction when the party was fully engaged in the struggle against reaction. He followed the line of nationalist-chauvinist policy.[27]

Dej's decision to place Pătrăşcanu on trial was influenced by Malenkov's wish that Dej introduce collective leadership; while Pătrăşcanu continued to live Dej would be reluctant to take such a step. In November 1967, when the trial and execution of Pătrăşcanu were examined by a party commission, Dumitru Petrescu, a veteran Communist, recalled a visit to Moscow in January 1954 made by a Romanian government delegation composed of Dej, Miron Constantinescu, Alexandru Bîrlădeanu and himself. During the visit Constantinescu confided to Petrescu that he was taking to Malenkov a fifty-page dossier in Russian containing charges to be brought against Pătrăşcanu and a demand for the death sentence. When asked by Constantinescu for his opinion Petrescu declined to give one; when Constantinescu returned from seeing Malenkov, Petrescu stated, 'He told me he had solved the problem. In what sense he did not say, but I understood "solved" to mean that the Soviets

26 Ionescu, *Communism in Rumania*, p.152.

27 *Ibid.*

had given their agreement to Pătrăşcanu's execution.'[28]

On 14 March 1954, it was announced that the Romanian Politburo had decided 'that the trial of the group of spies headed by Pătrăşcanu should now go ahead'.[29] It was held *in camera* between 6 and 13 April 1954. No word had been published of Pătrăşcanu's arrest or interrogation and nothing was revealed about the conduct of the trial. The only information disclosed concerned the charges –which were summarised under their legal headings as articles of the penal code but not defined – the findings of the Military Tribunal, and the execution of Pătrăşcanu and Remus Kofler which were reported in a communiqué published in *Scînteia* on 18 April. It was only after Ceauşescu's downfall in 1989 that fuller details of Pătrăşcanu's ordeal were made public.

Pătrăşcanu was tried with ten co-defendants, Remus Kofler, Herbert (Belu) Silber, Ion Mocsony-Styrcea, Alexandru Ştefănescu, Jack Berman, Emil Calmanovici, Victoria Sârbu, Harry Brauner, Lena Constante, and Herant Torossian. The list of their alleged crimes ran to thirty-six pages. Pătrăşcanu himself was charged on the following main grounds: (*a*) 'crime against peace, in that he served as an agent of the "Fascist and bourgeois-landowners" police, and of the British Secret Service in trying to break up the Communist Party from within and paralyse its actions in the fight against Fascism and the imperialist war, and had supported Antonescu and the war against the Soviet Union'; (*b*) 'the crime of high treason, in that as minister of justice he led a group of conspirators who, with the help of the Anglo-American imperialists and their intelligence agencies, worked for the violent overthrow of the democratic regime installed on 6 March 1945 with a view to destroy the independence of the Romanian state'; and (*c*) 'the crime of high treason, in that he passed to the British and American intelligence agencies after 23 August 1944 secret information regarding the security of the Romanian state'.

The same three charges were levelled against Silber and Ştefănescu, while Kofler, Berman, Calmanovici were accused of (*a*) and (*c*). Only one charge was brought against Sârbu (*a*) and Mocsony-Styrcea (*b*). Constante was accused of (*a*) 'high treason, in that

[28] C. Popişteanu, 'Un epilog neaşteptat: Malenkov aprobă lichidarea lui Lucreţiu Pătrăşcanu', *Magazin Istoric*, no.3 (March), 1992, p.39.

[29] Nestorescu-Bălceşti, 'Structura Conducerii Superioare a PCR', p.363.

she passed secret information to the British Secret Service regarding the security of the Romanian state', and (*b*) 'complicity in Pătrăşcanu's actions designed to destroy Romania's independence'. Brauner and Torossian faced these same charges, except that the latter was alleged to have passed information to the CIA.[30] According to an eye-witness account published in Athens in May 1958, certain Communists were paraded for the prosecution, among them Ecaterina Borilă, wife of Dej's associate Petre Borilă, who testified that Pătrăşcanu was plotting to gain power, and Ana Toma, wife of DGSS chief Gheorghe Pintilie (Bodnarenko). Ilka Wassermann, director of the Russian-language publishing house *Cartea rusă* alleged that Pătrăşcanu had connections with Western agents, was a nationalist and anti-Semite, and that he had collaborated with the *Siguranţa*. No proof of the allegations was provided. If Pătrăşcanu listened with disgust at the fabrications of his former Communist colleagues, he found the use of Gheorghe Tătărescu, King Carol's prime minister and a Communist puppet, too much to stomach. Rising from his seat he protested:

> 'Such scum of history are brought to this trial as witnesses against me, who am a Communist. If such an individual has to prove that I am not a Communist, it is only a proof of the low level of the Romanian Communist Party which needs such elements, as well as evidence of the total lack of proof in this odious trial, so that it has been necessary to resort to such a witness.'[31]

Neither Borilă, Toma nor Wassermann figure in the list of the eighty-seven to be called which was annexed to the charge sheet drawn up by Colonel Rudolf Rosman, deputy chief military procurator, on 30 March 1954.[32]

[30] Popişteanu, 'Cazul Grupului Pătrăşcanu (I)', pp.64-6. Among the declarations extracted from Kofler under interrogation was one giving the identity of those who provided financial support for the RCP after the disbandment of the Comintern in 1943. The principal contributors were Kofler's fellow defendants, Calmanovici (8.4 million lei in 1943 and 12 million up to 23 August 1944), Berman (7 million lei in 1943 and 3.4 million and £1,000 to August 1944) and Ştefănescu (2 million lei in 1943 and 6.1 million to August 1944). The industrialist Max Auşnit donated 7.5 million lei in the period January-August 1944. (L. Betea, 'Recunoştinţa' partidului pentru cei care l-au subvenţionat', *Magazin Istoric*, no.7 (July), 1997, p.25.

[31] Quoted from Ionescu, *Communism in Rumania*, p.156, n.17.

[32] Popişteanu, 'Cazul Grupului Pătrăşcanu (I)', p.66.

The nature of the charges against Pătrăşcanu – 'crimes against peace', 'having supported Antonescu and the war against the Soviet Union' and being 'an agent of British espionage' – brought the trial within the competence of a military court according to Romanian law.[33] It was therefore conducted in front of a military tribunal, made up of Colonel Ilie Moisescu, the chairman, Colonel Alexandru Demeter, and Colonel Ion Ciulei. The prosecuting team were Colonel Aurel Ardealeanu, Colonel Grigore Râpeanu, Colonel Rudolf Rosman and Major Ioan Pohonţiu.[34] Details of the conduct of the trial were given by Moisescu to the party commission in April 1967. The order in which the witnesses were to be called, and the examination of the accused to take place, had been prearranged by Iosif Chişinevski, a member of the Central Committee secretariat, the chief interrogator Ioan Şoltuţiu, and Moisescu himself. Neither the defendants nor their counsels, who were appointed by the court, were given the opportunity to question the witnesses, and the defendants' statements, with the exception of those of Pătrăşcanu and Ştefănescu who were said to have had nothing to say in their defence, were all self-incriminating.[35] Pătrăşcanu, in a pre-trial interview with Moisescu, expressed doubts as to whether Moisescu and his colleagues were ready to serve the interests of justice and declared the trial to be a 'frame-up'. He considered the charges against him were not in the tribunal's competence and could only be heard by the party leadership. Moisescu informed Chişinevski of Pătrăşcanu's attitude but Şoltuţiu 'guaranteed' that Pătrăşcanu would talk at the trial. In the event the interrogator was wrong. Pătrăşcanu refused to recognise the tribunal and remained silent. During the trial Moisescu was constantly summoned to the telephone by Chişinevski who instructed him as to how to proceed; on one occasion Moisescu was told to keep his questions of the accused to a minimum. Even the sentences were prescribed by the party leadership and dictated to Moisescu by Chişinevski while Dej followed the results of this stage-management by listening to the proceedings on a tape-recorder.[36]

33 *Principiul Bumerangului. Documente ale Procesului Lucreţiu Pătrăşcanu*, Bucharest: Editura Vremea, 1996, pp.12, 846.

34 Popişteanu, 'Finalul Cazului Pătrăşcanu', p.23.

35 Popişteanu, 'Cazul Grupului Pătrăşcanu (VII)', p.89.

36 Popişteanu, 'Finalul Cazului Pătrăşcanu', p.23, and 'Epilog neaşteptat: Lucreţiu

The court's findings, announced in *Scînteia,* were that between 1940 and 1944 'the accused Pătrăşcanu, Kofler, and their accomplices, together with the spy Alexandru Ştefănescu and the *agents provocateurs* and spies Ştefan Foriş, H. Zilber, E. Calmanovoci and J. Berman, had sought to weaken the struggle of the democratic forces against Fascism...' Investigations had shown that since 1940 Pătrăşcanu had been in contact with the Iron Guard head of the *Siguranţa,* Alexandru Ghica, and that he had been one of its most unscrupulous agents. During the war these agents and spies had betrayed many anti-Fascist patriots. In 1943, the court maintained, Pătrăşcanu arranged with Piki Vasiliu, the under-secretary of state at the Ministry of the Interior, to be interned for several months in the camp at Tîrgu-Jiu to avoid any suspicion of contact with the *Siguranţa.* After 23 August 1944, Pătrăşcanu was said to have received instructions from 'some imperialist powers' to keep his office at any cost so that he could work against the interests of Romania. The court argued that he had organised a plot against the state and that about 24 February 1945 he had transmitted to Rădescu, via the American spy L. Madison, his agreement for the organisation of a coup.[37]

With the help of the American 'spies' Thomas Hall and William Hamilton, Pătrăşcanu and his group made contact with the 'conspiratorial' group of Iuliu Maniu, Victor Rădulescu-Pogoneanu, Grigore Niculescu-Buzeşti, Constantin Vişoianu, and Ion Mocsony-Styrcea in order to organise a coup against the 'people's state'. The link man between the two groups was Zilber. Pătrăşcanu was entrusted with leadership of the coup and in February 1947 he made contact abroad with Vişoianu and Niculescu-Buzeşti who had fled the country (Pătrăşcanu travelled to Paris at this time for the signing of the Peace Treaty). In the event of the coup's failure Pătrăşcanu was to be smuggled out of the country by Hall and Hamilton, but the two American agents were forced to leave the country unexpectedly and Pătrăşcanu was therefore forced to make his own arrangements to flee.[38]

Pătrăşcanu's disgust and contempt at the trial proceedings, and at the behaviour of his old friend, Zilber, overflowed in court.

Pătrăşcanu', p.39.

37 *Scînteia,* 18 April 1954.

38 *Ibid.*

During Zilber's final statement, Pătrăşcanu continually interrupted him, accusing him of being 'a wretch' who defiled his (Pătrăşcanu's) name when he uttered it. He condemned the trial as an outrage. When invited by the judge to make his own final statement, Pătrăşcanu said that he had nothing to say 'except to spit on the accusations made against him'.[39]

On the morning of 14 April, after the capital sentence on Pătrăşcanu and Kofler had been decided upon *by unanimous vote in the Politburo*, the court's verdict was pronounced.[40] Pătrăşcanu and Kofler were sentenced to death; Zilber, Ştefănescu and Calmanovici to hard labour for life; Mocsony-Stârcea and Torosian to fifteen years' hard labour; H. Brauner and L. Constante to twelve years' hard labour; J. Berman to ten years' hard labour; and V. Sârbu to eight years'.[41] Pătrăşcanu refused to request a pardon, unlike Kofler who was nevertheless denied one. His execution took place at Jilava prison at 3 a.m. on 17 April 1954 by firing squad, more than six years after he had been arrested.[42] Iosif Moldoveanu, an officer in the Directorate of Penal Investigation who had interrogated Pătrăşcanu, confessed in a suicide note, left after Pătrăşcanu's rehabilitation in 1968, to having shot Pătrăşcanu in the back of the neck on Dej's orders during the night of 16 April 1954 at Jilava. Dej was said to be fearful that Pătrăşcanu at his execution would divulge Dej's part in his demise. These details were given by Ion Pacepa, formerly deputy head of the Romanian Intelligence Service, after his defection in 1978

39 *Cartea Albă a Securităţii*, vol. II, docs. 202-3, pp.459-60.

40 As a member of the Politburo, Emil Bodnăraş raised his right hand in favour of Pătrăşcanu's execution. With the same hand he wrote an article in 1968, at the time of Pătrăşcanu's rehabilitation, in which he lamented the loss of a great personality and a good friend. He might have even decorated Pătrăşcanu's wife in 1971 on the occasion of the 50th anniversary of the RCP, had Mrs Pătrăşcanu not left the room where the medals were being handed out in disgust. It was at this same ceremony that General Pintilie was decorated by Nicolae Ceauşescu, despite having being named by the party investigative committee in 1968 as one of those responsible for the murder of Foriş (T. Chiper, 'De la ideal la idol. Convorbire cu o fostă ilegalistă', *Dilema*, vol.II, no.72 (27 May-2 June), 1994, p.16).

41 Calmanovici died of heart failure in Aiud prison on 12 March 1956, according to his death certificate (Sfatul popular, Aiud, no.39/1956). Family friends say that his death occurred after he went on a hunger strike to protest his innocence.

42 Popişteanu, 'Finalul Cazului Pătrăşcanu', p.26.

but unfortunately, there is no corroborating evidence for them.[43] According to Ministry of the Interior records Kofler was executed on 17 April.[44] Recalling at a plenary meeting of the Central Committee in 1961 the steps taken against Pătrăşcanu, Dej is said to have declared: 'I dealt with him as he should have been dealt with!'

At the very same Politburo meeting that determined the fate of Pătrăşcanu, Dej demonstrated his confomity to the new Soviet model by introducing collective leadership. On the same day that *Scînteia* published the communiqué about the trial – 18 April – it was announced that a plenary session of the Central Committee had decided to abolish the post of secretary-general and replace it with a secretariat headed by a first secretary. Dej resigned as secretary-general of the party but remained president of the council of ministers. His friend Gheorghe Apostol was elected first secretary of the RWP while the other three secretaries were all new: Nicolae Ceauşescu, Mihai Dalea and János Fazekas. Ceauşescu and Drăghici were at the same time made candidate members of the Politburo, a sign that both were on their way up the party hierarchy and that the dominance of one would require the removal of the other. The timing of Ceauşescu's promotion, coming as it did after the Pătrăşcanu trial and execution in which Drăghici as minister of the interior was deeply implicated, proved extremely convenient fourteen years later when Ceauşescu could claim his innocence in the affair whilst proclaiming Drăghici's guilt.

By executing Pătrăşcanu Dej was able to preempt any Soviet attempt to impose a post-Stalinist restructuring of the party. Unlike Poland or Hungary where such victims of Stalinist terror as Gomulka and Nagy were elevated to the party leadership, Romania now lacked a living martyr. Moreover, Dej could argue that Stalinists had already been purged from the Romanian party by pointing to the removal of Pauker and Luca. To underline his point he ordered the trial of Luca in October 1954. Unlike the Pătrăşcanu trial, foreign correspondents were admitted, but this time the defendant's replies were read into the record by the president of the tribunal in order to avoid the embarrasment caused in the Pătrăşcanu trial

43 *Moştenirea Kremlinului*, Bucharest: Editura Venus, 1993, pp.125-6.

44 His dossier is listed under no. 40002 in 'Service C' of the former Directorate General of State Security.

by the latter's outbursts.[45] Luca's trial lasted four days. He was found guilty of charges of sabotage of the economy and conspiracy, and sentenced to death on 10 October. After his entering a plea for clemency, the sentence was commuted to forced labour for life.[46]

A trial of Ana Pauker was not to be excluded. Debates over her fate appear in October to have caused the postponement, for the second time, of the party congress. This was announced only two days before it was due to convene and followed more than two months of intense congress propaganda. The announcement said that the congress would be held 'after the completion of necessary autumnal agricultural work' but, as the British minister to Bucharest reported, it was doubtful whether there could have been any sudden economic crisis of sufficient gravity to necessitate a last-minute postponement after so much advance publicity. The minister suggested a (more plausible) reason derived from his Yugoslav colleagues: that in fact it was a political matter, concerning the 'disposal of Ana Pauker who had not yet been tried'; and that there were two factions, one led by Dej, the other by Bodnăraş, with the latter supporting Pauker's rehabilitation. Some colour was given to this theory by the non-appearance of Bodnăraş at any official function for three months from early November. Nevertheless, the manner in which Dej was toasted by the Soviet ambasssador at the November banquet marking the anniversary of the Bolshevik Revolution showed that he retained the confidence of the Kremlin.[47]

In fact, Dej had remained a convinced Stalinist. Stalin's death had had little impact on Romania's internal affairs: there had been

45 See the deposition of Vasile Varga, a deputy judge at Luca's trial, dated 23 March 1968, for the party commission of inquiry set up to investigate the charges against Pătrăşcanu (copy in possession of the author).

46 Under the provisions of decree no.3 of 1963, the sentence was modified to twenty-five years' hard labour. Luca was first imprisoned at Râmnicul Sărat where ironically he shared his incarceration with, amongst others, Ion Mihalache and Corneliu Coposu, two of the leading figures in the NPP whom Luca's own party had jailed in November 1947 (Mihalache died in the prison on 5 March 1963). He was later transferred to Aiud where he died of a heart attack on 23 July 1963. ('Documentar Referitor la Procesul Privind pe Vasile Luca', Archive of the Executive Committee of the Central Committee of the RCP, no. 264/19. 18.02.1972, p.2).

47 PRO, FO 371/116579. Annual Report for 1954.

no major change in the party leadership, no decentralisation of the economy, and no stop to the collectivisation of agriculture. There was, however, a short-lived amnesty of political prisoners in 1955 and a slight relaxation in cultural policy. It was upon Romania's relations with the Soviet Union that Stalin's death had greater influence, one which with the advantage of hindsight proved emblematic. Work on the Danube-Black Sea Canal was abandoned after Khruschev failed to share Stalin's interest in the project, the Soviet government dissolved the Sovroms, the joint-stock companies set up in the late 1940s to exploit Romania's natural resources,. by selling its interest to the Romanians in the summer of 1954. The sole surviving companies, involved in oil and uranium exploration and mining, were sold in 1955 and 1956.

A clear sign that there had been no concession to Khrushchev's sanitised party was Dej's resumption of the position of first secretary in December 1955 and the re-election to the Political Bureau of the same figures as had been chosen in May 1952 when the purge of Pauker and Luca had taken place.[48] Two new members were added, Ceauşescu and Drăghici, thus confirming the parallel rise of the two up the party ladder. It was not long, however, before Dej had to face the implications of another reappraisal of the Stalinist legacy by the new Soviet leadership.

Until February 1956, to be known as a 'Stalinist' was the highest accolade in the Soviet Union and in its satellite states. Their leaders had all risen to power and been confirmed in it through their declared loyalty to Stalin.[49] Then, during the night of 25 February 1956, Nikita Khrushchev turned this ascription on its head. Khrushchev's speech in closed session at the Twentieth Congress of the Communist Party of the Soviet Union accused Stalin of often violating all norms of morality and Soviet laws, of mass arrests and deportations of many thousands of party members, of execution without trial and without normal investigation, and of creating conditions of fear and despair. Although Khrushchev did not mention the satellites in his speech, he had nevertheless raised

48 M.E. Fischer, *A Study in Political Leadership*, Boulder, CO, and London: Lynne Rienner, 1989, p.51.

49 I have taken this phrasing from a paper by Maurice Pearton in a volume of essays written by him and Dennis Deletant entitled *Romania Observed: Studies in Contemporary Romanian History*, Bucharest: Encyclopaedic Publishing House, 1998, p. 217.

a problem for Stalin's placemen who enjoyed office at Stalin's direction or with his compliance.

The speech threw Dej completely off balance and it took him a month to regain his composure. Dej had led the Romanian delegation to the Congress – the other members were Iosif Chişinevski, Miron Constantinescu, and Petre Borilă – but it was only on 23 March that his first comment on the Congress's conclusions was made in a report of the Romanian delegation to an enlarged plenum of the Romanian Central Committee and this was only published in abridged form in *Scînteia* six days later. Dej admitted merely that Stalin had soiled his reputation by indulging in the personality cult and by allowing the security police to use terror; he added that Stalin's 'departure from the Marxist-Leninist concept of the role of the personality' had a 'negative influence'. Nothing was said about Khrushchev's 'secret' speech.[50]

Dej tried in his report to anticipate and deflect criticism of his own allegiance to Stalinism by pointing to, although not naming, Pauker, Luca and Georgescu as the real Stalinists in the party. Since the dismissal of these leaders the party, he alleged, had taken decisive steps to democratise itself, citing the second party congress of December 1955 as the beginning of the new phase by which collective leadership and internal democracy had been reintroduced. In an allusion to the use of terror by the security police, he recognised that although the security forces had achieved great successes, especially in unmasking Western spies, they had gone beyond the bounds of legality during, he implied, the period of Georgescu's office. The only way to counter this was to consolidate party control of the *Securitate.* Drăghici emerged unsullied but ironically the arguments marshalled by Ceauşescu twenty-one years later to denounce Drăghici and to call for a return to legality by the Ministry of the Interior were startlingly like those presented at this plenum by Dej.

Dej's vulnerability over the indictment of Stalin was exposed by the attack made on him during the plenum by two other delegation members, Constantinescu and Chişinevski, who accused him of following Stalinist principles and employing Stalinist methods. The convergence of their opposition to Dej brought the two together. Both were driven by opportunism, attempting to displace

[50] Ionescu, *Communism in Rumania*, p. 259.

Dej by exploiting the developments in Moscow. Chişinevski himself was heavily implicated in the Pătrăşcanu affair, as was Constantinescu according to the testimony of Dumitru Petrescu cited earlier. Constantinescu saw the Khrushchev speech as an opportunity for discussion on the need for liberalisation in the party and country, and as a means of removing Dej.[51] For Dej, on the other hand, the demolition of Stalin's personality cult was most unnerving in view of his pliancy in the hands of the Soviet dictator, and he did his best to play it down, reserving it, as a US source remarked, as 'matter for party cabal and not for public discussion'.[52]

Dej's caution in this respect is shown by his convocation of a secret meeting at the Floreasca sports hall at the end of March 1956, only a few days after the Central Committee plenum. The audience of 3,000 represented the party elite. The meeting was chaired by Dej and it was announced that note-taking was forbidden. Dej read out a shortened version of Khrushchev's secret speech to the Soviet Twentieth Congress, commenting that the speech had no relevance to the Romanian Party since 'thanks to the consistent Marxist-Leninist policy of the Central Committee' the excesses of the personality cult had been eliminated in 1952. Gheorghe Apostol made a fawning speech in favour of Dej and in the others that followed, all made by minor figures in the party, only one showed a discordant tone, calling for an assessment of the party leaders' actions in the light of Khrushchev's criticisms. Dej's speech fixed the party line for the next three years; it placed the RCP amongst the most hardline of the Communist camp. The meeting itself was of major significance. It was the only one in Romania in which Khrushchev's text was presented even to a limited public; it showed the resistance of the party leadership to the process of de-Stalinisation; and finally, it highlighted the weakness of opposition to Dej within the party.[53]

The absence of speeches at this meeting from major figures in the party except Apostol reflected the divisions in the Poliburo

51 *Ibid.*, p.261; see also V. Tismăneanu, 'Miron Constantinescu or the Impossible Heresy', *Survey*, vol.28 (winter 1984), p.182.

52 S. Verona, *Military Occupation and Diplomacy: Soviet Troops in Romania 1944-1958*, Durham, NC: Duke University Press, 1992, p.88.

53 G. Haupt, 'La Genèse du Conflit Soviéto-Roumain', *Revue Française du Science Politique*, vol.18, no.4 (August 1968), p.676.

over Dej's refusal to embark on de-Stalinisation, and Constantinescu and Chişinevski renewed their attack on Dej in Politburo meetings held on 3, 4, 6 and 12 April. The minutes of these meetings show Dej on the defensive, faced with criticism from Constantinescu and Chişinevski over the abuses of the *Securitate* for which he was held ultimately responsible, and over the repression of the previous decade. Constantinescu went on to emphasise the need for a wide-ranging discussion of the consequences of the personality cult surrounding Dej which had led to a weakening in the role of the party. These views unleashed a fury in Dej which he confined himself to expressing in notes in the margins of the minutes. There Dej expressed his disgust of Constantinescu, whom he suspected of trying to take his place, and of Chişinevski, whom he accused of betrayal.

Constantinescu launched into his attack on Dej from the very opening of the meeting on 3 April. He claimed that despite the improvement in health in the party following the purge of Pauker, Luca and Georgescu in 1952, some worrying signs had appeared since then. Of particular concern were the 'abnormalities' in the activity of the Ministry of the Interior. Among these he highlighted the presence of *Securitate* officers in various ministries and institutions without the knowledge of ministers, especially when those ministers and heads of institutions were Politburo members. He listed a number of cases in which citizens had been beaten and blackmailed into working as informers, and some of these he had reported to Dej:

> 'I am not saying that the Ministry of the Interior encouraged these abuses, but it allowed them to take place and tolerated them. The Ministry of the Interior does not, however, work independently; the minister is in contact with comrade Gheorghiu-Dej. I ask myself: how was it possible for comrade Gheorghiu-Dej not to take steps once he had been informed of these abuses? Comrade Gheorghiu-Dej did not bring the Politburo in on overseeing the activity of the Ministry of the Interior. [...]
>
> I think the work of the Ministry of the Interior and of the *Securitate* should be placed firmly under the control of the Politburo. Perhaps even the *Securitate* should be separated from the Ministry of the Interior and placed under the control of a committee. I believe that comrade Drăghici can be of great help

to the Politburo since he is aware of many cases of abuse. There is no point in us hiding these things because they keep on appearing all the time. [...]

I think that the Ministry of the Interior has had a bad influence on comrade Gheorghiu-Dej. He spent hours on end reading the reports of the ministry. Comrade Gheorghiu-Dej was in the habit of making notes in the margins and writing instructions on almost all the reports which he received. [...] Some might say that I am bringing up irrelevant things about comrade Gheorghiu-Dej. However, no one in our party is infallible and even if only part of what I say is true, it is still of assistance. [...]

Comrade Gheorghiu-Dej's merits are well-known to us. However, I want to highlight some of his negative traits. Comrade Gheorghiu-Dej is one of the party leaders but he is not the only one because there are also others. Comrade Gheorghiu-Dej often pays no heed to Politburo members and even goes so far as to mock their views. [...]

Comrade Gheorghiu-Dej does not pay attention to how he behaves. In January 1956, en route to Moscow for a meeting on economic matters, comrade Gheorghiu-Dej spoke only in the first person when talking about the monetary reform to a comrade in the Central Committee. It was as though the party, the Central Committee and the Politburo did not exist. [...]

Regarding myself, I have made numerous mistakes. I played an important part in spreading the personality cult, I embraced and supported the theory of intensifying the class war, I employed aggressive methods, and on several occasions I have made ill-tempered outbursts. But my faults cannot cover the faults of others, nor those of comrade Gheorghiu-Dej. I have never criticised comrade Gheorghiu-Dej and I was wrong not to do so.

[...] In conclusion, I propose that we discuss things openly and then we concentrate on the powers of the Politburo, of the secretariat, on the methods of working in the Politburo, and that the role of the control commission be strengthened.'[54]

Drăghici was the first to respond. He put a number of questions to Constantinescu: did he know of the existence of prison camps?

[54] V. Tismăneanu, 'Arhivele secrete şi istoria comunismului românesc', *Sfera Politicii*, no.25 (February 1995), pp.16-18.

Had he not put pressure on the Ministry of the Interior in 1952 to evacuate citizens from the Jiu Valley in order to make way for the building of flats for miners? Constantinescu gave unconvincing replies, arguing that he did not know of the existence of prison camps, only of labour camps, and that he did not put pressure on Drăghici to evacuate people, but 'proposed' that the evacuation take place. Other Politburo members came to Dej's aid. Gheorghe Apostol, Chivu Stoica and Alexandru Moghioroş challenged Constantinescu's affirmations. Stoica asked Constantinescu why he had chosen this moment to launch his attack on Dej and reminded him that he had contributed to the personality cult. It was left to Apostol to sum up the meeting:

> 'At the opening of the Politburo meeting, Miron Constantinescu accused comrade Gheorghiu-Dej of not taking measures to ensure that the report of the delegation to the Twentieth Congress was compiled collectively, he alluded to the lack of collegiality in the Politburo's work, and criticised the method of taking decisions without consulting all the members of the Politburo. Why has comrade Miron seen and sees only the faults in our activity? I think that it is necessary for us to see the faults, but let us see in the first place the good results as well. Can it really be said that the activity of the Politburo has been slack compared with the period before the removal of the deviators [Pauker, Luca and Georgescu]? I do not think so. On the contrary.'[55]

Dej, by refusing with the backing of the party cadres to embark on de-Stalinisation, managed to reinforce his own control of the party and to bind it more closely to his person. His success in resisting attempts to 'liberalise' the party proved, ironically, to be a boon for Khrushchev later in the year in the midst of major challenges to Communist authority in Poland and Hungary.

The most fundamental implications of de-Stalinisation concerned Poland. There, the entire Communist Party had been liquidated on Stalin's orders in 1938 as an agency of German espionage. De-Stalinisation meant the rehabilitation of Stalin's victims and the evidence upon which the liquidation had been carried out was officially declared – on 19 February 1956 during the Twentieth Party Congress – to have been faked. A few days later, the Polish

[55] *Ibid*, no.26 (March 1995), pp.12-13.

Party leader Boleslaw Bierut, a committed Stalinist, who headed his party's delegation at the Congress, fell ill and died in Moscow. His funeral in Warsaw provoked an anti-Soviet demonstration. On 20 March Khrushchev arrived in Warsaw to procure the election of Edward Ochab. Ochab began to implement a policy of moderate liberalisation. Many of Stalin's victims were released from jail, among them a veteran Communist Wladislav Gomulka. The Polish intelligentsia wanted more radical change, though within socialism. In June, Polish workers added their voice. In Poznan, the rumour that a metal-workers' delegation to Warsaw had been arrested led to a protest march by their colleagues. The protest turned into a riot which was put down by Polish security forces at a cost of fifty-four dead and 300 wounded. The Polish party newspaper blamed 'enemy agents' for the riot, as did the Soviet leadership, for whom the event was a great shock. Khrushchev saw in it the beginning of the counter-revolution which the West, led by the United States, had organised in order to detach Poland and other satellite states from the Soviet bloc.

Public interest in Romania in the events in Poland was, according to a British legation report, 'intense', but Romania was able to insulate itself against what was happening in Poland; it was less able to do so against Hungary. Hungary was a neighbour, Hungarians formed the largest minority in Romania, and Romanian workers, students, and intellectuals shared the same problems as their Hungarian counterparts. In Romania itself discontent was rising in the summer of 1956. The same British source reported:

> It was already evident in August that the harvest would be a bad one; an anticipatory scarcity of food, with a consequent rise in prices, began to show itself long before the crops were in and it grew throughout the autumn. There was no sign of any appreciable amelioration of the appalling housing shortage and even though the gradual improvement in the availability of clothing and household equipment which Mr Macdermot [a legation official] had noted seemed to be continuing, prices were high and the majority of workers were too ill-paid to buy much. Food and housing continued to be the most important elements in the standard of living, which could therefore be said to have suffered at least a temporary decline. Discontent was evidently rising, and reports of trouble at Poznan encouraged it; the establishment of

the Gomulka régime in Poland and the revolt in Hungary made it stronger.[56]

If Dej was dilatory in handling the economic discontent, as suggested by this report, his reaction to the political manifestations was swift and firm. The Hungarian uprising allowed Dej to demonstrate amply his fidelity to the Soviet Union. The repercussions of the revolt, which began with a massive popular demonstration in Budapest on 23 October 1956 during which the Stalin monument was destroyed and the national flag hoisted with the emblem of the People's Republic removed, were soon felt in Romania.

At the time of the outbreak of the revolt, Dej was in Yugoslavia, returning a visit which Tito had made to Romania during the summer. He did not return immediately but remained in touch with Bucharest by telephone where Nicolae Ceauşescu responded at the other end of the line. The Romanian Politburo met on 24 October. It decided to place heavy censorship on news reporting from Budapest, to strengthen the guard at the frontier points with Hungary, to avoid measures which would antagonise the Hungarian and German minorities, and to 'display tact and political judgement over arrests so as not to anger the population needlessly'.[57] The initial public reaction of the regime in Romania was to play down the demonstrations in Budapest. The British legation reported on 27 October:

> The first brief news of the disturbances in Budapest was only given by the Romanian radio on the evening of October 24 and in the press the following morning, which rapidly sold out. The press attributed the trouble in Hungary to the work of subversive reactionary organisations incited by foreign reaction, explained that the Hungarian Government had asked for Soviet help and alleged that Hungarian workers who continued to support the Communist Party and friendship with the USSR were hostile to the revolt. [...] Anyone dependent entirely on the Romanian press and radio for his news would get little idea of the nationalist and anti-Soviet nature of the developments.[58]

56 *Roumania: Annual Review for 1956*, PRO. FO 371/128892.

57 Mihai Retegan, 'Actul decizional în timpul revoluţiei ungare', *Dosarele Istoriei*, no.3(8), 1997, p.45.

58 PRO. FO 371/122699.

On 26 October, with Dej still absent, the Politburo met again. Aware that the food shortages could bring people out onto the streets, the party leaders approved a set of measures designed to improve food supply and to raise wages. However, these steps came too late. On the following day, there were student and workers' demonstrations in Bucharest, Cluj, Iaşi and Timişoara. The emphasis of the student protests was to press for the abolition of the teaching of Russian in schools and universities. At the polytechnic in Timişoara a group of students – Caius Muţiu, Teodor Stanca, Aurel Baghiu, and Ladislau Nagy, to name but a few –backed by a lecturer Gheorghe Pop, held a secret meeting on 28 October 1956 at which they decided to convene a general meeting of students from all the educational establishments in Timişoara to discuss the meagreness of food in the student canteens and shortcomings in the teaching. The meeting was arranged over the heads of the polytechnic administration and the party organisation and took place at the faculty of mechanical engineering on 30 October. More than 1,000 students attended. According to a report prepared by the Party Regional Committee at the time, the party representatives, headed by Petre Lupu and Ilie Verdeţ, were jeered and forced to leave the hall, whereupon army units were called in to seal off the polytechnic campus and arrests were made.[59] The protests, however, made their mark. On 5 November Miron Constantinescu addressed a student meeting in Cluj and promised that compulsory classes in Russian at universities would be abolished and living conditions raised. Two weeks later Constantinescu was made minister of education. The appointment of one of the toughest men in the party, and number seven in the Politburo, to a post hitherto held by a comparatively undistinguished ex-professor, was a clear sign that Dej was not satisfied with his regime's grip on the country's youth and was determined that it should be tightened.

Other potential sources of dissaffection were brought into line. Mihai Beniuc, secretary of the Writers' Union, condemned 'the bandit-like acts of the counter-revolutionary Fascist elements in Budapest', while writers of the Hungarian Autonomous Region addressed a letter to the Central Committee denouncing 'the Horthy-Fascist savage forces in Hungary'.

59 *NU*, no.108 (6-13 May 1993), p.9.

In the meantime, Dej had returned to Romania on 28 October. He had doubtless discussed the Hungarian crisis with Tito. A non-Communist Hungary suited neither leader. The archives do not provide, as yet, details of the discussions, but immediately after Dej's return Aurel Mălnaşan, the deputy foreign minister, and Valter Roman, a senior Romanian Communist Party official who in the early 1940s had got to know Imre Nagy, the newly-appointed Hungarian prime minister, in Moscow when he worked for a Soviet-backed Romanian radio station, were sent to Budapest to provide on-the-spot reports to Dej and to the Soviet leadership.[60] On 29 October, railwaymen at the Griviţa yards in Bucharest held a protest meeting calling for improved conditions of work and in Iaşi there were street demonstrations in support of better food supplies. Hundreds of arrests were made in the centres of protest, especially among students who participated in meetings in the Transylvanian capital of Cluj and in Timişoara. One of the largest meetings took place in Bucharest. In the clamp-down persons amnestied in 1955 were also re-arrested. Khrushchev himself alluded to the demonstrations in an address to the Moscow Comsomol on 8 November 1956 when he said that there were 'some unhealthy moods' among students 'in one of the educational establishments in Romania' and he congratulated the RCP on having dealt with them quickly and effectively.[61] On 30 October the Timişoara, Oradea and Iaşi regions were placed under military rule as Soviet troops based in Romania were concentrated on the frontier with Hungary. To placate the workers the government announced on 29 October that the minimum wage would be raised, and special concessions were given to railwaymen in the form of free travel. On 2 November Gheorghe Apostol addressed

[60] A record of a verbal account of their experience in Budapest, given to the party leadership on 2 November 1956, has been published in *Sfera Politicii*, no.42, pp.29-31 and no.43, pp.32-4. Valter Roman (real name Ernest Neulander), was a Hungarian-speaker from Oradea who had fought in the International Brigade in Spain and was believed by Nagy, and prominent figures in the RCP, to be an NKVD officer: see Nagy's own notes on his discussion with Bodnăraş and Roman on 26 November 1956 while in detention in Romania (*Dosarele Istoriei*, no.1, 1996, p.40).

[61] Ionescu, *Communism in Rumania*, p.272.

a railwaymen's meeting and promised help. Dej, himself a former railwayman, stayed away.[62]

Convergence of interest with the Soviet Union and not just slavish obedience determined the stance adopted by Dej and his colleagues. They had two main concerns: a successful revolt in Budapest against Communist rule might spread to the two-million strong Hungarian community in Transylvania, thus sparking an anti-Communist rising in Romania; and a non-Communist Hungary might lay claim to parts of Transylvania. Their fears had been fuelled by the participation of Hungarian students and workers in demonstrations in Cluj, Timişoara and the Autonomous Magyar Region. On 30 October an emergency 'General Command' was set up by the Romanian government with orders to 'take all measures necessary in order to guarantee public order throughout the entire territory of the Romanian People's Republic'. Among the command's attributes was 'the coordination and extension of intelligence gathering in order to identify subversive action', 'to ensure security at all party and state buildings, at communications centres, and on all road, rail, air and sea links', and to put down any action which threatened the control of the state'. The army and the Interior Ministry were placed under the command of this new body which was headed by Emil Bodnăraş. The other members of the command were Nicolae Ceauşescu, Alexandru Drăghici, and Leontin Sălăjan, the latter being minister of the armed forces.[63]

Khrushchev, in the mean time, was holding a series of emergency meetings with Communist leaders, including a delegation from China, in which he told them that Moscow would use force if necessary to resolve the crisis. There were no objections, not even from Tito and Gomulka.[64] On 1 November, Khrushchev met

62 *Ibid.*, p.269.

63 *Sfera Politicii*, no.42, p.33.

64 Csaba Békés, 'The 1956 Revolution and World Politics', *Hungarian Quarterly*, vol.36, (summer 1995), p.112. Khrushchev and Malenkov are said to have paid a secret visit to Bucharest on 1 November 1956 to discuss the Hungarian crisis with Romanian, Bulgarian and Czechoslovak leaders and, according to one report, Khrushchev demanded that Romanian troops be used to crush the Budapest revolt. Dej and Bodnăraş allegedly replied that, owing to a large Hungarian minority in the Romanian army and general sympathy for Hungary, the army could not be relied upon for such an operation (Richard Lowenthal. *The Observer*, 25 November 1956, quoted from Verona, *Military Occupation and Diplomacy*,

Dej and Bodnăraş. The Romanians pushed for firm military intervention against Imre Nagy's government, indeed Soviet troops based in Romania had been among the first to cross the Hungarian border on 26 October to reinforce the Soviet presence. Bodnăraş was a key figure in the Romanian Party's support for Soviet intervention in Hungary. During the uprising he was appointed minister of transport and communications and in this capacity he supervised the widening of roads of strategic importance to Soviet troops for their transit through Romania.

Dej was as anxious as Khrushchev to bring the Hungarians back into the socialist fold; the two leaders agreed that a Romanian delegation, led by Dej, should travel to Budapest on 3 November to hold discussions with Imre Nagy. Nagy attempted to coordinate a plan whereby Dej would petition Khrushchev for a Soviet-Hungarian summit. On that very same day, however, the Soviet leadership was holding a meeting of a very different nature with János Kádár, the purpose of which was to coordinate the violent overthrow of the Nagy government.[65] At dawn on 4 November, Soviet troops regrouped around Budapest, and began to move in. Red Army tanks opened fire on the barricades erected by the rebels. A few hours earlier, the authorised representatives of the Nagy government, Generals Maleter and Kovacs, who had been invited to Soviet headquarters to continue negotiations begun on 1 November, were arrested. The Soviet intervention quickly overcame the rebels' resistance.

In deposing the Nagy government, Khrushchev invoked the Warsaw Treaty which, as the Soviet delegate in the UN Security Council underlined, empowered the Soviet Union 'to protect Hungary against subversion'. An appeal was made to the Soviets by Kádár, who on the morning of 4 November, announced his break with Nagy over the radio and the formation of a 'revolutionary workers' and peasants' government'.

The establishment of the Kádár government allowed Dej to follow up his rapprochement with Tito by establishing his position with the new Hungarian leadership. On 4 November the Romanian Central Committee sent a message of greeting and congratulation

---

p.103. The Khrushchev memoirs claim, by contrast, that offers of military assistance were received from the Romanian and Bulgarian leaders (*ibid.*, p.103).

65 Bêkés, '1956 Revolution', p.112.

to the Revolutionary Worker-Peasant Government. This was followed by the visit, from 21 to 25 November, of a full Romanian delegation led by Dej and Bodnăraş. The main object of the visit was to demonstrate, like the Czechoslovak and East German governments before them, the Romanians' support for the Kádár regime. But there was another, significant purpose to it: the question of what to do with Nagy was nagging at the Soviets.

Nagy had taken refuge in the Yugoslav Embassy in Budapest on 4 November with several colleagues from his government. He was offered political asylum by the Yugoslavs and accepted it. Following negotiations between the Yugoslav and Hungarian governments, a convention was signed under which both governments agreed that Nagy, his colleagues and their families, could leave the Yugoslav embassy as free persons and return to their homes with a guarantee from the Hungarian government of their personal security.

At 6 p.m. on 22 November a bus arrived, as agreed, at the Yugoslav embassy to take Nagy and his colleagues home. However, the Yugoslav military attaché was indignant at discovering that the bus driver was a Russian and that there were several other Russian 'passengers'. Nagy appealed to the Yugoslav Ambassador to intervene and the latter ordered the first secretary of his embassy, and the military attaché, to accompany Nagy in the bus to his home. The moment the bus set off, two Soviet armoured cars drove out and sandwiched the bus between them, escorting it to the Soviet military headquarters. There, the two Yugoslavs were sent away and Nagy and his group were placed under Soviet guard. The bus continued its journey to a military school where Nagy and the others were effectively prisoners. They were placed in separate rooms and forbidden to speak to each other.

At 10.30 the same evening, Nagy was summoned from his room with a message that Valter Roman wanted to talk to him. His discussions with Roman lasted almost two hours. Roman said that he had the authority of Dej and Kádár to transmit their joint request that he (Nagy) should go to Romania where he would be treated in the best possible manner until the political situation in Hungary returned to normal. This would take two to three months, after which Nagy could return to Hungary and take part in political life. Nagy's departure for Romania was advisable since his life was in danger if he remained in Hungary. Roman suggested to Nagy that he put in writing his intentions in order to pacify public opinion.

Nagy told Roman that 'as a prisoner of the Soviet security authorities I am not prepared to declare anything since I am not in a position to act freely. As a Hungarian citizen, in full possession of my freedom of action, I am happy to talk things over with fellow comrades'. He went on: 'I emphasised to Valter Roman my determination not to leave Hungary voluntarily. I said that they could remove me from Hungary by force, because they have sufficient power, but I would never agree to this'. Roman said in reply to Nagy that he would not be removed against his will and with that he left'.[66]

The following afternoon, Nagy and his colleagues were herded into two windowless military buses. They were joined by György Lukacs, Zoltan Szanto and Zoltan Vas together with their wives. This latter group had left the Yugoslav embassy three days before Nagy and his associates, accepting Kádár's promise that they were free to return to their homes. The buses took them to an airport where they boarded two Soviet planes, one of which was the aircraft which had brought Dej and his delegation to Bucharest. The pilots were Russian and their guard was made up of Soviet soldiers and KGB officers. They arrived at Bucharest after a two-hour flight and were met by Alexandru Moghiroş, a member of the Romanian politburo. It was only on seeing Moghioroş that Nagy realized that he was in the Romanian capital.

To give a semblance of formality to Nagy's kidnapping, a memorandum was signed between Kádár and Dej bearing the title 'The understanding via an exchange of letters between the government of the Romanian People's Republic and the government of the Hungarian People's Republic regarding the assistance given to Imre Nagy and persons in his group on the territory of the Romanian People's Republic'. Although the understanding appeared to be a simple arrangement between Dej and Kádár, it was overseen by the Kremlin, in particular by a 'crisis team' composed of Malenkov, Suslov and Aristov, who acknowledged in a report compiled on 23 November the role played by Roman in keeping them informed of his efforts to persuade Nagy to leave Hungary voluntarily for

66 I have taken this account from Nagy's own notes, published in Romanian translation with an introduction by Florica Dobre in *Dosarele Istoriei*, no.1, 1996, pp.37-40.

Romania. Suslov instructed both Kádár and Dej over the wording of their memorandum.[67]

Nagy was held, along with other members of his government, in a *Securitate* safe house in a locality just north of Bucharest, where their interrogation was coordinated by Boris Shumilin, chief KGB adviser 'for counter-revolutionary affairs'.[68] They were not allowed the visits from UN officials promised by Grigore Preoteasa, the Romanian foreign minister, to prove that he was not under duress. Shumilin allowed Bodnăraş and Roman, to question Nagy and the others.[69]

During his visit with Dej to Budapest in late November, Bodnăraş also offered help with the reorganisation of the Hungarian security service, the AVH, which had been decimated during the uprising as the result of the shooting by demonstrators of hundreds of its officers. Several hundred *Securitate* agents of Transylvanian Hungarian background were sent to Budapest and Bodnăraş's extended stay in the Hungarian capital indicates that he was closely involved in this operation. A second Soviet agent in Romanian clothing who assisted Bodnăraş was Wilhelm Einhorn, a Hungarian Transylvanian who had been recruited by the NKVD, had fought as a volunteer in the International Brigades in the Spanish Civil War, and had been appointed director of the secretariat of the *Securitate* in autumn 1948 with the rank of major. It was as deputy director of Directorate 1 for Foreign Intelligence of the *Securitate* that Einhorn was sent to Budapest under the cover of counsellor of the Romanian embassy, becoming chief of the newly-created Romanian foreign intelligence station there.[70]

Romania was the Soviet Union's most active ally during the Hungarian crisis. Its support of the Soviet Union went beyond

67 Retegan, 'Revolutiei ungare', p.46.

68 Andrew, *KGB: Inside story*, p.435.

69 Judit Ember, *Menedekjog-1956*, Budapest: Szabad Ter Kiado, 1989, pp.146-8.

70 Ion Pacepa, *Red Horizons*, London: Heinemann, 1988, p.359. *Securitate* participation in Soviet-supervised security and intelligence operations in Hungary had also taken place before the uprising and had again involved Transylvanian Hungarian officers. Many such officers from the First Directorate were sent as visitors to Hungary via the West on false Austrian, West German, French and Italian passports to identify Hungarian 'counter-revolutionaries' and the information they gathered was transmitted to Bucharest. This particular campaign was supervised by Ceauşescu with the assistance of a KGB adviser (*ibid.*).

the political arena into the domain of practical assistance and open encouragment. Dej and Bodnăraş were among the first foreign leaders to visit Budapest after the Soviet invasion and in their official communiqué they opined that the Soviet action 'was necessary and correct'.[71] The Romanian delegation congratulated Kádár on the steps taken to crush the uprising and on the use of Soviet troops for that purpose. Dej's fulsome praise was doubtless driven by relief that a repressive regime had been restored to power in Hungary instead of a government pledged to introduce liberal measures which might well have stimulated discontent and demands for similar treatment at least among the Hungarian minority in Transylvania, if not more widely in Romania.

[71] Verona, *Military Occupation and Diplomacy*, p.103.

12

FROM SUBSERVIENCE TO THE SOVIET UNION TO AUTONOMY, 1957-1965

The events of October and November 1956 in Hungary had a particular impact in Romania by reason of its large Hungarian minority. But the impact had not been confined to Romanian citizens of Hungarian origin. It had filtered through to workers, students and the intelligentsia. The uprising and the response to it in Romania had reminded Dej and the Russians how dependent he was on force, and on the Soviet Union as the source of his power. Accordingly, the Russians were prepared to give little away to Dej. This soon became clear from the visit made by Chivu Stoica at the head of a Romanian delegation to Moscow on 24 November 1956.

The Soviet leaders, for their part, had advanced two main arguments in confronting the crises in Poland and Hungary. The first was that the Poznan riots and the Budapest uprising were the work of the West, led by the United States, and were an attempt to wrest Poland and Hungary from the socialist bloc. The second was that Nagy's actions threatened the Soviet gains in the Second World War, achieved at massive cost by the Red Army. It was essential, Khrushchev concluded, that extra precautionary measures be taken to cement members into the Soviet bloc and therefore new troop-stationing agreements were to be signed with his allies. Such an agreement was signed with Romania in April 1957, but the basis for it was decided during Stoica's visit to Moscow in December 1956. The presence of Soviet troops on Romanian territory had been regulated by the Soviet-Romanian Armistice Agreement of September 1944. The Peace Treaty of February 1947 with Romania had given the Russians the right to station troops there in order to ensure lines of communication with the Soviet forces in eastern Austria. A US army intelligence report of January 1950 estimated the Soviet presence in Romania at two divisions, totalling 30,000 troops, supplemented by a 2,000-strong security force.[1]

In a joint statement released by Tass on 3 December 1956, the two governments were of the view that the stationing of Nato forces near socialist countries presented a threat to the latter's security. In these circumstances, 'the temporary stationing of Soviet armed forces in the Romanian People's Republic' was deemed necessary by both sides and was 'in conformity with the Warsaw Treaty international treaties and agreements'.[2]

From the Romanian point of view the agreement was wanting in several respects. No time limit was laid down for the stationing of Soviet troops, there was no provision for it to be terminated by one of the parties, and it could only be amended with the consent of both sides. This meant that in practice the Soviet government would be able to keep its troops in Romania as long as it wished. Moreover, a provision exempting Soviet troops from Romanian jurisdiction enabled them to ignore Romanian law. The publication of the agreement which was contrary to normal practice, demonstrated that Soviet troops were in Romania legally, and with the consent of the Romanian government, thereby countering Western claims that they were not.

The Romanian delegation also discussed economic cooperation in Moscow. But comparisons between the Polish-Soviet agreement, reached only days before Stoica's visit, and the Romanian-Soviet text, showed that the Romanians had been treated less generously. The Poles won the concession that all Polish 'debts' arising from credits given between 1946 and 1953 should be considered settled, whereas in the case of the Romanians, the Soviet Union agreed only to postpone for four years the repayment of credits granted between 1949 and 1955. In the words of a British newspaper, the Soviet-Romanian communiqué gave 'the appearance of having been signed between two equal partners but it is clear from its

[1] Donald R. Falls, 'Soviet Decision-Making and the Withdrawal of Soviet Troops from Romania', *East European Quarterly*, vol. XXVII, no.4 (winter 1993), p. 490.

[2] *România. Retragerea Trupelor Sovietice, 1958*, ed. Ioan Scurtu, Bucharest: Editura Didactică şi Pedagogică, 1996, p.240. This is a collection of Soviet and Romanian official documents on the conclusion of the withdrawal agreement of 1958 and on its implementation.

terms that the Romanians are less equal than the Poles'.[3]

The lesson for Dej given by the Hungarian uprising – that the position of the Communist Party in Romania continued to be dependent on repression of all opposition – translated itself into new measures. The strength of the *Securitate* was increased: in August 1956, it had numbered 13,155 officers and men, and 5,649 civilian employees and in March 1957, its forces were supplemented by the addition of 2,059 officers and 429 men.[4] But there were no immediate large-scale arrests; the number of arrests rose from 2,357 in 1956 to 3,257 the following year.[5]

At the same time, Dej used the political credit which he had gained through his fidelity to Moscow during the Hungarian uprising to strengthen his personal hold on the party and to take action against his remaining rivals. The grounds he used against them were that they were 'Stalinists'. The 'Stalinists' in question were Miron Constantinescu and Iosif Chişinevski, both of whom in March of the previous year had used the same charge of 'Stalinist' against Dej in the debate on the 20th Congress of the Soviet Party. On 4 July 1957 it was announced in *Scînteia* that Constantinescu and Chişinevski had been removed from their posts at a Central Committee plenum held on 28 and 29 June, and 1 and 3 July. The plenum resolution, published five days later, stated that both 'members of the Politburo of the RWP have been responsible for grave anti-party expression of opinion directed against the unity of the party and against its leadership'. The direction they supported in debates on the 20th Soviet Congress 'would have produced confusion within the ranks of the party...and have undermined the policy of the party and the state'. There was a lesson to be learned from Hungary in their actions: 'The events in Hungary are most instructive in this connection'. To add weight to the charge of treachery, Constantinescu and Chişinevski were linked to the 'anti-party fractionist group of Luca and Pauker'.

It is difficult to dismiss the disclosure of this Romanian purge and the announcement on the very same day, 4 July, in Moscow that the Soviet Central Committee in plenary session from 22 to

3 *Manchester Guardian*, 4 December 1956. Quoted from Ionescu, *Communism in Rumania*, pp.274-5.

4 *Cartea Albă a Securităţii*, vol.II p.21.

5 *Ibid.*, vol.III, p.159.

29 June had dismissed the 'anti-party' group of Malenkov, Kaganovich, Molotov, and Shepilov from their posts, as a coincidence. Yet only by having advance warning of the *Pravda* announcement could Dej have linked his own one. In seeking an explanation for this close parallelism, the Soviet ambassador's departure for Moscow on 26 June and his return to Bucharest on 1 July should not be overlooked. It is quite possible that Soviet and Romanian policies were linked, despite the difference in outlook between Dej and Khrushchev. The charges of disloyalty to the party may have been similar, but the reasons behind them were precisely the opposite. Malenkov was opposed to de-Stalinisation whereas Constantinescu had advocated it.

The conclusion of Ian Dudley, the British minister to Bucharest, was that 'although it is likely enough that the infringement of Party unity... was the essential reason for getting rid of Constantinescu and Chişinevski, nevertheless the decision to get rid of them for this reason was taken in Moscow rather than here'.[6] Maurice Pearton has pointed out:

> Although they had been allied tactically the two men [Constantinescu and Chişinevski] had little in common. Chişinevski, as the indictment confirmed, was an *apparatchik* of long standing, whose mind and experience revolved exclusively around doctrine and tactics. He struck Mr Dudley as "an evil, intelligent weasel". Constantinescu, by contrast, could discuss with the British minister "the relative importance of culture and economics". Constantinescu was a geniune intellectual in a party whose leadership was deficient in that category, and naturally appealed to all those members who disliked the anti-intellectual bias in the running of its affairs. [...] How far his personal enthusiasm for de-Stalinization went was and remains problematical – he told Togliatti that he thought Khrushchev's explanations of Stalin's behaviour as "the cult of the personality" over-simplified – but within the Romanian leadership he did offer an alternative to Gheorghiu-Dej.[7]

In the unsettled situation in Moscow, Dej could not be certain

[6] Quoted from an article by Maurice Pearton entitled 'The Romanian Leadership and its Problems, 1956-1957-1958', in Pearton and Deletant, *Romania Observed*, p.257.

[7] *Ibid.*, p.255.

that he himself would not be thought indispensable. Furthermore, like Pătrăşcanu before him, Constantinescu represented a class of party member with whom Dej never felt comfortable.

However the decision had been reached and to whatever degree it had been coordinated with Khrushchev, Dej had removed yet more potential rivals to his leadership. From now on, Dej was to proceed unchallenged, with the party firmly united behind him, to distance Romania from the Soviet Union. A foretaste of this came in the speech of Emil Bodnăraş on the fortieth anniversary of the Russian Revolution, which emphasised the role played by the RCP in overthrowing Marshal Antonescu, thereby overshadowing the contribution of the Red Army which hitherto had been given prominence in official accounts of the 23 August coup. Bodnăraş boldly revised the official line: 'The party was the organiser and leader of the armed insurrection of 23 August 1944 which, under the favourable conditions created by the victories of the USSR... overthrew Fascist dictatorship and led to Romania's passing over to the side of the anti-Hitler coalition headed by the USSR.'[8]

Impetus to the apparent distancing of Romania from the Soviet Union came with the unexpected announcement on 24 May 1958 at a meeting of the Warsaw Pact in Moscow that the Soviet Union was withdrawing its troops from Romania. The decision was implemented with remarkable speed, and by 25 July the last of the 35,000 had crossed the border.[9] What, then, prompted this *volte face*?

According to Khrushchev's memoirs it was Bodnăraş who, as minister of war, first raised the question of the withdrawal of Soviet troops from Romania during Khrushchev's visit to Romania in August 1955.[10] The idea of withdrawal had been conceived by Dej who feared that Khrushchev might try to purge him as a Stalinist. Withdrawal was, therefore, a question of survival for Dej and was advanced out of personal considerations, not from ideological ones.[11] Dej's timing was influenced by the signature of the Austrian treaty on 15 May 1955, which established Austria's neutrality and by which the Soviet Union agreed to withdraw its

8 *Ibid.*, p.261.

9 Falls, 'Withdrawal of Soviet Troops', p.491.

10 Verona, *Military Occupation and Diplomacy*, p. 83.

11 Author's interview with Alexandru Bârlădeanu, 8 August 1996.

troops. Without the need to maintain lines of communication with its forces in Austria, the Soviet Union lost its justification for keeping troops on Romanian – not to mention – Hungarian territory.

Displaying his usual prudence and cunning, Dej chose Bodnăraş to broach the subject because of his impeccable credentials: his past services to the Soviet Union; the confidence and respect which Khrushchev acknowledged he enjoyed among the Soviet leaders; and his senior position – he was one of the first three deputy prime ministers. Khrushchev records that Bodnăraş asked him his reaction to the idea of withdrawing Soviet troops from Romania. The Soviet leader flew into a rage. Bodnăraş justified the subject by pointing out that there was little threat to Soviet security interests because Romania was hemmed in by other Communist countries and that there was 'nobody across the Black Sea from us except the Turks'.[12] Seeing that he was not making any impression, Bodnăraş went on:

> 'All right, if that's how you feel, we'll withdraw the question. We just didn't want you to think that we were standing firmly on a socialist position only because your troops are stationed on our territory. We just want you to know that we sincerely believe in the building of socialism and in following Marxist-Leninist policies, and our people recognise us as their leaders and support us completely.'[13]

These comments made no impact upon Khrushchev who lectured Bodnăraş on his underestimation of the West's strength and determination. Dej, in his turn, showed his annoyance with Khrushchev by not going to Bucharest airport to see off the Soviet leader.[14] If Khrushchev judged the idea to be premature in the international context of 1955, he did not abandon it and was to use it at the time he regarded most appropriate.

That judgement had to be made firstly, in the context of a wider scenario composed by Khrushchev in 1958 for his policy

[12] N.S. Khrushchev, *Khrushchev Remembers – The Last Testament*, translated by Strobe Talbott, Boston: Little, Brown and Co., 1974, p. 228, and Verona, *Military Occupation and Diplomacy*, p.83.

[13] Quoted from Falls, 'Withdrawal of Soviet Troops', p.491.

[14] Author's interview with Alexandru Bârlădeanu, 8 August 1996.

of a new opening towards the West, and secondly, with regard to the Romanian party's ability to ensure internal security. The key foreign policy element was the unilateral Soviet move to withdraw a limited number of troops from Eastern Europe as a whole which, Khrushchev hoped, might prompt a similar response from Nato. In order to attract the maximum publicity and to demonstrate Moscow's peaceful intentions, the notice of withdrawal was timed on 24 May to coincide with the announcement of Warsaw Pact troop-cuts of 119,000 men – this in addition to an earlier Soviet decision to slice 300,000 from the Red Army in 1958.[15] Romania's strategic position, flanked as it was by other Warsaw Pact states, made it a safer proposition for the Soviet Union on security grounds for a troop withdrawal, and any fears about Romania's reliability as an ally had been dispelled by its actions during the Hungarian revolution. By the same token, the precautionary measure of keeping a large number of Soviet troops in Hungary after the revolution allowed Khrushchev to partially offset any overall reduction of Soviet troops in the area.

For Romania, the most significant impact of Soviet withdrawal upon the Romanian leadership was its psychological one. While Romania was still firmly enmeshed within the Soviet bloc – Soviet divisions in southern Ukraine and across the Prut in the Moldavian Republic could descend at once in an emergency – Dej could present it as a concession wrung from the Soviets. Furthermore, the departure of Soviet troops relieved the Romanians of an economic burden and removed a source of irritation. With the confidence thus gained Dej could embark, albeitly cautiously, on policies which placed Romanian above Soviet interests.

A signal of Dej's immediate priority was given in his speech at the investiture on 25 July of Soviet generals marking the departure of Soviet forces. After praising the 'valiant Soviet armies who, by delivering crushing blows to the fascist hordes, freed Romania from the yoke of Hitlerist imperialism', honouring the memory of the Soviet soldiers who fell in that struggle, and evoking the 'atmosphere of warm friendship which accompanied the departure of Soviet troops from our country', Dej turned his attention to the internal situation:

[15] Falls, 'Withdrawal of Soviet Troops', p.497. The communiqué on the meeting was published in *Scînteia* on 27 May and reprinted in Scurtu, *România*, pp.280-3.

'At the same time, we should not forget the wretched wrecks of the old exploitative classes, remnants of the former fascist reactionary groups, who still wallow in the hope that the march of history might be reversed, and that Romania might be returned to the state of slavery and backwardness which it experienced in the time of the bourgeois-landowners' regime. Let it be clear to all these lamentable ghosts of the past, to all those whom our people have thrown into the dustbin of history, that their dreams will remain empty, and that the hand of the working people and its people's democracy will not hestitate in the future as well to strike mercilessly against all those who attack the revolutionary conquests of the people.'[16]

The violence of Dej's language foreshadowed the violence that was to be used against the imagined enemies of his regime. To compensate for the Soviet withdrawal, and to allay Soviet fears that it might demolish the underpinning of the Romanian regime Dej approved the immediate introduction of stringent internal security measures in order to maintain the party's control.[17] Amendments were made to the penal code which were even more draconian in their remit than the provisions for the death penalty enacted in 1949. Decree 318 of 21 July 1958 defined new crimes attracting the death penalty. Article 9 imposed it on any Romanians contacting foreigners to perpetrate an act 'which could cause the Romanian state to become involved in a declaration of neutrality or in the declaration of war'. This was clearly designed to deter those who might be tempted by the example of Imre Nagy in Hungary who, during the 1956 revolution, proclaimed his country's neutrality and thus, implicitly, its withdrawal from the Warsaw Pact. The definition of 'economic sabotage' in the code was enlarged to include theft and bribery, as was that of so-called 'hooligan' offences

[16] Scurtu, p.359.

[17] Foreign diplomats noted an increase in domestic tension throughout 1957 and in the last few months of the year the British head of mission opined that 'the government was behaving in a highly nervous manner which I thought must mean that they had solid reasons to anticipate trouble.' (PRO FO 371/143326. XC15773) His impressions were justified in mid-January 1958 by the outbreak of serious peasant disturbances in southern Moldavia which were put down with bloodshed. The rapid crumbling of the demonstrations was due not only to the severity with which they were curbed, but also to a one-metre snowfall which covered the region when the trouble was at its height.

committed by juveniles. By the autumn of 1958, the first death sentences for the new crimes were applied.[18]

In his desire to give Moscow a guarantee of his Marxist-Leninist orthodoxy, Dej launched a campaign of 'revolutionary vigilance', designed to expel from the party and to punish all those who were deemed to have strayed from the party line. These expulsions were accompanied by the arrest, and in some cases re-arrest, of political and cultural personalities from the pre-Communist period who were officially considered to pose a threat to the stability of Dej's regime. This new wave of arrests began in July 1958. *Securitate* figures show that between 1 July and 8 August, 1,103 persons were detained, the majority of them on charges of 'agitation of a hostile character' or 'membership of a counter-revolutionary organisation'.[19] The arrests continued over the following months, producing a total for the whole year of 6,362 persons.[20]

Among those who fell victim were two groups of writers and scholars, who were arrested over twelve months from December 1958 and tried together on 24 February 1960 on a charge of 'conspiring against the social order'. They included the philosophers Constantin Noica, Nicu Steinhardt and Alexandru Paleologu, the celebrated epigrammist Alexandru 'Păstorel' Teodoreanu and the literary critic Constantin Pillat. Their crime was having received works written by Emil Cioran and Mircea Eliade, who were both living in the West, and having discussed them in private together. Cioran and Eliade were branded by the authorities as Iron Guardists. Noica was alleged to have written works which were hostile to the Communist regime – he had written an unpublished study on Hegel – and to have organised with the co-accused meetings in which they 'prepared the violent overthrow of the regime of people's democracy in the Romanian People's Republic'. In statements extracted by their *Securitate* interrogators through beatings and threats, some of the accused 'confessed' to the charges but Noica steadfastly refused. In his declaration before the court he denied that he had given certain statements to his interrogators in which he was alleged to have used the terms 'hostile', 'illegal', and 'banned'. Noica was sentenced to twenty-five years' hard

18 Ionescu, *Communism in Rumania*, p.290.

19 *Cartea Albă a Securităţii*, vol.III, p.132.

20 *Ibid.*, p.159.

labour, as was Pillat, while Paleologu received fourteen years and Teodoreanu seven.[21]

The flow of convicts sentenced to forced labour under the new measures was channelled into penal colonies established in the marsh areas of the Danube Delta, notably at Periprava, where the prisoners plucked reeds in the extreme temperatures of winter and summer for the recently constructed cellulose plants at Maliuc-Mahmudia and at Chişcani near Brăila, financed jointly by Romania, Poland, Czechoslovakia and East Germany.[22] It was estimated that a labour force of 25,000 would be required to gather the reeds and this was supplied by transferring political and common law prisoners to join the newly sentenced convicts. An article in *Scînteia* of 5 February 1959 eulogised the achievements of the workers in the delta without mention of their status or of the appalling conditions in which they lived and worked. Although many intellectuals and peasants passed through these camps, the majority of labourers were young opponents of the regime between the ages of sixteen and twenty-five, large numbers of whom succumbed to the ravages of malaria and tuberculosis. In fact, the production figures from the camps were so disappointing that the regime was forced to recruit 'voluntary' labour whose working conditions were far better than those of the convicts and who received a wage.

A former detainee described the conditions in these penal colonies in an emigré journal in the early 1960s. The camps were located in four areas in the delta: the Balta Brăilei, north of Hîrşova, where there were about ten camps; near the village of Feteşti, where there were a number of smaller camps; around the village of Periprava, where the largest numbers of camps were situated; and around lake Dranov. The largest camps, like that of Salcia in the Balta Brăilei, housed up to 6,000 prisoners, and it was estimated that the total number in the delta approached 60,000. The convicts had to work exclusively with their hands, standing waist-deep in the water and cutting the reeds with a scythe-blade

[21] The interrogations and trial proceedings are published in *Prigoana. Documente ale Procesului C. Noica, C. Pillat, N. Steinhardt, Al. Paleologu, A. Acterian, S. Al-George, Al. O. Teodoreanu etc.*, Bucharest: Editura Vremea, 1996. All the accused were released in 1963 and 1964. Noica was released in 1964 and died in 1987.

[22] See the description of one colony in Petru Dumitriu, *Incognito*, London: Collins, 1964, pp.384-90.

attached to a pole. After gathering the reeds into sheaves weighing about 50 kilos, they were forced to carry them on their backs for over a kilometre without allowing the reeds to touch the ground. Specially trained dogs bit the men's heels if they wavered. The daily quota for each convict was fifteen sheaves and those who failed to fulfil it had their food ration reduced and were sometimes beaten on the soles of their feet. Prisoners who bore the letters CR, meaning 'counter-revolutionary', on the back of their hand were particularly maltreated. Food consisted of several slices of bread and jam, and a cup of coffee substitute in the morning, and a piece of cold polenta and soup at lunchtime and in the evenings.

The areas to be harvested were sealed off with barbed wire and electrified fences and patrolled by guards on horseback and by teams of dogs with handlers. Machine-gun posts and floodlights were set up around the perimetre fences. The convicts returned each day having worked in the water to unheated and uninsulated wooden huts, and not surprisingly regularly fell prey to illness, especially malaria. Medical care was virtually non-existent with a total absence in some camps of medicines and dressings. The death-rate was high, inviting the charge that the authorities deliberately sought to liquidate the detainees but such motives are difficult to reconcile with the need to fulfil production targets. Camp conditions were more testimony to a mentality which saw the convicts as expendable slaves, worthy only of the barest of essentials to ensure work capacity but denied any care which might enhance it or indeed protect it.

The delta colony's population was increased at the beginning of 1959, as the example of the Stoieneşti camp in the Balta Brăilei showed. Some 2,000 'convict' students were brought to this camp, containing about 1,400 peasants opposed to collectivisation, in February 1959. Many of the students had been caught trying to leave the country clandestinely. They were quartered in three outbuildings for sheep, each 6 metres wide and 80 metres long, with walls only a metre high. Poorly clothed for the extreme winter temperatures, lacking running water and adequate sanitation, many of the students developed dysentry and typhoid. Despite this, they were forced to build a dam in sub-zero temperatures. After three weeks more than 400 had to be moved to Galaţi for treatment, of whom forty died *en route*. A medical commission was ordered to the camp and more than 1,500 prisoners were found to be in need of hospital treatment, but instead of being sent to Galaţi, the prison authorities, the General Directorate of Prisons, moved them to the colony at Periprava where many died after a few days.[23] Their numbers were made good by more than 1,000 prisoners transferred from Gherla prison at the beginning of April 1960. The latter were herded into railway wagons during the night of 2/3 April and spent four nights without adequate sanitation or food before reaching Periprava. Some did not survive the journey.

A further decree of 1958 signalled another wave of purges from government employment of former officers in the royal army, former landowners, persons with a record of 'political' crime, and children of all the above. On a much more petty scale, divulging the location of Romanian archives also attracted the death penalty.[24] At Gherla alone, the prison records show that thirty people accused of belonging to anti-Communist partisan groups were executed in 1958.[25] In the prisons discipline itself became noticeably harsher. Annie Samuelli, a prisoner for almost twelve years between 1949 and 1961, remembered how the warders' behaviour worsened overnight. 'They suddenly had a free hand to apply regulations literally, and that included a fresh range of punishments, maliciously meted out'.[26]

The effects of the clampdown were also felt by Western missions. Those who employed Romanian staff saw a number of them arrested, and police surveillance of all staff was tightened. In September 1958 the authorities insisted that all British nationals should either take Romanian citizenship or leave the country; similar demands were made of other Western citizens. In his Annual

[23] 'Les Camps de la Mort du Delta du Danube', *La Nation Roumaine*, no.215 (Nov.1962-Jan.1963), p.6.

[24] Ionescu, *Communism in Rumania*, p.290.

[25] Information provided by Dr Ioan Ciupea, head of the contemporary history department of the National History Museum of Transylvania. A memorial erected in 1995 by the Association of Former Political Prisoners in Romania in Gherla cemetery bears the names of forty-seven persons executed in the Cluj region between 1948 and 1958. Among them is the brother of Gavril Dejeu, minister of the interior in the Ciorbea government.

[26] A. Samuelli, *The Wall Between*, Washington, DC: Robert B. Luce, 1967, p.187.

Review for 1958, the British head of mission commented that the new repressive measures, coupled with the granting of exit permits to large numbers of Jews, 'all seemed to flow from the same objective of eliminating alien and bourgeois influences'.[27]

It was not just the exceptional severity of these new measures which sent a clear signal to the Romanian people that the regime of terror was not to be relaxed; the failure to publicise them in the press or on the radio (the provisions were merely printed in the *Monitorul Official*, the record of legislation) generated uncertainty about the legislation and so amplified the fear inculcated into the population. The apparent randomness in the legislation's application by the instruments of the police state served perfectly to enhance the regime's control by terror at the moment when the most public Soviet symbol of power, the Red Army, had been withdrawn.

Dej was making a distinction between the Soviet model and the Soviet Union. In opting for the former, Dej took his party and the country on a new course of autonomy from his Soviet overlord. Dej's motives were initially economic and were manifested in his refusal to accept for Romania the role within Comecon of 'breadbasket' for the industrialised members such as East Germany and Czechoslovakia. There was also a paradox here: Dej's commitment to the Leninist-Stalinist values of industrialisation turned him into a 'national communist'.[28]

The rift with Moscow developed gradually. It was fuelled by the mutual dislike felt by Khrushchev and Dej which came to the fore in 1957. Even after the Hungarian uprising, Dej continued to fear that Khrushchev would attempt to purge him as a relic of Stalinism. His distrust and dislike of the Soviet leader was amplified by the latter's unpredictable and often violent outbursts. During a visit to Romania in 1957, Khrushchev upbraided Dej during the dinner of welcome for allegedly having a policy of slaughtering pigs when they reached a weight of 25 kilos. 'Perhaps you are thinking of sucklings', Dej replied. 'No', stormed Khrushchev. Dej explained that the Romanian policy was to kill pigs at 100 kilos. In an attempt to have the last word on the subject, Khrushchev telephoned Dej that evening to admit that the figure of 25 kilos was incorrect but to claim that the true one was 50

27 Public Record Office, Kew. FO 371/143326. XC15773.

28 As pointed out by Shafir, *Romania*, p.48.

kilos. During the three-hour train journey to Constanţa, the two men did not exhange a single word, and when they arrived at the port they quarrelled over the method for sowing maize. At a rally marking the end of his visit, Khrushchev introduced an 'off-the cuff' remark into his speech to a packed football stadium that the Romanians did not know how to sow maize![29]

The frostiness of relations between Dej and Khruschev is confirmed by the memoirs of Arkady Shevchenko, the Soviet under secretary-general of the United Nations who defected to the United States in April 1978. Khrushchev travelled by sea to New York to attend a session of the UN and was accompanied on the voyage by Dej, and the Hungarian and Bulgarian leaders, Janos Kádár and Todor Zhivkov. Describing the atmosphere during the trip, Shevchenko has this to say:

> The Romanians...kept themselves aloof, and there was an obvious chill between them and the Soviet delegation. At his table in the dining room, Gheorghiu-Dej generally remained silent. Khrushchev was annoyed at this but did not display his feelings toward the Romanians publicly, except on one occasion when he lost control of himself before a small group of Soviets and declared that Gheorghiu-Dej was not a bad Communist in general, but that as a leader he had no force; he was too passive. He added that in Romania, and even in the ranks of its Communist Party, pernicious nationalistic and anti-Soviet attitudes were developing which must be cut off at the very root. 'A firm hand is required for that,' he declared. 'The *Mamalyzhniki* [a derogatory Russian nickname for Romanians, based on the Romanian word *mămăligă* meaning "maize porridge"] are not a nation, but a whore.' Khrushchev stopped short, realising he had gone too far. 'I am referring', he added lamely, trying to extricate himself, 'to pre-revolutionary Romania.'[30]

The campaign to establish Romania's new course was at once active and reactive. It was not only in furtherance of Dej's aim to distance Romania from the Soviet Union, thereby gaining greater popularity for his party, but it was also a reaction to two major

[29] Author's interview with Alexandru Bârlădeanu, 8 August 1996.

[30] Arkady N. Shevchenko, *Breaking with Moscow*, New York: Alfred Knopf, 1985, p.97.

developments which posed a threat to Romania's new course. The first was Khrushchev's plan, presented in Moscow on 3-5 August 1961 to members of Comecon, to give the body a supranational planning role which, if accepted by Romania, would have obliged her to remain a supplier of raw materials, and to abandon her programme of rapid industrialisation, thus risking economic chaos at home. Such a move would have made the country susceptible to further economic exploitation by the Soviet Union, which was precisely what Dej had sought to avoid by embarking on the policy of industrialisation.

The second major development was the Sino-Soviet rift, which first emerged at the Third Congress of the Romanian Communist Party in June 1960. Dej used the Chinese formula of equality of all socialist states to justify his own autonomous policies towards the Soviet Union and received Chinese backing for his rejection of the Comecon plan.[31] The rift was indispensible to Dej's challenge to Khrushchev,[32] but the Romanian leader was careful to preserve neutrality in the dispute. In an effort to mediate in the conflict a Romanian delegation led by Ion Gheorghe Maurer visited Peking from 2 to 10 March 1964 but it returned empty-handed and this led only to further 'arm-twisting' by Khrushchev to bring the Romanians back into line. One source states that Khrushchev formally, but not publicly, raised the question of territorial revision in Transylvania during the Romanians' stopover in Moscow on their return from China, and even indicated a willingness to hold a plebiscite in Bessarabia as well as in Transylvania.[33] This linkage of the Transylvanian issue with the Sino-Soviet conflict unnerved the Romanians and pressure from Moscow was stepped up in the same month when a plan to create an economic region encompassing much of the Moldavian SSR, half of Romania, and part of Bulgaria was launched in the Soviet capital. Known as the Valev plan after its author who was a professor of economics at Moscow university, it met with a hostile response from the Romanian government which publicly condemned it in the Romanian media.[34]

31 R.R. King, 'Rumania and the Sino-Soviet Conflict', *Studies in Comparative Communism*, no.4, 1972, p.375.

32 Fischer-Galati, *The New Rumania:*, pp.78-103.

33 *Ibid.*, p.101.

34 I. Alexandrescu, 'Obsesia protecţionismului', *Dosarele Istoriei*, no.3, 1997, p.38.

These signals from Khrushchev, coupled with the realisation that the Chinese were unable to help the Romanians economically, drove the Romanians into a public declaration of their autonomy which, apart from pre-empting any move by the Kremlin, would also stake a claim to Western political and economic support against Moscow. The Romanian policy was formally legitimised in the 'Statement on the Stand of the Romanian Workers' Party Concerning the Problems of the World Communist and Working Class Movement' which was published in *Scînteia* on 23 April 1964. At the same time, in deliberate response to the Soviet threats the Party's Central Committee authorised the publication of a manuscript on the Bessarabian problem and highly critical of Russia by Karl Marx.

Khrushchev's removal on 14 October 1964 as Soviet leader offered Dej a further chance to consolidate his break with Moscow. Exploiting the change in the Soviet leadership, he summoned the Soviet ambassador on 21 October and requested him to withdraw the KGB counsellors from Romania. Moscow reacted quickly and furiously. On the following day, the Chairman of the KGB, Vladimir Yefimovici Semichastny, sent a telegram to Drăghici reminding him that Romania lived 'under the Soviet protective umbrella' and that it would regret Dej's move. A similar telegram from General Alexsandr Sakharovsky, the head of the First Chief Directorate and former MGB adviser in Bucharest, landed on the desk of General Nicolae Doicaru, the head of the Foreign Intelligence Directorate of the *Securitate*. In November, Sakharovsky arrived unexpectedly at Bucharest, followed by Semichastny.[35]

Irritation over the presence of KGB counsellors in the Romanian Ministry of the Interior had surfaced in the spring of 1963 when the issue was raised at a meeting of the Romanian Politburo chaired by Dej in May; Dej informed his colleagues that 'comrade Jegalin had been to see him and had raised the matter of the counsellors' (Jegalin was one of them). Dej repeated to Jegalin Drăghici's view that 'there was no point in the counsellors sitting around and just reading newspapers' and that nothing was served by the counsellors remaining since there were solid links between the Romanian and Soviet Ministries of the Interior. Drăghici himself told the Politburo that Jegalin had brought a letter to him from the chairman of the KGB, Vladimir Yefimovici Semichastny,

[35] Pacepa, *Moştenirea Kremlinului*, p.253.

offering to withdraw the counsellors if Drăghici continued to question their usefulness. Drăghici told Jegalin that he did and Jegalin asked when he could leave. Drăghici said that he could go the very next day, to which Jegalin replied that he would go if his own government gave the word – in fact, the last Soviet counsellor did not leave until the end of the following year. Drăghici complained to the Politburo that there were times when the Soviet counsellors tried to do the *Securitate*'s work for them and that they had lost agents because of this. He derided the effectiveness of cooperation between the Romanian and Soviet services, complaining that the Soviets passed on information that was, in some cases, seven years old!

> Whatever you say to the counsellors, they still go their own way. In effect, we have no counsellors, the professional ones left in 1956. For the past year, all they have done is sit in the office and read the newspapers, occasionally fishing for information from the odd person. In Pintilie's time, they spent the whole day in his office and of course Pintilie kept them informed.[36]

The discussions between Dej and Brezhnev in connection with the withdrawal of KGB counsellors from Bucharest allegedly went on until the end of November and also involved Aleksandr Shelepin, who until December 1961 had been KGB chairman and had been moved to head the Committee of Party and State Control which oversaw the work of the KGB. Sakharovsky was particularly wounded, since he had nursed the *Securitate* into being in 1948, but eventually the Soviet leadership abandoned its standpoint and in December 1964 the counsellors were withdrawn, being allowed to take all the contents of the flats which they had requisitioned. Thus the Romanian security and intelligence services became the first such agencies of a Warsaw Pact country to get rid of its Soviet counsellors, and, as regards the Foreign Intelligence Directorate, the DGIE, the only foreign intelligence agency in the Eastern bloc to enjoy this privilege down to the collapse of Communism in 1989. This did not mean that it ceased to collaborate with the KGB.

A condition of the withdrawal of KGB counsellors was that the DGIE should continue to meet Romania's obligations under the Warsaw Pact to play its part in the espionage activities

[36] Scurtu, *România*, p.391-2.

coordinated by the Soviet Union. Moscow established the defence field as the chief priority of intelligence gathering in the 1960s and emphasis was placed on scientific and technical espionage. Both the First Chief Directorate of the KGB, charged with foreign intelligence, and the GRU, Soviet military intelligence, set the agenda for their counterpart bodies in the Warsaw Pact states, in Romania's case, the DGIE and the *Departamentul de Informaţii al Armatei* (DIA).[37] Soviet activity in scientific and technical espionage was coordinated by the Military Industrial Commission (VPK) and the United States, West Germany, France and Britain chosen as the principal targets.

Collaboration between the KGB and the DGIE, on the one hand, and the GRU and the DIA on the other, served a dual purpose for the Soviets; not only was the intelligence gathered for Soviet needs, but the Romanian officers concerned were not asked, in their operational activities in the 1960s, to distinguish a loyalty to Romania from one to the Soviet Union, since the intelligence needs of both countries coincided. Furthermore, the Soviet training of most of the Romanian intelligence and security officers, cemented an extra bond with the Soviet master. It was in these conditions that an ambiguity in Soviet-Romanian relations emerged. For while Dej's anti-Russian measures of 1963, which

[37] The DIA was the successor to the Second Section of the Romanian Army General Staff (*Secţia a II-a de pe lângă Marele Stat Major)* which was charged with gathering military intelligence. By 1 July 1945 all Romanian military attachés had been withdrawn from foreign countries and most of the officers in the section purged or arrested on Soviet orders. In 1948 the first postwar appointment of a military attache was made by the Soviet-controlled Ministry of National Defence, to the Romanian embassy in Moscow. On 15 February 1951 the Second Section was transformed into the *Direcţia Informaţii a Marelui Stat Major* (Directorate of Information of the General Staff) and at the same time military counter-espionage activity was tranferred to the DGSP. The work of the DIMSM, which was subordinated to the Ministry of National Defence, was supervised by GRU counsellors who trained young Romanian officers. After the withdrawal of Soviet troops in 1958 the Soviet counsellors were withdrawn from the DIMSM. Contacts were strengthened with other armies but Alexandru Drăghici's desire, as minister of the interior, to extend his power by adding military intelligence to the military counter-espionage activities which he already controlled, led to the subordination of the DIMSM to the Ministry of the Interior by an order signed by both Drăghici and the minister of national defence on 22 October 1962. This supervision by the Ministry of the Interior was removed on 18 October 1968.

involved closing the Russian Institute in Bucharest, eliminating Russian as a compulsory school subject, and replacing the Russian names of streets and public buildings with Romanian ones, signalled a cooling of relations with Moscow, the rift was not so deep as to stop Romanian collaboration in intelligence and security matters.

Indeed, the DGIE scored a number of notable successes on behalf of the KGB in the early 1960s. In 1962 Mihai Caraman, a DGIE officer in Paris, recruited François Rousilhe, a Frenchman who worked in the library of NATO headquarters, to provide him with hundreds of secret documents. Caraman's catch was considered so important by the KGB that they decided to pay the Frenchman in gold coins which Caraman received from Moscow. In the following year Caraman took over the running of a Turkish colonel, Nahit Imre, who had been recruited by the DGIE in Ankara and transferred to Paris at deputy financial director of NATO. In order to exploit to the full these two contacts, Caraman was summoned on several occasions to Moscow. In 1965 the KGB was so impressed by the amount of material coming from NATO via Caraman that they sent one of their own officers, Vladimir Arhipov, to work with Caraman. All went well until 1969 when Colonel Ion Iacobescu, Caraman's deputy in Paris, asked for political asylum in the United States. Shortly afterwards Rousilhe and Imre were arrested, and Caraman was withdrawn.

Dej's rift with Moscow, by striking the chord of deep anti-Russian sentiment felt by most Romanians, attracted some support for his regime. Drawing on this sentiment offered Dej a simple way of increasing the regime's popularity while at the same time putting a distance between himself and his Soviet master.[38] With these changes in Romania's relationship with the Soviet Union came a notable shift in the severity of police rule.

The number of persons sentenced to imprisonment for crimes 'against state security' (i.e. against the one-party state), stood in January 1960 at 17,613. The first notable decrease occurred between January and December 1962 when the number fell from 16,327 to 13,017 as many former Iron Guardists were freed. In the next twelve months, following pardons decreed by Gheorghiu-Dej in

38 It was at the beginning of the 1960s that a new wave of young diplomats, all with university degrees and completion of postgraduate courses in international relations, restored professionalism to the Romanian diplomatic corps.

1963 (nos 5 and 767), the figure fell to 9,333 and in 1964 (nos 176 of April and 411 of July) most of the remainder were released.[39] The amnesty marked the end of an era of political terror which had cost the lives of tens of thousands of Romanians, ranging from the pre-Communist political, economic, and cultural elite, but the instrument of that terror, the *Securitate* remained intact, unreformed, and ubiquitous. It and its powerful and ambitious head, the Minister of the Interior Alexandru Drăghici who had first been appointed to this post in May 1952, remained a constant reminder of the past and a threat to the future.

[39] *Cartea Albă a Securităţii*, vol. III, p.33. According to official figures, in 1965 only 258 persons were arrested by the *Securitate* for 'actions hostile to the state'; in the following year, 294 were arrested and in 1967, 312 (*ibid.*, p.95).

13

CONCLUSION

In late January 1965 Dej showed signs of serious illness. A London surgeon had visited Bucharest in the spring of the previous year to perform a prostate and bladder operation on him, but he was now treated for cancer of the lungs. Despite this Dej carried on working. On the advice of Maurer, he travelled to Poland to attend a meeting of the Warsaw Pact since Maurer did not relish the prospect of facing the Soviet leader Leonid Brezhnev alone, but the Romanian delegation left immediately after the conclusion of the proceedings. The cancer quickly spread to Dej's liver, and foreign doctors were called in, among them Dr Geraint Evans, a Harley Street chest specialist, and his wife, a liver specialist, who flew out on the weekend of 6 March. On his return to London, Dr Evans told officials at the Foreign Office that Dej was dying and that he had 'gained the impression that the news would be made public in about a month, and that the choice of Dej's successor as head of state and first secretary of the party was at present under consideration'.[1]

But the Romanian public had already had an opportunity to see the deterioration in Dej's condition. On 5 March Dej had recorded for television and radio what turned out to be his last speech, delivered two days before elections to the National Assembly. Paul Niculescu-Mizil, the senior party official who supervised the recording in Dej's villa on Lake Herăstrău, was alarmed by the faltering nature of his voice and was obliged to ask him to re-read his text. In comparison with his usual speeches, the brevity of his message could not fail to provoke comment among foreign observers, especially on Radio Free Europe which commented that Dej's performance 'provided the most recent and

[1] Note by H.F.T. Smith, 12 March 1965, Public Record Office, FO 371 182734.

most alarming indication of his state of health'.[2]

Dej made his last public appearance on the evening of election day 7 March at a polling station. *Scînteia* published two photographs of him the following day, the first showing him casting his vote with a smile, and the second in the company of Maurer, Ceauşescu and other comrades. It was only on 18 March that the secrecy surrounding Dej's illness was lifted. A medical bulletin, signed by the minister of health and seven Romanian doctors, announced that Dej was suffering from a lung disease and liver complications. The news was enough to cause public expressions of alarm throughout the party. The Central Committee sent Dej an open letter expressing its affection and devotion. A second medical bulletin appeared the following day saying that Dej's condition was unchanged, together with a telegram of good wishes from Mao Tse-tung, and messages from every corner of the country. But the end came rapidly. Shortly after 4 p.m. on that same day, 19 March 1965, the party secretary lapsed into a coma and within two hours he was dead. The fact was announced one hour later on Romanian radio.[3] Three days later, on 22 March 1965, Nicolae Ceauşescu was 'elected' as the first secretary of the Romanian Communist Party.[4]

[2] Quoted from Pierre du Bois, 'Ultimele zile ale lui Gheorghiu-Dej', *Dosarele Istoriei*, no.3, 1997, p.49.

[3] *Ibid.*

[4] On paper Ceauşescu was but one of a number of senior party officials who could put a case for election to the leadership. Yet only he, Alexandru Drăghici, Chivu Stoica and Gheorghe Apostol were not ruled out from the post by virtue of their ethnic origin, the other Politburo members being of Bulgarian (Coliu), Ukrainian (Bodnăraş) or German (Maurer) background. The manoeuvres which enabled Ceauşescu to emerge as first secretary were not made public and it was only after 1989 that some light was shed upon them. Although Dej appears to have designated Apostol as his successor, Ion Gheorghe Maurer, who had been elected president of the council of ministers (prime minister) as recently as 12 March, proposed Ceauşescu as first secretary. Maurer gave the reasons for his choice in a number of interviews after Ceauşescu's overthrow, the principal one being that he regarded Ceauşescu as having the courage to stand up to the Russians; at the same time Maurer let it be understood that he regretted his action. (See the interviews with Apostol, Maurer and Alexandru Bîrlădeanu in 'Cum a venit la putere Nicolae Ceauşescu', *Magazin Istoriç*, vol.29, no.7 (July, 1995), pp.3-7). Drăghici, as the long-serving minister of internal affairs, was feared by everyone, Stoica was not considered up to the job, and Apostol was deemed too headstrong. According to one inside source, Maurer did a deal

Large crowds attended Dej's funeral on 24 March. They listened in silence as four members of the Politburo delivered eulogies. The rhetoric which had followed him for much of his life accompanied him in death. This was its final flowering. Chivu Stoica, who had been elected to the titular position of president of the Council of State on that same day by the Grand National Assembly, spoke first, followed by Gheorghe Apostol, Ion Gheorge Maurer, and Ceauşescu. All stressed Dej's dedication to the principles of Marxism-Leninism and his decisive role in the triumph of Communism in Romania, but at the same time they gave great weight to Dej's contribution to the 'people's happiness'. Ceauşescu described him as the 'beloved leader of the party and the state' and lauded Dej's 'life-long devotion to the happiness of the people' which 'has earned you the unanimous esteem, trust, and love of your closest colleagues, of the Central Committee, of the party, and of the entire population.'[5]

The eulogists were right: Dej's role 'in the triumph of Communism' *was* decisive. But it was Ion Gheorghe Maurer who came closest to the truth that day in the closing words of his speech. After praising Dej for the 'lofty moral qualities' and the 'permanent osmosis that existed between his thoughts and deeds...and those of the people', he concluded:

> 'As we follow with unswerving consistency his instruction and his stimulus, having ever present before us in our minds and in our hearts the lofty example of devotion to the cause of the people's happiness...we and those who come after us will forever feel as we step towards the future the presence alongside us of the man who was and will remain in our history the builder of socialist Romania: Gheorghe Gheorghiu-Dej.'[6]

Maurer spoke better than he knew. Dej's presence was represented most enduringly by the terror which marked Romanians'

---

with Ceauşescu: Ceauşescu would support Maurer's nomination as prime minister (he did so on 12 March) and, in exchange, after Dej's death, Maurer would propose Ceauşescu as party secretary. (E. Mezincescu, 'Din nou despre fantoma lui Dej', *Romînia literară*, no.41 (16-22 December 1992), p.14). In this way Maurer outmanoeuvred Apostol. Stoica was bought off with the post of president of the Council of State.

[5] *Scînteia*, 25 March 1965, p.3

[6] *Ibid.*

lives for a generation after his death and upon whose effect Ceauşescu was to draw so successfully. It is only now that its imprint is beginning to fade.

Dej's body was laid to rest in a hideous mausoleum built in the 'Park of Liberty' in the southern part of the capital. In 1968, barely three years after his funeral tribute in which he praised Dej as 'a dear colleague' whose memory he would 'cherish in his mind and in his heart', Gheorghe Apostol gave a very different appraisal of Dej and his rule. As a fellow railway worker who had joined the Communist Party at the age of eighteen, who had been imprisoned alongside Dej in Tîrgu-Jiu, and had served as first secretary of the party between April 1954 and October 1955, and as a close personal friend, Apostol was well-placed to pass judgement on the Dej era. On 30 April 1968, only days after the plenary meeting of the Central Committee which rehabilitated Foriş and Pătrăşcanu and removed Alexandru Drăghici from his party and government positions, Apostol sent an article to the party daily *Scînteia*. The covering note read:

> We send you this article with a request that you publish it in *Scînteia* after, of course, some stylistic fine-tuning. 'You' does not mean 'you' as a group but as a figure of respect since I imagine that the comrade censor does not know the difference. If, indeed, freedom of the press exists, let us see if you can publish articles which express personal opinions.

IN WHICH DIRECTION ARE WE HEADING?

We are witnessing a toppling of idols which should have taken place a long time ago. Gheorghiu-Dej and other beloved leaders can be firmly placed in the category of assassins. But all the blame has fallen upon comrade Drăghici. Our view is that Drăghici was the most innocent since all he did was to apply the party line, and where there is a line there is no messing around. In fact, that can be seen from the fact that his speech [at the plenum of April 1968] has not been published. As is the case in civilised countries, the defence and not just the prosecution should have been heard. But he would probably have brought a whole chain of people down with him and that is not yet desirable. I would give a great deal to see his reply in print and even more to see it in manuscript. Certain measures should be taken, however, since it is not only a question of Foriş and Pătrăşcanu but also of hundreds and thousands of unknown persons who, like them, finished up with a bullet in their back.

Let us also examine the reason for these notable murders. It seems that the struggle for power between different groups explains the case of Foriş. But there is another explanation for the Pătrăşcanu case. Here the reason is the ideology [of Communism] itself which brings out the *petit bourgeois* in intellectuals. This occurred at the very time of the Russian revolution and also caught on in our country. However, it is clear to everyone that a modern state cannot be run by shepherds and railwaymen. You need a wide vision and broad beliefs which only the highest education in at least law and history can give you. But what education did Gheorghiu-Dej and Chivu Stoica have when they seized power? How did they know how to run a country? And how do even the present leaders know? In fact, this is obvious from the measures and laws which change from one day to the next. Our view is that the real people behind the policy of assassination of Foriş and Pătrăşcanu were the Soviet comrades. There must be a document somewhere which shows this more clearly, even though there is information about this in the papers of the plenum. Many Romanians, whose names we have now learned, were similarly killed in Russia without a trial. Let us not forget that the Russian army withdrew from Romania in 1957 [*sic*!] but that Pătrăşcanu was liquidated in 1954. The only fault of the poor fellow was that he was more of a patriot than others, and more cultivated and intelligent. The policy of cutting off a head which thinks for itself was successfully applied by the Soviet Union in the Baltic States, Poland and Moldavia, so that perhaps Dej's guilt and that of Drăghici is not so great. In fact, the insinuations of thefts of documents and of escape abroad [levelled at Pătrăşcanu] confirm that there is still something fishy about it all.

Let us see now what guarantees there are that similar deeds will not take place again. We regret to say that there are none. We only have to read comrade Ceauşescu's speech of 27 April 1968 to realize this; when we see how many mistakes it contains, since it was written very hastily, and how many errors it proclaims loud and clear. It is clearly the case that the law is one thing for members of the party, and another for those who are not members. As long as that is the case, it is obvious that discretion will rule unfettered. A senior member of the party will be able to trample over a non-member but the law will not be used against him until his colleagues allow it.

Another problem is that a resolution of the party has the force of a law. In such circumstances we ought to act according to what the newspapers say and not according to the constitution and codes of law etc. The law is what appears in the *Official Bulletin* after it has been passed by the Grand National Assembly. A party resolution is an instruction for the drafting of a law but it does not take the place of a law and cannot anticipate it.

Yet the party's role is confused with that of the state. The party is not the state and must not be ubiquitous. For this reason, the *Securitate* have the duty to monitor every person in the country and to report to the prime minister, not to the first secretary. Legislative, executive and judicial power form a perfect amalgam with the party. They should be completely separated from each other to prevent any influence of one upon the other. As it stands, if the president of the State Council falls out with someone, he passes a special law against him and in his capacity as first secretary instructs the courts how to conduct the trial so that the person found guilty can be buried alive.

There have been, and there still are, so many patent abuses of the law that our leaders believe that only the more lowly are obliged to respect it. It is commonplace to recount them. We limit ourselves to showing that two accused men [Foriş and Pătrăşcanu] were thrown out like servants without the least respect for legal formalities being shown. At least in Drăghici's case these formalities were respected.

It is with bitterness that we ask ourselves what to believe in and to whom we can express a positive opinion, if we have one. No one pays any attention to us, because no view has any value unless it is flattery. Public debate is a farce and all that is published of it is that which the censorship allows, and nothing against the line imposed by two or three imbeciles.

Gentlemen, set up a press without censorship and you will see the result immediately. Do you think that it gives us any pleasure to see you arguing amongst yourselves for good jobs if you are not doing anything for the country? Enormous sums are being spent for extraordinarily little benefit. The reason? Because there is no free press to denounce the guilty.[7]

As long as the biggest zero, a man who thinks his opinion is infallible, is there at the top, as long as the deputies in the assembly are robots who raise their hand and applaud, we will do nothing with pleasure, and what we do will be done with disgust and dissimulation. We will always be behind all other states in the world. Nothing can be done just by decrees and arbitrary measures, and without freedom.

Gh. Apostol
30 April 1968

The article was not published.[8]

Since Stalin had been the only person who could call Dej to account, Dej had been able to do what he wanted, subject to Stalin's agreement. As long as Stalin was alive, Dej behaved according to Soviet interests, regarding them as his own; but once Stalin's successors departed from Stalinism he did not think in the same fashion.

With the imposition of Communist rule Romania was forced to turn its back on the West and face eastwards. The most graphic feature of this new stance was the adoption of the Stalinist practice of mass arrests and imprisonment without trial. The application of the Soviet model in the Romanian legal system brought with it the notorious show trial which allowed the regime to dispose of its opponents under a cover of spurious legality. This was in marked contrast to the pre-war judicial regime which, despite its many flaws, was not the instrument of a single political party. The pre-war Romanian governments did not seek the elimination

[7] The sentence that follows is ungrammatical and unintelligible. It reads: 'We do not have nuclear physics and electronics. Yet we have a commission. What a great discovery was made by our party secretary in that until now it was the dustmen who were responsible for these, and not the "party" and the ministers.'

[8] Apostol was Ceauşescu's main rival and was bitter at his failure to win the backing of his colleagues in the Politburo as Dej's successor. The article was found in the archive of the SRI and passed to me by a friend who requests anonimity. Apostol's jibe at the lack of education of Dej and Chivu Stoica is tantamount to the pot calling the kettle black, as is clear from the ungrammatical structure of this article. I have reflected some of its structure in my translation to give it a more authentic ring but not, I hope, at the expense of meaning. Text in square brackets has been added by me for the reader's elucidation.

of a political class, nor did they rely upon the principle of guilt by association.

The methods used by Dej against the Romanian people were also used against party members – the most prominent being Pătrăşcanu, Pauker, Luca and Georgescu – to keep them in line, all the time. This involved the violation of party statutes. Dej's interest in following the results of the stage-management of Pătrăşcanu's trial by listening to the proceedings on a tape-recorder echoes Stalin's presence on the balcony overlooking the Moscow show trials in 1937. Both Communist leaders embodied the intrusiveness of the police state, encapsulated in George Orwell's caption from *1984*, 'Big-brother is watching you!'

In the 1960s, there was a partial return to the West. Credits from Western governments enabled Romania to develop new industries and to redirect some of its trade away from the Communist bloc, and at the same time there was a de-Stalinisation of Romanian cultural policies. In a certain sense, these developments can be interpreted as the triumph of the culture of Romanian behaviour over the culture of Communism. But they were not allowed to pose a threat to Communist rule in Romania, and could be accomodated within the principles of Marxism-Leninism.

It was Dej who created the conditions for the emergence and continuation of 'the biggest zero', Ceauşescu, as Romania's leader. Dej's removal of all his opponents impoverished the political landscape and perverted Romanian society. Imprisoned husbands divorced their wives – and *vice versa* – so that partners and children would not carry the stigma of a political detainee which was a bar to higher education and to employment, and led to dismissal from work. The children of political prisoners were denied entry to higher education until 1963. It was precisely these children who left Romania at the first opportunity in the 1960s and 1970s with dire consequences for the formation of an opposition to Ceauşescu.

APPENDIXES

1

ACCOUNT BY EMIL BODNĂRAŞ OF HIS ACTIONS BETWEEN NOVEMBER 1942 AND APRIL 1944

As a result of a pardon [of former Romanian army officers] issued by Antonescu I was due to be released on 2 November 1942. A few days beforehand, I was summoned by Gheorghiu-Dej and Chivu Stoica (fellow-prisoners in Caransebeş jail) and they discussed with me what I should do after my release. [...] Dej and Stoica were unable to clarify a number of details about my activities in the Soviet Union which continued to be of interest to them, especially when in 1936 I was given Soviet citizenship after being stripped of my Romanian one. [...] After losing the latter, I requested Soviet citizenship on the advice of the Soviet legation with whom I was in contact through my brother Manole and my mother. A few weeks later, a secretary from the legation brought me the news that I had been granted Soviet citizenship and that on the expiry of my sentence I should go to the legation.

These details made the comrades [Dej and Stoica] realise that they were dealing with someone who had contacts which were of interest to them. [...] They told me that 50,000 lei had been put aside and would be sent to me at my brother's address in Brăila, that I would have 10,000 lei upon my release and that my task was to organise the escape from prison of comrades Gheorghiu-Dej, Chivu Stoica, and Teohari Georgescu. To this end a series of contacts had been established which I could use: General Precup, Iuliu Orban, and several names which Teohari Georgescu had been given. [...] In order to carry out this mission I was told to avoid the party, but without being given a reason. [...] This insistence upon avoiding the party was linked, I supposed, to the need to preserve secrecy about it. [...]

When I was questioned by the *Siguranţa* [in Bucharest] I found them very interested in my opinions and activities and extremely anxious about the outcome of the war. I had three interviews in the space of five or six days with the deputy director Rânzescu. [...] He asked me if I did not want to stay in Bucharest and in reply I said that I wanted to go to Brăila, to be with my brother. [...] Once I arrived at Brăila, I began to set up some contacts. In February 1943, I went to Bucharest and got in touch with Precup and Orban. Precup was a person who had access to money, but he was also connected to the party. I warned him not to talk to anyone else about the help he was giving me but he understood this to mean anyone outside the party and he gave details of his meetings with me to Nicolae Apetri [Petrea], whose code-name was Sorin, the party secretary for Bucharest.

Marius [code-name of Foriş] learned that I had been released... but did not know my whereabouts and was surprised that I was not interested in contacting the party. Apetri told him about my meetings with Precup and Foriş gave instructions for me to be summoned. Around March, Precup passed on the message and I chastised him for divulging our meetings. I went back to Brăila.[...]

In the mean time, I went to Caransebeş to discuss escape plans but since work-details outside the prison had been curtailed, this was no simple task. Precup continued to insist that I meet Foriş and since I did not know the real reason for avoiding him, I decided to go. That was about June 1943. By this time I had already set up the first safe house in the Vatra Luminoasă district [of Bucharest]. I went to the meeting with Apetri. He received me with reproaches and kept me in his safe house. At night he took me to another safe house in the district of Ferentari to see Foriş. I realised then that there was a close relationship between him and Foriş. With Foriş I found Mira [code-name for Victoria Sârbu, Foriş's wife] who had been brought into the party leadership by him and dealt with a series of matters.

Foriş chided me, but gently, and I later attributed his attitude to his desire to stop any action which, unsupervised by him, could become dangerous. He was also anxious to discover my role. He knew about the other detainees but very little about me and my contacts. [...] That's why he kept me there for two days. He put it to me that there was a war on, that soldiers who were Communists were needed, and expressed surprise that I was not taking any action. Seeing myself in front of the general secretary of the party,

I said to Foriş: 'Look here, I must tell you why I didn't make contact [and that is because] I received orders to organise Gheorghiu-Dej's escape.' He replied: 'You will organise his escape, we are in agreement with that, rather than working in the party's military structure, which is rather lame and is led by comrade Mihail, that is Rangheţ.' [...]

Pleased that I had established a serious link with the general secretary, I wrote to Gheorghiu-Dej using my contacts. He was now in the Tîrgu-Jiu internment camp. I related everything I had said to Foriş. Dej's reply was a disaster for me. In short it was this: 'We greatly regret that you did not follow your instructions. Please cease any further action on the plan we discussed and get on with your own work. We are stopping all contact.' [...] That made me stop and think. It is not so easy to be told to break off all contact. I had known Foriş for only a week, but Dej I had known since 1935-36. I sent a letter to Dej asking for an explanation but got no reply. The comrades were reserved, they were frightened because of what they knew, but I knew nothing.

In order to keep an eye on me and to win me over, Foriş often called me to his place. This happened every two, or at most three weeks, and he kept me overnight. I slept in the same room as him and he made the coffee, smoked, and reminisced all the time. What surprised me about him was that he tried to discredit Rangheţ and spoke prejoratively about him to me. He criticised almost everyone and the only person he had a high opinion of was himself. He began to allude to Gheorghiu-Dej more and more often in the belief that he had won me over enough in order to reveal his true feelings about him.

I didn't tell Foriş about the reply which I had received from Dej because I realised the reason behind it. [...] One night, Foriş attacked the problem of Dej and told me that he had drawn up a document which would compromise him, saying that Dej was carrying out divisive activity in Tîrgu-Jiu, and that he had isolated the prisons and the camp from the party. What Foriş was after was extremely dangerous: he wanted a list of members who had been caught, together with the positions which they held. [...]

I then realised that I was dealing with a dishonest person, especially when you added the fact that he as party leader was cut off from the party and had no links with it. The only job of Petrea, the party secretary for Bucharest, was to bring us coffee, a small packet of *halva*, and black-market goods. Mira, the woman who lived with Foriş and whom he had made a member of the Central Committee, was a woman whose nastiness was intolerable enough in a person who had no responsibilities, let alone in one who was in the leadership of an organisation which had a historic mission in war-time.

There was also the total lack of contact with the Comintern. Just gossip, a lot of idle talk, Foriş liked to hear himself talk and he wrote for hours on end. A number a things, then, made me realise that I was dealing with a dishonest person and led me to understand why Dej and the other comrades were so cautious as to break off links with me after I contacted Foriş.[...]

Eventually comrade Gheorghiu said that the time was ripe for a talk with me. They decided to summon me to Tîrgu-Jiu. Comrade Gheorghiu organised this meeting by arranging for himself to be moved to hospital where I should join him. I left for Tîrgu-Jiu in the guise of a salesman. I had an attack of appendicitis at about 2 p.m. when there was only one nurse in the hospital, a girl named Maria, and she signed me in as a patient. I was given a dressing-gown. [...] In the room in which Gheorghiu-Dej was staying there were two empty beds but Gheorghiu-Dej complained that he didn't need any bourgeois salesmen. The gendarmes guarding him were paid off and eventually Gheorghiu-Dej had the heart to receive the salesman. [...] This was in August (1943). And there, after I expressed my misgivings, I found out about Marius and why I had been advised not to make contact with him. And there too, the solution presented itself, for I was in possession of a radio. By 5 a.m., when I left the hospital via the morgue, the plan of action had by and large taken shape.

Step 1: the removal of Foriş and the whole of the bourgeois leadership. I should forget about the escape (of Dej), that was of no interest now. The main thing was to sort out the situation in the leadership. In the mean time, other deeds had demonstrated the bourgeois behaviour of the leadership.

Step 2: the unity of action by the working class; the United Workers' Front; finding the solution for working with the Social Democrats; what name we should give to the democratic parties' front; Romania's exit from the war; the creation of our own armed units; sabotaging the war effort; infiltrating the army; winning-over the army. Our exit from the war could only take place after a fight because we were dealing with traitors. And so the two plans of action took shape in those discussions with comrade Gheorghiu-Dej: one for 4 April, the other for what was to come –on 23 August. Our discussion there was developed in detail in correspondence which followed, a part of which must be in the archives and the rest looked for. It was given to [Gheorghe] Pintilie. We should find out what he did with it. Perhaps we ought to ask comrade Pîrvulescu. [...]

It was decided that Rangheţ should be sounded out for his opinion about Foriş. I should also seek out others, including Pîrvulescu, for he had been isolated by Foriş. A group was to be set up to oust Foriş and they were to use force if necessary. [...] It was only around December [1943] that I was able to discuss the Foriş problem with Rangheţ. In a meeting I had with him in my safe house in Vatra Luminoasă, I saw that his opinion about Foriş coincided with that of comrade Gheorghiu-Dej and so, in another meeting with Rangheţ, I told him about my own meeting with Gheorghiu-Dej.

After I informed comrade Gheorghiu-Dej about my discussions with Rangheţ, he was of the opinion that I should go ahead. By 1 January 1944, we were clear [...] Foriş was no longer in command. I had many contacts, I had a car, I and Rangheţ could get around without Foriş knowing. We looked for Pîrvulescu. [...] Foriş complained to me that Rangheţ did not maintain contact with him and that he was hesitant. Rangheţ was indeed very cautious. [...] Foriş proposed that I should in effect take over the party leadership. Up to then Rangheţ was in charge. I was his assistant. I should take over the whole organisation and take a number two. How about Pîrvulescu?

I thought at first that it was a provocation. My mind turned to Rangheţ. Had he, somehow, let something out of the bag? I let myself be persuaded and Mira (Victoria Sârbu) put me in touch with Pîrvulescu. I knew him from my time in prison and on the very first night that we were alone together I spoke to him. Comrade Pîrvulescu agreed with our view of Foriş and with the opinion of the comrades in interment that we should get down to work, although we were concerned with how to deal with Rangeţ who was in danger of being pushed aside. [...]

Pîrvulescu and I finalised the plan to remove Foriş. I also discussed it with Filipescu – real name Chioreanu – who confirmed my view that we were dealing with a traitor. This Chioreanu was a comrade who had been parachuted into Romania from the Soviet Union with his wife in order to restore links with the RCP, because they had been broken. He had been dropped in the wrong place, in Bessarabia instead of Bucharest. He managed to make contact with the party but instead of being used, he was put in mothballs. Later, Rangheţ came across him, working as a carpenter, and handed him over to me. I sent him to look for his radio-transmitter but he could not find it because the house in which he had hidden it had been destroyed. Chioreanu's attitude towards Foriş convinced me that the latter was not interested in links with leading organs of the Communist movement.[...]

I was in particular disagreement with Foriş over the use of our armed units and sabotage groups. We managed to put together several groups and they didn't work badly. We also made contact with a number of partisan groups which had been dropped by parachute and we thought it necessary to use these groups deep behind the front-line, not immediately behind it. [...] It is easier to work a long distance behind the front line in order to carry out sabotage and I expressed this view to Foriş. He was in total disagreement. True to his treacherous conduct, he felt the need to disorganise what had been organised. [...] He argued for sabotage right behind the front line and I showed him that this would quickly lead to the destruction of those groups which, with great difficulty, we had managed to assemble in adverse conditions. He was unwilling to accept a contrary opinion, especially when it was expressed in the presence of others, and we fell out over this matter in front of Pîrvulescu, Sârbu and Apetri, who had been summoned to a meeting in one of the three safe houses which he used on 30 March [1944].

At this meeting, attended by Pîrvulescu, Rangheţ, Sârbu, Petrea and me, Foriş without much ado raised the problem of Spătaru, that is, me: that Spătaru disagreed with the party line, that he was out of step with the party's actions during the war, and that therefore – he had drawn up a document to this effect – I should be replaced. This development was unexpected; it was an interesting one, however. In drawing up our plan to remove Foriş we had considered various ways of doing this. Rangheţ had a naive idea, one which I, at one point, went along with and reported to Tîrgu-Jiu, that we should talk frankly to Foriş and tell him to step aside since he was incompetent and made mistakes. We also considered another plan, that of ousting Foriş without warning, and for this we counted on a factor which we felt that Foriş would attach importance to in our relations with him. This was Foriş's ignorance of the contacts I made when I was in the Soviet Union and when I was active [as an agent] on my return from the Soviet Union to Romania. He tried on a couple of occasions to raise the subject of my activities but did not insist, which again was characteristic of a traitor who, seeing that I avoided the topic, did not press the point, but waited in the hope that he could discover these contacts later. [...]

What was the plan? It involved concocting a story that a senior contact of mine was trying to get in touch with me, a contact which had been set up when I returned to Romania and who had turned up asking me to meet him. The senior contact could only be from the Soviet Union and not from Romania because Foriş knew that no party body in Romania had given me a mission. We were counting on the fact that Foriş, learning that this senior contact was trying to get in touch with me, would be interested to find out details of it, and we would then come to him with a message that a decision had been made that the leadership should be changed, pretending that this decision had been taken at a higher level [by the Comintern].

We considered that Foriş could not check the veracity of this decision; he knew, however, that I had links (with the Soviet Union), especially in 1936 when I was given Soviet citizenship, a status which was not given to just anybody. This would possibly lead Foriş to believe in the likelihood of my having contacts and that these were at a high level. This was the hypothesis upon which the plan was based. A few days before 30 March, I had told Foriş among other things during one of our meetings, that I had received a message that a contact was looking for me. Foriş said: 'OK', but he didn't seem too interested because he had got the idea into his head that he would deal with me in his own way.

On 30 March, our meeting took place. [...] After Foriş announced the agenda, that it was the matter of Spătaru (Bodnăraş) and his disagreement with the party line, and Sârbu and Apetri nodded in accord, there were only the three of us, Pîrvulescu, Rangheţ and me, to combat him. He spoke for a hour and a bit and then called for a break about 10 a.m...and left the room.

We three quickly consulted each other as to what to do. [...] We decided that I should tell him that my contact person had arrived and had asked for a meeting with me in the next few days, namely on 3 April. I went to look for Foriş. He was drinking a cup of coffee. I said to him:

'Comrade Marius, I have something to report. [...] You didn't give me time to mention it before because you started straightaway with this Spătaru business. My contact has arrived.'

'Really?' he replied.

'Yes, and on 3 April he has asked me to meet him. All the indications I have point to the fact that it is a serious matter and I want your opinion as to what to do.'

'You should go,' he said.

'Good, I'll go, but afterwards?'

'You'll report to me and we'll see.'

'All right, when should I report?'

'The very next day.' And he summoned Sârbu.

'What have we got on that day, do we have something planned?'

I was told to come at 10 p.m. on 4 April.

He finished his coffee and the meeting re-started. It was as if the Spătaru problem had never been raised. He didn't feel obliged to give the slightest explanation but said simply:

'Comrades, we raised a problem, we'll postpone it since it requires studying more closely.'

That shows the effrontery of this satrap (Foriş) regarding elementary procedure. We passed on to other business on the agenda. [...] In the afternoon, we went through some papers and in the evening we left the house without mentioning the Spătaru case again.

On the evening of 4 April, the meeting took place, except that in the meantime, Bucharest had been bombed. Foriş was convinced of a link between this bombing and what I had told him. I found him livid, especially as some bombs had fallen nearby. The bombing had been to our great advantage. In the first place, because Foriş's driver, a man called Romeo, who had been told to take me to Foriş, had not been able to come with his car, and therefore the problem of Ranghet and his men having to follow Romeo's car to find out where he was taking me did not arise. My own car had not been requisitioned because my driver paid the police 1,000 lei each month not to take it, and so I was the only one with a car when I met Romeo. When I got to the rendezvous, I saw the bomb craters next to the house and found Foriş sprawled out on the floor. Kofler was also there. I discovered that after half an hour. Foriş had summoned him the evening before. Things could go to plan, with the exception of Rangheţ's intervention with his armed men which couldn't take place because of the unforseen sequence of events.

We imagined that after I entered the house, Foriş would ask me to give him a report on the meeting with my contact and I had written down the three points of a resolution:
(1) The present leadership of the party is dismissed, effective from the date of my communication of the resolution;
(2) A new leadership is to be formed from designated comrades;
(3) All contacts, together with code-names and codes are to be handed over to comrade Spătaru and the former leadership should await instructions from the new one.

Foriş, in order to hide his nervousness, caused first by the bombing and second, by the unknown nature of the report and the fact that he had shown his hand to me on 30 March, it being better that I had not known his intentions, began to deal with his assistant Romeo whom he had not seen for two days and who had brought messages from the contacts. Now, according to the plan, the driver Matei should find Rangheţ, who was in Carol Knappe street, close to the Filantropia district. Rangheţ had with him a group of armed men and a car and was waiting for word from my driver that I was in such and such a place.

While Foriş was busy with his assistant, there was the screech of a car outside, but I hadn't yet managed to report anything (to Foriş). For me to go to open the door (for Rangheţ) was difficult, because in the house we were in, there were three doors from the room I was in to the front entrance and in addition there was also the verandah. Before I could move, I heard some sobbing [and] the landlady thought the *Siguranţa* had arrived. Rangheţ got out of the car, came to the door, but seeing that it was locked and the house was in darkness, thought that I was in another safe house.

Foriş was becoming more and more agitated, but I could see that he got a grip on himself and carried on working with Romeo.

After about fifteen minutes the car returned. The householder, who had been alarmed by the first incident, broke into a fit of hysteria. She was a poor woman with five children and a husband who worked for the post office. At this point Foriş became alert. I couldn't move, I put my hand on my pistol and said

'No need to worry, it's our car.'

'What does that mean?'

'You'll see straight away.'

But at that very moment the car left. I got Romeo out of the room and told Foriş that my contact had come and the message was the following. I was probably nervous, I spoke in a harsher voice, took out the piece of paper, put it on the table and did the same with the pistol. He read it, turned white, and then said that he would comply. I was then convinced that I was dealing with a traitor. Sârbu was cleverer than he was. When she was later summoned to hand over the party archive to me, she raised the matter: 'But comrade, we should call a meeting.' 'There'll be no meeting,' I said, 'it's too late.'[43]

I told Foriş to call his assistant and to tell him that there had been a change of leadership and that the contact man was Spătaru (Bodnăraş). I called Romeo and when he heard his eyes were filled with astonishment. I called him to one side after Foriş had passed on the news, and told him that if he did not carry out orders, it would be bad for him. He said that he would obey. I then told him to put it in writing. And then Foriş, trembling, told me that Kofler was in the house. 'Why did you bring him here? I asked. 'Well, you see, he stayed on overnight,' Foriş replied. I detained Kofler as well and Sîrbu was summoned to hand over the archive. At about 12.30 a.m. – the whole operation lasted some two hours – I finished. I checked all the papers and all the correspondence. It was all in a briefcase. [...] I took the briefcase and left Romeo there. I told him that he was responsible with his life to make sure that no one left the house. He said that he would do his best. The house in which Foriş received me was in Domenii Square.

I went to Filipescu and found him with his wife and Nae Mutulescu. When they saw me they were very surprised and thought that I hadn't succeeded, especially as Rangheţ had been there twice. Rangheţ had dismissed his men and he had gone. I gave Filipescu a gun, left the papers with his wife and with Mutulescu, and returned to Foriş. When he saw Filipescu, he realised that he was the one who had been dropped by parachute. I arranged with Romeo to move Foriş to a neighbouring house and sent Romeo to wake up the occupiers. They were understanding and we moved them (Foriş, Kofler and Sârbu) on foot about 2 or 3 a.m. It was easy to carry out the move because there was total chaos in the area, with people wandering the streets looking for wounded, while others were carrying their belongings.

We moved them and left them with Filipescu with strict instructions that no one should leave the house. Filipescu carried out these orders faithfully, although I could not relieve him for two days. Afterwards I returned to Carol Knappe street, picked up the briefcase, took Nae Mutulescu and went on foot towards Vatra Luminoasă. I left Mutulescu near Mihai Bravu street and entered Vatra Luminoasă district alone. And then there was an interesting coincidence. In a backstreet – it was about 3.30 a.m. – a woman coming out of a courtyard called out to me: 'Sir, for God's sake, help me, I'm giving birth!' I thought to myself, 'What kind of trap is this?' I saw a shadow in the street. On a nearby corner, I knew that there was a public watchman's post and I thought that this woman was trying to pick me up. I shouted: 'Watchman, there's a woman here giving birth, get her help as quickly as you can and here's 100 lei!' And then I though how symbolic this all was: here as a child is born, so too is a new party leadership.

I got home. Pîrvulescu had stayed there with Ana Toma, who was his assistant, and Florica. Rangheţ had dropped by, had heard nothing, and then left. The next day, Pîrvulescu was due to leave the house. I found them all very nervous because something else had happened. After Rangheţ had returned and reported that he couldn't find me and that his men were preparing for the worst, the doorbell began to ring incessantly at about 2 a.m. They were there with our archive and the bottle of paraffin next to it ready to burn it if necessary. The householder took fright – he was a timorous man – and didn't go to the door and so Florica decided to go downstairs, leaving Ana with the archive, and discovered that it was a short-circuit. How it occurred they could never discover. They were nervous as a result of this and about 4 a.m. I appeared. The next morning I sent word for Rangheţ. We held the first meeting and the communiqué was issued which is in the Party archives. That is how things happened on 4 April.[1]

* * *

[The trial of Lucreţiu Pătrăşcanu and Remus Kofler, Foriş's deputy, in April 1954, offered more about the reasons for Foriş's removal although we should remember that much of the evidence presented by the prosecution had been extracted under torture from the defendants. A statement for the prosecution from Nicolae Petrea (Apetri) was produced at the trial in which he declared:

> Foriş's instigation of the conflict with Petre Gheorghe and his personal and hostile actions against the latter, only emerged clearly in summer 1943 when Foriş drew up a party document which he distributed to activists and members in which he referred to Petre Gheorghe. He went so far as to call Gheorghe a 'Fascist', in spite of the fact that the latter had been arrested some time before and had behaved heroically in the hands of the *Siguranţa* and in front of the execution squad, defending with his life the cause of the party to which he proved his devotion to the end.[2]]

[1] Institutul de Studii Istorice şi Social-Politice de pe lîngă CC al PCR (Institute of Historical and Socio-Political Studies of the Central Committee of the Romanian Communist Party), dosar 1404, fond XIII, Documente şi Memorii Privind Alăturarea României la Coaliţia Antihitleristă (1943-1947), vol.1, pp.402-21. The documents in this volume were prepared in 1968 for the sole use of members of the Central Committee and of the above-mentioned institute and were classified as 'strictly secret'.

[2] Under interrogation on 7 February 1950 after her arrest on 15 December 1949 as an associate of Lucreútiu Pătrăşcanu , Sârbu gave this account of these events: 'On the evening of 4 April 1944, comrade Bodnăraş came with a type-written order that comrade Foriş and I should hand over all our contacts and papers and that we should chose a house where we could stay and await new instructions, since it was a question of an inspection which would last at most a few days. Comrade Bodnăraş said that this order came from the Soviet Union.' See Levy, 'Power Struggles', p.79, n. 3. Betea, 'Testamentul lui Foriş, p.44.

2

THE REPORT OF V. LESAKOV

The divisions in the Romanian Party leadership were echoed in a detailed report on the political situation in Romania compiled by a senior official in the Section for International Relations of the Soviet Communist Party, V. Lesakov. Lesakov visited Romania between 7-20 August 1947, and six days after his return to Moscow submitted his findings to his chief, L.S. Baranov.

TOP SECRET

Annex No. 6
For Comrade L.S. Baranov

During the period of my stay in Bucharest, between 7-20 August, I had meetings with leading activists of the RCP's Central Committee, including secretaries Gheorghiu-Dej, Ana Pauker and Vasile Luca, and also with the deputy head of the Allied Control Commission, comrade Susaikov. Besides helping me to resolve the problems connected with my mission (gathering materials for articles and information about the party) Susaikov, Ana Pauker and Luca raised the matter of serious differences of opinions between the Central Committee secretaries, namely between Dej on the one hand, and Pauker and Luca on the other, in the course of their discussions with me. In this respect I consider it necessary to report to you the content of those discussions.

In the discussion which I had on 8 August, comrade Susaikov told me of the existence of two groups in the leadership of the party's Central Committee: one group consists of Dej and 'his men': Maurer, the deputy minister of industry, Zeiger, Dej's private secretary, and Gaston [Marin]; the other group is made up of Vasile Luca and Ana Pauker, although the latter has fewer disputes with Gheorghiu-Dej than Luca. The principal cause of these divergencies lay, in Susaikov's view, in Dej's unwillingness to discuss the major issues in the Politburo and to take decisions on them alone. Gheorghiu-Dej virtually ignores the party and is very sensitive in his reactions to proposals made by Pauker and Luca since he fears that their authority in the party may grow.

Comrade Susaikov believes that Gheorghiu-Dej is striving to remove Pauker and Luca from the party leadership. As an example, he mentions the occasion when Dej, during the parliamentary election campaign, proposed that Pauker and Luca should not be included on the list of candidates on the grounds that they were not Romanian and had come from the Soviet Union. When the International Federation of Women was set up, Dej proposed that Pauker be elected to the federation's leadership and sent on a permanent posting to Paris.

Comrade Susaikov noted that independent actions, which are not discussed in the Politburo, produce gross political errors. Thus, for example, Dej prepared two laws on finance which were in essence correct, but did not inform any of the Communists about them and presented them to the minister of finance, the Liberal Alexandrini, who brought them before the budget commission. At the commission, Luca and other members who backed the Communists, declared themselves against the laws, particularly because they had been proposed by Alexandrini. The latter declared that he was personally against these laws, but that they had been proposed by the Communists. Only the wise behaviour of Ana Pauker allow this chapter to be closed.

In July and August, trade union elections were held. Pauker suggested to Gheorghiu-Dej over the phone that they meet and discuss a series of measures related to this matter, but Dej replied that he did not have time and that at the same time he was meeting the Social Democrats Voitec and Rădăceanu to discuss the elections. At Pauker's suggestion that Luca be invited to this meeting as a knowledgeable person regarding the organising of elections – Luca as a Central Committee secretary dealt with the unions – Gheorghiu-Dej replied that he would meet the Social Democrats alone.

Comrade Susaikov considers that all these actions of Dej can be ascribed, in large measure, to the influence of Maurer and Zeiger who are cautious members of the party. Pauker and Luca are trying to weaken Maurer's influence on Dej. To this end, they have proposed that Miron Constantinescu, a Politburo member, be named general secretary of the Higher Economic Council in place of Maurer, but Dej has not been willing to accept this for some time. The Politburo took the decision to appoint Constantinescu to this position at the meeting which took place during Dej's visit to Moscow. Maurer, who was present at this meeting, did not dare to vote against. When Luca telephoned Dej in Moscow with news of this decision, Dej said: 'if Maurer agrees, then I agree.'

On 15 August, I had a meeting with Vasile Luca. Regarding the situation in the party leadership, Luca declared that we (referring to himself and to Pauker) want the party to run the country and the ministries – where there are Communist ministers – and not the ministries to run the party as is happening at present. Luca repeated what comrade Susaikov had told me. Luca considers that Pauker and Teohari Georgescu are largely in agreement with him, although the latter is trying to keep at arm's length from these disputes.

Luca said that when tasks were being assigned to the Central Committee secretaries, Dej tried to remove him (Luca) and Pauker from the party leadership. Gheorghiu-Dej proposed that Pauker should head the administrative and women's sections, Luca the unions; the organisation and Agitprop sections Dej reserved for himself, that is, as Luca put it, 'for his own people'.

Luca reported that there were many bourgeois economists in the Ministry of Industry who, by working with Maurer, influence the ministry's work. There are also many old hands in the Ministry of Justice (the minister is the Communist Pătrăşcanu) who are sabotaging the ministry's work. 'Honest people can be expelled more quickly than Fascists from this ministry,' said Luca. The ministry drags its feet when looking into the cases of various criminals or even supports them. Even though he is aware of this situation in the Ministry of Justice, Gheorghiu-Dej has not taken a single step against Pătrăşcanu.

According to Luca, Maurer is the man who at present is aiming at establishing economic ties with the West. It was at his insistence that last year the greatest Romanian capitalists, Auschnit and Malaxa, were sent to set up economic links with the United States; they are there at this moment and are spreading reactionary propaganda. Maurer in his work consults with the General Union of Romanian Industrialists instead of relying on and taking advice from the unions. Luca is of the view that Maurer is consciously trying to discredit trade with the Soviet Union by taking measures so that machinery acquired from the Soviet Union is sold under-priced in Romania. In Luca's opinion, Dej allows himself to be influenced by such people as Maurer and also commits political errors because Dej does not have sufficient political training and has difficulty handling economic problems.

Luca believes that without the involvement of the Central Committee of the Soviet Communist Party he and Pauker cannot get positive results since they do not carry authority in Dej's eyes and the latter will resolve all problems on his own. At the same time, Luca stated that this discord was not known to anyone outside the Politburo and that it is not reflected in the party's activity. Luca said that all the Politburo members tried to uphold and to strengthen Dej's authority as general secretary of the party in their speeches. He emphasised that no one aspired to this position and that they were no other candidates in the party for the post, but we [Luca and Pauker] want the party and not the ministries to solve all the major problems.

In conclusion, Luca requested that the Central Committee of the Soviet Communist Party be informed about these differences of opinions and asked for help in removing them.

On 19 August I had my second meeting with Ana Pauker. At the first meeting, which took place on 8 August, Pauker did not raise the problem of differences of opinion in the leadership of the party. At the second meeting, she did express her opinion, which was in essence similar to those of comrade Susaikov and Luca.

With regard to the sending of Auşnit and Malaxa to the United States, she declared that Dej's approval of Maurer's initiative was prompted by the fact that they, 'the national Communists', had to show concern for the country's economy, whereas 'the Muscovite group' thought more of the Soviet Union.

Pauker said that when fixed prices were set after the introduction of the monetary reform on 16 August, Dej ordered Apostol, the unions' leader and a member of the Politburo, as well as the leaders of the party organisation in Bucharest, to organise working groups and to 'lynch' all those who were going to put up the prices of goods. This decision of Dej was adopted at the Politburo meeting of 18 August.

Following a proposal by Tătărescu, Dej agreed to hold weekly meetings with Groza, Rădăceanu and Tătărescu in order to discuss current major problems. In Pauker's opinion, the Communists, who were in a majority in the government, not to speak of parliament where they had an absolute majority, should not have taken part in these meetings. Nevertheless, Dej agreed with Tătărescu's proposal and took part.

Pauker considers that all of Gheorghiu-Dej's errors can be ascribed to his lack of political and general training. He does not apply his knowledge to the problems which he has at present to resolve. He is very preoccupied with his work in the ministry and barely deals with party matters. Similarly, he does nothing to improve his ideological and political level.

On the evening of 19 August I had a discussion with Gheorghiu-Dej. At my request, he addressed the current political problems facing the country. With regard to the role of the party, he emphasised that the principal problem facing him was the poor political training of party members and, in this respect, of its leadership. Dej believes that as a result many mistakes are made but at the same time, the fundamental political line is correct.

He did not refer to the problem of differences of opinion in the party leadership but, when speaking about the struggle with the Social Democrats and the discord among the latter, Dej remarked that 'we, too, have our differences in the party and we are at each other's throats sometimes'.

V. Lesakov, 29 August 1947

3

STATEMENT BY GHEORGHE PINTILIE, FORMER HEAD OF THE SECURITATE, DATED 15 MAY 1967 AND PRESENTED TO THE PARTY COMMISSION CHARGED WITH INVESTIGATING THE DEATH OF ŞTEFAN FORIŞ

The undersigned Gheorghe Pintilie, being questioned by Vasile Patilineţ at the Central Committee about what I know about Ştefan Foriş, and my views in connection with this matter, have the following to say. Personally, I did not see a single document from the period of the bourgeois regime which showed any trace of contact between Foriş and the bourgeois *Siguranţa,* nor do I have any knowledge that such a document might exist. We interrogated former police and agents of the bourgeois *Siguranţa* for years on end without finding any sign of such a link. As regards what happened to Foriş I know the following:

In 1941, some of the comrades who were in jail, including me, began to feel that something was not right with the party leadership. It was a very vague feeling. We were concerned about the large number of arrests of Communists at that time.

In 1941 or 1942, the party leadership sent a leather jacket to the prison to be given to Dej. The jacket was accompanied by a letter from the party leadership which, among other things, used the form of address to Dej as 'you, as a future commisar'. It was I who received the jacket and I took it to Dej. On learning that it came from the party leadership, he refused to accept it with the words: 'Screw him, he wants to buy me. You can do what you want with it, tear it, throw it away, whatever.'

Later, on another occasion, Dej spoke to me of Foriş as someone whom he didn't trust or about whom he was unhappy. At the same time, he told me to keep my mouth shut about his views of Foriş. I thus realised that the other Communist prisoners did not know of Dej's attitude. All of this took place in Caransebeş jail. It was known in the jail that 'fractionist' sentiments had appeared in the party and that these had made themselves felt in the prison as well. Sometime in 1942, this 'fractionism' grew and each group sought to establish links with those in jail to persuade them that they were right. Dej gave orders that none of the jailed Communists should get in touch with any of the groups on the grounds that we didn't know what was going on outside and who was in the right. In insisting that no contacts were to be made with any group, Dej made a point of stressing that this applied to Foriş's group in particular. No one was to respond to any communication, and although messages came from the Central Committee, no replies were given.

It was against this background that a document came from the Central Committee asking us for the names of all the Communists belonging to the party in jail. Dej handed me this document with the words: 'There, there's your proof!' My view about this document was that if it wasn't an act of betrayal, it was in any case a grave error and a gross lack of vigilence. It was at this very same time that the number of party members arrested increased.

From this point onwards word got around amongst other party leaders in jail such as Teohari [Georgescu], Vinţe and Chişinevski that Foriş was a traitor. At the same time, the secretaries of party groups began saying that something was amiss in the party leadership. At this time, Dej was concerned about the whereabouts of Costică Pîrvulescu since he had been sought in several places and could not be found. It was in this atmosphere that a number of comrades were primed in prison to 'sort out' the party leadership, starting with Foriş.

After 23 August 1944, I was given the task of keeping Foriş under guard. After Foriş was released at the beginning of 1945, it was also I who was instructed in June 1945 to re-arrest him and detain him. The order was given by Dej. Ana Pauker might have been present as well when this order was given. I kept Foriş in the following places: in a room in the headquarters of the Central Committee, in a basement in the building where I lived, and in a house on Popa Şapcă street. As Foriş's guard I used two or three comrades, yet they didn't know the identity of their prisoner. During the whole period of his detention, Foriş was very obedient and disciplined, doing everything he was asked. For example, he was told not to go near the window, so as not to be seen from outside, told not to shout or to speak to anyone, not to give his name. He followed all these instructions.

Each day, sometimes every other day, I was summoned by Dej and asked about Foriş, how he looked, what his attitude was. During Foriş's detention, Dej visited him several times and talked to him. What they discussed I do not know. I never saw Dej emerge from their meetings with anything on paper. Sometimes their discussions were very animated, with them shouting at each other. Sometimes Dej was accompanied by another comrade from the party leadership when he went to talk to Foriş. Among those who went with Dej were, I remember, Ana Pauker and Teohari Georgescu. No one, however, contacted Foriş without Dej being present. In summer 1946, I received instructions from Dej and, separately from Teohari Georgescu, that I should do away with Foriş.

When Dej gave me these instructions, I asked how I should proceed. he replied: 'Haven't you got a brain? You sort it out!' Over the following days I was continually asked by Dej if I had dealt with Foriş. Eventually, when I kept saying 'not yet', he chided me with 'why do you keep pussy-footing around with him, as though you were about to give up?' When I told him that Foriş had been liquidated, Dej said, 'Thank goodness we've finished with that wretch.'

In getting rid of Foriş I was assisted by Bulgaru and my former chauffeur, who later left for the Soviet Union. It was also they who helped me to get rid of Pîrgariu, who was buried in the same place as Foriş. I was the only person among us who knew the identities of the murdered persons. Foriş and Pîrgariu were buried in a house on Aleea Alexandru which I have indicated on the spot.

(Cristian Troncotă, 'Ghiţă Ordonă, Pantiuşa execută', *Dosarele Istoriei*, no.3, 1997, pp.33-4)

NOTE

The report of the party commission, drawn up by Gheorghe Stoica, Vasile Patilineţ, Ion Popescu-Puţuri and Nicolae Guină, concluded that 'Foriş's execution was carried out by Gheorghe Pintilie, aided by his chauffeur Dumitru Necin, through blows administered with an iron bar. The body was thrown into a specially-prepared pit in the grounds of the building in which he was killed. A few days after Foriş's murder, two other persons were killed in the same place and in the same way, only one of whom was identified as N. Pîrgariu. All three were thrown into the same pit and their bodies covered with earth and rubble (stenograma of Gheorghe Pintilie's deposition before the Commission).

Regarding the disappearance of Foriş's mother, it has been established that since she came to the Central Committee headquarters on repeated occasions in tears, shouting from the street for the return of her son, she was arrested in the summer of 1946 and sent to Oradea under the supervision of the local party committee. According to the declaration of Zoltan Eidlitz, former secretary for the cadres in the Bihor county, and Adolf Vogel, in whose house Foriş's mother was held, it emerges that the latter died at the beginning of 1947. Since she had been brought in exceptional circumstances to Oradea – as the two witnesses declare – her disappearance had to be engineered in the same way. In order to remove any trace of her, her body was thrown into the river Crişul Repede, with a stone attached to her neck (Declarations of Laurentiu Cziko, Zoltan Eidlitz, Dumitru Cernicica, former party secretary of Bihor county, and Adolf Vogel, *ibid.*, p.35).

Pintilie gave a similar account to Lt.-Gen. Grigore Răduică, a senior *Scuritate* officer, who had also been ordered by Nicolae Ceauşescu to investigate Foriş's fate in 1967 (Ştefănescu, *Istoria Serviciilor Secrete Româneşti*, p.251). A party obituary of Foriş dates his arrest to 9 June 1945 and his murder to the summer of 1946 (Florea, 'Ştefan Foriş', p.153). This chronology is corroborated by George Fotino, a private secretary to the minister of the interior, Teohari Georgescu. Georgescu himself described under interrogation in May 1953 how the decision was taken to get rid of Foriş: 'In spring 1946 General Nicolski came to me and asked me "What are we going to do with Foriş? He has been under arrest for some time." I told him that I would make inquiries and let him know. A few days later, I went to the party general secretary and asked him, "What are we going to do with Foriş. We've held him for a long time, shall we get rid of him?" Comrade Gheorghiu told me that he agreed with my proposal. After that I looked for Vasile Luca and Ana Pauker. I found them together in a room of Pauker's on the first floor. I asked them, "What are we going to do with Foriş?" in the sense that we should get rid of him. Both were in agreement.' (ASRI, Fond P, file 40009, vol.1, pp.230-40. Marius Oprea was kind enough to show me this document.) Fotino recalled an attempt made by Foriş's mother to seek an unscheduled audience with Georgescu in the early summer of 1945 to ascertain the whereabouts of her son. When Fotino, who had never heard of Foriş, went into the minister's office to tell him that a certain 'Mrs Foriş' was in the ante-room and would like to see him, Georgescu went bright red and told him to tell her that he had been called away to a meeting, adding an instruction to Fotino that 'the woman was not to be allowed into the ministry again' (author's interview with G. Fotino, 9 April 1994). Pintilie was coopted as a member of the RCP Central Committee at a plenary meeting on 10-11 June 1948 (*Scînteia*, 13 June 1948, p.1). Despite being attacked in the April 1968 Central Committee plenary meeting for his role in Foriş's murder, Pintilie was decorated by Ceauşescu in May 1971 on the 50th anniversary of the party. Pintilie's chaffeur, Dimitrie Necin (Dumitru Mitea), had orginally been sent to Romania as one of a three-man NKGB group parachuted in May 1944 into the area of Predeal with a radio transmitter to communicate to the Red Army information on German military activity (Mircu, *Dosar Ana Pauker*, p.130, n. 21). Pintilie consistently denied to

Eduard Mezincescu that he had wielded the iron bar, claiming that the chauffeur Mitea struck the mortal blows (E. Mezincescu interview with the author, 16 June 1994), but his sadistic impulses were revealed in a drunken confession he once made at a party to Tatiana Brătescu, Ana Pauker's daughter, in the early 1950s. He told her that as a member of the Comsomol in the Ukraine he had discovered a priest holding a service on the edge of his village in a hollow. He gathered other youths and together they pinned down the priest and buried him alive by piling earth over him with tractors (interview with T. Brătescu, 30 July 1994).

4

FORMATION OF THE GROZA GOVERNMENT

Dej confirmed in a meeting of the Romanian Politburo on 29 November 1961 that the idea to remove Pauker was planted in his mind in January 1946 by Vyshinski; see 'Stenograma Şedinţei Biroului Politic al CC al PMR din ziua 29 noiembrie 1961' pp.12-13, reproduced in *Sfera Politicii*, no. 48, 1997, p.36. At the Moscow Conference in December 1945, the United States proposed that the Groza government should be reorganised to include members of the opposition parties. Stalin made a limited concession in this respect in the agreement signed on 26 December, in which the three Allies recommended that the Groza government should include one member each of the National Peasant and Liberal parties. Vyshinski, Harriman and Clark-Kerr arrived in Bucharest from Moscow in 31 December to oversee the implementation of the agreement. The opposition parties nominated Ion Mihalache and Dinu Brătianu. The Groza government rejected these nominations, and finally Emil Haţieganu and Mihail Romniceanu were included in the cabinet to represent the national Peasants and Liberals respectively. The relevant passage in the Politburo minutes reads as follows:

> *Comrade Gh. Gheorghiu-Dej*: 'Vyshinski arrived on behalf of the Soviet Union, Harriman for the Americans and Clark for the British. Vyshinski got in touch with us, explained the whole business and we consulted with Groza and Tătărescu and those responsible for these matters. We agreed to accept a representative from each of these parties, as well as the date proposed by them for the elections. We agreed amongst ourselves not to accept leading figures from these two parties but only second-rate people. We then settled upon Romniceanu and Haţieganu, if you recall. Then Groza, who was in constant touch with Vyshinski, told him of our position. [...] In the evening we went to the theatre. I, Groza and Ana were there. There were many of us. Vyshinski was there as well, if I'm not mistaken.

Comrade E. Bodnăraş: No, Vyshinski wasn't there.

Comrade Gh. Gheorghiu-Dej: Towards the finale Ana got up and called me. She continued to play the role of leader, although I was the general secretary. She still pulled all the strings and summoned me and said: 'My dear Ghiţă, look, there's a problem. You've got to go to Groza and inform him that we have to substitute Bebe [Dinu] Brătianu for Romniceanu.' I asked, 'Why?' I think she gave the following reason: 'It will be easier, things will be understood more easily.' It seemed that this proposal was supposed to help Vyshinski. From the way she spoke to me, I took it to be a suggestion. This was her way of doing things, these things emerged from somewhere. She was never precise about it, but the suggestion was that they came from the highest Soviet circles.

Comrade E. Bodnăraş: All the more because we knew that Susaikov was leaning towards Brătianu.

Comrade Gh. Gheorghiu-Dej: We didn't know that then. We found out afterwards. So I went to Groza after the theatre and told him: 'Look, here's the problem. You remember that we settled on Romniceanu and Haţieganu, but now there's a proposal that we change Romniceanu for Bebe Brătianu.' He gazed in surprise at me. Then I told him the same story that there would be heated discussions and that a solution must be found, and we should give Vyshinski a helping hand. When he heard this he said: 'OK'.

The next day, Groza told Vyshinski what I had told him. Vyshinski hit the roof when he heard. Vyshinski, Susaikov and their translator went to Groza's house. When Vyshinski heard the whole story he got very angry. Groza said afterwards that Vyshinski was almost shouting: 'What is the meaning of this? Have I come here, sent by my government, with an easy task? Am I one to run away from problems? I don't understand you.' In other words, a pretty heated discussion. 'Why did you make this last-minute change?' Groza did not say at the outset that Dej had come to see him. Then he related how Dej had come to see him and what I had said.

And so Vyshinski sent for me and I went to Groza's house. I realised that the atmosphere was glacial. There was me, Groza, Vyshinski, Susaikov and the translator. Vyshinski then asked me:

'Comrade Dej, you came by last night. Listen to what Mr Groza has to say. Well, then? What happened? Why?' Again the temperature rose. I said: 'Look here, Comrade Vyshinski, Ana went to the theatre last night and made a concrete proposal to ease the discussions with the two representatives of the US and Britain in terms that suggested that it came from the Soviets. I then came and informed Groza in the exact words used by Ana to me.'

Vyshinski calmed down, but it was now the turn of Susaikov. The penny dropped later. I wondered why Ana had raised the matter of Romniceanu's replacement by Bebe Brătianu. Susaikov then put the question: "But who is the general secretary?" In other words he was asking: "Why have you come with this story involving Ana when you are the general secretary." I then asked him: "But who really is the general secretary?" I knew that he and Ana were close, they visited each other and talked. This happened less frequently with me.

Susaikov said nothing and Vyshinski took me to one side and said: 'Comrade Dej' – the others heard, perhaps, because he wasn't speaking softly, but fairly loudly – 'how is Ana of help to you?' I said, 'You can see for yourself what help she gives me, and if this was not the only example.' He thought for a little and said, 'Wouldn't it be better if she was removed?' 'Removed' could be understood in the sense that she should be removed from the leadership or removed from Romania.

I then said to Vyshinski: 'Comrade Vyshinski, such a thought never crossed my mind, but I shall think about it and reflect on what you have said. And with that it was over.'

On a later occasion, Vyshinski criticised Ana and Teohari Georgescu very harshly over the question of the Iron Guardists.

5

THE ROMANIAN FOREIGN MINISTRY

On 23 August 1944 there were 279 diplomats and consuls (out of a total of 957 employees) working in the ministry. A characteristic feature of the diplomatic service was its core of high quality personnel who had gained their experience in the inter-war period. They were marked by their professionalism and patriotism, and displayed both in the difficult period after 23 August 1944, and after the imposition of the Groza government. As a result of the increasing number of states with which Romania established diplomatic relations, a new law on the organisation of the Foreign Ministry was adopted in March 1946 which led to an increase of about one hundred in the number of diplomats. On 30 April 1946, there were still ninety-one posts vacant in the ministry, among them fifteen heads of mission and thirty-one counsellors. The parties supporting the Groza government were quick to profit from this situation and used the new law to place their own members or supporters in diplomatic posts. Of the forty-five persons taken on, the main beneficiary was the Liberal Party whose leader, Gheorghe Tătărescu, was foreign minister. The Communists occupied second place, with eleven posts, followed by the Ploughmen's Front with ten. Up to January 1947, there was a continuous rise in the number of diplomatic personnel taken on but after that date economy measures began to bite. On 1 June 1947, nine diplomats and six consuls were dismissed, and on 1 September the numbers were reduced by a further thirty-six. None of those dismissed were members of the Communist Party.

The 'Communisation' of the diplomatic corps began only after the removal of Tătărescu from the Foreign Ministry and his replacement by Ana Pauker on 7 November 1947. After this date, the Romanian Foreign Ministry was literally occupied by Communists. Those employees who were not members of the Communist Party were denied access to the ministry. But when the Communists realised that they did not have the experience to deal with certain matters, they appealed briefly to some of the older diplomats. However, these, too, were dismissed on 20 November. At the same time new recruits were taken on, using the criteria of their social background and political persuasion. 268 new staff were recruited between November 1947 and March 1948, the prime consideration for employment being the extent of their activity on behalf the Communist Party.

A detail which shed lights on the way in which Pauker ran the Ministry of Foreign Affairs is her sponsorship of Ana Toma. On 1 December 1947 Toma was appointed to the Foreign Ministry with the rank of first secretary (head of chancery). On 8 May 1948, under a decree signed by the president of the Presidium of the Romanian People's Republic, Professor C. Parhon, and countersigned by Pauker, Toma became secretary-general of the Foreign Ministry. Even before that date, Toma had been granted exceptional powers within the ministry. An example is the authorisation for Toma, signed by Pauker on 29 January 1948, to approve expenditure 'in the major interest of the state' within the budget agreed by the Ministry of Finance for any sum for which receipts could be shown, and up to a maximum of 20% of the budget when receipts could not be shown. In the latter case, a written order of Toma, specifying that payment was to be made without receipts, would suffice. How much money passed through Toma's hands on the basis of the authorisation will probably never be known. These funds could have be used for espionage or propaganda exercises on behalf of the regime. The diplomatic historian Ion Calafeteanu does not rule out the theory that Pauker used the money to support the Zionist movement and to facilitate Jewish emigration from Romania, actions which would have discredited her in Stalin's eyes and contributed to Gheorghiu-Dej's victory in the struggle for power.

(Ion Calafeteanu, 'Schimbări în aparatul diplomatic românesc după 6 martie 1945' in *6 Martie 1945*, pp.164–71).

6

CONDITIONS IN THE AIUD CENTRAL PENITENTIARY

(*written in English by an anonymous former member of Antonescu's cabinet in 1947*)

The Aiud Central Penitentiary has the following staff:
Director: Alexandru Gutan, a Communist from Cetatea Albă.
Deputy-Director: Mareş, an ex-inmate of the prison, whether as political or common-law offender I do not know.
Warders: These have in their care the cells of the prison where only political prisoners are kept.
(*a*) *Head Warder*: I. Urdărianu
(*b*) *Warder*: Furda
(*c*) *Warder*: Filimon
(*d*) *Warder*: Onica

The cells contained (30 March 1947) about 400 political offenders. I have now been informed that the *Sumanele Negre* have also been brought here.

Types of prisoner

— War criminals (Romanian and Hungarian)
— National Peasant Party members
— Iron Guard members

Accommodation

The prisoners are kept in 4 × 2-metre cells, containing one iron bed each. The necessary linen is supposed to be brought from their respective homes. The bed excepted, prisoners have the right to keep a suitcase each in their cells. All cells, without exception, are densely inhabited by bed bugs. The central heating is almost nonexistent – about 6 metres of tubing and no radiators, through which, during the last winter, circulated small quantities of warm water for two or three hours daily.

On entry in the prison each detained person is subjected to a search. I will here recount what happened to the former Antonescu cabinet ministers, of which I was one.

We arrived on 6 March 1947 and were taken under escort to the prison. We were put six in a cell without any search having been made and with all our luggage. The cells were quite empty and contained no beds. At about 1900 hours, the director came, asking us each our names, and left in a very civilised manner.

At about 0030 hours, we were awakened by bangings on the door and obscene language. Lacking any sort of sleeping space, we had put our baggage next to the doors. We got up, took away the baggage and the following persons burst through the door, the deputy director Mareş and an Iron Guardist, whose name I do not know. Two of us (General Sichiţiu, a seventy-year-old man, and Colonel Cristea Manea) were unable to get up. Both had arrived ill, especially Colonel Manea, who has a perianal fistula with twelve craters, which had just formed an abcess.

They were kicked by Mareş for their inaction, General Sichiţiu receiving a blow on the right eye-socket and several on his back. Colonel Manea was also severely kicked. After having got up, they were again hit with the butt end of a Schmeisser' sub-machine-gun, with which the deputy director was armed. After having asked us our names, Mareş left.

The second evening, we were subjected to a search under the supervision of Mareş. [...] Clothes were torn, personal belongings messed up, medicines spilt. They stole everything they found and took a liking to. I can give one example: General Arbore had his gold pencil stolen. On 27 March he told this to his wife in the presence of the head warden, Urdărianu, in the parlour. The latter immediately reported this conversation to the deputy director and on 12 April, just before Easter, he was not allowed to receive any food parcels. [...]

Treatment

The food consists of a lump of about 300 grams of maize meal, together with a cloudy water called soup, morning and night, or five slices of unskinned potatoes in perfectly crystalline water. Most of the time, the prisoners eat the potatoes, keeping the water in order to wash their more intimate parts, as this is the only warm water which they receive. Thosè who were on a diet received plenty of soup. [...]

All prisoners, excepting those condemned to hard labour, have the right to receive 3 kg of food parcels from home. For Christmas, they were approved 5 or 6 kilos each, but immediately after Christmas the deputy director made a midnight search, confiscating all the remaining food.

The prison has a canteen from which political prisoners are forbidden to buy anything, except those who are ill, who receive a little booklet where the man in charge of the canteen writes the quantities and sums to pay, and the prison cashier pays these sums from the money sent to the prisoners by their families. [...] Water is distributed normally through a pump system, which draws it to the highest storey and then distributes it to the respective wash-basins. The pumps broke down in the autumn of 1946 and were not repaired. Today water is distributed to the prisoners in buckets, about 2 litres daily, because excepting a plate, a spoon and a bottle of water, all other receptacles were confiscated from the cells. This water must suffice for washing both body and clothes and for drinking.

The W.C. is a real calamity. Every floor has ninety cells. On some floors there are two and even three political prisoner in each cell. All these have to use six drain holes without water, which fill up after being used three times. They are only cleaned once every twenty-four hours. Rats circulate in legions through the prison drain system.

The prisoners are taken out of their cells for five to ten minutes morning and night in order for the cells to be cleaned, and half an hour morning and afternoon to take exercise in the quad. The rest of the time they stay in their cells. [...]

The Aiud prisoners have lived and probably still live days and nights of real terror. The deputy director Mareş used to search the cells five nights a week. The technique was as follows:

The door opened and Mareş, accompanied by one or two Iron Guardists, of whom one was usually Boian-Moisescu, the former chief of Iron Guard police, came in. They stripped you to the skin and started searching. They tore the mattress open, strewing all its contents on the floor, and then threw the inmates' salt, food, medicine, clothing etc. on top. They confiscated everything they liked and the Iron Guardists cut suitcases and shoes or boots open with a knife if these seemed suspicious. Woe befell he who protested.

I will now quote two cases, that of Romulus Daianu and of Reinhardt.

The first was a journalist and the second a police officer, formerly in the Bucharest Prefecture of Police. Daianu worked for two days to tidy up his cell after such a visit and Reinhardt was put in 36 lb. chains for nine days for having concealed a small icon on which was written a sentence from a sermon preached in prison and censored by the administration – icons were completely banned, as well as family photographs. [...]

Family visits are allowed in the parlours twice a month only, on the 12th and 27th of each month. The families are received at the station by the police, escorted from there to the police station, hotel and prison and immediately after, taken out of town. They are forbidden to contact anyone in Aiud, even if they have relatives or friends in this town. [...]

7

ORGANISATION OF THE ROMANIAN SECURITY SERVICE, 1948-1965

All information presented below on the organisation of the Romanian security services down to 1965 is taken from *Organizarea şi funcţionarea Organelor Ministerului de Interne de la Infiinţare pînă în prezent* (Bucharest: Ministry of the Interior, 1978, 144 pp.). I am grateful to the relevant authorities in Romania for allowing me to consult this document.

1. The organisation of the DGSP (*Direcţia Generală a Securităţii Poporului)* as established by decree on 30 August 1948:

Directorate I	Domestic Intelligence
Directorate II	Counter-sabotage
Directorate III	Counter-espionage in the Prisons and Police
Directorate IV	Counter-espionage in the Armed Forces
Directorate V	Penal Investigation
Directorate VI	Protection of Ministers
Directorate VII	Technical
Directorate VIII	Cadres
Directorate IX	Political (responsible for party purity)
Directorate X	Administration

Auxiliary departments dealt with interception of mail, surveillance and eavesdropping and further included a cipher section and a secretariat.

Thirteen regional directorates, including that for the city of Bucharest, were established

2. On 30 March 1951, by Decree no. 50, the DGSP is referred to by the new name of the DGSS (*Direcţia Generală a Securităţii Statului)* which was structured as follows:

Directorate A	Foreign Intelligence
Directorate B	Counter-espionage
Directorate C	Counter-sabotage
Directorate D	Transport
Directorate E	Counter-espionage in the Militia

Directorate F	Surveillance
Directorate G	Penal Investigation
Directorate H	Counter-espionage in the Armed Forces
Directorate I	Protection of Party leadership
Directorate J	Cadres and Schools
Directorate K	Administration
Directorate L	Political

There were also departments for accounts, records, interception of mail, transport of secret documents, and a secretariat. To reflect the local government reorganisation of September 1950 when the counties *(judeţe)* were combined to form twenty-eight regions, the number of regional directorates was increased to match this figure.

3. The Ministry of State Security (*Ministerul Securităţii Statului)* was set up as a body distinct from the Ministry of the Interior on 20 September 1952. It incorporated the DGSS.

4. On 7 September 1953 the Ministry of State Security was amalgamated with the Ministry of the Interior.

5. The Ministry of the Interior was reorganised on 11 July 1956 and divided into two departments: the Department of Security (DS) *(Departamentul Securităţii)* and the Department of the Interior *(Departamentul Internelor)*. The latter was given responsibility for the militia and prisons while the former inherited the structure of the DGSS with the following modifications:

Directorate I	Foreign Intelligence
Directorate II	Counter-espionage
Directorate III	Domestic Intelligence
Directorate IV	Counter-sabotage
Directorate V	Counter-espionage in the Armed Forces
Directorate VI	Transport
Directorate VII	Surveillance
Directorate VIII	Penal Investigation
Directorate IX	Protection of Party leadership
Directorate of Cadres and Schools	
Directorate of Administration Secretariat	
Department B	Radio counter-intelligence
Department C	Records
Department D	Transport of prisoners
Department F	Interception of mail

Department H Cipher
Department K Counter-espionage in the prisons and militia
Department T Technical

A school for training officers and one teaching foreign languages were also placed under the control of the DS as were the security troops and the frontier guards.

6. On 30 May 1963, control of the security troops was removed from the DS and placed under a separate department within the Ministry of the Interior. By the same decree of 30 May Directorate I (Foreign Intelligence) of the DS was redesignated UM (*Unitate militară*) 0123/1 and given the name *Direcţia Generală de Informaţii Externe* (DGIE).

8

ARREST AND INTERROGATION OF HERBERT (BELU) ZILBER

We have to thank Herbert Zilber for shedding further light on how his own arrest and interrogation was used to implicate Pătrăşcanu in the charge of being an agent of the *Siguranţa*. This he did in an autobiographical memoir written in the early 1970s but published only in 1991under the pseudonym of Andrei Şerbulescu, (*Monarhia de Drept Dialectic*, Bucharest; Humanitas). Zilber had been Pătrăşcanu's number-two in the talks conducted in 1944 with the opposition parties to plan Romania's *volte-face* but in May 1947 he was expelled from the Communist Party for failing to follow the 'party line' and on suspicion of being 'an Anglo-American spy'. His expulsion should have been a warning to Pătrăşcanu who had attracted the enmity of Dej. Being ostracised by his friends prompted Zilber to write to Ana Pauker in November 1947 with a request that his innocence be established through a full investigation ofhis activities (*ibid.*, p.46). In a letter to Ceauşescu, dated 6 September 1966, Zilber outlined the ordeal that followed:

> I was arrested by order of the Central Committee on 6 February, 1948. A long and detailed interrogation carried out by the organs of the Ministry of the Interior (February 1948-December 1951) on the initiative and under the direction of the party proved without any doubt my total innocence. This conclusion was communicated to me during the interrogation and after the completion of the investigations (*ibid.*, p.182).

Zilber's interrogation began on 2 April 1948 at the hands of Marin Jianu, secretary-general of the Ministry of the Interior, and Alexandru Nicolski, the chief interrogator of the Ministry of the Interior, who sought to extract a declaration from him that he had been an agent of the *Siguranţa*. A 'confession' by Zilber would be enough to implicate his friend Pătrăşcanu. In the evenings he was brought before Rangheţ and Drăghici who were responsible for the party investigation. Zilber's interrogation ceased in December

1951 when he thought that he might be released, but it was resumed in September 1952 with a new team of interrogators

> ....among whom I only know the names of the Minister Alexandru Drăghici, Colonel Şoltuţiu, Captain Moraru and Captain David. On the night of 17-18 September 1952 I was beaten for the first time, while on the night of 24-25 September 1952 I was beaten three times on the soles of my feet. Comrade Colonel Şoltuţiu, said to me, these are his very words: 'Your protectors have gone. The Party is now in strong hands. You must declare all the crimes you committed with Pătrăşcanu and others.' Since I did not know what crimes I had committed or who the 'others' were, I asked the young officer who was supervising my beating that evening in the cellar of Malmaizon, tearing the hair from my head. The latter enlightened me: 'You should declare all the crimes you have committed with Lucreţiu Pătrăşcanu, Ana Pauker, Vasile Luca, Teohari Georgescu, Ion Gheorghe Maurer, Ştefan Voitec, Aurel Vijoli, Petre Năvodaru, Mihnea Gheorghiu, Ilie Zaharia, Carol Neuman and others. It is the order of the secretariat [of the Party]'. [...] Later Colonel Şoltuţiu added to the list Emil Calmanovici, Jack Berman, Remus Kofler, Alexandru Ştefănescu, Luiza Năvodaru, Vera Călin, Petea Petrescu (Gancev) and others. I realised that a trial on the model of those in Moscow, Sofia, Budapest, Prague and Warsaw was being organised in which I had to play the role of the criminal spy. With my swollen feet I reflected upon the álternative which was placed before me and I concluded that any resistance was futile. I had to declare all the crimes that were usual in such interrogations. [...] I declared that I was an agent of the *Siguranţa*, an Anglo-American spy, a conspirator, an assassin, and a traitor. I did not hesitate to declare that I intended to spread the plague in working-class districts, that I organised inflation and sabotaged the stablisation programme, that I handed over the Banat to Yugoslavia in a deal with Mosha Piajde etc. Everything, of course, in complicity with Pătrăşcanu, Vijoli, Maurer, Voitec and all the other conspirators suggested by the interrogators. I admitted the final plot at the express demand of Alexandru Drăghici on 5 May 1953, a demand which he made in his very office in the presence of Colonel Şoltuţiu. It was a question of a 'plot' which was the imagination of Radu Buzeşti (convicted in the Maniu trial), a person of whom I had never heard and whom I met for the first time at a so-called

'confrontation' in July 1953. Naturally this Radu Buzeşti not only declared that he knew me, but he even dictated my whole life story, exactly as I had written it down [for the interrogators]. I specifically mention this plot because it was on the basis of this fiction that Pătrăşcanu was condemned to death and executed, while I and others spent many terrible years in prison. (*Ibid.*, pp.182-3)

BIBLIOGRAPHY

UNPUBLISHED PRIMARY SOURCES

Arhiva Serviciului Român de Informaţii [Archive of the Romanian Security Service], Bucharest.

Public Record Office, Foreign Office Records

FO 371: Political Correspondence of the Foreign Office.

PUBLISHED MEMOIRS AND SECONDARY SOURCES

6 Martie 1945. Inceputurile Comunizării României, Bucharest: Editura Enciclopedică, 1995.

Andreescu, Ştefan, 'A Little-Known Issue in the History of Romania: The Armed Anti-Communist Resistance', *Revue Roumaine d' Histoire*, vol.33, nos 1-2, 1994, pp.191-7.

Andrew, Christopher, and Oleg Gordievsky, *KGB: The Inside Story of Its Foreign Operations from Lenin to Gorbachev*, London: Sceptre, 1991.

Arhivele Totalitarismului

Bacon, Walter M., Jr, 'Romanian Secret Police' in J. R. Adelman (ed.), *Terror and Communist Politics: The Role of the Secret Police in Communist States*, Boulder; CO: Westview Press, 1984.

Bacu, D., *The Anti-Humans*, Monticello, IL: TLC, 1977.

Baier, Hannelore (ed.), *Deportarea Etnicilor Germani din România în Uniunea Sovietică*, Sibiu: Forumul Democrat al Germanilor din România, 1994,

Barker, Elisabeth, *British Policy in South-East Europe in the Second World War*, London: Macmillan, 1976.

Beeson, Trevor, *Discretion and Valour: Religious Conditions in Russia and Eastern Europe*, London: Fontana, 1974.

Bellu, Ştefan, *Pădurea răzvrătită*, Baia Mare: Editura Gutinul, 1993.

Betea, Lavinia, *Maurer şi lumea de ieri. Mărturii despre stalinizarea României*, Arad: Fundaţia Ioan Slavici, 1995.

Biddiscombe, Perry, 'Prodding the Russian Bear: pro-German Resistance in Romania, 1944-45', *European History Quarterly*, vol.23, no.2 (April 1993), pp.205-12.

Bishop, R., and E.S. Crayfield, *Russia astride the Balkans*, London: Evans, 1949.

Borsody, S. (ed.), *The Hungarians: A Divided Nation*, New Haven, CT: Yale Center for International and Area Studies, 1988.

Bossy, Raoul, 'Religious Persecutions in Captive Romania', *Journal of Central European Affairs*, vol.15, no.2 (July 1955), pp.161-81.

Braham, Randolph L. (ed.), *Genocide and Retribution: The Holocaust in Hungarian-ruled Transylvania*, The Hague: Nijhoff, 1983.

Brătescu, G. (ed.), *Lichidarea lui Marcel Pauker*, Bucharest: Univers Enciclopedic, 1995.

Broun, Janice, 'The Latin-Rite Roman Catholic Church of Romania', *Religion in Communist Lands*, vol.12, no.2 (Summer 1984), pp.168-84.

Brucan, Silviu, *Generaţia irosită*, Bucharest: Universul/Calistrat Hogaş, 1992.

———, *The Wasted Generation*, Boulder, CO: Westview Press, 1993, p.181.

Buzatu, G., *România cu şi fără Antonescu*, Iaşi: Editura Moldova, 1991.

Campbell, J., and P. Sherrard, *Modern Greece*, New York: Praeger, 1973.

'Les Camps de la Mort du Delta du Danube', *La Nation Roumaine*, no.215 (Nov.1962-Jan.1963), p.6.

Captive Rumania. A Decade of Soviet Rule, London: Atlantic Press, 1956.

Carp, M. *Cartea Neagră. Suferinţele Evreilor din România, 1940-1944*, Bucharest: Socec, 1946.

Cartea Albă a Securităţii, 6 vols, Bucharest: SRI, 1994-95.

Chiper, Ioan. Constantiniu, Florin. Pop, Adrian (eds), *Sovietizarea României. Percepţii anglo-americane*, Bucharest: Iconica, 1993.

Cipăianu, George, 'Une Eglise "réduite au silence". Les gréco-catholiques roumains et le communisme', *Transylvanian Review*, vol.6, no.1, 1997, pp. 71-82.

Congresul Partidului Muncitoresc Român. Bucureşti, 21-23 februarie 1948, Bucharest: Editura PMR, 1948.

Constante, E., *The Silent Escape*, Berkeley: University of California Press, 1995.

Constantiniu, F., A. Duţu, M. Retegan, *România în război, 1941-1945*, Bucharest: Editura Militară, 1995.

Coposu, Corneliu, *Dialoguri cu Vartan Arachelian*, Bucharest: Editura Anastasia, 1992.

Cretzianu, A., *The Lost Opportunity*, London: Cape, 1957, p.47.

Deletant, Dennis, 'The *Securitate* and the police state in Romania, 1948-1964', *Intelligence and National Security*, vol.8, no.4 (October 1993), pp.1-25.

———, 'The *Securitate* and the police state in Romania, 1964-89', *Intelligence and National Security*, vol.9, no.1 (January 1994), pp.22-49.

———, *Ceauşescu and the Securitate. Coercion and Dissent in Romania, 1965-89*, London: Hurst, 1995.

———, 'New Light on Gheorghiu-Dej's Struggle for Dominance in the

Romanian Communist Party', *The Slavonic and East European Review*, vol.73, no.4 (October 1995), pp.659-90.

Documents on the Expulsion of the Germans from Eastern-Central-Europe, vol. III: *The Fate of the Germans in Rumania*, Bonn: Federal Ministry for Expellees, Refugees and War Victims, 1961.

Dosarele Istoriei

Dumitriu, Petru, *Incognito*, London: Collins, 1964.

Dura, Ioan, *Monahismul românesc în anii 1948-1989*, Bucharest: Harisma, 1994.

Ember, Judit, *Menedekjog-1956*, Budapest: Szabad Ter Kiado, 1989.

Falls, Donald R., 'Soviet Decision-Making and the Withdrawal of Soviet Troops from Romania', *East European Quarterly*, vol. 27, no.4 (winter 1993).

Fildermann, Willy, and Sabin Manuila, 'Regional Development of the Jewish Population in Romania', *Europa şi Neamul Românesc*, no. 247 (January 1993), pp.21-33.

Fischer, Mary Ellen, *Nicolae Ceauşescu: A Study in Political Leadership*, Boulder, CO: Lynne Rienner, 1989.

Fischer-Galaţi, Stephen, *The New Rumania: From People's Democracy to Socialist Republic*, Cambridge, MA: MIT Press, 1967.

———, *Twentieth Century Rumania*, New York: Columbia University Press (2nd edn), 1991.

Fisher, J.S, *Transnistria: The Forgotten Cemetery*, New York: Thomas Yoseloff, 1969.

Floyd, David, *Rumania: Russia's Dissident Ally*, London: Pall Mall Press, 1965.

Franck, N., *O Infringere în victorie*, Bucharest: Editura Humanitas, 1992.

Fuiorea, N., *Divizia Stalinistă 'Tudor Vladimirescu' în umbra Steagului Roşu*, Bucharest: Pan-Arcadia, 1992.

Gafencu, Grigore, *Prelude to the Russian Campaign*, London: Frederick Muller, 1945.

Galloway, George, and Bob Wylie, *Downfall: The Ceauşescus and the Romanian Revolution*, London: Futura, 1991, p.73.

Gavrilă-Ogoranu, Ion, *Brazii se frâng, dar nu se îndoiesc*, vol.1, Timişoara: Editura Marineasa, 1993; vol.2, 1995.

Georgescu, Vlad, *The Romanians: A History*, Columbus: Ohio State University Press, 1991.

Gheorghiu-Dej, Gheorghe, *Articole şi cuvântări*, Bucharest: Editura pentru literatura politică, 1952.

———, *Articole şi cuvîntări*, Bucharest: Editura politică 1963.

Giurescu, Dinu, *Romania's Communist Takeover: The Rădescu Government*, Boulder, CO: East European Monographs, 1994.

———, *Five Years and Two Months in the Sighet Penitentiary (May 7, 1950-July 5, 1955*, Boulder, CO: East European Monographs, 1994.

Golopenţia, A. and D.C. Georgescu, 'Populaţia Republicii Populare Române la 25 ianuarie 1948' in R. Mănescu (ed.), *Probleme Economice*, Bucharest, 1948, pp.28-35.

Haupt, G., 'La Genèse du Conflit Soviéto-Roumain', *Revue Française du Science Politique*, vol.18 (1968),. no.4 (August), pp.669-84.

Hazard, Elizabeth W., *Cold War Crucible: United States Foreign Policy and the Conflict in Romania, 1943-1953*, Boulder, CO: East European Monographs, 1996.

Hillgruber, Andreas, *Hitler, König Carol und Marschall Antonescu. Die Deutsch-Rumanischen Beziehungen*, 1938-1944, Wiesbaden: Franz Steiner, 1965.

Hitchins, Keith, 'The Romanian Orthodox Church and the State' in B.R. Bociurkiw, J.W. Strong (eds), *Religion and Atheism in the USSR and Eastern Europe*, University of Toronto Press/London: Macmillan, 1975, pp.314-27.

Hitchins, Keith, *Rumania, 1866-1947*, Oxford: Clarendon Press, 1994.

Hodoş, G., *Show Trials: Stalinist Purges in Eastern Europe, 1948-1954*, New York: Praeger, 1987.

Ioanid, Ion, *Inchisoarea noastră cea de toate zilele*, 5 vols, Bucharest: Editura Albatros,1991-7.

Illyes, E., *National Minorities in Romania: Change in Transylvania*, Boulder, CO, East European Monographs, 1982.

Ionescu, Alexandru, *Dacă vine ora H pe cine putem conta*, Piteşti, 1992.

Ionescu, Ghiţa, *Communism in Rumania, 1944-1962*, London: Oxford University Press, 1964.

Istoria militară a poporului român, vol.1, Bucharest: Editura Militară, 1984.

Istoria Romîniei, vol.1, Bucharest: Editura Academiei Republicii Populare Romîne, 1960.

Istoria RPR. Manual pentru învăţămîntul mediu, Bucharest: Editura Ştiinţifică, 1956.

Janos, Andrew C., 'Modernization and Decay in Historical Perspective: The Case of Romania' in Kenneth Jowitt (ed.), *Social Change in Romania, 1860-1940*, Berkeley, CA: Institute of International Studies, University of California, 1978, pp.72-116.

Jela, Doina, *Cazul Nichita Dumitru. Incercare de reconstituire a unui proces comunist, 29 august-1 septembrie 1952*, Bucharest: Humanitas, 1995.

Jowitt, Kenneth, *Revolutionary Breakthroughs and National Development: The Case of Romania, 1944-1965*, Berkeley and Los Angeles: University of California Press, 1971.

Khrushchev, N.S., *Khrushchev Remembers – The Last Testament*, trans. by Strobe Talbott, Boston: Little, Brown and Co., 1974.

King, Robert R., *Minorities under Communism: Nationalities as a Source of Tension among Balkan Communist States*, Cambridge, MA: Harvard University Press, 1973.

——, 'The Escalation of Rumanian-Soviet Historical Polemics over Bessarabia', *RFE Research. Romania Background Report, no.28* (12 February 1976).

——, *History of the Romanian Communist Party*, Stanford, CA Hoover Institution Press, 1980.

Kirschen, Leonard, *Prisoner of Red Justice*, London: Arthur Barker, 1963.

Kopeczi, Bela, ed., *Erdely Tortenete*, 3 vols, Budapest: Akadémiai Kiadó, 1986.

Lampe, John R., and Marvin R. Jackson, *Balkan Economic History, 1550-1950*, Bloomington: Indiana University Press, 1982.

Lee, A.G., *Crown against Sickle*, London: Hutchinson, 1950.

Levy, Robert, 'Did Ana Pauker Prevent a "Rajk Trail" in Romania?', *East European Politics and Societies*, vol. 9, no.1 (winter 1995), pp.143-78.

Litani, Dora, *Transnistria*, Tel Aviv, 1981 (in Romanian).

Lungu, Dov, *Romania and the Great Powers, 1933-1940*, Durham, NC: Duke University Press, 1989, pp.149-50.

Lupu, M., C. Nicoară, and G. Onişoru, (eds), *Cu Unanimitate de Voturi*, Bucharest: Fundaţia Academia Civică, 1997.

Magazin Istoric.

Marineasa, Viorel and Vighi, Daniel, *Rusalii '51. Fragmente din deportarea în Bărăgan*, Timişoara: Editura Marineasa, 1994.

Marineasa, Viorel, Daniel Vighi amd Valentin Sămînţă, *Deportarea în Bărăgan*, Timişoara (no publ), 1996.

Marinescu, A., 'Pagini din rezistenţa armată anticomunistă', *Memoria*, no.7 (1992), pp.47-51.

Markham, Reuben H., *Rumania under the Soviet Yoke*, Boston: Meador, 1949.

Matichescu, Olimpia, *Doftana. Simbol al Eroismului Revoluţionar*, Bucharest: Editura Politică, 1979.

Memoria.

Memorialul Ororii. Documente ale Procesului Reeducării din Inchisorile Piteşti, Gherla, Bucharest: Editura Vremea, 1995.

Mezincescu, Eduard, 'Din nou despre fantoma lui Dej', *România literară*, no.41 (16-22 December 1992), p.14.

Michelson, Paul, 'Myth and Reality in Rumanian National Development', *International Journal of Rumanian Studies*, vol.5 (1987), no.2, pp.13-14.

Mihalache, V., Suciu, I.P., *Jandarmeria Română. Pagini dintr-o istorie nescrisă. 1850-1949*, Bucharest: Ministerul de Interne, 1993.

Mircu, Marius, *Dosar Ana Pauker*, Bucharest: Editura Gutenberg, 1991.

Montias, John Michael, 'Background and Origins of the Rumanian Dispute with Comecon', *Soviet Studies*, vol.16 (October 1974), pp.125-52.

Muşat, Mircea and Ion Ardeleanu, *Viaţa Politică în România, 1918-1921*, Bucharest: Editura Politică, 1976.

Oldson, William, *A Providential Anti-Semitism: Nationalism and Polity in Nineteenth century Romania*, Philadelphia, PA: American Philosophical Society, 1991.

Organizarea şi funcţionarea Organelor Ministerului de Interne de la Infiinţare pînă în prezent, Bucharest; Ministry of the Interior, 1978.

Pacepa, Ion, *Red Horizons*, London: Heinemann, 1988.

———, *Moştenirea Kremlinului*, Bucharest: Editura Venus, 1993.

Partidul Muncitoresc Romîn. Congresul al II-lea al PMR, 23-28 Dec. 1955, Bucharest: Editura Politică, 1956.

Partidul Muncitoresc Romîn. Congresul al III-lea al PMR, 20-25 Iunie 1960, Bucharest: Editura Politică, 1960.

Pascu, Ştefan, *A History of Transylvania*, Detroit, MI, Wayne State University Press, 1982, p.53.

Pătrăşcanu, Lucreţiu, *Sub trei dictaturi*, Bucharest: Editura Politică, 1970 (2nd edn).

Pearton, Maurice, *Oil and the Romanian State*, London: Oxford University Press, 1971.

Pearton, Maurice and Dennis Deletant, 'The Soviet Takeover in Romania, 1944-48' in Gill Bennett (ed), *The End of the War in Europe 1945*, London: HMSO, 1996, pp. 204-20.

———, *Romania Observed. Studies in Contemporary Romanian History*, Bucharest: Encyclopaedic Publishing House, 1998.

Persecuţia Bisericii din România sub Dictatura Comunistă, Freiburg: Coresi, 1983.

The Perversion of Education in Rumania, Washington, DC: Rumanian National Commitee, 1950.

Peter, Laszlo (ed.) *Historians and the History of Transylvania*, Boulder, CO: East European Monographs, 1992.

La Population Juive de la Transylvanie, Bucharest: Section de Roumanie du Congrès Juif Mondial, 1945.

Porter, Ivor, *Operation Autonomous: With SOE in Wartime Romania*, London: Chatto and Windus, 1989.

Prigoana. Documente ale Procesului C. Noica, C. Pillat, N. Steinhardt, Al. Palelologu, A. Acterian, S. Al-George, Al. O. Teodoreanu, Bucharest: Editura Vremea, 1996.

Principiul Bumerangului. Documente ale Procesului Lucreţiu Pătrăşcanu, Bucharest: Editura Vremea, 1996.

Prison Conditions in Rumania: Conditions for Political Prisoners, 1955-1964, London: Amnesty International, 1965.

Prunduş, S.A. and Plaianu, C., *Cardinalul Alexandru Todea*, Cluj: Ordinul Şfintul Vasile cel Mare, 1992.

Quinlan, Paul D., *Clash over Romania: British and American Policies towards*

Romania: 1938-1947, Los Angeles: American Romanian Academy, 1977.

Raţiu, A., and W. Virtue, *Stolen Church: Martyrdom in Communist Romania*, Huntington, IN: Our Sunday Visitor, 1978.

Rizea, Elisabeta, *Povestea Elisabetei Rizea din Nucşoara*, Bucharest: Humanitas, 1993.

Roberts, Henry L., *Rumania: Political Problems of an Agrarian State*, New Haven, CT: Yale University Press, 1951.

România în anii celui de-al doilea război mondial, vol.1, Bucharest: Editura Militară, 1989.

Les Roumains dans la Résistance française, Bucharest: Meridiane, 1971.

Rusan, Romulus (ed.), *Memoria ca formă de justiţie*, Bucharest: Fundaţia Academia Civică, 1994.

——— (ed.), *Instaurarea Comunismului – între rezistenţă şi represiune*, Bucharest: Fundaţia Academia Civică, 1995.

——— (ed.), *Anul 1946-Inceputul Sfârşitului*, Bucharest: Fundaţia Academia Civică, 1996.

Samuelli, Annie, *The Wall Between*, Washington, DC: Robert B. Luce, 1967.

Scarfe, Alan, 'The Evangelical Wing of the Orthodox Church in Romania', *Religion in Communist Lands*, vol.3, no.6 (Nov.-Dec. 1975), pp.15-19.

——— 'Patriarch Justinian of Romania: His Early Social Thought', *Religion in Communist Lands*, vol.5, no.3 (autumn 1977), p.164-69.

——— 'The "Lord's Army" Movement in the Romanian Orthodox Church', *Religion in Communist Lands*, vol.8, no.4 (1980), p.315-16.

Schöpflin, George, and Hugh Poulton, *Romania's Ethnic Hungarians*, London: Minority Rights Group, 1990.

Scurtu, Ioan (ed.), *Viaţa politică în Documente*, Bucharest: Arhivele Statului, 1994.

——— *România. Retragerea Trupelor Sovietice, 1958*, Bucharest: Editura Didactică şi Pedagogică, 1997.

Seton-Watson, Hugh, *The East European Revolution* (3rd edn) London: Methuen, 1956,

Seton-Watson, Robert William, *A History of the Roumanians*, Cambridge University Press, 1934.

Sfera Politicii.

Shafir, Michael, *Romania: Politics, Economics and Society*, London: Pinter, 1985.

Shevchenko, Arkady N., *Breaking with Moscow*, New York: Alfred Knopf, 1985.

Simon, T., *Pacepa: Quo Vadis?*, Bucharest: Odeon, 1992.

The Soviet-Yugoslav Dispute, London: Royal Institute of International Affairs, 1948.

Stehle, Hansjakob, *Eastern Politics of the Vatican, 1917-1979*, tr. Sandra Smith, Athens, OH: Ohio University Press, 1981.

Stănescu, Marin C., *Moscova, Cominternul, Filiera Comunistă Balcanică şi România (1919-1944)*, Bucharest: Silex, 1994.

Suppression of Human Rights in Romania, Washington, DC: Romanian National Committee, 1949.

Şerbulescu, A. [Belu Zilber], *Monarhia de Drept Dialectic*, Bucharest: Humanitas, 1991.

Ştefănescu, P., *Istoria Serviciilor Secrete Româneşti*, Bucharest: Divers Press, 1994.

Tismăneanu, Vladimir, 'Miron Constantinescu or the Impossible Heresy', *Survey*, vol.28, no.4 (winter 1984), pp.175-87.

—— 'The Tragicomedy of Romanian Communism', *East European Politics and Societies*, vol.3, no.2 (spring 1989), pp.329-76.

—— *Arheologia Terorii*, Bucharest: Editura Eminescu, 1992.

—— *Fantoma lui Gheorghiu-Dej*, Bucharest: Editura Univers, 1995.

Tökes, Laszlo, *With God, For the People*, as told to David Porter, London: Hodder and Stoughton, 1990.

Tomaziu, G., *Jurnalul unui Figurant*, Bucharest: Univers, 1995.

Trial of the Group of Spies and Traitors in the Service of the Espionage of Tito's Fascist Clique, Bucharest, 1950.

Tupper-Carey, Fiona, 'Romania', *Religion in Communist Lands*, vol.18, no.2 (summer 1990), pp.181-2.

Turnock, David, *An Economic Geography of Romania*, London: G. Bell, 1974.

Urwich-Ferry, J., *Fără Paşaport prin URSS*, Munich: Iskra, 1977.

Verca, Filon, *Paraşutaţi în România vândută. Mişcarea de rezistenţă 1944-1948*, Timişoara: Editura Gordian,1993.

Verdery, Katherine, *National Ideology Under Socialism*, Berkeley: University of California Press, 1991.

Verona, Sergiu, *Military Occupation and Diplomacy: Soviet Troops in Romania 1944-1958*, Durham, NC: Duke University Press, 1992.

Watts, Larry, *Romanian Cassandra. Ion Antonescu and the Struggle for Reform, 1916-1941*, Boulder, CO: East European Monographs, 1993.

Weber, Eugen, 'Romania' in Hans Rogger and Eugen Weber (eds), *The European Right*, Berkeley: University of California Press, 1966, pp.501-74.

Weiner, Robert, *Romanian Foreign Policy and the United Nations*, New York: Praeger, 1984.

Woolf, Robert Lee. *The Balkans in our Time*, Cambridge, MA: Harvard University Press, 1956.

Wurmbrand, Richard, *In God's Underground*, London: W.H. Allen, 1968.

Interviews

Gheorghe Apostol, 7 May 1990.
Alexandru Bîrlădeanu, 8 August 1996.
Gheorghe Brătescu, 30 July 1994.
Tatiana Brătescu (née Pauker), 30 July 1994.
George Fotino, 6 April 1994.
Father Tertullian Langa, 31 May 1993.
Eduard Mezincescu, 30 December 1992, 7 April 1993, 16 June 1994.

INDEX

Aftenie, Bishop Vasile 98, 101, 103-4
Agiu, Constantin 27
agriculture 12-13, 85, 87
Ajutorul Roşu (Red Aid) 7
Aldea, Gen. Aurel: 48; Interior Minister 49; arrest of 77 and n.; coordinates resistance 225-6
Alexandrescu, Anton 70,71
Antonescu, Marshal Ion: 31 and n., 34, 36, 39, 41, 44-5, 46, 51n., 153n., 157n., 175, 273, 298; anxious to prevent Soviet occupation of Romania 35; and events of 23 August 1944 47-50, 52
Antonescu, Mihai 34, 46, 51n.
Apostol, Gheorghe: 16, 27n, 65, 160, 161, 251, 255-8 *passim*, 262, 290n., 291, 312; appraisal of Dej 292-5 cit.
Armistice: 36, 48, 52, 53, 168, 269; negotiations in Cairo 35, 39,44-5; as mechanism of Soviet takeover 54-7, 60-1;
Arnăuţoiu, Toma 225, 230-2
Arsenescu, Gheorghe 225, 230-2
Avramescu, Gen. Gheorghe 69n.

Bălan, Bishop Ioan 98, 101, 104
Bălănescu, Mircea 16n.,
Becescu, Florin 42-3
Bessarabia: 1, 9, 12, 22, 24, 39; disputes over sovereignty 4, 5, 11; Soviet annexation 19, 22, 24n., 55, 122
Bîrlădeanu, Alexandru 24 and n., 32n., 127, 245, 290n.
Bodnăraş, Emil (Engineer Ceauşu): 13, 29, 32, 37n. 40n. 41n. cit, 57, 63, 104-5, 161, 165, 166, 252, 268, 298-309 cit.; questions over real loyalty 41-3; role in coup 43-4, 49-50; secretary-general 72-3, NKGB agent 73; Minister of War 81; and removal of Foris 149-51; and removal of Pătrăşcanu 170n.; placed in charge of General Command in 1956 263; meets Khrushchev 263-4; helps reorganise Hungarian security sevice 267; distancing Romania from Soviet Union 273-4
Borilă, Petre 16, 20, 25n., 243n., 247, 254
Brainer, Bela 22, 24
Brătianu, Constantin 38, 46, 47, 50, 70, 71, 76, 197
Brătianu, Gheorghe 47
Brezhnev, Leonid 289
Brucan, Silviu viii-ix, 163
Bucicov, Valerian (Vasile Bucikov) 16, 118n., 181, 184
Bukovina, Northern 2, 22, 39, 55
Bulgaria 11, 44,
Burcă, Mihai 20, 25n., 143 and n., 196

Caracostea, Dumitru 135,
Caransebeş prison 19, 23n., 27 and n., 43, 115, 116, 314-15
Casablanca conference 34
Ceauşescu, Nicolae: vii, 15, 16, 27n., 29, 126n., 141, 151, 152, 250n., 251, 260, 291, 292, 293, 296; first secretary of RCP 290 and n.; phone tapped 127;
Chişinevski, losif (Roitman): 7, 23n., 27n., 28n., 118n., 127, 171, 188, 192, 219, 235, 237, 238, 248, 254, 271, 315; attacks Dej 256; *apparatchik* of long standing 272 cit.
Chişinevski, Liuba 19, 127,
Cluj prison 17, 20n.
Codreanu, Corneliu 7
Coliu, Dumitriu (Dimitur Kolev) 8, 25n.
Collectivisation 79, 129, 135-42, 210

Comecon 213, 281, 283
Cominform 141
Comintern: 1, 2n, 6, 9, 17, 21, 22, 30, 40n., 147, 161 and n., 162, 242, 300; and SDP 3; and RCP 4, 5, 7, 23, 27; training school 16, 18
Communist Party, Romanian (RCP): vii, x, 13, 19, 21-2, 24, 39, 40n., 44, 52, 55, 57, 61, 62, 78, 86, 124, 156, 162, 163, 180, 195, 255, 302; role of minorities 6, 7, 8; front organizations 9; factionalism 6; early years 1-10; 1930-1944 11-33; ban on 1, 4, 18; congresses 4, 5, 6, 7, 17, 18, 169, 177, 283; membership figures 4, 8, 9 and n., 22 and n., 40n.; 'Moscow bureau' 25, 147 and n., 237, 312; 'prison group' 27, 29, 147 and n., 161, 237; distorted historiography of 23 August 1944 coup 36, 49, 273; in Groza government 71-3; merger with SDP 82-3, 169; takes over Foreign Ministry 322-3; verification campaign 84-5; party organisation 85; policy toward Roman Catholic Church 92; relationship to Soviet Union 146-8, 168, 194; struggle for leadership 146-169 *passim*; collective leadership 251; congratulates Kádár government in Hungary (q.v.) 264;
Constante, Lena 183 and n., 184-6 *passim*, 246, 250
Constantinescu, Alecu 2
Constantinescu, Miron: 27n., 127, 147n., 235, 238, 245, 254, 261, 271, 310; attack on Dej 255-6, 256-7 cit.; alternative to Dej 272 cit.;
Coposu, Corneliu xi, 40n., 158n., 252n.
Corbu, Gustav 27-8
Corps of Detectives 56n., 72 and n., 122
Cristescu, Gheorghe 4, 5, 217
Crosneff, Gheorghe 8

Danube-Black Sea canal project: 131, 205-6, 212-24; numbers of political prisoners 216; show trials of saboteurs 219-20
Dej (Gheorghe Gheorghiu-Dej): vii, ix-x, 13-15, 27, 29, 52, 62-3, 70, 71 cit., 103, 110, 128, 135, 159, 192, 207, 211, 223, 235-68; 276 cit, 292, 293 cit., 297-308 *passim*, 309-13, 319-21 cit.; myth of role in coup of 23 August 36-7, 148-9; in Doftana jail 15-17, 43n., 165; denounced by workers 65n.; and Soviet Union 17, 42, 146-8, 168, 178, 194, 251-2, 269; and Stalin 64n., 146-8, 164-5, 188, 196, 235, 237, 254, 295; and ousting of Ştefan Foriş 29-33, 149, 150, 314-16; condemned by Ceauşescu for 'assassination' of Ştefan Foriş 150-1; Minister of Communications 62, 167; Minister of National Economy 168; first-secretary 81, 83, 167; and Patriarch Justinian 90; phone tapped 127-8; and collectivisation 136, 139-41; consolidates power 147-8, escapes from prison 154 and n.; and Pătrăşcanu 154-160 *passim*, 170, 172-3, 177-80, 190, 196, 236 cit., 244, 245; and Ana Pauker 165-6, 237, 319; and Luca 238, 240, 251; doctors Politburo minutes viii; party history according to 242n.; accused of Stalinism 254-8, 271; accuses opponents of Stalinism 271; fears accusation of Stalinism 273, 281; visits Yugoslavia 260; and Hungarian crisis 262-8, 271; visits Budapest 265, 267; memorandum with Kadar (q.v.) 266-7; distances Romania from Soviet Union 273-4; snubs Khrushchev 274; launches campaign of 'revolutionary vigilance' 277-8; rift with Moscow 281-3; requests withdrawal of KGB counsellors 284-5; anti-Russian measures 286-7; illness and death 289-90; eulogies 291

Deportations 142-4, 237
DGSP *see Securitate*
DIA (*Departmentul de Informaţii al Armatei*) 286 and n.,
Didenko, Vania 148, 151, 170n.
Dimitrov, Georgi *see* Dimitrov, Gheorghe
Dimitrov, Gheorghe 3n, 21, 23 and n., 147, 161-2, 176
Dobrogeanu-Gherea, Alexandru 2, 5, 6, 8 and n., 19 and n.
Doftana prison 15-16, 27n., 165,
Doncea, Constantin 15, 20, 127
DPS(*Direcţia Poliţiei de Siguranţă*) *see Siguranţa*
Drăghici, Alexandra 16, 19, 27n., 82n., 110, 132, 133, 144, 149n., 180, 191, 195-6, 212, 216, 219, 223-4, 239 and n., 251, 254, 257-8, 263, 284-5, 288, 290n., 292, 331, 332
Dulgheru, Mişu 132, 190 andn., 192 and n., 219

elections: 9, 12, 36, 76-7; of 1946 78 and n.; of 1926 2; union 65; Groza (q.v.) cit. 78

Fabian, David 19 and n.
Fascists: 66, 70, 117, 223; as defined by RCP 58, 62, 72, 73, 79, 181
Florescu, Mihail 20,
FLP (*Formaţiunile de Luptă Patriotice*) see Patriotic Guards
Foreign Intelligence Directorate (DGIE) 285-7
Foriş, Ştefan: 6-7, 8, 16n., 23, 24, 31n., 120, 146, 147, 179, 181, 249, 250n., 292, 297-308 *passim*; removal from post as RCP secretary-general 29-33, 149; arrest and murder 150-4, 314-18
Frenţiu, Bishop Valeriu Traian 98, 101, 104

Galaţi railway yards 13
Gavrilă-Ogoranu, Ion xi, 225, 233-4
Georgescu, Teohari: 23 and n., 24, 27 and n., 57, 63, 127, 152, 159, 161, 180, 194, 207, 237, 256, 296, 297, 315, 316, 317; Deputy Minister of the Interior 61; Minister of the Interior 71, 168 and n. cit.; RWP secretariat 83; denounces Pătrăşcanu 177-8; arrested 181, 242; accusations against him 191, 239, 243, 254; released 244; and Ana Pauker 235, 236
Germany 34, 44-5, 69n.
Gheorghe, Petre 30-1, 32, 308
Giurescu, Professor Constantin 197-9
Goncearuc, Pyotr (Petea Goncearuk): 16, 116, 132, 148, 180, interrogation of Pătrăşcanu 184-6
Graiul Nou 66
Greek Catholic Church *see* Uniate Church
Griviţa railway yards: 262; strike 14, 15, 19, 24n., 195
Groza, Petru: 74-78 *passim,* 81, 114, 117, 165, 168-9, 171, 313; Deputy Prime Minister 64; Russain choice as leader 68-70; formation of government 71-3, 319-21; and Uniates 104 cit.

Haţieganu, Emil 76
Holostenko, Vitali 6
Hossu, Bishop Iuliu 98, 100, 101, 104-5
Hungarian Minority: 92, 171, 225, 259, 260, 261, 268, 269; demonstrations in 1956 263
Hungary 11, 44, 55, 77, 258-60, 275, 276

Industrialisation 12, 283
Ionniţiu, Mircea 46, 48, 49
Irineu, Metropolitan of Moldavia 89, 90
Iron Guard: 7, 13, 57, 62, 72, 74, 125, 200, 228, 236 and n.; rounded up 84; and church 110, 112; many former Guardists freed 287

Jewish minority 10, 11, 13, murdered at Odessa 75n.; Zionists 146, 200, 236-7; property 174-5; in Com-

munist Party 7-8; granting of exit visas 281
Justinian, Patriarch: 99 cit., 103, 106-13; and Dej 90

Kádár, Janos 264, 266, 268, 282
KGB 285-7
Khrushchev, Nikita: 110, 189, 253-5, 269, 272 cit., 283-4; during Hungarian crisis 262-4; withdrawal of Soviet troops from Romania 273-5; upbraids Dej (q.v.) 281, 282 cit.
Koblos, Elek (Bădulescu) 5, 6, 8, 19
Kofler, Remus: 7, 27, 32 and n., 132, 152n., 179, 189, 192, 247n., 249, 307, 308; torture and 'confession' 181; execution 194, 246, 250-1
Kollontay, Madame Alexandra 44, 46 and n.
Korosi-Krizsan, Sandor (Georgescu) 5

labour camps (*colonii de muncă*): 129, 134-5, 145, 196, 210-12; memoir literature 217, 221-2; regime at Capul Midia 218; conditions in Danube Delta 278-80; *see also* Danube-Black Sea Canal
land reform 12, 62, 64, 130; *see also* collectivisation
Luca, Vasile (Laszlo Luka): 6, 24 and n., 25, 26, 61, 62, 67, 71, 127, 147, 149, 157, 159, 163, 171, 173, 175, 207, 235, 254, 256, 296, 309-13; Minister of Finance 80-1; RWP secretariat 83; purged 238-41, 251-2
Lucian, bishop of Roman 89

Macici, Gen. Nicolae 75 and n.
Malenkov, Georgi 244, 245, 266
Malinovsky, Marshal Rodion 51, 67n., 69 and n.
Maniu, Iuliu 34-5, 38, 40n., 44-5, 50, 63, 71, 76, 77, 80 and n., 197, 249
Maurer, Ion Georghe 19 and n., 31n., 40n., 127, 150, 154, 283, 289, 290 and n., 291 cit., 311
Mazuru, Vladimir 119 and n., 124, 219
Mezincescu, Eduard 20n., 31n., 116, 151n., 152 and n., 180, 318
MGB 119 and n., 120
Michael, king of Romania: 35, 37 and n., 45, 46, 60-1, 64, 79, 148; and events of 23 August 1944 47-50; acquiesces to Soviets 67- 8; requests Groza's resignation 76, 159, abdication 80-1
Mihalache, Ion 80 and n., 252n.
Militia (*Direcţia Generală a Miliţiei*) 129 and n., 138, 144, 212
Ministry of Cults 89-90; 93, 94, 100
Ministry of the Interior 30, 66 cit. and n., 72, 84, 97, 103, 104, 117, 128, 129, 133, 135, 196, 210, 211, 216, 230, 240, 256, 258, 263, 284, 330
minorities 5, 6, 7-8, 10, 11, 124-5
Mocsony-Styrcea, Ion 46, 47, 148n., 181, 182n., 246, 249, 250
Moghioroş, Alexandru 16, 19, 27n., 139, 171, 238, 258, 266
Moghioroş, Stela (Esther Radoshovetsky) 19
Moldavia 11-12, 141, 276n.
Molotov-Ribbentrop pact 21-2
Molotov, Vyacheslav: Soviet Foreign Minister 53, 54, 164, 165, 168, 236, 241, 242
MOPR (*Mezhdunarodnaia organisatsiia pomoshchi bortsam revoliutsii*) 7, 31n.

Nagy, Imre 262 and n., 264-7, 269, 276
Nanu, Frederick 38-9, 44 and n.
National Democratic Bloc (NDB) 37, 40n., 44, 45, 49, 148
National Democratic Front (NDF) 57-61, 65, 68, 70, 71
National Liberal Party: 44, 60, 68, 70, 76, 78; arrests 79, 80, 159; dissolution 82
National Peasant Party (NPP): 2, 19, 24n., 44, 60, 68, 70, 76, 78, 79,

159, 200; arrest of leadership 80; dissolution 82
National Resistance Movement (*Mişcarea Naţională de Rezistenţă*) 77
Nicolski, Alexandru: 72 and n., 119, 121-3, 124, 127, 132, 153, 219, 331; directs re-education programme (q.v.) 199, 200, 205, 206
Niculescu-Buzeşti, Grigore: 38, 46, 47, 48, 159; Foreign Minister 49
Nikonov, Serghei (Serghei Nicolau) 16, 42, 115, 117, 148, 184
NKGB 64, 65, 114, 115, 117, 119 n., 120 and n.
NKVD 31, 38, 41, 42, 72, 114, 120, 122, 132, 147, 148n., 170n.
Novikov, Nikolai 40, 44

O'Hara, Papal Nuncio 94-6, 100 cit., 101-2
Orthodox Church: 88, 95, 106-13; purged 89; reliant on state support 90-1; merger with Uniates 100-1, 103, 106

Partisans: 225-34; National Resistance Movement 225; and CIA 226- 7; political affiliations 228-9
Parvulescu, Gen. Nicolae 23n.
Patrascanu, Lucretiu: 9, 13, 27, 31 n., 53, 61 n. cit, 71n., 116, 132, 154, 157 n., 158 n., 163, 169 and n., 220, 235, 243 n., 272, 292, 296, 308, 311, 331-3; background 155; intellectual 156; account of 23 August coup 36 cit., 37 and n.; part played in coup 41, 46, 49-50, 156, 159; Minister of Justice 56, 61, 74; purges legal system 86; trial of 131, 147, 155n., 245-50; shot 250; Soviet backing 40 and n.; Soviet suspicions 157-60; downfall 170-195; and Hungaraian minority 171-5 *passim*; attempts suicide 185
Patriotic Guards: 50, 52, 63, 65, 170n.; enlarged 57; and *Siguranta 62,*
Pauker, Ana: 2n, 7, 13, 24, 52, 61, 67, 71n., 83, 117 n., 127, 147, 149, 159, 176, 195, 215, 243 and n., 252, 254, 256, 271, 296, 309-13, 319-21; worship of Stalin 9 and n.; Stalin's opinion 164; origins and early activity 17-19; recruitment activity for Red Army 25 and n., 26; Foreign Minister 80-1, 168-9, 322; RWP secretariat 83; and collectivisation (q.v.) 137-40; and Foris 152 and n., 315-16; and Patrascanu 159, 173-5, 174, 187, 194n.; returns from Soviet Union 161-2; leading role in RCP 162-3; purged in 1952 165-6, 207, 241-2 reasons for downfall 235-7, 239-40, 242 n.,
Pauker, Marcel (Luximin) 3 and n., 6 and n., 7, 8 and n., 13, 17, 18
Pavlov, Andrei 69 n., 70
Penescu, Nicolae 59 and n., 60
Petrescu, C. Titel 4, 37, 41, 46, 49, 82 and n.
Petrescu, Dumitru 15, 25 n., 26, 159, 245
Pintilie, Gheorghe (Pantelimon Bondarenko): 16, 117, 124, 144, 148, 153, 181, 187, 194, 212, 219, 222, 223, 247, 250n., 285 cit., 301; oversees *Siguranta* 80; 115-6; heads *Securitate* 118-9; philosophy 120, 121 cit.; phone tapped 127; role in death of Foris 314-16 cit., 316 n.
Pintilie, Ilie 15, 16,
Pîrvulescu, Constantin 16, 27, 29 and n., 147-50 *passim*, 154, 161, 301-3 *passim*, 307, 315
Poland 258-60
Popescu, Eremia 143
Posteuca, Vasile (Misha Postanski) 16, 148, 170
prison: 79, 145; Giurescu's description 196-9; Pitesti 199, 200 n.; Gherla 280 and n.; description of Aiud 324-7; communists' experience of 1, 15-16, 18-19, 29, 195; communist recruitment from 25

Rabinsohn, Ana *see* Pauker, Ana

Rădăceanu, Lother 62, 82, 310
Rădescu, Gen. Nicolae: 27n., 56, 60-2 and nn., 63, 68 n., 75, 249; government 57, 64, 164; removal from office 66-7
Rajk, Laszlo 173, 178, 183-4, 187, 189
Rangheţ, Iosif 27, 29, 149-50, 173, 180, 196, 301-8 *passim,* 331
Răutu, Leonte (Lev Oigenstein) 7, 24, 147 n., 237
Red Army: 35, 45, 52, 55, 265, 269; Tudor Vladimirescu Division 25n., 26, 84n., 85; Horia, Cloşca and Crişan 25n., 26, 84n.
Re-education: 199-210, 212; psychiatric abuse 199; reason for location at Pitesti 200; methods 201-5; and ODCC (Organisation of Prisoners with Communist Convictions) 201-2; extended to Gherla 205, reason for ending 207
Roman, Valter (Ernst Neulander): 7, 24, 127, 243n, 267; offers Nagy (q.v.) refuge in Romania 265-6
Roman Catholic Church 88, 91-8, 99, 135
Romania Liberă 25, 36, 151
Romanian Workers Party (RWP) *see* Communist Party, Romanian
Romniceanu, Mihai 76
Rusu, Bishop Alexandru 98, 101, 104-5

Sakharovsky, Alexsandr Mikhailovich 178-9, 184, 187-92 *passim,* 193n., 238, 284
Sănătescu, Gen. Constantin: 38, 46, 47, 77; Prime Minister 48; government 56, 58-60, 61 and n., 156, 168
Sârbu, Victoria 151-2, 182, 246, 301-8 *passim,* 308 cit
Schubert, Bishop Joseph 95, 96, 97 and n.,
Schuyler, Brigadier 68-70
Scînteia 60 cit, 66, 73, 82n., 83n., 154, 156, 163, 167, 175, 215, 239, 246, 249, 271, 284, 292
Securitate (DGSP, *Direcţia Generală a Securităţi Poporului*): vii, x, 72 and n., 82 n., 87, 94, 101, 103, 120, 123, 186n., 190, 206, 207, 217, 219, 222, 238, 255, 256, 284, 294; reports on Orthodox Church 109-12; formation and remit 118-21; social make up 123 n., 124-5; organisation 328-30; anti-espionage activity 125-6; anti-subversive function 126-7; and army 126n., eavesdropping 127-8; 128, informers 128-130; legal framework and *Procuratura* 130-1; torture during interrogations 132-3, 241, 277; numbers of arrests 133-5, 196n. 271, 277, 288; role in collectivisation 136-7, 141; deportations from Banat 142-4; and May Day 144-5, interrogation of Pătrăşcanu 178-9; investigates deaths in labour camps 216, 218; and armed resistance to communist rule 225, 227, 23-1; role in Hungarian crisis 267 and n.
Siguranţa (Security Police): 1, 18, 23n., 30-3 passim, 56, 62, 72, 114, 151 n., 155, 195, 217, 243, 247, 249, 297, 314, 331; RCP appointees 84; reorganisation 117-8
Social Democratic Party (SDP): 17, 19, 44, 57, 313; maximalist and minimist factions 2-3; centrists 3; expulsion of centrists 4; membership 4; and 1946 elections 77; merger with RCP 82-3
Socialismul 18
Şoltuţiu, Ioan: 192, 332; interrogation of Patrascanu 191 and n. cit., 193 cit., 248
Soviet Union: x, 1, 8, 11, 20, 61, 167, 244, 253-4, 270, 272; agents of in RCP 16, 41n., 80, 117; Romania attacks with Germans 27, Second World War 34; armistice with Romania 44, 52, 53, 60; demands reduction in Romanian police force and army 56, 74; military presence in Romania 67-8, 269-70; Moscow Agreement 76; treaty of friendship, cooperation and

mutual assistance 82, 168; as totalitarian model 86, 295; penetration of Romanian security services 114-24 *passim*; behind death of Foriş 151-3, 293; role in purge of Pătrăşcanu 159-60, 187-94 *passim*, 245-6; and Danube-Black Sea Canal 213, 253; intervention in Hungary 264; most active ally Romania 267; source of Dej's power 269; Sino-Soviet rift 283-4
Spanish Civil War: Romanian fighters 19-20, 243
Şraier, Iosif 16n., 40n., 52
SSI (*Servicul Special de Informaţii*): 40n., 42, 56 and n., 73, 84, 114, 165, 173, 180, 184, 185, 186 n., 189-90; organisation and role 115-17
Stalin, J.V.: 20n., 31n., 33, 35, 54, 55, 64, 88, 142 152n., 153, 159, 172, 176, 194, 236, 241, 244, 253-4, 296; purges 8, 19, 42, 237; campaign to eliminate Romanian opposition 80; favours Dej as RCP leader 164-5, 169; kept Dej under control 295
Steel, Christopher 39 cit,
Stoica, Chivu: 15, 29, 149, 258, 290 n.: heads delegation to Moscow 269-70
Stoica, Gheorghe 16, 25n.
Suciu, Bishop Ion 98, 100, 101, 103, 104
Susaikov, Col.-Gen. Ivan 67, 68 and n, 69, 76, 160, 166-7, 309-13, 319-21
Ştefanov, Boris (I. Draganov) 2 and n., 6 and n., 21-2, 24 n.,
Ştefanski, Alexandru (Gorun) 6,
Şteflea, Ilie 34,

Tătărescu, Gheorghe 62-3, 70, 71n., 71-2, 79 cit., 197, 247, 313, 322
Tîrgu-Jiu internment camp 27-8, 31n., 40 n., 443 and n., 249, 292, 299
Tito, J.B. 16, 142, 176, 184, 237, 260, 263
Toma, Ana 117 and n., 247, 307, 323
Transylvania 5, 9, 10, 22, 39, 44, 55, 77, 88, 99 cit., 171, 197, 263, 267, 268, 283
Trupele de Securitate 129, 143
Ţurcanu, Eugen 200-10
Ţurcanu, Nicoae 38, 40

Uniate Church 88, 93, 98-106, 135

Vişoianu, Constantin 39, 40, 45, 54 n., 159, 172 and n ., 249
Voitec, Stefan 82, 310
Vyshinski, Andrei 54n., 60-3, 67-70 *passim*, 74, 76, 80, 130-1. 158 n., 166, 169, 188, 319-21

Warsaw Pact 289
Worker-Peasant Bloc (*Blocul Muncitoresc-Ţărănesc*) 9, 10

Yugoslavia 142, 176-8, 181, 260

Zilber, Belu 132, 160, 174, 181, 194 n., 249, 250, 331-3
Zlătescu, Col.: commandant of Tîrgu-Jiu (q.v.) 28 and n.